D0886959

Exiled Royalties

Exiled Royalties

MELVILLE

AND THE LIFE

WE IMAGINE

Robert Milder

OXFORD

UNIVERSITY PRESS

2006

OXFORD
UNIVERSITY PRESS

Oxford University Press, Inc., publishes works that further
Oxford University's objective of excellence
in research, scholarship, and education.

Oxford   New York
Auckland   Cape Town   Dar es Salaam   Hong Kong   Karachi
Kuala Lumpur   Madrid   Melbourne   Mexico City   Nairobi
New Delhi   Shanghai   Taipei   Toronto

With offices in
Argentina   Austria   Brazil   Chile   Czech Republic   France   Greece
Guatemala   Hungary   Italy   Japan   Poland   Portugal   Singapore
South Korea   Switzerland   Thailand   Turkey   Ukraine   Vietnam

Published by Oxford University Press, Inc.
198 Madison Avenue, New York, New York 10016

www.oup.com

Oxford is a registered trademark of Oxford University Press

Library of Congress Cataloging-in-Publication Data
Milder, Robert.
Exiled royalties : Melville and the life we imagine / Robert Milder.
p. cm.
Includes bibliographical references and index.
ISBN-13 978-0-19-514232-7
ISBN 0-19-514232-2
1. Melville, Herman, 1819–1891.   2. Melville, Herman, 1819–1891—
Political and social views.   3. Literature and Society—United States—History—
19th century.   4. Novelists, American—19th century—
Biography.   6. Democracy in literature.   I. Title.
PS2386.M487   2006
813'.3—dc22   2005006680

To the memories of MY MOTHER

AND GRANDMOTHER,

AND TO GAIL

what a lie, and what a sign of the debasement of culture, that books are somehow presented as though they were library things, dead paper & cardboard & vellum, instead of what they are forever to any writer, the live things that some other man made as you yrself are trying to make live things—a book—too, are trying to get yrself as human being so totally inside the written word that it stands in your stead as—YOURSELF, yr life, yr vision, yr commitment, your ACT OF LANGUAGE, like theirs was . . . .

—Charles Olson to Merton M. Sealts, Jr.

'Tis to create, and in creating live
A being more intense, that we endow
With form our fancy, gaining as we give
The life we imagine, even as I do now.

—Byron, *Childe Harold's Pilgrimage*

ACKNOWLEDGMENTS

Parts of chapter 2, originally appeared in "'Nemo Contra Deum. . . .': Melville and Goethe's Demonic," in *Ruined Eden of the Present*, ed. G. R. Thompson and Virgil L. Lokke (West Lafayette, Ind.: Purdue University Press, 1981), pp. 205-244. Reprinted with permission.

Early versions of sections of chapter 4 were first published in "Moby-Dick: The Rationale of Narrative Form" in *Approaches to Teaching Melville's "Moby-Dick,"* ed. Martin Bickman (New York: Modern Language Association, 1985), pp. 35-49. Reprinted with permission.

Most of chapter 6 first appeared in "'The Ugly Socrates': Melville, Hawthorne, and Homoeroticism," *ESQ: A Journal of the American Renaissance*, 46 (2000): 1-49. Reprinted with permission. Copyright © 2001 by the Board of Regents of Washington State University.

Chapter 7 was first published in "An Arch Between Two Lives: Melville in the Mediterranean, 1856-57," *Arizona Quarterly*, 55 (1999), 21-47. Reprinted with permission.

Early versions of sections of chapter 8 were originally published in "The Rhetoric of Melville's Battle-Pieces," *Nineteenth-Century Literature*, 44 (1989): 173-200. Reprinted with permission. Copyright © 1989 by the Regents of the University of California.

Portions of chapter 10 were originally published in "Melville's Late Poetry and Billy Budd: From Nostalgia to Transcendence," *New Essays on "Billy Budd"* (New York: Cambridge University Press, 1987), pp. 493-507.

PREFACE

I will keep this brief. Except for the chapters on democratic tragedy and *Moby-Dick*, the ten essays in this book were conceived independently and are unified chiefly by my belief that "Melville's work," as Charles Olson said, must "be left in his own 'life.'"[1] The quotation marks are Olson's and reflect his feeling that writers' "lives" are things that within the boundaries of informed scholarship and responsive criticism we bring forth ourselves. Why should we bother? John Bryant broached the question when he asked whether by "Melville" we mean "the man or the text," "the biographical person—a writer writing—or the sum total of his work—the writings alone."[2] There are other things we might mean, among them "Melville" as a function of or index to the various discourses of his time. Bryant's position—that "literary scholarship has its own 'desire'": "to discover evidence of the writer writing, and to give a meaning to that process"[3]—is close to my own, save that I believe "literary scholarship" is a house with many windows and that authorial criticism (the writing as it emerges from and relates to the writer) is only one of them.

Carlyle argued the case for an authorial criticism when he claimed that

> it is Biography that first gives us both Poet and Poem, by the signifi-
> cance of the one elucidating and completing that of the other. That
> ideal outline of himself, which a man unconsciously shadows forth
> in his writings, and which, rightly deciphered, will be truer than any
> other representation of him, it is the task of the Biographer to fill-up
> into an actual coherent figure, and bring home to our experience, or at
> least our clear undoubting admiration, thereby to instruct and edify us
> in many ways.[4]

I would shear away Carlyle's "undoubting admiration" and retailor his "instruct and edify" to mean the kind of satisfaction that comes with broadly contemplating the shape of a writer's career. What I would emphasize is "that ideal outline of himself, which a man unconsciously shadows forth in his writings," and which the authorial critic tries to understand both within the writer's terms and apart from them. Wayne Booth defined what he called the "career-author" as "the sustained creative center implied by a *sequence* of implied authors,"[5] that is, the successive "Melvilles" inferable from *Typee, Omoo, Mardi*, and so on as they cohere (or not) in a figure we denominate "the writer." An authorial criticism takes Booth's career-author as its starting point, but it places the sequence of implied authors within the known or conjectured extratextual life. It is concerned with how and why particular texts come into being from the pressures of personal and collective experience and how on some level they serve the writer as stylized resolutions of what he or she could not resolve in life.

With Melville, conjecture is indispensable if we are to have anything beyond the canon itself and a life of bare facts. The dense, highly nuanced authorial criticism that is possible with Emerson, Thoreau, and Hawthorne (all compulsive journalizers and/or correspondents) is not possible with Melville; the primary sources are too meager: a volume of letters, only a handful of which are of prime importance; laconic travel journals from trips to England and the Continent in late 1849–50 and to the Mediterranean in 1856–57; reading marginalia, mostly in the form of underlinings, sidelinings, *X*s, and checks; testaments of contemporaries, few of whom were intimate acquaintances; and family reminiscences and legends, notably those included with commentary (and with who knows what omissions and palliations) in his granddaughter Eleanor Melville Metcalf's *Herman Melville: Cycle and Epicycle* (1953). Authorial critics must make do with these materials, saturate themselves in the writing, and guess, as Newton Arvin so fruitfully did in *Herman Melville: A Critical Biography* (1950), even when he guessed wrongly or aslant. A great deal has been learned since Arvin's time, but much of it is about the people surrounding Melville, though valuable pieces of evidence like a fragment of the *Typee* manuscript and Melville's annotated edition of Milton have also come to light. An authorial critic will be specially in debt to Hershel Parker's two-volume *Herman Melville: A Biography* (1996, 2002), which makes available in lively, intelligent form more than any reasonable person would want to know about the outward particulars of Melville's life while leaving room for new imaginative uses of its material.

The present book is not a biography, but it is "authorial" insofar as Melville the writer is prominently in mind as a context for the work and often, especially in the later chapters, as an open subject. If the book has any particular donnée, it would probably be the letter of [June 1?] 1851, in which Melville confided to Hawthorne the consciousness of mental unfolding so crucial to any interpretation of his character and work. Reading the letter years ago I was struck by its remarkable premonition of decay: "But I feel that I am now come to the inmost leaf of the bulb, and that shortly the flower must fall to the mould" (*Corr* 193). The question I asked then, and continue to ask, is why a thirty-one-year old writer just beginning to realize his powers should have felt himself on the verge of dissolution. And yet *Pierre* followed within months. Warner Berthoff spoke of the book as having "a certain air of inevitability";[6] E. L. Grant Watson called it "the center of Melville's being."[7] To understand Melville, it seemed necessary to ask "Why *Pierre*?" and to explore the relationship of the book to those that preceded and followed it, to the logic of Melville's development, to his childhood, to the outer and inner lives he fashioned for himself, to his domestic and vocational situation in 1851–52, and, increasingly, I came to feel, to his friendship with Hawthorne as it grew out of and reawakened needs and traumas from the past. My first published essay, "Melville's 'Intentions' in *Pierre*,"[8] was a preliminary effort to address a few of these questions; chapter 6 here, "Melville, Hawthorne, and the Varieties of Homoerotic Experience," is another attempt and a fulcrum on which my reading of Melville turns.

For the most part, I would prefer to let the essays declare themselves. The title piece, "Exiled Royalties," takes its name from the passage in *Moby-Dick* in which Ishmael acknowledges "the larger, darker, deeper part" of Ahab that "remains unhinted" after the analyzable motives for the hunt have been explored (*MD* 185). All of Melville's characters of thought, from Babbalanja onward, are exiled royalties—outcast children of a divinity who may or may not exist—as Melville imaginatively felt himself to be. "Ah, exile is exile though spiced be the sod," he had a speaker exclaim in a late poem, "The Devotion of the Flowers to Their Lady" ("WW" 42). The "sod" is the worldly garden of delights we inhabit and love even as we "languish with secret desire" for a problematic "garden of God" ("WW" 42). How to live nobly in exile—how to be "godlike" in the perceptible absence of God—was a lifelong preoccupation for Melville and will be a recurrent theme in this book. The phrase from my subtitle, "The Life We Imagine," is from Byron's *Childe Harold's Pilgrimage* and refers to writers' efforts to address this feeling of exile by staging a drama of spiritual life in their work. In lieu of church, theology, and positive belief, the emotions formerly attached to religion are transposed not to a religion of art but to a religion *in* art, a self-contemplative sublimity whose defining quality is a posture of aspiration beyond "the clay-cold bonds which round our being cling."[9] Byron's "we" are poets, who come to live in their writing, but in works of authorial criticism "we" should also be understood as ourselves, their interpreters, as we bring to life a version of them from our own imagining.

But I do not wish to make the essays seem monolithic or thesis-ridden. Leonard Woolf titled a volume of his autobiography *The Journey Not the*

Arrival Matters. While I hope that each of these essays, as well as the book collectively, "arrives," one of the great pleasures in writing it has been the assumed freedom of looking at what is to be seen along the way. There was a great deal to be seen: Melville's writings, of course, with sustained attention to the second half of his career; his attitudes toward society, history, and politics, from large ideas like "democracy" to neighborhood events like the Astor Place riot; his attitudes toward sexuality and, in nearly all chapters, toward religion; his relationship to America and his American audience; his relationship to past and present writers; his relationship to his wife, Lizzie, to Hawthorne, to his dead father, and to identic images of himself. Among literary figures, Hawthorne and Emerson figure prominently in the book, but so do Byron, Carlyle, and Arnold. As Lawrence Buell rightly observed, "it did not come naturally to Melville to think of himself simply and cleanly as an American man of letters."[10] His intellectual affinities were less with his American contemporaries than with his European ones, the English and German Romantics and the thought-burdened post-Romantics who lived in their afterglow and were precursors of modernity. To "historicize" Melville involves considerably more, and sometimes considerably other, than situating him within the social, political, and cultural context of ante- or post-bellum America. As to coverage, I have not felt obliged to be comprehensive. Some writings fall by the wayside, though the outlines of what might have been a chapter on the magazine pieces of 1853–56 are visible in my introduction to *"Billy Budd, Sailor" and Selected Tales* (Oxford's World's Classics, 1997).

Most of these essays are new. Those that have been previously published, with the exception of chapter 7, have all been enlarged and substantially revised or reconceived. I would like to thank the original publishers for permission to reprint or adapt portions of early articles. Intellectual debts are numerous, but I particularly wish to acknowledge the work of Charles R. Anderson, Newton Arvin, Warner Berthoff, Walter E. Bezanson, William B. Dillingham, Jay Leyda, F. O. Matthiessen, Hershel Parker, and Merton M. Sealts, Jr. To the late Merton Sealts also goes deep gratitude for years of friendship, encouragement, and generous sharing. I would like to thank Thomas L. Philbrick, a masterful teacher who introduced me to Melville; John Bryant and Randall Fuller, who read portions of the manuscript; Birgit Noll, with whom I discussed Melville and German Romanticism; Janet Duckham, who helped me think freshly about Melville's family; and graduate students Adam Sonstegard, James Spicer, and Tamara Taylor, who made useful suggestions about the Melville/Hawthorne relationship and about *Clarel.* I am grateful to Edward S. Macias, Dean of the Faculty of Arts and Science at Washington University, and David Lawton, Chair of the English Department, for a sabbatical leave that enabled me to complete the manuscript, and to Robert E. Thach, Dean of the Graduate School of Arts and Sciences, for financial support through a Faculty Research Grant. Always, and above all, I would like to thank my wife, Gail, for her love, patience, and support, and for her insightful comments on the manuscript. She is my best critic.

CONTENTS

ABBREVIATIONS

FOR FREQUENTLY CITED SOURCES

BB   *Billy Budd, Sailor (An Inside Narrative)*. Ed. Harrison Hayford
      and Merton M. Sealts, Jr. Chicago: University of Chicago Press,
      1962.

BP   *The Battle-Pieces of Herman Melville*. Ed. Hennig Cohen. New
      York: Thomas Yoseloff, 1963.

C   *Clarel: A Poem and Pilgrimage in the Holy Land*. Ed. Harrison
      Hayford, Alma A. MacDougall, Hershel Parker, and G. Thomas
      Tanselle. Vol. 12 of *The Writings of Herman Melville*. Evanston,
      Ill., and Chicago: Northwestern University Press and The New-
      berry Library, 1991.

CM   *The Confidence-Man: His Masquerade*. Ed. Harrison Hayford,
      Hershel Parker, and G. Thomas Tanselle. Vol. 10 of *The Writ-
      ings of Herman Melville*. Evanston, Ill., and Chicago: North-
      western University Press and The Newberry Library, 1984.

Corr *Correspondence*. Ed. Harrison Hayford, Hershel Parker, G. Thomas
      Tanselle, and Lynn Horth. Vol. 14 of *The Writings of Herman
      Melville*. Evanston, Ill., and Chicago: Northwestern University
      Press and The Newberry Library, 1993.

J   *Journals*. Ed. Harrison Hayford, Hershel Parker, and G. Thomas
      Tanselle. Vol. 15 of *The Writings of Herman Melville*. Evanston,
      Ill., and Chicago: Northwestern University Press and The New-
      berry Library, 1989.

M   *Mardi; and a Voyage Thither*. Ed. Harrison Hayford, Hershel
      Parker, and G. Thomas Tanselle. Vol. 3 of *The Writings of Her-
      man Melville*. Evanston, Ill., and Chicago: Northwestern Uni-
      versity Press and The Newberry Library, 1970.

MD   *Moby-Dick; or, The Whale*. Ed. Harrison Hayford, Hershel
      Parker, and G. Thomas Tanselle. Vol. 6 of *The Writings of Her-*

man Melville. Evanston, Ill., and Chicago: Northwestern University Press and The Newberry Library, 1988.

O   *Omoo: A Narrative of Adventure in the South Seas.* Ed. Harrison Hayford, Hershel Parker, and G. Thomas Tanselle. Vol. 2 of *The Writings of Herman Melville.* Evanston, Ill., and Chicago: Northwestern University Press and The Newberry Library, 1968.

P   *Pierre; or, The Ambiguities,* Ed. Harrison Hayford, Hershel Parker, and G. Thomas Tanselle. Vol. 7 of *The Writings of Herman Melville.* Evanston, Ill., and Chicago: Northwestern University Press and The Newberry Library, 1971.

Poems   *The Poems of Herman Melville.* Ed. Douglas Robillard. Kent, Ohio: Kent State University Press, 2000.

PT   *The Piazza Tales and Other Prose Pieces, 1839–1860,* ed. Harrison Hayford, Hershel Parker, and G. Thomas Tanselle. Vol. 9 of *The Writings of Herman Melville* (Evanston, Ill., and Chicago: Northwestern University Press and The Newberry Library, 1987.

R   *Redburn: His First Voyage.* Ed. Harrison Hayford, Hershel Parker, and G. Thomas Tanselle. Vol. 4 of *The Writings of Herman Melville.* Evanston, Ill., and Chicago: Northwestern University Press and The Newberry Library, 1969.

T   *Typee: A Peep at Polynesian Life.* Ed. Harrison Hayford, Hershel Parker, and G. Thomas Tanselle. Vol. 1 of *The Writings of Herman Melville.* Evanston, Ill., and Chicago: Northwestern University Press and The Newberry Library, 1968

WJ   *White-Jacket; or The World in a Man-of-War.* Ed. Harrison Hayford, Hershel Parker, and G. Thomas Tanselle. Vol. 5 of *The Writings of Herman Melville.* Evanston, Ill., and Chicago: Northwestern University Press and The Newberry Library, 1970.

"WW"   "'Weeds and Wildings Chiefly: With a Rose or Two' By Herman Melville." Ed. Robert C. Ryan. Ph.D. diss., Northwestern University, 1967.

Exiled Royalties

I

Anticipating Freedom: Melville and Polynesia

If sex is repressed, that is, condemned to prohibition, non-existence, and silence, then the mere fact that one is speaking about it has the appearance of a deliberate transgression. A person who holds forth in such language places himself to a certain extent outside the reach of power; he upsets established law; he somehow anticipates the coming freedom.

—Michel Foucault, *The History of Sexuality*, vol. 1

The myth of eternal return states that a life which disappears once and for all, which does not return, is like a shadow, without weight, dead in advance, and whether it was horrible, beautiful, or sublime, its horror, sublimity, and beauty mean nothing.

—Milan Kundera, *The Unbearable Lightness of Being*

Casting Off

In *Memories of a Catholic Girlhood*, Mary McCarthy wonders what course her life might have taken if she and her siblings had not been orphaned during the influenza epidemic of 1918 and lodged with unsympathetic relatives at a young age. She may, she imagines, have become "rather middle class and wholesome. I would probably be a Child of Mary. I can see myself married to an Irish lawyer and playing golf and bridge, making occasional retreats and subscribing to a Catholic Book Club. I suspect I would be rather stout." Vocation, McCarthy implies, does not inevitably assert itself; it may even require the stimulus of adversity. "Was it a good thing, then," she speculates, "that our parents were 'taken away,' as if by some higher design? . . . I do not know myself."[1]

To Allan Melvill, an importer of French goods in New York City, his second son, Herman, not quite seven years old, seemed "very backward in speech & somewhat slow in comprehension," though "of a docile and aimiable [amiable] disposition"[2] and probably not unsuited to commerce. It is unimaginable what Melville would have made of life, and life of him, had not his father died a bankrupt when Melville was twelve, blighting Melville's middle-class expectations and forcing him, as he would say of Redburn, "to think much and bitterly before my time" (*R* 10). The trauma of Allan's failure and premature death would be lifelong for Melville and would imprint itself deeply on his thought and art as well as on his emotional and perhaps his psychosexual life. The "good things" that issued from this early reversal of fortune were Melville's going to sea as a common sailor (a sourcebook for his writings through *Moby-Dick*) and his chancing to arrive in the Pacific at a moment when the past, present, and future of two civilizations, Polynesia's and the West's, were simultaneously available for observation or inference in a way that prompted questions about the nature of civilization itself.[3]

In the absence of letters, journals, and the testimony of associates, Melville's ascertainable life between his departure from Fairhaven, Massachusetts, on the whaleship *Acushnet* in January 1841 and his landing in Boston on the frigate *United States* in October 1844 is almost entirely a matter of places, dates, and occupations, save for what is recorded with varying degrees of reliability in his fiction or may be extrapolated from its attitudes and themes. Although Melville would later tell Hawthorne he "had no development at all" until his "twenty-fifth year" (*Corr* 193), the unfolding of mind that began with his writing of *Typee* (1846) had a long foreground, crucial to which were the more than three and a half years he spent in the Pacific. Ontologically, his experience of the wonder and terror of the sea, above all of its sublime indifference, bred in him an existential naturalism that would ripen from impression into idea under the stimulus of his subsequent reading and thinking. Politically, life aboard ship taught him the impertinence of class distinctions and arbitrary rule measured against the worth of the individual, whom he came to regard as universally possessed of natural rights, if not (as forecastle living also taught him) of natural goodness.

Not least, Melville's wanderings in the Marquesas, Society, and Sandwich (Hawaiian) islands supplied an otherwise provincial American with an outsider's perspective on matters of race, class, sexuality, social organization, progress, and history. Hawthorne remarked on this heterodoxy when, reviewing *Typee* for the *Salem Advertiser* in 1846, he praised Melville for "that freedom of view—it would be too harsh to call it laxity of principle—which renders him tolerant of codes of morals that may be little in accordance with his own."[4] In short, Polynesia did for Melville what a night and a day with Queequeg did for Ishmael. While the brevity of his residence in Typee (less than four weeks) and his rudimentary grasp of the language kept him from comprehending native customs on their own terms, he saw enough to realize, or idyllically imagine, that in their relationship to nature, to each other, and to their own bodies the Typees exemplified a mode of being antithetical to that of his own culture. What he previously took for "life" came to appear to him a particular arrangement of life. There were alternative arrangements; there might even be new and better arrangements.

Melville did not arrive at this view all at once, nor did he intellectualize it to himself either at the time or soon thereafter. In the Marquesas, his modern editors note, "he had been a naïve and inexperienced observer who was probably not to form his opinions concerning the relative merits of civilization and savagery until he had been exposed to more striking contrasts in Tahiti and Hawaii."[5] Even as he began *Typee* he had "no set political agenda"[6] and probably intended little more than to write a marketable book. Revisiting his experience, however, Melville began to interpret it, and as the demands of supplementing and explaining his recollections led him to consult earlier visitors to Polynesia—David Porter, Charles S. Stewart, Georg H. von Langsdorff, William Ellis, and Otto von Kotzebue, among others—he found himself gradually "discovering an ideology"[7] that situated Polynesia within the course of history and measured it socially and ethically against the Christian/capitalist West.

Completing *Typee* did not finish the process of coming to terms with the Marquesas. In a revised edition forced on him by his American publisher in response to criticisms in the religious press, Melville muted erotic passages in his book and excised many of its attacks on Western missionaries. In doing so he bowdlerized two of his chief themes, the despoiling of Polynesia by the Christian imperialist West and the personal and cultural effects of unrepressed sexuality. He would return to these themes almost immediately in *Omoo* (1847) but more as an extension of his account in *Typee* than as a conceptual development of it. The pervasive, if largely unformulated question in both books is the relationship between sexuality and the tenor and organization of social life. In part, as Newton Arvin pointed out, "Melville was debarred, as a writer for the general public, from reproducing all that he had certainly observed,"[8] but the elusiveness of *Typee* also stems from Melville's uncertainties about sexuality as a feature of Marquesan life. His remark about Typee religion—"I saw everything, but could comprehend nothing" (*T* 177)—applies nearly as well to Typee eroticism. Sexuality was omnipresent and, evidently, socially constitutive but in ways that Melville could glimpse only as outcroppings of cultural practice. The foundations, rationale, and psychodynamics of Marquesan sexual life he could only guess at.

Wanting adequate experience and even a rudimentary analytic vocabulary, Melville intuited but could not overtly ask, let alone answer, questions about the interdependency of eroticism and social structure that would engage theorists from Freud through Foucault and beyond. Because Melville saw relatively little, comprehended less, and was hindered from freely expressing what he did see, reading *Typee* for his psychosocial attitudes involves a process of triangulation. There is the text itself, scanned for what Arvin called its "discreet intimations" (Arvin 57) as well as its statements; there is Melville's engagement with his sources, whose opinions he adopts, revises, transforms, or contests as he shapes and enunciates his own; and there is the larger Melvillean context in which "Polynesia" is at once a constant retaining a core significance over the span of Melville's career and a variable receiving its local import within a particular literary or biographical gestalt. If Melville's thinking about sex and society—the erotic underpinnings of personal and communal relations—is not entirely comprehensible in *Typee*, neither is his later thinking on the subject comprehensible without *Typee*.

"In the Name of Christ and Trade"

When Melville jumped ship in Nukuhiva in July 1842, the Marquesas were at what might be called a threshold moment. Only weeks earlier Rear-Admiral Du Petit Thouars had taken possession of the islands in the name of France. Others had done so before, most notably Captain David Porter, who had claimed the northern Marquesas for America in 1813 and laid waste to the valley of the resistant Taipis.[9] Porter, however, came and went without permanently altering the fabric of island life, and Melville was largely justified in claiming that "in every respect" the inland tribes were "unchanged from their earliest known condition" (*T* 11). His initial descriptions of the Typee valley present this precontact state as Edenic, in contrast not only to shipboard life and life in the civilized West but, as the book unfolds, to conditions in the Society and Sandwich islands, where missionary civilization was well established. Commentary on *Typee* has typically focused on primitivism and civilization as opposing panels of a cultural diptych, but the book is also concerned with historical process and is imbued with a grim foreknowledge of "the change a few years will produce in [the Typees'] paradisaical abode" (*T* 195). Whatever sailor Melville's first impressions might have been, writer Melville cannot think of Typee apart from the afterimage of "the once smiling and populous Hawiian [*sic*] islands, with their now diseased, starving, and dying natives" (*T* 124).

Raymond Williams observed that in the nineteenth century the word "civilization" came to signify two things that "were historically linked: an achieved state, which could be contrasted with 'barbarism,' but now also an achieved state of *development*, which implied a historical process and progress" culminating in "the metropolitan civilization of England and France."[10] To be civilized meant to resemble bourgeois Westerners, or to adopt the amalgam of puritanical Christianity, consumer capitalism, and sentimental domesticity that defined respectable Euro-American life. In *Polynesian Researches*, a chief source for both *Typee* and *Omoo*, British missionary William Ellis underscored the relationship of virtue to consumption when he acknowledged that a "principal aim" of his colleagues in Tahiti "was to encourage habits of industry; and this, from the heat of the climate, the spontaneous productions of the soil, and other causes, appeared likely to be done by the introduction of what might be called *artificial wants*, which should operate on the native minds with power sufficient to induce labour for their supply."[11] To be fully and permanently Christianized, Ellis maintained, the islanders had to abandon their paradisaical economy and adopt a work ethic that would enable them to buy the "decent clothing" and enjoy "the comforts and conveniences" that were a requirement and measure of civilized life (Ellis 2:278). A benchmark moment for Ellis was the introduction of hats and bonnets among the Tahitians in the 1820s, soon followed by the passion among native women for the decorative ribbons and strings worn on the bonnets of missionary wives and daughters. Ellis notes with satisfaction that "European articles of dress are in the greatest demand; and there are few, who, by preparing arrow-root, feeding pigs, manufacturing cocoa-nut oil, or other labour, cannot purchase from the shipping a suit of foreign clothes"—a development, he adds, that has served to swell the "market for British manufactures the consumption of which, among the islands of the Pacific that have received the gospel, is already considerable" (Ellis 2:397). Ellis is sensitive to the absurdities of cultural imitation, such as affecting "a thick, shaggy great coat" in the oppressive Polynesian heat (Ellis 2:397), and to the charge that an obsession with Western finery may have encouraged worldly pride among the islanders. Yet Ellis never doubts that fashion-induced wants are not only an index of cultural progress but, among a people otherwise disinclined to labor and delayed gratification, an indispensable *means* for such progress, even if the rage for English clothes consigns the natives to feeding pigs.

Like other travelers, Melville would have observed the profound dislocations of missionary civilization in the Pacific, but he probably did not conceptualize his impressions until he returned home and began to sift them with the help of his sources. As he wrote *Typee* his indignation was strong enough to lead him beyond his immediate subject to sketch a fuller picture of the Polynesian world, one in which "the spontaneous fruits of the earth, which God in his wisdom has ordained for the support of the indolent natives," have been sold off to visiting ships and the "famished" islanders "are told by their benefactors to work and earn their support by the sweat of their brows!" (*T* 196). "Habituated to a life of indolence," he adds, the Polynesian "cannot and will not exert himself; and want, disease, and vice, all evils of foreign growth, soon terminate his miserable existence" even as his conquerors announce the triumph of Christianity over "the abominations of Paganism" (*T* 196).

Melville deleted this and similar passages for the "Revised (Expurgated?—Odious word!) Edition of Typee" (*Corr* 60), but he returned to his theme of the imposition of the Protestant ethic in the central chapters of *Omoo*, using Tahiti as a test case for the effects of missionary rule in the Pacific. Countering religious with nonreligious sources, Melville takes Ellis as his tacit point of departure—"It has been said, that the only way to civilize a people, is to form in them habits of industry" (*O* 189)—then proceeds to observe, echoing the reports of Charles Wilkes and Otto von Kotzebue, that the Tahitians are actually *less* industrious under missionary civilization than they had been in their native state: "Instead of acquiring new occupations, old ones [such as tappa-making] have been discontinued," and "native tools and domestic utensils" have been superseded by European manufactures bought with the earnings from menial labor or, as frequently happened, too expensive to be bought at all (*O* 189).[12] Deprived of their native employments and traditions—"denationalized," Melville presciently calls it (*O* 183)—the Tahitians have grown more licentious despite the efforts of a Taliban-like religious police to suppress even the most innocent native amusements. Islanders are herded to Sunday services under threat of forced labor and made to profess an austere form of Christianity foreign to their understanding and antipathetic to their "constitutional voluptuousness" and "aversion to the least restraint" (*O* 175). "Calculated for a state of nature, in a climate providentially adapted to it, [the Tahitians] are unfit for any other. Nay, as a race, they can not otherwise long exist" (*O* 190).

Melville's sorrow and anger at the destruction of Polynesia would not ease with time. The "authentic Edens in a Pagan Sea" he would later celebrate in the poem "To Ned" belong to more than his own nostalgically recollected youth; they belong to the world's youth "ere Paul Pry cruised with Pelf and Trade" (*Poems* 295), and they will not return. The note of elegy for a vanished time, place, and idyll of personal and cultural liberty grew stronger as Melville aged, but it never displaced his profound feeling of outrage at civilization's trespasses upon primitive innocence; in this respect, *Billy Budd, Sailor* is "Typee Revisited." In *Clarel*, Melville has the self-exiled American Ungar, himself part Indian, declaim against the predations of Christian/capitalist imperialism. The bitterness and hyperbole of Ungar's indictment are his own, but substantively Melville is speaking through him as he could only partially speak in *Typee* and *Omoo*:

> The Anglo-Saxons—lacking grace
> To win the love of any race;
> Hated by myriads dispossessed
> of rights—the Indians East and West.
> These pirates of the sphere! grave looters—
> *Grave, canting, Mammonite freebooters,*
> *Who in the name of Christ and Trade*
> (Oh, bucklered forehead of the brass!)
> Deflower the world's last sylvan glade!
>
> (*C* 4, 9: 117–25)

Eros and Snivelization

Within the mid-nineteenth-century debate on imperialism, Melville's position is that, whatever its achievements, Western civilization has little to offer a people living in natural abundance and temperamentally unsuited to the "strict moralities" (*O* 175) of otherworldly Christianity. Civilization, he writes in *Typee*, "may 'cultivate [the native's] mind',—may 'elevate his thoughts,'—these I believe are the established phrases—but will he be the happier?" (*T* 124). Melville, however, is also concerned with the level of happiness within civilization itself, and his eulogy of the primitive's idyllic, if preintellectual state quickly evolves into a polemic against the "heart burnings, the jealousies, the social rivalries, the family dissensions, and the thousand self-inflicted discomforts" attendant on "refined life" (*T* 124–25). In *Redburn* Melville would offer a comic version of this critique through one of Redburn's shipmates, Larry, who has lived in Madagascar and developed "a sentimental distaste for civilized society" (*R* 100):

> "And what's the use of bein' *snivelized?*" said he to me one night during our watch on deck; "snivelized chaps only learns the way to take on 'bout life, and snivel. You don't see any Methodist chaps feelin' dreadful about their souls; you don't see any darned beggars and pesky constables in *Madagasky*, I tell ye. . . . Blast Ameriky, I say!"
> (*R* 100)

For Melville in *Typee*, as for Larry, the issue is not simply what civilization can or cannot do for the precivilized; it is what civilization has done to the West, whether in the form of sin-obsessed piety or poverty-ridden capitalism. "It is impossible to read this pleasant volume," a British reviewer wrote of *Typee*, "without being startled at the oft-recurring doubt has civilization made man better, and therefore happier?"[13] Beneath its mix of travelogue, episodic plot, genial anecdote, and anti-imperialist rhetoric, *Typee* takes up the paradox later explored by Freud in *Civilization and Its Discontents*: that "what we call civilization," developed to protect human beings from nature and from one another, "is largely responsible for our misery."[14] With hindsight, Melville saw the arrival of the French in Nukuhiva as the beginning of a historical process that doomed the Marquesas to follow the course of Tahiti and the Sandwich islands. Beyond that, he seems to have regarded the incursion of the West as symbolic of a decisive anthropological moment in which a subsistence culture devoted to the senses was replaced by one of economic productivity, delayed (or denied) gratification, and social coercion.

In effect, what Melville witnessed in Nukuhiva in 1842 was an enforced historical version of Freud's mythological social contract: the origin of civilization in the passage from the pleasure principle to the reality principle. In this epochal transformation, according to Freud, human instincts toward a free, polymorphous sexuality, along with the drive toward aggression, were abandoned or checked in the name of communal stability, and the original gratifications of the self were channeled into work and sublimated into the "higher psychical activities" of science, art, and cognitive thought (*CD* 44). From the standpoint of the individual's liberty and happiness, this exchange was not a felicitous one. Because sublimated pleasures were less intense than instinctual ones and available only to a gifted few, civilization was inherently unsatisfying and prone to insurgencies from the thwarted instincts. Suppression was thus the very condition for order. Toward sexuality in particular, civilization felt obliged to adopt the stance of a police state, channeling all permissible sexual expression into monogamous "heterosexual genital love" (*CD* 51–52), stigmatizing alternative pleasures as perversions, and "disregard[ing] the dissimilarities, whether innate or acquired, in the sexual constitution of human beings"—all this, Freud observed, at a cost not merely of personal frustration but of "serious injustice" (*CD* 51).

As a product of the civilization Freud describes, the young Melville would have regarded its deprivations and denials as a condition of life even if his acquaintance with civilized unhappiness had not been compounded by the aftermath of his father's bankruptcy and death. In Typee he encountered a precivilized world in which "there seemed to be no cares, griefs, troubles, or vexations" (*T* 126) and happiness seemed perpetual. He was particularly struck, or became so after reading the accounts of David Porter and others, by the fact that the Typees maintained an "unparalleled" social harmony without the regulation of government and laws (*T* 200). "How are we to explain this enigma?" (*T* 200), Melville asks. Although the mysterious taboo imposed a host of restraints on even "the minutest transactions of life" (*T* 221), it could not account for the overwhelming spirit of "concert and good fellowship" (*T* 200) that permeated the valley; rather, Melville argued, it was to an "indwelling, . . . universally diffused perception of what is *just* and *noble*, that the integrity of the Marquesans in their intercourse with each other is to be attributed" (*T* 201).

"Know what he thinks a savage is and you have the key to his work,"[15] Clifford Geertz remarked of his fellow anthropologists. With less than a month's firsthand experience and a library of conflicting sourcebooks, Melville did not know what a savage was. A late addition to the manuscript, his praise of the natives' innate virtue was a rhetorical strategy, not a testament of belief. In the service of what Charles R. Anderson called his "brief against civilization,"[16] Melville found it useful to invoke the idea of the noble savage as a norm of reason and sentiment against which to measure and indict the perversions of the West. As a fledgling anthropologist, however, he was aware that the Typees were not *precivilized* but *alternatively* civilized and as much fashioned by the customs and traditions of their world as Euro-Americans were by the West's. Fayaway may seem "a child of nature," but the "audacious hand" that inscribed her countenance with minute tattoos was the hand of culture (*T* 86), which writes upon character from birth through a network of identity-defining practices and relationships.

The social conditions to which Melville ascribed Marquesan happiness were twofold, economic and sexual. Natural abundance enabled the Typees to dispense with money, "that 'root of all evil'" responsible for "those thousand sources of irritation that the ingenuity of civilized man has created to mar his own felicity" (*T* 126). Although private property and differences in wealth existed in Typee, the mental habits of competition, acquisitiveness, and material envy visibly did not. The question was whether moneylessness was the cause of the Typees' amity or itself the manifestation of a fraternalism with other roots. Reviewing *Typee* in the Brook Farm periodical the *Harbinger*, John Sullivan Dwight fastened on the economic theme and argued that through an equitable system of production and distribution the West could create the abundance that nature bestowed on the Marquesans, with a resulting "peace and good will" superior to theirs because of "our greater refinement and intelligence, and our higher religious development."[17] Brook Farm itself was a monument to this belief that "the work of human regeneration" had "a material basis."[18] What Dwight and his colaborers overlooked, and what Hawthorne made a dominant theme in his fictive treatment of the community, was the power of sexual rivalry to undermine brotherhood and sisterhood even in a materially egalitarian world. As

Freud would argue against socialism, human aggression, while expressing itself in a lust for property, was not created by private property or curable by its abolition: "If we do away with personal rights over material wealth, there still remains prerogative in the field of sexual relationships, which is bound to become the source of the strongest dislike and the most violent hostility among men who in other respects are on an equal footing" (CD 60–61).

It was in the context of sexual prerogative that Typee was particularly a revelation. Most Western travelers regarded the Marquesans as the comeliest of Polynesian peoples and "their eroticism" as "among the most elaborate";[19] yet beyond the remarkable beauty and voluptuousness of the natives, what impressed Melville was their unabashed innocence and want of sexual jealousy, along with a freedom from those frustrations and neuroses endemic to Western sexual and familial life. "There were no cross old women," Melville observes, "no cruel step-dames, no withered spinsters, no love-sick maidens, no sour old bachelors, no inattentive husbands, no melancholy young men" (T 126). In place of these things, among other customs, were a socially encouraged practice of youthful promiscuity and a marital system of polyandry and domestic homoeroticism in which an older suitor married both a young woman and her lover, "all three thenceforth liv[ing] together as harmoniously as so many turtle doves" (T 191).

With shipboard sexual practices fresh in his memory and Anglo-Saxon repression behind and probably still partially within him, Melville observed Marquesan sexual freedom, almost certainly availed himself of it, and came later to find it exonerated, even commended, in his more tolerant secular sources. While "virtue among [the Marquesans], in the light which we view it, was unknown," he would have read in Porter, the natives "attached no shame to a proceeding which they not only considered as natural, but as an innocent and harmless amusement, by which no one was injured."[20] Like Porter, Melville managed to purge his treatment of Marquesan sexuality of nearly all vestiges of Anglo-Saxon moralism and prurient sniggering. Beyond that, it is hard to gauge what relationship he saw between Marquesan eroticism and Marquesan communal harmony. He could scarcely have avoided posing the question; it was thrust upon him by his readings. In missionary Ellis's account, the Tahitians were as playful and good-natured as the Typees: "they do not appear to delight in provoking one another, but are far more accustomed to jesting, mirth, and humour, than irritating or reproachful language" (Ellis 1:96). Ellis's appreciation turned to horror, however, when he considered the Tahitians' sexual practices: "Awfully dark, indeed, was their moral character, and notwithstanding the apparent mildness of their dispositions, and the cheerful vivacity of their conversation, no portion of the human race was ever perhaps sunk lower into brutal licentiousness and moral degradation, than this isolated people" (Ellis 1:97). The litmus test of morality for Ellis was conformity with Western norms of sexual propriety, as it was for navy chaplain Charles S. Stewart, who found "all that [was] pleasing and praiseworthy in the nature and condition" of the Marquesans vitiated by one's "disgust at [their] licentiousness" and "moral deformity."[21] It did not occur to Ellis and Stewart that the qualities they admired in the natives might flourish because of, not despite, their eroticism. Did it occur to Melville as he wrote *Typee*?

There are indications that it did, despite Melville's limited grasp of the workings of Marquesan society. Ellis had found the Tahitians wanting in "that high satisfaction expressed by members of families more advanced in civilization" (Ellis 1:95). Melville notes a similar absence in Typee, but he regards it positively. Instead of dividing the community into family units, "the love of kindred . . . seemed blended in the general love" so that the whole valley "appeared to form one household, whose members were bound together by the ties of strong affection" (*T* 204). What Melville seems to be describing is the effluence of sexual and familial love into fraternity as the pleasures of the body and of kinship, detached from exclusive love-objects, become a source of cohesion within the body politic. A community bonded through affection is what Freud had in mind when he called civilization "a process in the service of Eros, whose purpose is to combine single human individuals, and after that families, then races, peoples and nations, into one great unity," and whose driving force is not necessity or a rational understanding of "the advantages of work in common" but libido (*CD* 69). However sacrosanct in bourgeois ideology, the nuclear family was not, in Freud's view, a historically climactic or entirely benign social institution; it could even exercise a retarding influence on the progress of civilization, since "the more closely the members of a family are attached to one another, the more often do they tend to cut themselves off from others, and the more difficult it is for them to enter into the wider circle of life" (*CD* 50). The relative weakness of Polynesian family ties that Ellis took as a measure of primitivism might, from another point of view, indicate a highly evolved civilization, and one whose foundation was precisely the eroticism Ellis deplored.

The issue raised by Marquesan society was whether Eros could form the operative principle of a civilization *without* discontents. Freud was radically divided on this question in ways that reflect on Melville's own nascent understanding of it. Within Freud's theory of the instincts, Eros was disruptive both for the community and for individuals, who in pursuing sexual fulfillment exposed themselves to rejection by the love-object; within, however, his apocalyptic vision of a world-struggle between creation and destruction, life and death, Eros was the only force powerful enough to counter the instinct of aggression. In *Civilization and Its Discontents* Freud tried to resolve his deep ambivalence by dividing Eros and enthroning a rarefied form of it. Against anarchic sexuality he set a decorporealized mode of libido that "avoid[ed] the uncertainties and disappointments of genital love by turning away from its sexual aim and transforming the instinct into an impulse with an '*inhibited aim*'" (*CD* 49). Eros of this kind was an "evenly suspended, steadfast, affectionate feeling" whose object was not a specific individual but humanity in general (*CD* 49), and which therefore was not inimical to civilization but conducive to it. Freud even went so far as to reverse his antireligious stance in *The Future of an Illusion* (1927) and praise the utility of those consummate forms of aim-inhibited Eros, the Christian principles of "love thy neighbor as thyself" and "love thine enemies" (*CD* 56, 57). It was precisely because human beings were naturally aggressive and *un*worthy of love that love became an essential means for curbing the instincts and advancing the cause of civilization (*CD* 59). Freud's fear that this struggle might prove to be a losing one, or a pyrrhic victory achieved at the cost of chronic unhappiness, stemmed from his belief that the desire for order was aligned *against* powerful instincts rather in accord with them. Aim-inhibited libido was a much-diluted substitute for sexuality, which, denied open expression, would flow darkly into the byways of sadism and violence. The paradox of Freud's position, as Herbert Marcuse pointed out, was that by making culture require "continuous sublimation" Freud impaired the power of Eros as a "builder of culture" and further unleashed the "the destructive impulses" that culture was meant to contain.[22]

Distrustful of Eros, Freud was unable to enlist it on civilization's behalf except in so decathected a form as to deprive it of whatever motive power it might have. The example of Typee implied a counterhypothesis: that rather than being distinct and antagonistic, sexuality (genital Eros) and communal love (aim-inhibited Eros) were naturally *continuous* and tended to diverge only when culture intervened to stigmatize pleasure and separate body from soul. At one point in his argument, Freud broached this possibility himself as he speculated on the path civilization might take if it "allow[ed] complete freedom of sexual life, and thus abolish[ed] the family"; all he felt sure of was that aggression would find some other outlet (*CD* 61). Marquesan society as Melville encountered it came close to actualizing Freud's liberationist state. Without abolishing the family, it weakened its bonds and inverted the psychosocial pyramid so that it rested on its broad instinctual base (sexuality) rather than tottering on its apex (sublimation buttressed by vigilant repression). The miseries of sexual life Freud ascribed to dependence on a single love-object were minimized for the Marquesans by the diffusion of sexuality among a plurality of love-objects held in affection but without possessiveness. The younger Marquesan women, Porter observed, were intelligent and vivacious but wholly without "fidelity" in the Western sense, which "they do not consider as necessary," nor "is it expected of them by their husbands," despite strong affection on both sides: "every woman was left at her own disposal, and everything pertaining to her person was considered as her own exclusive property" (Porter 2:59). Marriage did not involve sexual appropriation, yet neither did it imply continuing promiscuity. "After they have advanced in years, and have had children," Porter continued, the women "form more permanent connexions, and appear then as firmly attached to their husbands, as the women of any other country" (Porter 2:60–61).[23] Melville follows Porter's account closely, down to insisting on marital constancy. "Infidelity on either side is rare," he writes, and though "the matrimonial yoke sits easily and lightly," virtue in wedlock, "without being clamorously invoked, is, as it were, unconsciously practised" (*T* 191, 192).

Cumulatively through picture, anecdote, and commentary, *Typee* portrays a culture in which a guiltless, exploratory eroticism among the young developed into a stable but sexually tolerant adult order distinguished by feelings of community more consonant with the Christian ideal of brotherly love than anything Melville had witnessed in Christendom itself. With the examples of Typee and Christianized Tahiti in mind, Melville would have looked askance at William Ellis's claim that "unless habits of industry" were encouraged among the Polynesians they "would develop but partially the genius and spirit of Christianity, and exercise very imperfectly its practical virtues" (Ellis 2:282). The "genius and spirit of Christianity"— its ethical teachings—were precisely what the Marquesans *were* following, against the so-called practical virtues of Protestant capitalism, whose heartlessness Melville knew firsthand from his 1839 voyage to Liverpool as well as from the trials of his family in 1830s America. "J[esus]. C[hrist]. should have appeared in Taheiti" (*J* 154), he would later write—not, he felt, that the Polynesians were in special need of redemption but that their nature and society were particularly suited to Jesus' gospel of love.[24] The paradox Melville would come to exploit in book after book—that cannibals were the fraternal Christians, and professing Christians the predatory cannibals—was not an empty rhetorical flourish; it grew from his admiration for the social life of putative savages, and it lies at the moral center of his thinking in *Typee*. Like Freud in *Civilization and Its Discontents*, Melville sets Eros against Death, but he makes "primitive" culture the repository of Eros and civilization itself the primary agent of Death: "The fiend-like skill we display in the invention of all manner of death-dealing engines, the vindictiveness with which we carry on our wars, and the misery and desolation that follow in their train, are enough of themselves to distinguish the white civilized man as the most ferocious animal on the face of the earth" (*T* 125).

In eulogizing Marquesan community, Melville does not romantically slight the fact of aggression—the Typees' periodic skirmishes with neighboring tribes—but he presents it as a violence "expend[ed] on strangers and aliens" rather "than in the bosom of the community" (*T* 204). Freud euphemistically called such behavior "*the narcissism of minor differences*," a form of aggression frequent in "communities with adjoining territories, and related to each other in other ways as well," which functions as an outlet for an ineradicable human instinct and as a source of internal cohesion" (*CD* 61). A group solidarity facilitated by extragroup hatred can be a horrific thing, but Marquesan wars were largely ceremonial and bloodless, save for Westerner Porter's devastation of the Taipi valley in 1814. Like Freud, Melville seems to understand aggression as an ineradicable human instinct that is best deflected into relatively harmless cathartic rituals, as in Typee, rather than empowered in the service of material, national, or ideological aggrandizement, as in the West.

The issue of cannibalism was more problematic for Melville because of its loathsomeness to the civilized mind and its status as the very mark of primitive depravity. Whether or not Melville had ground to believe the Typees practiced cannibalism, the idea served him well as the core of his suspense plot and the reason for Tommo's flight from Typee. Caleb Crain argues that Melville "associate[s] . . . cannibalism and voluptuousness with one another."[25] I would emphasize the contrary: that Melville carefully *dissociates* them in order to make cannibalism a lightning rod for reader anxieties normally associated with sexuality. Invoking the image of a "heart of darkness," T. Walter Herbert, Jr., describes the unsettling shock of recognition experienced by Westerners in Polynesia as they found themselves involuntarily magnetized by an eroticism they condemned.[26] Foucault uses an identical trope—"the fragment of darkness that we each carry within us"—for the nineteenth century's obsession with sexuality as "harboring a fundamental secret" of our being.[27] The gnawing sweetness of a secret is that it may not be told and at the same time cries out to be told. This is the impression delivered by William Ellis's remark that "the veil of oblivion must be spread over" the licentiousness of the Tahitians' character (Ellis 1:98). To proclaim a need for silence is itself to invite prurient fantasy—a veil both hides and calls attention to the thing being hidden—but Ellis goes further and all but supplies the fantasy by alluding to the first chapter of Romans, with its references to hetero- and homo-sexual sodomy, as "afford[ing] but too faithful a portraiture" of the islanders' sins (Ellis 1:98).[28] The disgust of observers like Ellis was unquestionably sincere, yet it may also have involved, as Herbert speculates, a latent fascination that threatened the basis of civilized self-definition and required emphatic denial. "It is one thing to be tempted by a recognizable devil," Herbert remarks; "it is quite another to find oneself doubting that the attractive pleasure is in fact devilish" and so be forced to question one's very discourse about sin.[29]

By sensationalizing the threat of cannibalism, Melville makes *it* the lurid secret beneath the idyll of Marquesan life and directs reader anxieties about the primitive away from sexuality. From Tommo's first imaginings about the Marquesas ("Naked houris—cannibal banquets" [T 5]), the voluptuous and the cannibalistic are presented as opposite poles of savage life, as they remain through the climactic revelation of cannibalism that confirms Tommo's desire to escape. While Marquesan eroticism is portrayed as innocent pleasure, the pornographic titillation belonging to travel narrative is transferred to the prospect of cannibalism both as a device for narrative suspense and as a locus for the islanders' "heart of darkness." If, as Herbert says, the savage in Polynesia functions as "a source of testing . . . for the civilized self,"[30] Melville's handling of cannibalism allows the reader to say "I am not *that*—a cannibal" without identifying cultural self-definition with sexual morality.

Melville's success in naturalizing the sexual is shown by the fact that "though the Victorian Age had begun, common readers seem not to have been offended" by the eroticism of *Typee*.[31] Indeed, it was precisely the *un*exceptionableness of *Typee*'s eroticism that agitated readers like Horace Greeley, who conceded the "charm" of "Melville's graphic pages" in *Typee* and *Omoo* but found the books "unmistakably defective, if not positively diseased in moral tone. . . . Not that you can put your finger on a passage positively offensive; but the *tone* is bad."[32] An instance of this "tone" might be Melville's early description of Fayaway: "for the most part [she] clung to the primitive and summer garb of Eden. But how becoming the costume! It showed her fine figure to the best possible advantage; and nothing could have been better adapted to her peculiar style of beauty" (T 87). Hawthorne seems to have remembered Melville's words in *The Blithedale Romance* when he had Zenobia playfully tell Coverdale, "As for the garb of Eden, . . . I shall not assume it till after May-day!"[33] Coverdale's reaction is like Greeley's, an instinctive pleasure immediately checked by a blushing self-rebuke as if visions of Zenobia in a fig-leaf were "hardly . . . quite decorous, when born of a thought that passes between man and woman."[34] The achievement of *Typee* is to depuritanize sexuality by ridding it of Anglo-Saxon leering and reactive guilt. Melville's phrase "showed her fine figure to the best possible advantage" invites the reader to envision Fayaway nude, to delight in that nudity even to the point of arousal, but to accept arousal as a happily natural human fact. Melville tests the limits of such a stance when he describes the moonlight dances of the Marquesan girls as being "almost too much for a quiet, sober-minded, modest young man like myself" (T 152)—his "almost" performing the multiple functions of evoking the overheatedness of the scene, disclaiming a priggish reaction to it, reaffirming (archly) his status as a respectable member of his culture and class, and confessing his swooning enjoyment of the dance.

Foucault notes that unlike many classical, Middle Eastern, and Asiatic societies, the West has never had an *ars erotica*, in which "truth is drawn from pleasure itself" apart from "an absolute law of the permitted and the forbidden" and from the "criterion of utility."[35] An *ars erotica* was precisely what Melville discovered in Typee, where the chief business of youth was to anoint and beautify itself to enhance sexual attractiveness and where even venerable chiefs like Mehevi "carr[ied] on love intrigues with the maidens of the tribe," sometimes in tandem with a young man (*T* 190). Physical pleasure, however, was more than an elaborately cultivated pastime in Typee; the natives' *ars erotica* was also, Melville seems incipiently to have understood, the psychological and social basis of their *ars politica*.

Was eroticism a bond in primitive cultures only or could it serve as the foundation for a regenerated civilized life? This is the implicit question that gave Polynesia a significance for Melville well beyond the idyllic and the elegiac. Though Melville was never a social theoretician—his known readings conspicuously omit Tocqueville, Marx, Mill, Fourier, Spencer, and Comte—*Typee* has strong affinities with the tradition of the Freudian Left, particularly with Herbert Marcuse's *Eros and Civilization*, which raised the possibility of "a non-repressive civilization, based on a fundamentally different experience of being, a fundamentally different relation between man and nature, and fundamentally different existential relations" (Marcuse 5). In generalizing from the model of his own culture, Marcuse argued, Freud had confused the reality principle with what Marcuse called the "performance principle," or the "prevailing historical form" the reality principle took in a given society (Marcuse 35), in Freud's case "an acquisitive and antagonistic society in the process of constant expansion" (Marcuse 45). Freud had also failed to distinguish between the renunciations of the pleasure principle required for social order and the "surplus-repression" (Marcuse 35) exacted by a particular society in the service of economic and political domination (or, Melville might have added, of religious ideology).

Pertinently for *Typee*, Marcuse imagined the future development of civilization as involving a regression "behind the attained level of civilized rationality" in order to "reactivate early stages of the libido which were surpassed in the development of the reality ego" (Marcuse 198). Civilization, that is, needed to go forward by harking back. The chief element to be recovered was Eros—not the "aim-inhibited Eros" of Freud but sexuality itself. In truth, Marcuse worried about an orgiastic sexuality nearly as much as Freud did. What he envisioned with the dismantling of prohibitions was not an upsurge of genital sexuality but what he called a "'libidinal rationality'" that differed from Freud's aim-inhibited Eros chiefly by *diffusing* rather than sublimating or repressing the sexual instinct and that was "not only compatible with but even" productive of "higher forms of civilized freedom" (Marcuse 199). His phrase "the transformation of sexuality into

Eros" (Marcuse Ch 10) refers to a special kind of *"self-sublimatiom of sexuality"* (Marcuse 204) in which genitality is freer and more variously expressed than in Western society but in which sexuality is nonetheless marked by "a spread rather than explosion of libido" (Marcuse 201). For the individual, this change involved an eroticism that permeated the entire body and personality, as it hypothetically did before culture (not biology) fixed it narrowly upon the genitals; for society, it implied nothing less than a metamorphosis of human values and activities, including a "disintegration of the institutions in which the private interpersonal relations have been organized, particularly the monogamic and patriarchal family" (Marcuse 201).

"The transformation of sexuality into Eros" is an apt phrase for what Melville saw at work in Typee. If the effect of Western repression was a proliferation of sexualized objects and an elaborate taxonomy of forbidden behaviors—as Foucault says, an obsession with sex even as sex was seldom publicly discussed—the effect of Marquesan freedom was the reverse: a naturalization of sexuality that made it readily available, morally and culturally acceptable, and a source not only of innocent, nonpossessive delight but of a generalized affection that nourished communal bonds. In place of Freud's desexualized aim-inhibited Eros, Melville, like Marcuse, came to imagine the eroticized body as the fount of an alternative or complementary mode of consciousness for which the savage stood as an instructive type. Even missionaries who deplored Polynesian sensuality recognized its importance to the natives' mode of thinking. "When speaking of mental or moral energies," Ellis noted with surprise, the Tahitians eschew Western language of the head and heart and "invariably employ terms for which the English 'bowels' is perhaps the best translation" (Ellis 2:423)—"gut feeling," we say. Kory-Kory and Queequeg have this kind of visceral consciousness, related on one side to nature and sexuality and on the other to a sense of the (comm)unity of the species.

D. H. Lawrence came closest to voicing Melville's attitude toward primitivism and civilization when he remarked apropos of *Typee* and *Omoo*, "We can't go back to the savages. Not a stride. . . . [But] we can take a great curve in their direction, onwards."[36] Ishmael takes such a curve in *Moby-Dick* when he weds his speculative Western consciousness to Queequeg's somatically based "calm self-collectedness of simplicity" (*MD* 50). Queequeg is what Melville came to make of Polynesia, not as a geographical or cultural entity but as a mode of being detached from its source and inserted into the historical world as a rebuke to Western ways and a touchstone for qualities civilization needed to recover. The West, Marcuse argued, required "a reversal of the process of civilization, a subversion of culture—but only *after* culture has done its work" and established the mental and material conditions in which libidinal freedom could thrive (Marcuse 198). For Ishmael, returning to the Spouter-Inn after Father Mapple's sermon, the sight of Queequeg seated cosily by the fire, whittling away at the nose of his god, represents a "subversion" of the austere, otherworldly yet Mammonish Christianity of the West. Ishmael does not regress to the primitive; rather, through Queequeg, he subsumes it, and his new-found condition of sensual and affective well-being radiates outward in a *trans-* (but not *de-*) genitalized fashion to suffuse his relationship to the world. The chapter "A Squeeze of the Hand" with its "abounding, affectionate, friendly, loving feeling" (*MD* 416) rooted in the (homo)erotic activity of communally squeezing the whale's sperm is Typee transposed to a whaleship. The tableau realizes its full meaning, however, only in the intellectual Ishmael's presentation of it. Ishmael must go back to the primitive but then *ahead* to a "libidinal rationality" rooted in sexuality but extending beyond it to a state of being in which sexuality, sensuality, personal happiness, fraternal benevolence, and self-conscious intellect are enfolded together in himself and others to create a harmonious civilization without discontents.

The Unbearable Lightness of History

In the "Letter to Emerson" that prefaced the 1856 edition of *Leaves of Grass* Whitman ascribed the vapidness of American life and culture to "the lack of an avowed, empowered, unabashed development of sex . . . and to the fact of speakers and writers fraudulently assuming as always dead what everyone knows to be always alive."[37] Melville would have agreed. His experience in Polynesia gave him the basis for a Marcusan critique of civilization, yet with the exception of *Pierre* (which has its own special history), *Clarel*, and the poem "After the Pleasure Party" the critique went largely unwritten. *Typee* and *Omoo* are indignant books, but they are not, as they might have been, pleas for sensuous liberation like *Leaves of Grass*.

Returning to America in October 1844, after more than three and a half years in the Pacific, Melville found his family and the nation substantially changed. The hard times that had sent him to sea had long passed. A presidential campaign was in progress, and his older brother, Gansevoort, was earning a reputation as a vigorous orator on behalf of James K. Polk. Both Gansevoort and Melville's younger brother Allan had been admitted to the New York bar; the Melville family was doing well. Within the next two years, Melville would write *Typee*, achieve celebrity, settle into a career as an author of popular travelogue, and become engaged to Elizabeth Shaw—daughter of Lemuel Shaw, a former friend of Allan Melvill, a longtime benefactor of the family, and now chief justice of the Massachusetts supreme court. Living in Manhattan after his marriage, Melville moved among Evert Duyckinck's Young America literary circle and shared in the turbulent cultural and political life of the city. Despite memories of youthful hardship, later to surface in *Redburn* (1849), the events of late 1844–47 combined to reattune him to contemporary society. His future seemed bright, and his ambition was to succeed within the competitive, bourgeois American world, not to overhaul it.

Career prospects would always bear significantly upon Melville's writing, but his failure to translate his Pacific experience into a thoroughgoing social critique may also have had another cause. Charles R. Anderson noted that "Melville carried his interest in religion with him through all his wanderings in the South Seas, attending church whenever possible" but also, Anderson added, "shouldering on 'Christian' the whole burden of the multitudinous ills attributable, in the eyes of an idealist, to Western civilization."[38] The "startling solecism" Melville would later address in *Pierre*—"That while, as the grand condition of acceptance to God, Christianity calls upon all men to renounce this world; yet by all odds the most Mammonish parts of this world—Europe and America—are owned by none but professed Christian nations" (*P* 207)—was nowhere more evident than in Polynesia, where Euro-Americans were irresistibly extending their dominion. To a Christian idealist—which Melville would always be, despite his skepticism toward Christian metaphysics—the destruction of peoples who were better practical Christians than their self-appointed civilizers was more than a bitter irony; it was a betrayal that called into question the fundamental governance of history.

The genocide Melville saw in process in Tahiti and feared for the Marquesas did not seem to him inherent in the collision of Western civilization and primitivism. As he read in Kotzebue, "true, genuine Christianity, and a liberal government, might have soon given to [the Tahitians], endowed by nature with the seeds of every social virtue, a rank among civilized nations. . . . Europe would have soon admired, perhaps have envied Tahiti: but the religion taught by the Misssionaries is not true Christianity;" it is "a libel on the Divine Founder of Christianity" that has sacrificed "many more human beings . . . than ever were [sacrificed] to [the] heathen gods."[39] In *Typee* Melville adopts a similar position: "Let the savages be civilized, but civilize them with benefits, and not with evils; and let heathenism be destroyed, but not by destroying the heathen" (*T* 195). Even as he wrote these words, however, Melville must have known from the experience of Tahiti and the Hawaiian Islands that they were wishful thinking. The Protestant ethic was the inflexible rule of missionary civilization, and, forced by their conquerors to enter the stream of history on Western religio-economic terms, the Marquesans would go the way of other post-contact societies. "The Anglo-Saxon hive," he grimly observes in *Typee*, "have already extirpated Paganism from the greater part of the North American continent; but with it they have likewise extirpated the greater portion of the Red race. Civilization is gradually sweeping from the earth the lingering vestiges of Paganism, and at the same time the shrinking forms of its unhappy worshippers" (*T* 195).

In lamenting the last of the Polynesians, Melville was not, like Cooper in his novels, shedding a sentimental tear even as he applauded the triumph of a more advanced and ethically superior culture; the ethical superiority of Western civilization is precisely what *Typee* questions. Not only was Marquesan society doomed, but the terms of its passing—a compelled submission to Western ways culminating in extinction—also seemed inexorable. Returning from the South Seas with a radical's intuition of social possibility, Melville also carried home a vexed sense of the limits of human intervention in the macrocosmic processes of change. History would grind on according to its own logic of power irrespective of human protests and of moral right.

Irrespective, too, it seemed to Melville, of a divine plan. The lesson imposed on him in the Pacific extended the lesson of the Liverpool slums: the indifference of a laissez-faire economic system with its casualties of individuals and classes was replicated in the indifference of a laissez-faire universe with its sacrifice of entire races. Shortly before Melville's warship docked in Boston, Emerson delivered an address that raised this same question of nature's economy as it pertained to subjugated peoples. "Emancipation in the British West Indies" (1844) is Emerson's stirring, if belated debut as an abolitionist, yet beneath its carefully wrought argument is a lingering uneasiness about the relationship between social activism and natural law, whose benign pitilessness (Emerson had proclaimed earlier that year) "resists our meddling, eleemosynary contrivances."[40] Emerson's solution in the emancipation address was to ascribe to nature a logic and calendar of amelioration that regulated reformist impulses (often to check but sometimes to encourage) and an internal measure of value independent of human ethics. Nature "will save only what is worth saving; and it saves not by compassion, but by power"; only when a race represents "a new principle" and provides "an indispensable element of a new and coming civilization" does cooperation with natural law oblige citizens to become the race's defender.[41]

In Polynesia Melville saw precisely such a principle, "new" because it was old (a recovery of what had been lost in the development of civilization) and "indispensable" because it was the psychic complement to the West's restless material and mental aggrandizement. What Melville lacked after watching history unfold in the Pacific was Emerson's confidence in a benign teleology, whether providential or immanent. "Power," which for Emerson came from an alignment with beneficent natural laws, was for

Melville a function chiefly of organized righteousness and rapacity backed by military/technological force. There seemed no relationship, other than a commonly inverse one, between value and survival, nor could history's cruelties be legitimized by an appeal to long-term benefits or casuistical reasonings about divine intent. In *Omoo* Melville's account of the "hopeless" prospects of the Tahitians ends with the chant of a deceased highpriest: "The palm-tree shall grow, / The coral shall spread, / But man shall cease" (*O* 192). Not man altogether, but man in Tahiti, man in Polynesia, over whom time would close as obliteratingly as the sea closes over the drowned. The truly terrifying fact of history—what Milan Kundera would call its "unbearable lightness"—was not that evils endured but that they did not: that horrors like the extinction of an entire people could be absorbed into history with scarcely a ripple, to be forgotten in a generation or a half century and to be succeeded by new horrors, themselves to be forgotten.

In the idealist's gulf between "is" and "ought to be" Melville found the beginnings of what he would later call "blackness" (*PT* 243). His tendency to regard historical problems *sub specie aeternitatis* as metaphysical problems did not arise from his reading, nor was it simply the legacy of his youthful exposure to Calvinism; it came from a perception of ethical and social right being hopelessly and chronically overmatched. The evils he had witnessed in England and America as well as in the Pacific were manifestly social evils, and yet the vastness of the problems involved, the epochal sweep of the forces that generated and maintained social behaviors, the persistence of human indifference, brutishness, and folly as if they were psychologically determined or genetically inbred, and the all but insuperable difficulties of practical reform[42]—these things, falling upon a nature deeply theistic by temperament and training but unsettled in belief, seemed to point beyond active human agency to a fundamental dissonance in the order of things. The want of divine superintendence Ishmael would call "an interregnum in Providence" (*MD* 320) was, Melville early came to feel, permanent and constitutional. Faced with sufferings that seemed to defy amelioration, the tender-minded Redburn looked to Time and the Fatherhood of God (*R* 140); Melville himself could not, except occasionally as a hand-wringing last resort, and even then more as an appeal to temporal process than as an expression of trust in Providence. "Oftentimes," he has Babbalanja say in *Mardi*, "the right fights single-handedly against the world; and Oro [God] champions none. In all things, man's own battles, man himself must fight" (*M* 533).

There was hope in this orphaned naturalism, for it made human beings potentially the authors of history. If "what we call Fate is even, heartless, and impartial," as White-Jacket would say, then "ourselves are Fate" so far as "in our own hearts, we mould the whole world's hereafters" (*WJ* 320–21). It was one thing, however, to champion reform of specific abuses like flogging in the navy (already under debate in Congress as Melville wrote *White-Jacket*) and quite another to address the wide-scale depradations in the Pacific, let alone their roots in militarism, imperialism, economic exploitation, racism, and sexual repression. Even a free and relatively historyless people like the Americans labored within the inherited mindset of the Protestant ethic and could not begin to remake social institutions and relations until they themselves had been psychically remade. In "Man the Reformer" (1841), his most bitter attack on the organized "sefishness" of capitalism as it permeated the entire fabric of socioeconomic life, Emerson ended by proposing the solution of "Love," by which he meant nothing less than a total reorganization of being akin to the Calvinist's grace.[43] Love is what Melville saw operating in Marquesan society, but it was an erotically rather than a religiously based love, and for that reason all the more quixotic as a cure for puritanical capitalist America.

In *The Burden of Southern History* C. Vann Woodward ascribed the tragic vision of twentieth-century Southern writers to the region's experience of defeat and frustration, which "did not dispose [it] very favorably toward such popular American ideas as the doctrine of human perfectibility, the belief that every evil has a cure, and the notion that every human problem has a solution."[44] Melville's life history from the bankruptcy and death of his father through his years in the Pacific impressed on him a comparable sense of limits. Though he never lost his idealist's indignation at social injustice or prophet's faith in alternative possibilities, he came to feel that while reformist effort was necessary and sometimes efficacious, history, even in democratic America, would continue to stumble along in its cruel and wasteful fashion, uncontrolled by human intelligence or divine will.

It is sometimes asked whether Melville is chiefly a tragic writer or a social one. It seems most accurate to say that he is a tragic writer partly *because* he is a social one. "Humanity cries out against this vast enormity:—not one man knows a prudent remedy," he wrote of slavery in *Mardi* (*M* 534) and might have written of any of the other social enormities that outraged him. The "startling solecism" he addressed in *Pierre*—the disparity between the Sermon on the Mount and the way of the world—retained its hold on him throughout his career, whether his response was angry (*Typee* and *Omoo*), philosophical (*Mardi*), pathetic (*Redburn*), satirical (*White-Jacket*), comically ironic (sections of *Moby-Dick*), tragically ironic (*Pierre*), tragicomic ("Bartleby, the Scrivener"), satiric and deconstructionist (*The Confidence-Man*), mythic (*Billy Budd, Sailor*), or most of the above (*Clarel*). Whatever the literary mode and degree of authorial distance, the underlying attitudes were a bitterness toward God for his detachment from history and a visceral indignation at the callousness of human beings. "We talk of the Turks, and abhor the cannibals," Redburn says, "but may not some of *them*, go to heaven, before some of *us*? We may have civilized bodies and yet barbarous souls. We are blind to the real sights of the world; deaf to its voice; and dead to its dead. And not till we know, that one grief outweighs ten thousand joys, will we become what Christianity is striving to make us" (*R* 293).

Melville was a tragic writer not because he ignored or rose above his age but because he responded acutely to its problems and, finding them intractable, transposed them ultimately to the plane of metaphysics, as though only "something, somehow like Original Sin" on the level of Creation could account for the vast and permanent imbalance between good and evil (*PT* 243). The young writer who began *Typee* in 1845 had much of the equipment of the social radical—a history of alienation from the dominant culture, a broad acquaintance with its sins, follies, and blindnesses, and a visionary intuition of a happier and more equitable social order. What kept him from mounting more than a series of guerrilla attacks on Western society, then or later in his career, was the feeling bred by his family hardships of the 1830s and reinforced by his Pacific experience that nothing short of a transformation of human character could have palpable effect on the direction of events. As things stood, and had always stood so far as he could tell from his reading, history was a scene of horror, and intelligence and good will had only limited influence upon its course.

Toward the end of *Civilization and Its Discontents* Freud remarked that "the fateful question for the human species" was "whether and to what extent their cultural development will succeed in mastering the disturbance of their communal life by the human instinct of aggression and self-destruction" (*CD* 92). Freud claimed to be optimistic, if only because the new technology of warfare had brought humanity to the edge of self-extermination and "it [was] to be expected that the other of the two 'Heavenly Powers,' eternal Eros, will make an effort to assert himself in the struggle with his equally immortal adversary" (*CD* 92). That Freud should portray this Armageddon as a clash of human instincts writ large as superhuman "Powers" suggests how little confidence he had in the ability of reason and free will to determine the future. Conscious on one side of the regenerative power of sexual/communal love (Eros) and on the other of the ceaseless advance of domination and repression (Death), Melville combined a Utopian vision of social possibility with a sober but hopeful Freudian realism about historical process. His intuition, like Freud's, was that human destiny was up for grabs and that his own century was pivotal. Meanwhile, it was enough for Melville simply to live in his century. He was twenty-six years old when *Typee* was published and he became an overnight celebrity, and even ardently idealistic young men have other things to think about than the future of civilization. As he went about building a life, Polynesia settled fondly into his mind as a physical and symbolic locus of libido, which it would remain. To think of Polynesia, however, was also, inevitably, to recall its fate, and to be instructed once again in the cruel, blundering, horrific, and unbearably *light* ways of history.

2

The Broken Circle:
Mardi and (Post-)Romanticism

For as this appalling ocean surrounds the verdant land,

so in the soul of man there lies one insular Tahiti, full of

peace and joy, but encompassed by all the horrors of the

half known life. God keep thee! Push not off from that

isle, thou canst never return!

—Melville, *Moby-Dick*

To the romantic, . . . childhood is over, its island is astern,

and there is no other.

—W. H. Auden, *The Enchafèd Flood*

Adam's Flight

In "The Figure in the Carpet," Henry James's parable of authors and readers, novelist Hugh Vereker tells a young critic of a buried intention or idea
that infuses his work and is responsible at once for its materials and its form.
As "the very string that my pearls are strung on,"[1] Vereker's figure in the
carpet is discoverably present in his novels, and among James's objects in
the tale is the retrospectively announced one of rebuking a criticism that "is
apt to stand off from the intended sense of things, from such finely-attested
matters, on the author's part, as a spirit and a form, a bias and a logic, of his
own."[2] Like any writer, James would have the critic defer to the pressure of
meaning objectified through structure and technique, with tactful reticence
toward the private springs of art and the shaping influences of history and

culture. "Intention," however, is a double-edged idea that works both for and against authorial claims for interpretive control of texts. It may refer to conscious aesthetic design, as it does for James; to a forming principle (conscious or not) that is inferably operative in a work or body of work;[3] or to the meaning of such work within what E. D. Hirsch calls the particular "horizon" of "the author's mental and experiential world."[4] Beyond or beneath the immanent purpose that James, like Vereker, may have inscribed in his writing are the cognitive and emotional structures that inscribed James himself and of which he could have been only partially aware. It is a commonplace that authors repeat themselves, ring changes on a constellation of themes, reenact dramatic postures, rehearse core fantasies, and refract discourses and ideologies of their times. In this they are instruments as much as creators of their recurring myths, and it would be problematic in some cases to decide whether authors are constructing their characteristic fables or the fables are constructing them.

There can be no single unequivocal figure in any literary carpet (all reading being a matter of construing and contextualizing), yet some authorial patterns obtrude themselves with special force. "Melville never wrote anything but the same book, which he began again and again," Albert Camus remarked of the "unappeasable" quest introduced in *Mardi*, consummated in *Moby-Dick*, subverted in *Pierre*, and dissected with vertiginous irony in *The Confidence-Man* (Camus seems not to have known *Clarel*).[5] "The voyage or quest was not simply a subject or an occasion" for Melville, Newton Arvin observed; "it was an archetypal pattern of experience to which his whole nature instinctively turned."[6] The mark of Melville's heroes (Ishmael included) is that they repudiate Ishmael's advice in "Brit" and "push off" from the safety of their "insular Tahiti" into "the half known life" (*MD* 274). The seeker Rolfe in *Clarel* speaks for the Melvillean quester generally when, fictively retracing his creator's experience as rendered in *Typee*, he rejects the pleas of his island hosts to remain with them, "abjures the simple joy" of their paradise, and "hurries over the briny world away'" (*C* 3, 30: 74–75). "Renouncer!" he chides himself years later: "is it Adam's flight / Without the compulsion or the sin? / And shall the vale avenge the slight / By haunting thee in hours thou yet shalt win?" (*C* 3, 3: 76–79).

The theme of Rolfe's soliloquy is the fall into knowledge, a willed lapse not through transgression but from an instinct that innocence, however alluring, is insufficient. Polynesia is nature, community, physical delight, and "simple joy," but with an emphasis on the adjective ("simple") that crucially devalues the noun. The other face of the Marquesans' sensuous fraternalism, so admirable on its own terms, is the mental childishness that makes their lives an aggregate of "the little trifling incidents of the passing hour," or "an often interrupted and luxurious nap" (*T* 144, 152). If on one side Polynesia represented for Melville a salvific complement to the domineering consciousness of the West, on another it was a lotus-eater's paradise fatal to the aspirations of humanity as intellectual and spiritual beings.

Through Rolfe, Melville is offering a version of the common Romantic reformulation of the Fall, in which, as Northrop Frye put it, "the older [biblical] myth of an unfallen state, or lost paradise of Eden," was recast as "a sense of an original identity between the individual man and nature which has been lost."[7] The new myth was rooted in socio-economic changes of the later eighteenth century, in the dissociation of sensibility that writers like Schiller posited long before Eliot coined the term, and in the rise of Hellenistic studies in pre-Romantic Germany, which established an idealized portrait of classical Greece as a foil to the inwardness of modernity. By the time of *Moby-Dick* Melville was saturated in Romantic myth; he had talked post-Kantian philosophy with German-American scholar George J. Adler, read Goethe, Schiller, and Jean Paul, sampled broadly in the English Romantics (especially Coleridge and Carlyle), and listened to and read Emerson. He had come to inhabit a transatlantic community of discourse modified in unique ways by New World conditions and possibilities yet sharing in the broader attitudes toward nature, the self, and the epochs of history that marked the transition from Enlightenment to Romantic thought. In fundamental ways, however, Melville's Romanticism anteceded his eclectic readings of 1848–50. It was rooted in his temperament and in his early infatuation with Byron, whose influence was incalculable, but it also grew formatively out of his residence in Typee, which acquainted him with the "undisfigured nature" that Schiller felt civilized man could possess only in remembrances of childhood and through the literary genre of idyll.[8]

Melville's special fate was to have known by experience a precivilized state that most Romantics could only theorize about, and to have known it historically in reference to the course of civilization as well as individually as a moment of freedom and prereflective delight. The myth of cultural development Schiller sketched in *Naïve and Sentimental Poetry* (in many respects the prototypal Romantic text[9]) corresponded in broad outline to the logic of Melville's development from his arrival in the Marquesas in 1842 through his completion of *Mardi* in 1848. The defining circumstance for both writers was the rejection of "innocent and contented mankind" (Schiller 146), which for Melville involved, on the one hand, the physical act of leaving Typee and, on the other, the intellectual act of undertaking the ambitious course of reading that would initiate him into "the world of mind" (*M* 556).

Romantic ideology as Melville later encountered it would help conceptualize the lesson he incipiently learned from his experience in the Pacific: that while individuals and societies could not regress to the primitive, they might ideally *pro*gress through life experience and history toward a kind of "higher primitivism" that recreated the personal and communal wholeness of the precivilized state but on the level of instructed mind. "All people who possess a history," Schiller wrote, "have a paradise, a state of innocence, a golden age," as do individuals whose childhood memories are glorified by poetical imagination (Schiller 148). The danger of literary representations of paradise (idylls)—Melville might have the same of actual paradises—is that, "set *before the beginnings of civilization*, they exclude together with its disadvantages all its advantages" and tempt us "backwards into our child-hood in order to secure to us . . . a peace which cannot last longer than the slumber of our spiritual faculties" (Schiller 149, 153). The legitimate use of idyll, Schiller felt, was not retrospective but prospective; idyll served to remind us of a condition of psychic wholeness and integration with the world that preceded civilization but was also, in a developed historical form, its ultimate goal (Schiller 147).

Symbolically, the flight from Polynesia was an intuitive declaration that the true paradise lay somewhere "over the briny world away" at the conclu-sion of a journey as uncertain as it was imperative. That it *was* imperative was a defining Romantic article of faith. Contrasting ancient (naïve or clas-sical) and modern (sentimental or Romantic) poetry, Schiller formulated the myth of a lapse from "*sensuous* harmony" with the world into self-conscious-ness, psychic fragmentation, estrangement from the community, and alien-ation from nature and the universe, a transitional phase through which both individuals and races needed to pass in their pilgrimage toward self-com-pletion (Schiller 111, 112). This midstate—humanity's home for the pres-ent and foreseeable future—was not a comfortable one. Whereas naïve (or natural) persons could be "perfect" within the limits of their "finite" being and the requirements of physical life (Schiller 113), moderns, impelled by "a restless spirit of speculation that presses on to the unconditioned in all its knowledge" (Schiller 177), were necessarily *im*perfect in relation to the ideal of moral unity toward which they strove. Since that ideal was "infi-nitely preferable" to the achievements of natural persons, even those of the ancient Greeks,[10] there was no question of civilization's value for the growth of the individual and the progress of the race (Schiller 113). Nonetheless, feeling themselves both inferior in harmony to earlier peoples and incalcula-bly distant from a higher harmony, moderns could never be certain of their relative worth, much less find ease in their amphibious state.

The predicament of Schiller's moderns is the predicament of Rolfe as he recalls the Polynesian idyll behind him and envisions only an endless search ahead. Typically, the plot of Romantic discourse was a celebratory one in which, as M. H. Abrams described it, "the Christian history of the creation, fall, and redemption was translated to the realm of human consciousness as stages, or 'moments,' in its evolving knowledge," beginning with an "initial act" of severance-through-intellection and leading ultimately to a "unifying and integrative" consciousness higher than the lost innocence (Abrams 188–89). In other words, the remedy for the dislocations of knowing was more knowing. Abrams called this plot, alternatively, "the ascending circle, or spiral" (Abrams 184), "the circuitous journey" (Abrams, chs. 3 and 4), and "the spiral journey back home" (Abrams 190). Under any name, its subject was "the painful education through ever expanding knowledge of the conscious subject as it strives—without distinctly knowing what it is that it wants until it achieves it—to win its way back to a higher mode of the original unity with itself from which, by its primal act of consciousness, it has inescapably divided itself off" (Abrams 190–91). Abrams's words are a fair summary of the intellectual plots of *Mardi*, *Pierre*, and *Clarel*, and of the pursuit of "the ungraspable phantom of life" (*MD* 5) that leads Ishmael to reject the familiarities of the land for the ontological mysteries of the sea. The difference between the Melvillean and the Romantic quests is that, while reproducing the pattern of Romantic myth, Melville's quests thematically abort it: the ascending circle in Melville's writings is never completed (save perhaps in *Billy Budd*), the more inclusive unity never achieved. Rather, Melville's heroes resemble, and openly draw upon, the legendary antiheroes (Ishmael, Cain, the Wandering Jew) sometimes featured as interim or crisis phases within the Romantic myth of fortunate return. In Melville, this "interim" phase is permanent, and any resolution of the quest, should there ultimately prove to be one, will occur beyond, not within, human time.

Morse Peckham disparaged Melville's relationship to his European predecessors and contemporaries when he argued that Melville "absorbed all at once all stages of Romanticism up to his own time, and . . . presented them in *Moby-Dick* in inextricable confusion."[11] This is partly true for *Mardi*, which Richard H. Brodhead called "the first draft of all [Melville's] subsequent works,"[12] and which, like many overambitious first drafts, is "a source-book for plenitude."[13] The larger truth is that in thought and feeling Melville replicated in condensed form more than half a century of Western literary and intellectual history. Two of Carlyle's modern editors refer to *Sartor Resartus* (1833–34) as "mark[ing] the transition from the Romantic to the Victorian period" and "enact[ing] within itself the dislocations of the passage."[14] *Sartor*, that is to say, "contains" Wordsworth and Byron and tries to subsume them to a new faith, or prophecy of a faith, pertinent to an age that has outgrown the traditional vestments of belief. *Mardi* also "contains" Wordsworth and Byron; by its rootedness in a common situation, it "contains" aspects of Carlyle as well; it reaches further still to anticipate the intellectual pyrrhonism and spiritual paralysis of Melville's near-contemporary Matthew Arnold, whose sense of belatedness vis-à-vis the Romantics and whose struggles with religious belief most nearly resemble Melville's own. What Peckham takes for confusion is, in *Mardi*, a function of the Romantic quest extending itself into a post-Romantic age and combining the exuberant self-dramatization of early Romantic quest narrative with a Victorian recognition of intellectual limits and feeling of spiritual ennui. A voyage of discovery through a circular atoll, *Mardi* is Melville's Schillerian *Bildungsroman*, save that the discovery is never made. Its journey is a spiral inward into greater complexity and ambiguity, not upward into higher unity and toward "home." "Let *me*, then, be the unreturning wanderer" (*M* 654), its hero Taji says at the last, prefiguring Melville's other seekers-turned-wanderers, Ishmael, Pierre, and the company of homeless figures in *Clarel*.

Idyll and Elegy

"We are off!" (*M* 3), *Mardi* begins. Who is off? Off to where? With its note of "excitement, unspecific and undirected,"[15] no opening could better announce a book whose protagonist is ambiguous (Taji or Babbalanja?), whose distance between protagonist and author is inconstant, whose reader is periodically enlisted as an accomplice in its intellectual adventure, and whose thematic and generic wanderings are as erratic as its geographical ones. For Melville, too, casting off is the keynote of *Mardi*. Having inaugurated his career with two semiautobiographical travelogues, Melville began his third book as a "narrative of *facts*" only to feel "irked, cramped & fettered by plodding along with dull common places" (*Corr* 106). *Mardi* would transform itself three times before Melville finally sent it to press, first into a "'Romance of Polynisian Adventure'" (*Corr* 106), then, in reponse to his readings of 1848, into a philosophical anatomy surveying a range of human thought and activity and focusing with increased urgency on the problems of knowledge, good and evil, faith and doubt, and immortality that would occupy Melville throughout his career. The protagonist of the romance is the shadowy first-person narrator, Taji, who wins, then loses a maiden named Yillah and searches for her unavailingly through the Mardian archipelago, Melville's symbol for the world. The protagonist of the anatomy is the philosopher Babbalanja, a quester of a more inward sort whose object is truth and the ideal way of life and whose dialogues and soliloquies come to form the book's center of gravity. Late in the compositional process, Melville inserted an extended political allegory prompted by events of 1848 in western Europe and America, supplementing *Mardi*'s philosophical themes with topically historical ones.[16]

The journeys of Taji and Babbalanja are complementary symbolic and intellectual embodiments of the Romantic search for unity in a postlapsarian world. Jerome C. McGann described Byron's *Childe Harold's Pilgrimage* as a work that "demands that the narrating poet be considered a participant in an action whose future progress he cannot know and whose ultimate issue he is, at all points prior to the climax, only partially aware of."[17] *Mardi* is

Melville's *Childe Harold*, prompted like Byron's poem by a feeling of satiety with ordinary life and a readiness to chance whatever comes.[18] The metaphoric vehicle for this spirit of adventure is wind and speed. Late in *Mardi* Melville will write of being "driven from my course, by a blast resistless" and "still fly[ing] before the gale" (*M* 557), but as in "The Lee Shore" in *Moby-Dick* he prefers the dangers of intellectual shipwreck to those of boredom and enervation. Against the enlivening breeze—a common Romantic image for the imagination—Melville sets the physical and metaphysical ghastliness of an oceanic calm, "a state of existence where existence itself seems suspended," "volition" is annihilated, and everything appears "gray chaos in conception" (*M* 9, 10, 48). To Taji, mental life aboard the whaleship *Arcturion* is a continuous calm. There was no one "who could page me a quotation from Burton on Blue Devils," he complains, no soul that was "a magnet to mine" (*M* 5, 4). Since Melville would not acquire a complete *Anatomy of Melancholy* until January 1848—he knew Burton through selections purchased the previous April[19]—Taji's impatience with commonplace life seems to reflect an awakening hunger on Melville's part for the speculative, the melancholic, and the meaning-laden more than an active acquaintance with these things. Impelled by the Romantic's "yearning for the yonder bank,"[20] Melville was a Romantic by inclination before his intellect reared up a superstructure of thought; the impulse to quest foreran any definite idea of what the quest might entail.

With the appearance of Yillah, *Mardi* enters the domain of Romantic myth. For Taji, Yillah is less an actual woman than "the earthly semblance of that sweet vision, that haunted my earliest thoughts" (*M* 158). Psychobiographers associate Yillah with Melville's pre-Oedipal relationship with his mother or his courtship and early marital happiness with Elizabeth Shaw, but Yillah might also be linked with Freud's "oceanic principle," a feeling of cosmic belongingness enjoyed by the ego before it "separates off an external world from itself."[21] Marginal in Freud, a form of the oceanic principle is prominent in Jung, who, in Martin Bickman's words, saw "the individual psyche" as originating "in a state of complete undifferentiated unconsciousness, a primordial wholeness that exists prior to and encompasses all opposites":

> As the ego grows and develops, it tends to separate itself from the rest
> of the psyche, setting up barriers between consciousness and what
> remains and what becomes unconscious. . . . Although this develop-
> ment is necessary for functioning in what we call everyday reality, . . .
> it creates an imbalance in the "self," the entire psychic unit, and leaves
> a person divided, with only a fragment of his or her potential realized.
>   Later in life, this unrealized potential beckons toward a rejoining of
> the ego with the rest of the self in a fuller integration of personality.[22]

Jung is especially pertinent to *Mardi* because his account of the process of individuation is rooted in the "circuitous journey" of the Romantics, itself a secularization of the Christian/neo-Platonic pattern of Paradise (unity), Paradise lost (the fall into division and self-division), and Paradise (to be) regained (a loftier unity ahead). Because the forward path toward integration is difficult and uncertain, there is a persistent temptation to fixate upon, lament, or try to recover the infantile past. In Romantic writings, Abrams notes, this desire to return to origins "is sometimes expressed as *Heimweh*, the homesickness for the father or mother and for the lost sheltered place; or else as the desire for a female figure who turns out to be the beloved we have left behind" (Abrams 194). In *Mardi* the female figure is Yillah, idealized in retrospect as Taji "look[s] back upon" their happiness from the standpoint of later "woes" (*M* 193): "The remembrance seemed the thing itself" (*M* 194). The loss of Yillah is Taji's imagined exile from paradise, and his quest to regain her, projected forward in time and across the breadth of the Mardian world, is essentially the Gatsbyan search for a putative bliss located at the beginnings of individual and cultural life.

Schiller divides "sentimental" (i.e., modern or Romantic) poetry into two chief categories: the satiric, whose "subject [is] alienation from nature and the contradiction between actuality and the ideal" (Schiller 117), and whose tone may either be comic or passionately earnest; and the elegiac, which looks wistfully backward to an imagined paradise, whether in longing (elegy itself) or in fancied attainment (idyll). Taji's brief possession of Yillah is cast as idyll, his loss of and obsessive search for Yillah as elegy. For Schiller the genuine elegiac note involves more than a sadness "at lost joys, at the golden age now disappeared from the world, at happiness departed with youth, with love, and so forth" (Schiller 126); its poetic significance rests on the moral symbolism of the lost object, which stands for an ideal of inner being mistakenly identified with a person or place, as if to recover *that* were to undo the Fall. For Taji in his restlessness and dissatisfaction, Yillah is the conduit backward to a glory overlaid by the mundaneness of civilization. Taji must win Yillah to be reminded of the wonder of life; this is the value of idyll: to help man "purify himself of the corruption of civilization" and rekindle the drive toward perfection (Schiller 148–49). But Taji must also lose Yillah, for the perfection of completeness lies ahead of him, through the trials of consciousness in the turbid world of experience, not behind in the simplicities of childhood. "In the typical *Bildungsweg*," Shirley M. Dettlaff observes of Romantic plots,

the protagonist falls from his innocent, instinctive life of the senses. Some trauma, often an unhappy love affair or death of a loved one, shocks him out of this naive unity with nature, and he enters the romantic state, one characterized by alienation, obsessive thought, interior conflict, melancholy, and unfulfilled yearning. He sets off to search for truth and for a return to this earlier paradise, but he discovers that he cannot go back and instead must struggle forward dialectically through reflection and freedom to achieve a new wholeness or reintegration.[23]

The story of Taji follows the Romantic pattern, with the exception that Taji never understands or accepts the developmental necessity of loss. Taji is a Romantic elegist, yet because of his fixation on the past he is not truly a Romantic quester. That will be the role of Babbalanja.

Romantic Satire

Babbalanja seems to have entered *Mardi* as an afterthought, probably in the early months of 1848 when, in response to his readings in a "remarkably varied but by no means random cluster" of "great and near-great writers"[24]— Burton, Sir Thomas Browne, Rabelais, Montaigne, Seneca, Coleridge, and Ossian, among others—Melville realized that he had cast off yet again and that his burgeoning philosophical interests required a more reflective protagonist than Taji and a more thought-conducive literary form than florid romance. Retaining Taji as a nominal but effaced narrator, Melville enfolded him intellectually within Babbalanja as a silent auditor of the quasi-Platonic dialogues that now commanded the book, available to act on call as if in consequence of them.

In *Pierre* Melville would have his author-hero intuit "that most grand productions of the best human intellects ever are built round a circle, . . . digestively including the whole range of all that can be known or dreamed" (*P* 283). In structuring *Mardi* according to this pattern, Melville created a home-grown version of German encyclopaedic Romance, as reviewers like George Ripley noted when they attacked the book for its abstruse content and ungainly form.[25] Although Melville would not read the Germans until after *Mardi* was completed, he drew from several of the same sources (Plato, Rabelais, Swift, Montaigne) that they did, and he seems intuitively to have reached some of Friedrich Schlegel's conclusions about modern literature: that it should be polyphonic and dialectical ("Novels are the Socratic dialogues of our time,"[26] Schlegel said); that it should be comprehensive, "a mirror of the entire surrounding world, a picture of its age," as the epic had been in earlier times;[27] and that it should be self-referential rather than objectively mimetic ("what is best in the best of novels is nothing but a more or less veiled confession by the author, the profit of his experiences, the quintessence of his originality").[28]

Mardi's "chartless" voyage (*M* 556) was a ready container for whatever provoked Melville in his reading or in contemporary events, but beyond that it was an autodidact's attempt to sift human knowledge in pilgrimage toward the reunification of experience that Abrams called "the redemptive goal of human life" for the Romantics (Abrams 189). With Wordsworth as his prime example, Abrams presents the Romantic journey as a triumphant one, yet beneath his claims about translucencies and correspondences, even Wordsworth suspects that the benignly instructive pantheism he finds in nature is of his own poetic making, a sermon imposed upon the stones of experience (allegory) rather than discovered within them (symbolism).[29] The awareness of Wordsworth and other Romantics of rhetorical sleight of hand—of a finessed gap between self and world, wish and fact—accounts for what Tilottama Rajan describes as a skeptical "counterplot within the apparently utopian narrative of Romantic desire, . . . initially hidden in the subtexts rather than the texts of works,"[30] though sometimes later, as in Wordsworth's "Elegiac Stanzas" or Coleridge's "Dejection: An Ode," surfacing in an overt repudiation of Romantic faith.

The legacy of the early Victorians was lamentationally to insist on what the Romantics tried to suppress. Robin Gilmour assigns "the first phase of the Victorian 'crisis of faith'" to the decade of the 1840s, among the post-Romantic generation "born between about 1810 and 1820."[31] (Melville was born in 1819; *Mardi* was published in 1849.) What Arnold in his 1850 eulogy of Wordsworth called the "doubts, disputes, distractions, fears" of "this iron time"[32] no longer seemed curable by Romantic affirmations and cloudy gestures of belief. "Wordsworth's eyes avert their ken / From half of human fate," Arnold wrote in "Stanzas in Memory of the Author of 'Obermann,'" as if weaning himself from a palliative he had long depended on. Melville's intellectual coming-of-age in the later 1840s coincided with the period when it came to be widely believed and openly acknowledged that, as Elizabeth S. Foster put it, "the benevolent hand of a Father" was no longer on "the tiller of the world."[33] *Mardi* testifies to this midcentury moment as both a personal moment in Melville's development and a historical moment of transatlantic spiritual crisis; except in its political themes, *Mardi* is an early Victorian book more than it is a provincially American one.

In the absence of compositional evidence, it is hard to determine how far *Mardi* consciously dramatizes the passage from faith to doubt and how far it autobiographically enacts it. Early in the book the narrator enthuses, "All things form but one whole; the universe a Judea, and God Jehovah its head. Then no more let us start with affright. In a theocracy, what is to fear?" (*M* 12). This is the Father at the tiller with a steadfast hand, but is Taji also speaking for Melville here, and are his words authoritative or intentionally or unintentionally ironic? Perhaps Melville is taking his cue from Sir Thomas Browne, whose "speculations operated as one of the strongest agents" in *Mardi*, sometimes "to the length of ventriloquism."[34] Or perhaps he has already abandoned such a position (if he ever held it) and is establishing a reference point for what he intends to be a journey of disillusion. Several of the early chapters (for example, chapter 48, appropriately titled "Something Under the Surface") contain structural ironies that undercut the narrator's blithe optimism, often by intruding evidence of the indifference or predatoriness of nature and the ubiquity of pain and death. The labored prose of these chapters anticipates the opening sections of *Pierre*, but though Melville seems not to be writing with the same openly parodic intent, his subversions preclude a naïvely literal reading. My own guess is that Melville was clumsily rehearsing his own initiation as a young sailor and drawing out the disjunctions between conventional belief and the metaphysical lessons of life at sea. Culture had instilled in him one reading of the universe, experience had imprinted another, and as yet he was intellectually straddling the two, unsure how (and whether) to translate his experience into an open interrogation of belief even as he nipped at its flanks.

Melville's readings of 1848 catalyzed his thought, but they also challenged him as a writer to rise to their example and trust his philosophical intuitions wherever they led him.[35] With the appearance of Babblanja, questions about nature, God, and immortality come soberly to the fore, in direct opposition to the early benevolism of Taji. "All vanity, vanity, . . . to seek in nature for positive warranty to these aspirations of ours," Babbalanja tells the poet Yoomy as they stand before the *memento mori* of a royal tomb: "Through all her provinces, nature seems to promise immortality to life, but destruction to beings" (*M* 210). Later in the voyage Babbalanja will return to this theme with reference to "the rise and fall of Nature's kingdoms" (*M* 415) as recorded in geological strata, a source of widespread evolutionary speculation and theological unease in the decades before Darwin.[36] Geology impressed Melville, as it did other literary intellectuals of the time, not simply for its challenge to the biblical account of creation but for its implication of a thoroughgoing naturalism that undermined ideas of Providence and human immortality. A year after *Mardi*, "trust[ing that] God was love indeed / And love Creation's final lore," Tennyson lamented that "Nature, red in tooth and claw / With ravine, shriek'd against [this] creed"[37] and showed no greater mercy for the species than for the individual. What Tennyson knew speculatively from the currents of the age and from books, Melville knew practically from his acquaintance with the sea, "a foe [not only] to man who is an alien to it," he would write in *Moby-Dick*, "but . . . also a fiend to its own offspring" (*MD* 274).

Almost invariably with Melville, one returns to the experiential basis of ideas in his observations of nature and history and his broad acquaintance with races, social classes, and "all kinds of that multiform pilgrim species, man" (*CM* 9). Though *Mardi* is an abstract book prompted in great part by

Melville's reading, its ideas are being tested by a man who has already been shaped by life and who holds books accountable to it even as he uses them to help crystallize his developing thoughts. Experience in Melville is the source and validating measure of ideas, with the proviso that all such ideas pertain only to time and finitude—the known or knowable world—and have no more than an inferential bearing on the transcendent world, if it exists. From *Mardi* through *Clarel*, Melville's questers will look to nature for evidences of supernature—confirmations of scriptural promise, testaments to providential order, hints of eternal life; they never find them, certainly not unambiguously. Early in the voyage Babbalanja meditates on the Mardian legend of a man "raised from the tomb" (*M* 237): "At best, 'tis but a hope. But will a longing bring the thing desired? Doth dread avert its object? An instinct is no preservative" (*M* 237). More than twenty-five years later Melville's characters will be asking this same question in *Clarel* (1876) and receiving the same unsatisfying non-answer.

Babbalanja's soliloquy on the resurrection is the young Melville's moment of open apostasy and identic self-assertion—his agnostic "coming out"—and the search for knowledge that follows is a novice's version of the Romantic quest to reunify the faith-emptied world by intellectually comprehending it. The chapter fitly titled "Babbalanja Discourses in the Dark" is a miniature of this effort, beginning with a bold assertion of man's will to know ("Let us aspire to all things. . . . What shall appall us? If eagles gaze at the sun, why not men at the gods?" [*M* 426]) and winding its way through a long and futile monologue on God's omnipotence, omniscience, omnipresence, and benevolence as they relate to matters of human freedom and identity and the pervasiveness of evil. Melville would never entirely shed these ideational categories of Christianity even though his sense of life inclined him in another direction, toward a proto-existentialist naturalism. Words, discourses, inherited paradigms of belief: these were what confounded thought by forcing it into straitened terms and generating insoluble problems that were actually functions of idiom. Recognizing the contingency of vocabularies, however, did little to help Melville free himself from their hold. Baffled by the conundrums of received theology—for example, "Oro [God] is *in* all things, and himself *is* all things—the old-time creed. But since evil abounds, and Oro is all things, then he cannot be perfectly good; wherefore, Oro's omnipresence and moral perfection seem incompatible" (*M* 427)—Babbalanja ends by despairing of the limits of knowledge: "Ah! Let us Mardians quit this insanity. Let us be content with the theology in the grass and the flower, in seed-time and harvest. Be it enough for us to know that Oro indubitably is" and that we can live "most happily, or least miserably . . . , by the practice of righteousness" (*M* 428). And "yet," he adds characteristically, prophesying Melville's own lifelong inconstancy, "too often do I swing from these moorings" (*M* 428).

Abrams describes Wordsworth's Romantic vision as predicated on "the awesome depths and height of the human mind," whose faculties can "consummat[e] a holy marriage with the external universe" and "create out of the world of all of us . . . a new world which is the equivalent of paradise" (Abrams 28). In *Mardi*, human faculties, considerably less than "awesome," run squarely up against the refractoriness of the external universe, which neither ministers to the self nor yields to its intellectual probings. The book's characters thus find themselves in the position of Schiller's moderns, lapsed from primal unity and sensible chiefly of their estrangement from the universe and of the dividedness of their self.

The clash between mind and world, ideal and fact, is the subject of that type of sentimental poetry Schiller calls "satiric," whose quality of earnestness or humor depends on whether the poet treats his theme ("alienation from nature") from the standpoint of the "will," which chafes at life, or of the "understanding," which laughs at it (Schiller 119, 117). The chief satiric Romantic poet in British literature is Byron, who cultivated both modes, the earnest in *Childe Harold's Pilgrimage*, *Manfred*, and *Cain*, the comic (or seriocomic) in *Don Juan*. Abrams omits Byron from *Natural Supernaturalism* on the ground that "he speaks with an ironic counter-voice and deliberately opens a satirical perspective on the vatic stance of his Romantic counterparts" (Abrams 13); from another perspective, it might be said that Byron enacts tensions within the vatic poets themselves, and in so doing anticipates the skepticism of the Victorians. Leslie A. Marchand described Byron's subject (he might equally have been describing *Mardi*'s) as "the inexorable dilemma of the romantic ego: the compulsive search for an ideal and a perfection that do not exist in the world of reality."[38] The paradox in Byron and *Mardi* is that the activity of thought, far from effecting a marriage of mind and world, only aggravates the mind's alienation from the world; as Manfred says, "they who know the most / Must mourn the deepest o'er the fatal truth / The Tree of Knowledge is not that of Life."[39]

Henry A. Murray believed that "the book which was most potent in fashioning Melville's ideal and thus affecting his personality and his writing was . . . [Thomas] Moore's *Life of Byron*, and, hardly to be separated from this, Byron's *Complete Works*."[40] Byron enters *Mardi* early in the quest as Donjololo, the androgynously handsome ruler of Juam, whose island is given more chapters than any other in the book and whose name is an apparent play on Don Juan (Donjololo is also likened to Sardanapulus, the eponymous hero of a Byronic verse tragedy). Allusions to Byron appear as early as Melville's 1839 "Fragments from a Writing Desk," but allusions barely suggest how resonantly Melville's themes and postures echo *Childe Harold* and the heaven-arraigning *Manfred* and *Cain*. Melville was not alone in his debt to Byron. Though sometimes considered anomalous among Romantics for his indifference to their ideas of nature and the imagination, it was Byron in his alienation who spoke most intimately to post-Romantic literary philosophers, even (or especially) to Carlyle, who openly disdained Byron's self-parading "*Sorrows of Lord George*,"[41] and to Arnold, who felt that he and his age had outgrown Byronism.

Melville would not read Carlyle until the summer of 1850 and Arnold for another dozen years, yet both writers illuminate *Mardi* as it enacts phases of the transition from Romantic quest to Victorian complaint. Among the chapters in *Sartor Resartus*, Carlyle's post-Romantic myth of the philosopher Diogenes Teufelsdröckh, are "Idyllic," recounting Teufelsdröckh's childhood before he enters the "fast-hurrying stream" of Time" (*Sartor* 70); "Romance," in which love awakens him to the sense of "'a certain prospective Paradise'" (*Sartor* 102), as Yillah awakens Taji; "Sorrows of Teufelsdröckh," where the abandoned lover, fallen into Time, begins a *Mardi*-like "perambulation and circumambulation of the terraqueous Globe" (*Sartor* 112), driven on in "the temper of ancient Cain, or of the modern Wandering Jew" (*Sartor* 119); and "The Everlasting No," in which his private unhappiness escalates into a crisis of belief much like Babbalanja's: "'Is there no God, then; but at best an absentee God, sitting idle . . . at the outside of his Universe, and *see*ing it go?'" (*Sartor* 121).

To this point Teufelsdröckh has retraced the journey of the Byronic hero, though in place of the deity Byron half-unbelievingly rails against, Teufelsdröckh's object of protest is the world of godless materialism advanced by eighteenth-century philosophy. The chapters that follow, "Centre of Indifference" and "The Everlasting Yea," are Carlyle's effort to transcend Byronism, and they are the chief reason why "for many a Victorian" *Sartor* "became a bible showing, above all, the way from doubt to faith."[42] Half insane with anger and the pressure to believe, Teufelsdröckh transforms empty materialism into a personified "devil" against whom he pits himself and, in an act of metaphysical defiance reminiscent of Byron, asserts his spiritual freedom.[43] From there, the Romantic satirist's frustrations with life, rather than issuing in a protest against God, become, astonishingly, a ground for absolute submission to him. "'Love not Pleasure; love God,'" Teufelsdröckh proclaims: "'This is the EVERLASTING YEA, wherein all contradiction is solved'" (*Sartor* 143).

Melville would record his opinion of such a solution in *Pierre* when he ridiculed the "preposterous rabble of Muggletonian Scots and Yankees" (Carlyleans and Emersonians) who pretend to have found the "Talismanic Secret" that reconciles the soul and the world (*P* 208). In *Mardi* he anticipates Carlyle by leading Babbalanja to the point of crisis and stranding him there—breaking the Carlylean circle and denying Babbalanja even the satisfaction of a cathartic "everlasting no." Despite their opposing worldviews,

Byron and Carlyle are alike in drawing energy from ontological resistance, but in *Mardi*'s naturalistic universe there is nothing to resist and no ground for demanding human exemption from the conditions of creaturely being. "'Though they smite us, let us not turn away from these things, if they really be thus,'" Babbalanja reads from his favorite text, the "Ponderings of old Bardianna." "'The ocean [of thought] we would sound is unfathomable,'" he quotes; "'eternity is not ours by right'"; "'unrequited sufferings'" on earth may not be redressed in an afterlife; "'how small;—how nothing, our deserts!'" (*M* 577).

Through Babbalanja Melville passes beyond both a "vatic" Romanticism and the neo-Romanticism of Carlyle to a post-Romanticism like that of Arnold, a "satirical" poet (in Schiller's sense) whose subject is the chasm between the actual and the ideal but a poet in whom the Romantic's abounding energy and claims upon life have given way to ontological humility and a cheerless resignation to duty. This is the situation Arnold portrayed in "Empedocles on Etna" (1852), a poem nearly contemporaneous with *Mardi* and akin to it in vision. Men are "ill at ease," Empedocles tells Pausanias, a would-be comforter, because "the lot they have / Fails their own will to please" ("Empedocles" I, 2: 148–50). Man's mistake is "not that he deems / His welfare his true aim" but that "he dreams / The world does but exist that welfare to bestow" ("Empedocles" I, 2: 173–76). Frustrated by cosmic indifference and "loath to suffer mute," human beings personify their discontent, "peopling the void air" with "Gods to whom to impute / The ills we ought to bear; / With God and Fate to rail at, suffering easily" ("Empedocles" I, 2: 277–81). (Melville would mark this stanza with a double vertical line in his 1867 edition of Arnold, long after he had created Ahab.)[44] This is Byron's error and Teufelsdröckh's in "The Everlasting No"; Empedocles scornfully rejects it: "Harsh Gods and hostile Fates / Are dreams!" ("Empdocles" I, 2: 304–5). He also rejects a Carlylean wishful belief in an omniscient, benevolent God and in eternal life:

> Fools! That in man's brief term
> He cannot all things view,
> Affords no ground to affirm
> That there are Gods who do;
> Nor does being weary prove that he was where to rest.
> ("Empedocles" I, 2: 347–51)

From its redefinition as symbolic romance nearly to its conclusion, *Mardi* develops from the Romantic idyll of Taji with Yillah (Wordsworth) through the Romantic quest of Taji and Babbalanja (Byron/Carlyle) to the post-Romantic resignation of Babbalanja (Arnold). Melville has not confused the stages of European Romanticism; in the course of a book he has traversed them and arrived with Empedocles at the neither/nor of groundless faith and delusional cosmic defiance. As a parody of the latter, Melville has Babbalanja reflect on the Plujii, mischievous spirits blamed for whatever minor evils capriciously afflict the islanders. Babbalanja finds the idea figuratively apt, "for, Plujii or no Plujii, it is undeniable, that in ten thousand ways, as if by a malicious agency, we mortals are woefully put out and tormented; and that, too, by things in themselves so exceedingly trivial, that it would seem almost impiety to ascribe them to the august gods" (*M* 264). Brooding on weightier ills and eliding Babbalanja's "as if," Ahab will ascribe "all the subtle demonisms of life and thought" to Moby Dick (*MD* 184). Empedocles and Babbalanja share Ahab's exasperation, but as naturalists they have lost the anthropocentrism that makes man's "*will* / The measure of his *rights*"("Empedocles" I, 2: 154–55); nor, being sane, can they project an antagonist in whom the evils of life are "visibly personified, and made practically assailable" (*MD* 184). As Babbalanja says, "No coward he, who hunted, turns and finds no foe to fight" (*M* 621).

In joining the Romantic quest to an early Victorian sense of nature and human limitation, Melville found himself not with the ascending circle of the Romantics but with a broken circle. Like Arnold in "Empedocles" he had contrived a situation "in which suffering finds no vent in action; in which a continuous state of mental distress is prolonged, unrelieved by incident, hope, or resistance; in which everything is to be endured, nothing to be done."[45] As the voyage nears its close, its feeling of tragic alienation, of an idyllic world left forever behind and an ideal one unattainably ahead, hardens into a diagnosis of the modern condition much like Schiller's. "This Mardi is not our home," Babbalanja says:

> Up and down we wander, like exiles transported to a planet afar: —'tis not the world *we* were born in; not the world once so lightsome and gay . . . . Then let us depart. But whither? We push ourselves forward—then, start back in affright. Essay it again, and flee. Hard to live; hard to die; intolerable suspense!" (*M* 619)

"Negative Romanticism"

Having traced the Romantic quest to its cul-de-sac in a perplexed anticipation of modernity, Melville faced the problems of how to end his book and how to reconcile its mood of frustration and ennui with his own excitement at an intellectual and vocational world opening before him. Uncertain what he finally believed, still less what would satisfy him, Melville knew what would not satisfy him: humanistic compromise, an acceptance of limits, and what Empedocles would oxymoronically call "moderate bliss" ("Empedocles" I, 2: 391). "Is it so small a thing," Empedocles asks,

> To have enjoy'd the sun,
> To have lived in the spring,
> To have loved, to have thought, to have done
> .... That we must feign a bliss
> Of doubtful future date,
> And, while we dream of this,
> Lose all our present state . . . ?
> ("Empedocles" I, 2: 397–400, 402-5)

On three occasions in *Mardi* (chapters 124, 135, 175) Melville brings Babbalanja to a similar "theology in the grass and the flower, in seed-time and harvest" (*M* 428). Reading from a book titled "A Happy Life" by an "antique pagan," closely modeled upon *Seneca's Morals By Way of Abstract* by Sir Roger L'Estrange,[46] Babbalanja comments, "No written page can teach me more" (*M* 389), yet he can no more follow the pagan's advice than he could the sage Bardianna's in a parallel chapter. Both scenes end with the reasoning Babbalanja lapsing from reason. In the first, he swoons; in the second, he falls into the persona of Azzageddi, his crazy-profound alter ego who represents the wild, nihilistic underside of truth-seeking ("Many things I know, not good to tell" [*M* 419].) Azzageddi is Babblanja brought to the edge of dissolution by too close and continuous a look at dark truth. His mode of discourse—the subversive descending into outright gibberish—is a dialect of the "irony" that Paul de Man called "unrelieved *vertige*, dizziness to the point of madness. Sanity can only exist because we are willing to function within the conventions of duplicity and dissimulation . . . . Once this mask is shown to be a mask, the authentic being underneath appears necessarily as on the verge of madness."[47]

As the visitations of Azzageddi become more frequent and debilitating, King Media urges Babblanja to settle for the world as he finds it and abandon his quest for the ideal: "Babbalanja, you mortals dwell in Mardi, and it is impossible to get elsewhere" (*M* 370). "Getting elsewhere," however, is precisely what Babbalanja wants. Stopping at Maramma, the island representing formal Christianity, Media asks Babbalanja why mortals try to climb the peak of Ofo (pilgrimage toward God), whose "rarefied air" would prove "unfitted for . . . human lungs" even if the summit could be reached (*M* 324). Babbalanja agrees, citing Bardianna's view that "the plain alone was intended for man" (*M* 324). Yet knowing human limits does little to help Babbalanja accommodate himself to them and to exorcise the drive toward God and truth that is the defining motive of his character.

In their acceptance of finitude, pragmatists like Media and stoic philosophers like Bardianna and the antique pagan are "natural" rather than "spiritual" beings or, in the language of Schiller and August Wilhelm Schlegel, "Southerners" rather than "Northerners." Schlegel in particular saw "the stern nature of the North" as "driv[ing] man back within himself," fostering a characteristic "earnestness of mind" in place of the Southerner's (or ancient Greek's) "free sportive development of the senses."[48] There were penalties to pay for the loss of playfulness and physical delight, but for Schlegel these were more than counterbalanced by the development of religion, without which humanity was "a mere surface without any internal substance."[49] The fall from Classic to Romantic, South to North, body to spirit, pleasure to earnestness was thus a fortunate one, though marked by a deep and chronic melancholy rising from the soul's dissatisfaction with temporal life and its "longing for its distant home."[50]

The oppositions sketched by the German Romantics were contained in Melville himself. "Gifted" like Ahab "with the high perception," Melville by no means "lacked the low, enjoying power" (*MD* 167), whether in his frank delight in eating, drinking, smoking, and genially conversing or, as Newton Arvin said, in his responsiveness to the "Greeklike cult of physical love" and the "unashamed and sometimes orgiastic sexuality" of Polynesia.[51] From *Typee* onward, Melville would work to balance these elements within himself (unavailingly, for the most part) while exploring their psychological, cultural, and historical *im*balance in Western society. When the impulses collided, it was usually the earnest "Northerner" in him that prevailed over the sensualist, even in its last, most articulated form of the contemplative epicurean. In *Mardi*, as in *Moby-Dick*, pipe-smoking is Melville's symbol for a sociable adjustment to life. Depressed by King Media's words "impossible to get elsewhere" (*M* 370), the voyagers "regale themselves with their Pipes" (*M* 371), a respite that makes even Babbalanja feel "the very gods must be smoking now" (*M* 372). But the mood passes as quickly as it came on, and three chapters later Babbalanja is once again reduced to the gibberish of Azzageddi. The problem is not simply that Babbalanja is unable to save himself through a virtuous hedonism but that he is *unwilling* to; as he says during one of the book's many feasts, "Some damned spirits would not be otherwise, could they" (*M* 594).

As the voyage draws to a close, it moves from spring to autumn, morning to night, and the quest openly becomes an image of perpetual homelessness terminated only by death. Almost immediately, however, the narrative turns about (chapter 185: "They sail from Night to Day") as the party lands at Serenia, the Christian paradise where "right-reason, and Alma" (Christ) have been reconciled (*M* 629), religion is chiefly ethical, and the doctrinal and ecclesiastical paraphernalia of Christianity have been winnowed down to a gospel of "Truth, Justice, and Love" (*M* 626). As Babbalanja listens to a wise Serenian expound his creed, it is as though Melville were catechizing the voyagers from William Ellery Channing's *Unitarian Christianity* (1819). (Melville's father, Allan, had been raised a Unitarian; Elizabeth Shaw Melville was a Unitarian; late in life Melville would become a member of All Souls Unitarian Church in New York City.) With the exception of Taji, the company is instantly converted. "'Oh, Alma, Alma! prince divine,' cried Babbalanja, sinking on his knees—'in *thee*, at last, I find repose. . . . Gone, gone! are all distracting doubts. Love and Alma now prevail'" (*M* 630). The chapter ends with the voyagers kneeling as "the setting sun burst[s] forth from the mists," as if to indicate heaven's approval (*M* 631).

While uncompleted, the ascending spiral of the Romantics seems to give promise of completion, if not in secular time, then beyond. "My voyage is ended," Babbalanja tells Taji: "Not because what we sought is found; but that I now possess all which may be had of what I sought in Mardi" (*M* 637). The implication is that Babbalanja may find what he sought *after* Mardi. Following his conversion, however, Babbalanja is given a mystical dream at odds with the ethical thrust of Serenian religion; he is conducted by an angelic spirit to Mardi's heaven, where is he surprised to hear sounds of "gladness" strangely "mixed with sadness" (*M* 633). "'Rude joy'" would be out of place in heaven, he is told (*M* 634), but there is a further reason why the blessed sigh: "'No mind but Oro's can know all; no mind that knows not all can be content; content alone approximates happiness'" (*M* 634); therefore, no mind but Oro's can be happy.

With this syllogism, *Mardi* breaks the Romantic circle once again, this time on the level of eternity. "'Know, then, . . . that when translated hither,'" the angel tells Babbalanja, "'thou wilt but put off lowly temporal pinings, for angel and eternal aspirations'" (*M* 634). Because the noble soul's hunger for truth can never be satisfied, on earth or in heaven, the condition of the soul must inevitably be one of deep and irremediable sadness. If suffering in *Mardi* is a pathway to knowledge—"We are fuller than a city," Babbalanja says: "Woe it is, that reveals these things. He knows himself, and all that's in him, who knows adversity" (*M* 594)—it is also an inevitable *consequence* of knowledge, since immortal spirits, knowing more, come more painfully to feel their exclusion from knowing all. Sadness is the price they pay for their immortality; it is the very mark of their immortality, as it is for sublunary beings as well. "'And hence it is,'" the angelic spirit instructs Babbalanja, "'that when ye Mardians feel most sad, then ye feel most immortal'" (*M* 636).

Profound constitutional sadness is not what Romantics envisioned as the destination of "the spiral journey back home" (Abrams 190). Against the affirmations of Wordsworth and others, Morse Peckham described a "negative romanticism" consisting of "the attitudes, the feelings, and the ideas of a man who has left static mechanism but has not yet arrived at a reintegration of his thought and art in terms of dynamic organicism";[52] this is the position of Carlyle's Teufelsdröckh in "The Everlasting No." In Melville, where Peckham's "not yet" is permanent, negative Romanticism is, instead, a condition of spiritual aspiration without an accompanying faith in its worldly or otherworldly fulfillment. The challenge for negative Romantics of this sort is not how to regain belief or even, despite a posture of expectation (Carlyle), how to conduct themselves in the interim; it is how to establish and maintain human spirituality—their feeling of the self as divinely created and divinely imbued; as "royal"—without the patent of the supernatural. What negative Romantics set in place of the divine is the soul's *yearning* for the divine and the pain of divine absence. In Byron, in Carlyle, in Arnold, and in Melville the locus of spirituality turns inward from the worship of a transcendent God to a mental state of self-contemplative suffering celebrated as "godlike" and ranging in mood from cosmic anger (the Byronic hero) to abject complaint (the speaker in many of Arnold's poems). "Man's Unhappiness," Teufelsdröckh says, "comes of his Greatness; it is because there is an Infinite in him, which with all his cunning he cannot quite bury under the Finite" (*Sartor* 141). For negative Romantics the converse is equally true: humans' greatness comes of their unhappiness; their greatness *is* their spiritual unhappiness, which testifies to the infinite in them. This is the significance in *Sartor* of quasi-sacramental phrases like the "*Sanctuary of Sorrow*," "the *Divine Depth of Sorrow*," and the "*Worship of Sorrow*" (*Sartor* 141, 143; emphasis Carlyle's), phrases that have analogues in Byron and Melville. "Of its own beauty is the mind diseased," Byron proclaimed in *Childe Harold* (IV, 1090); "All mortal greatness is but disease" (*MD* 74), Melville would write in *Moby-Dick*. Not disease (sickness) but dis-ease (worldly unrest) has become the source and measure of spirituality within the negative Romantics' new humanly centered religion of grief.

In Melville, the spiritualization of suffering shows itself in his heroes' attraction to darkly introspective characters who stand apart from commonplace life almost as emissaries from another world. In *Typee* the figure is Toby, "a strange wayward being, moody, fitful, and melancholy—at times almost morose" (*T* 32); in *White-Jacket* it is the sailor Nord with his "saturnine brow" and air of being "an earnest thinker" who has "been bolted in the mill of adversity" (*WJ* 51); in *Moby-Dick* it is Bulkington, "the deep shadows of [whose] eyes" contain "reminiscences that did not seem to give him much joy" (*MD* 16); in *Pierre* it is the dark, mournful Isabel; in *Clarel* it is Vine. With the exception of Isabel, these characters are all male; their distinguishing feature is melancholy. Beyond anything, their function is to serve as idealized projections of the hero's own undeveloped self. They are Jungian anima figures who beckon the self forward toward completion, in Melville's writings (save with Isabel) through union with a representative of the same, not the opposite, sex.[53]

As a resolution to *Mardi*'s quest, Melville could accept the Unitarian rationalism of Serenia only by enveloping it in an aura of supernal grief that transmuted it from a daylight gospel of works to a nocturnal mystery-religion evoking a sense of awe. As the angel tells Babblanja, "'Beatitude there is none . . . . Sadness makes the silence throughout the realms of space; sadness is universal and eternal; but sadness is tranquillity; tranquillity the uttermost that souls may hope for'" (*M* 636). By darkening heaven, conventionally a place of light and joy, Melville reconstitutes it for an imagination fascinated with melancholy. Even so, Melville seems bored or impatient with heaven's stasis, or perhaps with spiritual moorings of any sort, as well he might be at age twenty-nine. Spurning the plea to remain in Serenia, Taji casts off yet again in reaffirmation of the quest: "I am the hunter, that never rests! the hunter without a home" (*M* 638). *Mardi* has thus two endings, neither of which are satisfactory: on one side (Babbalanja), a "humble acceptance of limits" that amounts to a "submission" to life;[54] on the other side (Taji), a rash, half-suicidal persistence in the quest without hope of success or cathartic relief.

In the poem "A Summer Night," published close to the time of *Mardi*, Arnold juxtaposed two similar ways of life, the daily round of "most men [who] in a brazen prison live" and the quester's voyage through tempests toward "some false, impossible shore," ending in shipwreck and death (ll. 37, 69). "Is there no life, but these alone? Madman or slave, must man be one?" (ll. 74–75). In *Mardi* Babbalanja is the slave, Taji the Byronic madman. Told that to pass "through yonder strait" to open sea is "perdition," Taji proclaims, "Let *me*, then, be the unreturning wanderer" (*M* 654), echoing *Childe Harold*'s "wanderers o'er Eternity / Whose bark drives on and on, and anchor'd ne'er shall be" (*Childe Harold* III, 669–70). A reflection of Melville's own contempt for "the shore," where "naught new is seen" (*M* 556), Taji's intransigence resembles Childe Harold's in having no object beyond the perpetuation of the questing spirit itself. The tenor of the journey *is* the destination.

Byronism had its literary moment, but thirty-five years of cultural history rendered its histrionic melancholy, as Arnold said, "a pass'd mode, an outworn theme" ("Stanzas from the Grande Chartreuse," l. 100). *Mardi* represents a return to negative Romanticism but in a way that incorporates midcentury Victorian thought and marshals it in the service of a neo-Byronic defiance. Trapped within a received Christian vocabulary they could neither accept nor wholly expel, Byron and Melville were obsessed with an omnipotent God's responsibility for evil. "I never could / Reconcile what I saw with what I heard" (*Cain* I, 1: 165–66) Cain says of the gulf between experience and doctrine. Even in Babbalanja's dream of heaven, the problem of evil—"'why create the germs that sin and suffer, but to perish?'" (*M* 634)—is brushed aside by the angel as "'the last mystery which underlieth all'" and must remain hidden (*M* 634). Melville could never let it remain hidden, for he could never escape the theistic terms that made the problem inevitable. Ishmael would be an expression of the naturalistic strain in Melville, Ahab of this residual theism.

Despite Melville's divisions of mind and temperment, the failure of *Mardi*'s ending was finally less intellectual than imaginative. Melville could not vitalize Babbalanja's conversion, only half believing in it himself, nor could he infuse Taji's protest with sufficient import. His two endings to *Mardi* betoken a philosophical neither/nor, like Arnold's slave and madman, in which the intellect can only acquiesce to the conditions of life and the Romantic will only resist. Lacking the egocentrism of the Byronic hero and only fitfully, unusably mad (Azzageddi), Babbalanja was forced to concede that humanity had no rightful claim upon the universe and, in any case, no adversary to press its claim against. Instead of cutting the metaphysical knot through action, Babbalanja was condemned to trying to unravel it through reason, retreading the same barren casuistical ground to the point of psychic collapse.

To pass beyond *Mardi* Melville would need to go *usably* mad. Lionel Trilling ascribed the limitations of Hawthorne's work to "a conception of the artist's dealing with the world which [was] less bold and intransigent than it might [have been]" which submitted too readily to "the literal actuality of the world" and was only incipiently conscious of the powers and prerogatives of the imagination.[55] For all its fantasticalness, the world of *Mardi* was an allegorical replica of Melville's own world. This was its strength, indeed its raison d'être—the book's explorations were Melville's—but it was also its dramatic weakness, for in a mimetic world governed by the conditions of experience there was nothing, save recantation, suicide, or passive endurance, for the thwarted Romantic quester to *do*. Trilling's foil to Hawthorne is Kafka, who created a fictional world unconfined by probability or even possibility. Melville was not prepared to do that. Having embarked on what would be a lifelong process of self-education, he wanted to, and did, "blurt out everything" at once, as Friedrich Schlegel identified the "fault of young geniuses."[56] Nonetheless, Melville was right to tell Evert Duyckinck, "had I not written & printed 'Mardi,' in all likelihood, I would not be as wise as I am now, or may be" (*Corr* 149). The intellectual reconnoitering had to be done, if only so that it might be subsumed to the later work of imagination. To create Ahab and the white whale, Melville would need to unite Babbalanja (thought) and Taji (will) in a single figure raised to the level of myth. He would need to conceive a book about the impossible and symbolically enact what could not be enacted in life. He would need to understand that the Romantic circle could be completed, if at all, neither in temporal life nor in a problematic afterlife but only in the writerly life: in his creation of a work that would, in turn, re-create him.

3

The Theory and Practice of Democratic Tragedy (1): Melville's Metaphysics of Democracy: "Hawthorne and His Mosses"

[Democracy] is borrowed from the example of the perfect self-government of the physical universe, being written in letters of light on every page of the great bible of Nature. It contains the idea of full and fearless faith in the providence of the Creator. It is essentially involved in Christianity, of which it has been well said that its pervading spirit of democratic equality among men is its highest fact and one of its most radiant internal evidences of its origin.

—"An Introductory Statement of the Democratic Principle," *United States Magazine and Democratic Review* (1837)

Tragedy is a vision of nihilism, a heroic or ennobling vision of nihilism.

—Susan Sontag, *Against Interpretation*

Democracy, Christianity, Tragedy

In his preface to the 1855 *Leaves of Grass* Whitman likened America assuming its literary inheritance to an incoming tenant supplanting a deceased one, waiting patiently while "the corpse is slowly borne from the eating and sleeping rooms of the house," honoring the deceased as "fittest for its days" even as he knows that "he shall be fittest for his days."[1] Although America, Whitman claimed, did "not repel the past or what it has produced under its forms or amid other politics or the ideas of castes or the old religions" (Preface 1855, 150), it did tend to regard Old World achievements as time-bound and ideologically suspect. Among the outworn glories of the past was the tradition of high tragedy, which not only dealt with "splendid exceptional characters and affairs" more appropriate to aristocratic than to egalitarian times[2] but which seemed antithetical in spirit to the cosmic affirmation that progressive Americans saw as correlative to or foundational for the republic's political affirmation. Democracy, proclaimed the *Democratic Review* in 1837, is "a cheerful creed . . . of high hope and universal love" buoyed by faith in human nature and in divine nature,[3] while tragedy, despite its ultimate vindication of Law, radiated terror and gloom. "Perverse solicitors of woe," Emerson called the admirers of tragedy, ascribing their fascination to a morbid "appetite for grief" and voicing a widespread impatience among contemporary Americans that was only superficially at odds with the stage and schoolroom popularity of Shakespeare.[4]

Like Whitman in his poems and prefaces, Melville in *Moby-Dick* was engaged in trying to replace an old culture by a new.[5] "The Great Construction of the New Bible,"[6] Whitman called the enterprise at hand, whose poems he saw adopting a "different relative attitude towards God" and "the objective universe" from those of any poems ever written ("A Backward Glance" 564). What chiefly impelled the classic writers of the American midcentury—Emerson, Thoreau, Whitman, Melville, Fuller; Hawthorne was the chief exception—was not a particular nativist content or a new aesthetic form; it was the prospect of an emerging New World consciousness at once post-theological and spiritual, individualistic yet, as Whitman affirmed, "utter[ing] the word Democratic, the word En-masse."[7] In each of the writers save Melville, the modern personality represented in or prophesied by the work is "for freest action form'd under the laws divine" (Whitman, "One's-Self I Sing," l. 7); in Melville, the modern personality lives and acts in the perceptible *absence* of laws divine. Democracy in Melville's writings is not set against a backdrop of universal consonance and seen as its natural expression in society and politics; it is set against a backdrop of blackness, or tragic *dis*sonance, and advanced as a humanly wrought stay against nothingness and common victimhood.

As both a literary genre and a philosophical vision, "democratic tragedy" seems oxymoronic. Aristotle had confined tragedy to the "imitation of persons who are above the common level,"[8] not simply in their hierarchical status but in what Northrop Frye called their "power of action"[9] and their participation in a larger, more consequential world than that of common life. Frye saw Western literature descending over the centuries from higher to lower mimetic forms, as measured by the hero's stature vis-à-vis the community and nature. The shift reflected the wider historical progress in the West toward what Tocqueville, viewing America as its culmination, called "equality of condition."[10] Was high mimetic literature possible or even desirable in America? Because human beings "in democratic communities" are "all insignificant and very much alike," Tocqueville reasoned, American poets can "never take any man in particular as the subject of a piece";[11] they must write of human character and destiny at large, or, as Whitman understood it, of the representative self as it embodied universal capacities for knowing and being. In place of the heroic, martial, and class-based literature of the Old World, which has "been great," Whitman argued that "the New World needs the poems of realities and science and of the democratic average and basic equality, which shall be greater still ("A Backward Glance" 564).

As a reader and would-be writer of heroic literature, Melville was aware of the mimetic self-contradiction implicit in "democratic tragedy." In *Moby-Dick* he addressed the problem directly: wanting those "outward majestical trappings and housings" traditionally employed by the "tragic dramatist," he would rest the grandeur of his "poor old whale-hunter" chiefly on the intangibles of inner being (*MD* 148). In "The Ship" he foreshadowed some of these intangibles: "greatly superior natural force," "a globular brain and a ponderous heart," and a life experience conducive to independent thought and the development of a "bold and nervous lofty language" (*MD* 73). In "Knights and Squires" he went further and laid a theoretical basis for high mimetic democratic art, justifying his elevation of "meanest mariners, and renegades, and castaways" by appeal to the "great democratic God" who endowed all flawed beings with the capacity for a transfiguring heroism (*MD* 117).

Inspired partly by his own Christian socialist convictions and admiration for literary tragedy, F. O. Matthiessen fastened on this passage as a touchstone for Melville's "fusion of Christianity and democracy" within humanity's "dynamic struggle against evil," which Matthiessen saw as the core of Melvillean tragedy.[12] By "evil" Matthiessen meant largely moral and social evil—laissez-faire economics in *Redburn*, abuses of class in *White-Jacket*, overweening individualism in *Moby-Dick*—yet Matthiessen was also extraordinarily sensitive to the metaphysical strain in Melville. Where "Hawthorne was concerned with depicting the good and evil within man's heart," Matthiessen wrote, Melville was chiefly concerned "with titanic uncontrollable forces which seem to dwarf man altogether" (Matthiessen 441). The problem for Matthiessen was that in doing justice to Melville's sense of these forces he implicitly trespassed on Christian ideas of cosmic governance, as in his brilliant discussion of Melville and Gnosticism. Once he acknowledged the prominence of the transhuman in Melville, it was difficult for Matthiessen to confine Melvillean tragedy to the hero's "conflict with other individuals in a definite social order" (Matthiessen 179). The defining struggle in *Moby-Dick* is not between Ahab and Starbuck; it is between Ahab and the white whale as God or imputed "agent" of God (*MD* 164). The phrase "titanic uncontrollable forces" appeals to a conception of the universe prior to or apart from the Christian deity's omnipotent, benevolent rule; it evokes the kind of tragic vision that Richard B. Sewall called "primal, or primitive." The tragic vision

> calls up out of the depths the first (and last) of all questions, the question of existence: What does it mean to be? It recalls the original terror, harking back to a world that antedates the conceptions of philosophy, the consolations of the later religions, and whatever constructions the human mind has devised to persuade itself that its universe is secure. It recalls the original un-reason, the terror of the irrational. It sees man as questioner, naked, unaccommodated, alone, facing mysterious, demonic forces in his own nature and outside, and the irreducible facts of suffering and death. Thus it is not for those who cannot live with unsolved questions or unresolved doubts, whose bent of mind would reduce the fact of evil into something else or resolve it into some larger whole.[13]

In its vision of human vulnerability in a vast, incomprehensible universe, tragedy as Sewall describes it sets itself against the mix of Enlightenment, Romantic, and Christian ideas that passed for democratic metaphysics in mid-nineteenth-century America. The assumption among progressives was of a universe of benign laws that conduced to the growth and happiness of the individual, and therefore to the welfare of society, if left to function on their own.[14] In *The Confidence-Man* Melville caught the savor of this ersatz philosophy and teased out its self-contradictions: on one side Americans' tough-minded skepticism and reliance on hard facts, on the other their almost infantile credulity and attachment to fondly optimistic notions of humanity, nature, and God. It was here, in the gap between experience and professed belief, that tragedy interposed an un-American wedge of doubt. Through what Emerson called the "power of the imagination to dislocate things orderly and cheerful, and show them in startling disarray"[15] —perversely, in Emerson's view; insightfully, in Melville's—tragedy opened to inspection the discordance between ideal and fact that religion and ideology sought to hide. "This Shakespeare is a queer man," Melville has the Cosmopolitan observe in *The Confidence-Man*: "At times irresponsible, he does not always seem reliable. There appears to be a certain—what shall I call it?—hidden sun, say, about him, at once enlightening and mystifying. Now, I should be afraid to say what I have sometimes thought that hidden sun might be" (*CM* 172).

"A culture . . . is nothing if not a dialectic," Lionel Trilling remarked: "And in any culture there are likely to be certain artists who contain a large part of the dialectic within themselves, their meaning and power lying in their contradictions."[16] Melville never wrote a literary manifesto akin to Whitman's prefaces and retrospects; "Hawthorne and His Mosses" (*Literary World*, 17 and 24 August 1850) is his de facto manifesto, and threading through its ruminations on Hawthorne, Shakespeare, blackness, democracy, American literary nationalism, and his own burgeoning career is Melville's increasingly conscious attempt to synthesize the democratic and tragic strands within his own character—in Trilling's terms, the "yes" and "no" of his circumambient culture. The "yes" in Melville identifies Americanism in literature with "those writers, who breathe [the] unshackled, democratic spirit of Christianity in all things" (*PT* 248). The "no" in him, like the "NO! in thunder" he ascribed to Hawthorne (*Corr* 186), locates truth in a "blackness, ten times black" (*PT* 243) and literary greatness in the presentation of that truth. The relationship between these two things—what Julian Markels called their "millennialist connection in Melville's mind"[17]—is the key to Melville's argument in the "Mosses" essay and to his developing conception of democratic tragedy, an ontological vision with implications for politics, ethics, authorial vocation, and literary content and form that would guide his writing through much of *Moby-Dick*.

Dark Adamism

Melville's cultural "yes" in "Hawthorne and His Mosses" is associated with Emerson, who appears immediately after Hawthorne in Melville's list of distinguished American authors (*PT* 247), and who, as the leading prophet of New World possibility, stands as Hawthorne's complement and foil.[18] Melville's chief debt to Emerson in the "Mosses" essay is for the Adamism that made room for American writers crowded out by the density of the literary past. In at least one critical passage Melville seems almost to paraphrase Emerson. This is Emerson in "Literary Ethics" (1838):

> We assume, that all thought is already long ago adequately set down in books,—all imaginations in poems; and what we say, we only throw in as confirmatory of this supposed complete body of literature. A very shallow assumption. A true man will think rather, all literature is yet to be written. Poetry has scarce chanted its first song. The perpetual

admonition of nature to us, is, "The world is new, untried. Do not believe the past. I give you the universe a virgin to-day."[19]

And Melville:

Nor will it at all do to say, that the world is getting grey and grizzled now, and has lost that fresh charm which she wore of old, and by virtue of which the great poets of past times made themselves what we esteem them to be. Not so. The world is as young today, as when it was created; and this Vermont morning dew is as wet to my feet, as Eden's dew to Adam. Nor has Nature been all over ransacked by our progenitors, so that no new charms and mysteries remain for this latter generation to find. Far from it. The trillionth part has not yet been said; and all that has been said, but multiplies the avenues to what remains to be said. (*PT* 246)

For Melville, as for all those affected by Emerson, the Romantic quest for truth assumed special immediacy in a nation where truth seemed just beyond the doorstep. Yet America, as Emerson insisted, had compromised its unique historical position by replicating the forms and consciousness of the Old World. This is the meaning of Hawthorne's threshold symbol in *The Scarlet Letter*, the rusty, weather-stained prison door; Boston is scarcely a dozen years old and already its founders have sullied the New World with the oppressive social and ideological structures of Europe. Ishmael's New Bedford is similarly old, creaky, and hidebound in its ways, like the moss-grown villages Thoreau passes as he travels along the Concord River. Historically new, societal America was "old" in the sense of distant from the sources of life, which were ubiquitously available to Americans in the opportunity for an "original relation to the universe"[20] unmediated by traditions, institutions, and received ideas. To be an "American" meant to reject the historically constructed America for the New World of possibility. "The reason why an ingenious soul shuns society," Emerson wrote, "is to the end of finding society. It repudiates the false, out of love of the true."[21] The defining action of Emersonian midcentury literature is the flight from society to the physical or metaphysical frontier: Emerson going to the woods in *Nature*, Ishmael taking to sea, Thoreau removing to Walden Pond, Hawthorne's Coverdale leaving Boston for Blithedale, and Whitman rushing out of the house into the open air. Abandoning the settlements, the Emersonian writer-hero discovers truth in the direct confrontation of self with world and returns to the community, like Thoreau, to "say something" to his neighbors.[22]

Melville shared in this vision of New World possibility and the role it assigned the American writer as a kind of metaphysical scout. For this reason he deprecated the literalism of nationalists like Duyckinck associate Cornelius Mathews, who saw American literature reflecting "as from a faithful mirror, . . . the physical, moral, and intellectual aspects of the nation."[23] "It is not meant that all American writers should studiously cleave to nationality in their writings," Melville argued in the "Mosses" essay: "let [the American writer] write like a man, for then he will be sure to write like an American" (*PT* 248). For Emerson, literary "manhood" involved not simply shedding an acculturated Europhile sensibility but adjusting the angle of perception so that "the axis of vision" became "coincident with the axis of things" and illuminated nature as a wondrously interlocking system of laws.[24] For Melville, literary manhood presumed a comparable shedding—"no American writer should write like an Englishman, or a Frenchman" (*PT* 248)—yet the "axis of reality" (*PT* 244) that disclosed itself to the truth-seeker was radically askew. Beside Emerson's remark that the poet is a reconciler who "re-attaches things to nature and the Whole" and "disposes very easily of the most disagreeable facts,"[25] Melville would dryly comment, "So it would seem. In this sense Mr. E is a great poet."[26] For Melville, detachment from the Whole was the essence of temporal being and disagreeable facts were what willy-nilly obtruded themselves on all percipient natures. Responding with enthusiasm to Emerson's Adamicism, Melville inverted it epistemologically and ontologically so that the "intuitive truth" (*PT* 244) grasped by the profound thinker became a darkly empirical rather than a brightly transcendental one: the things that we cannot *not* know when our eyes are open and our minds free from the illusionary filters of moral and religious piety. To "write like an American" was simply to "write like a man," which meant to draw upon the same ever-available fund of sober truth that writers like Hawthorne and Shakespeare had drawn upon.

Melville had sounded these themes in *Mardi*, but, lacking a vocabulary adequate to his sense of experience, he had constrained his thinking within the framework of Christian theism, reasoning himself into the same logical and theological culs-de-sac. In the term "blackness" in the "Mosses" essay Melville found a liberating metaphor that allowed him to beg the question of ultimate reality while fronting what he would elsewhere call "the visable truth" (*Corr* 186). Neither an objective outward force nor a purely subjective inward feeling, blackness arose at the meeting point of mind and world. Like Camus's Absurd, it was essentially a *relationship*—in Camus's words, a relationship "between the human need and the unreasoning silence of the universe"[27]—that came into being as the perceived nature of reality, neutral in itself, impinged on human demands for order and meaning and called forth an almost visceral anger and revulsion. Camus's hero can defiantly laugh at the Absurd because his stance toward it is one of detached intellectual lucidity, yet even Camus could lapse into the emotive language of blackness with a phrase like "the primitive hostility of the world."[28] Without falling into cosmic personification, "black-ness" built upon a nearly involuntary sense of the antagonism of Creation. It expressed not only how humans *saw* the gap between need and fact but how they *felt* about it; it was a philosophical judgment charged with latent anthropocentric protest at life's betrayal.

"Blackness" enters the "Mosses" essay with Melville's account of the darker side of Hawthorne, but the conceit quickly overwhelms its prompt-ing subject to become a subject itself. Anticipating Henry James's ques-tion later in the century, Melville asks whether "Hawthorne has simply availed himself of this mystical blackness" for purposes of literary chiar-oscuro or whether he himself is possessed by "a touch of Puritanic gloom" (*PT* 243):

> —this, I cannot altogether tell. Certain it is, however, that this great power of blackness in him derives its force from its appeals to that Calvinistic sense of Innate Depravity and Original Sin, from whose visitations, in some shape or other, no deeply thinking mind is always and wholly free. For, in certain moods, no man can weigh this world without throwing in something, somehow like Original Sin, to strike the uneven balance. (*PT* 243)

The blackness in Hawthorne emanates from a sense of human fallenness, but when Melville extends blackness to a characteristic of every "deeply thinking mind" he reaches, as Matthiessen said, beyond the moral to the metaphysical. "This world" implies experience in its apprehended totality, while the phrase "something, somehow like Original Sin" converts a theo-logical doctrine into a metaphor for some fundamental wrongness at the heart of life, which alone can account for the preponderance of evil. "The infinite obscure of [Hawthorne's] back-ground" (*PT* 244), reminiscent of Shakespeare's, is the existential *mise-en-scène* of his writing; it is also its bur-ied subject, as fictive characters or the narrator himself periodically dive beneath the surface of the tale or sketch to insinuate truths that cannot be told directly.

Nina Baym remarked on Melville's visible impatience with "Haw-thorne's fabulating talents," a "skimmer's approach" to fiction confirmed by Melville's markings in his copy of *Mosses from an Old Manse*.[29] What absorbed Melville was not the actional apparatus of Hawthornean narra-tive or Shakespearean tragedy but its function in bringing a character to the point of extremity where, like Lear, he "tears off the mask, and speaks the sane madness of vital truth" (*PT* 244). One might almost say that with its aboriginal situation, stark setting, and naked thematic urgency, the Book of Job was the ur-tragedy for Melville and that all subsequent tragedies rep-resented (in Northrop Frye's terms) so many downward displacements to the world of human affairs and concessions to literary verisimilitude.[30] "It is our first, oldest statement of the never-ending Problem,—man's destiny, and God's ways with him here in this earth," Carlyle wrote of Job in *On Heroes, Hero-Worship, and the Heroic in History*, which Melville borrowed from Evert Duyckinck during the summer of 1850, shortly before encountering Hawthorne and writing the "Mosses" essay.[31] For Melville in 1850, the essence of tragedy was the declamatory spectacle of Job on his ash-heap or Lear on the heath "tormented into desperation" (*PT* 244) and delivering himself in rage and grief on the blackness of life.

It is hard to overestimate the importance of the term "blackness." Leon Howard aptly described Melville's response to Hawthorne as having all the transformational power of "a religious conversion."[32] "A mind," William James wrote of conversion, "is a system of ideas" that "alters . . . in the course of experience" and "may be undermined or weakened by this interstitial alteration just as a building is, and yet for a time keep upright by dead habit. But a new perception, a sudden emotional shock, or an occasion which lays bare the organic alteration, will make the whole fabric fall together; and then the centre of gravity sinks into an attitude more stable, . . . and the new structure remains permanent."[33] By 1850, Melville had explored most of the themes he would develop in *Moby-Dick*; stung by the reception of *Mardi*, however, and writing with an autodidact's mixture of exuberance and self-distrust, he had tried to contain his sense of tragedy within the bounds of an increasingly strained Christian democracy. His discovery of Hawthorne ratified the bent of his mind by showing him, as Howard P. Vincent put it, "that one American was expressively aware of the evil at the core of life, a perception toward which [he] had been groping for seven years of authorship and of self-scrutiny, but which he had not completely realized nor dared to disclose."[34] The significance of "blackness" was to coalesce this emergent sense of life in a trope of extraordinary evocativeness and power that could serve as a Jamesian "centre of gravity" in lieu of an articulated counterbelief to traditional theism. With "blackness" in mind, Melville no longer had to reason his way through to an ontological position, as he had tried to do in *Mardi*; it was enough to invoke the metaphor.

The Politics of Blackness

Melville was not the first to link Hawthorne with Shakespeare or to find a kindred darkness in them. Five years earlier Evert Duyckinck had ascribed the special fascination of Hawthorne's tales to their "occasional gloom and pale glimpses as it were of fiends starting up on the page," shadows of "Sin and Death . . . which fall alike upon the so called evil and the so called good, which darken all that is pure, and defile all that is sacred."[35] Duyck-inck had even gone so far as to liken Hawthorne to the "tempest-stricken Lear whose sagacity flashes forth from his exceedingly vexed soul like the lightning from the storm-driven clouds."[36] If Melville responded to Haw-thorne with a "shock of recognition" (PT 249), some credit should go to Duyckinck as a conductor of that shock. Duyckinck, however, only flirted with Hawthorne's blackness before retreating to conventionalism, conclud-ing with genteel condescension, "A truly pure, gentle and acceptable man of Genius is NATHANIEL HAWTHORNE!"[37] Duyckinck could neutral-ize the *un*acceptable in Hawthorne by platitudinizing it. "Young Goodman Brown," a tale Melville found "deep as Dante" (PT 251), is, for Duyckinck, "simply an enforcement of the old, well-known, often illustrated truth, that there is a capacity for evil in the best of us, and that it rests very much within our own choice whether we shall be angels or devils."[38]

Duyckinck's essay on Hawthorne is illustrative of how midcentury Americans were able to embrace tragic writers by morally regularizing and eviscerating them. If Shakespeare was "popular entertainment in nine-teenth-century America,"[39] as Lawrence W. Levine has said, it was partly because broadly histrionic acting styles appealed to a mass audience and partly because contemporary producers and critics worked to accommodate Shakespeare to mainstream American values. Theatergoers of Melville's time saw *Richard III* in Colley Cibber's barebones melodramatic version, which included the bombastic "'Off with his head! so much for Bucking-ham!'" that Melville disparaged as "rant, interlined by another hand" (PT 244). Similarly, Americans not only attended Nahum Tate's *King Lear*, in which Lear and Cordelia survive and virtue is rewarded, but preferred it to the original "on ideological grounds" as more consonant with national beliefs (Levine 45).

Even as readers, Americans commonly received Shakespeare through a filter of social and religious conservatism that established him as "preem-inently a *moral* playwright" (Levine 39). The most influential of Shake-speare's contemporary American editors and critics, Henry Norman Hud-son, was beyond a naïve didacticism—Hudson execrated the "Taitified Lear" as a "miserable work"[40]—yet even Hudson, or especially Hudson, was careful to show how this "teller of the truth" (Hudson 1:70) had an "unequalled ability to instruct us in the things about us, and to strengthen us for the duties that lie before us" (Hudson 1:vii). While often astute in his moral and psychological analysis of character, Hudson pointedly ignored the philosophical dimensions of the plays, other than to bring them in line with his own "conservative American Whig and High-Church Episcopalian doctrines on social, political, and moral matters."[41] Hudson was particu-larly vehement in using Shakespeare to attack that "restless fanaticism and incontinence in reform, which is not content to leave anything unreformed, and is even threatening to make war upon the heavens themselves, merely because they are old" (Hudson 1:108).

The reign of critics like Hudson is a chief reason why Whitman, privately an admirer of Shakespeare, felt publicly obliged to attack the plays as sharing in the monarchical and aristocratic character of English literature and having "the air which to America is the air of death."[42] In a major cultural coup, conservative Whigs managed to appropriate much of English literature for themselves. Where liberals looked primarily to the future for their writers, Whigs laid claim to Burke, Scott, Wordsworth, and Coleridge as well as Shakespeare, all of whom, Hudson proclaimed, "have unquestionably evinced a far more genial sympathy with man as man, than any of the root-and-branch democrats."[43] But Whigs were also quick to identify kindred spirits among their contemporaries, and in Hawthorne at least one prominent Whig critic believed he had found such a man. Reviewing *Mosses from an Old Manse* in 1846, shortly after Hawthorne began his tenure as a Democratically appointed surveyor of customs, Charles W. Webber remarked on "the ethical conservatism of [Hawthorne's] mind given in that fine allegory, 'Earth's Holocaust.'"[44] "Here," Webber wrote, "we have embodied and illustrated . . . the fundamental thought of that Higher Conservatism upon the eternal base of which all wise and true Whigs have planted their feet. It is ridiculous to contend or hope that Political Creeds ever were or can be separated from the Ethical and Religious. One always has and always will grow out of the other."[45]

For contemporary readers Webber's grounding of politics in ethics and religion was a familiar Whig strategy for condemning Democratic efforts at legislative reform. That Webber could plausibly enlist Hawthorne for the Whig cause despite Hawthorne's well-known party allegiance testifies to the conservative usability of Hawthorne's vision so far as it presented evil as arising morally from human nature rather than historically from flawed institutions and traditions. If the root distinction between Conservative and Reformer lay, as Emerson said, in their respective belief or disbelief in the reality of the Fall and consequently in the desired containment or liberation of the natural self,[46] then Hawthorne visibly qualified as a "Higher Conservative" despite his deep abhorrence for the pretensions of wealth and class.

Melville also signaled out "Earth's Holocaust" for its "profound, nay appalling" moral, which he took to be the futility of outward reform so long as "the all-engendering heart of man" is left untouched (*PT* 243). Melville would not have quarreled with Webber's view that political beliefs were inseparable from ethical and metaphysical beliefs. His objection to Whig interpretations of Shakespeare and Hawthorne would have been that they were timid. Intent on buttressing the social order, Whigs ignored how tragic writers called into question *all* human orders—social, moral, religious—

through an unsparing critique of sham, hypocrisy, empty conventionalism, intellectual sleight of hand, and ethical cowardice. By virtue of a skepticism that left nothing untested, Shakespeare and Hawthorne, as Melville read them—*mis*read them, in Hawthorne's case at least—went beyond Webber's "Higher Conservatism." They divested human beings of the class-based ideologies that the privileged have always tried to represent as universal truths. Moreover, through a stark vision that saw naked humanity as alone and undefended in a fearful universe they returned from the borders of nihilism with a gospel of democratic equality and love.

Democracy and Aristocracy

The politics of "Hawthorne and His Mosses" would have baffled progressives and conservatives alike, confounding as they did the common litmus tests for ideological and party allegiance. To the Whigs, the Democrats were latter-day Jacobins who, as Henry Norman Hudson charged, would "demolish whatever time has produced or spared, and thereby create a waste wherein to try [their] schemes and erect the trophies of [their] own inventive beneficence."[47] To the Democrats, the Whigs were oligarchs and traitors to the founding principles of American democracy, which "believes in [the] essential equality and fundamental goodness" of human beings, and whose "object is to emancipate the mind of the mass of men from the degrading and disheartening fetters of social distinctions."[48] Emerson put the issue succinctly when he observed that "conservatism stands on man's incontestable limitations; reform on his indisputable infinitude."[49] Melville shared in both of these beliefs at once—in humanity's potential infinitude and its actual limitations—just as he upheld an ideal of democratic equality without sentimentalizing the wisdom and virtue of the populace. As he told Hawthorne in 1851, "it seems an inconsistency to assert unconditional democracy in all things, and yet confess a dislike to all mankind—in the mass. But not so" (*Corr* 191).

Melville's creed had been sorely tested, or perhaps formatively shaped, two years earlier in a series of events involving Shakespeare, democracy, party politics, American literary nationalism, and the role of the writer/intellectual in public affairs. On May 10, 1849, at least twenty-one people were killed in New York City when militiamen opened fire on a stone-throwing mob outside the Astor Place Opera House where English tragedian William Charles Macready was playing *Macbeth*, to the fury of local workingmen whose nationalism and class consciousness had been turned against Macready by his American rival Edwin Forrest and by the inflammatory rhetoric of the Native American (Know-Nothing) Party.[50] The previous day a newspaper petition signed by Melville and forty-six other New Yorkers had asked Macready to continue his performances despite a violent disruption that had halted the production on May 7. Some of the signers of the petition were patrician conservatives with strong class prejudices and Anglophile tastes; others like Melville, Evert Duyckinck, and Cornelius Mathews were literary nationalists and moderate Democrats who deplored a shameful incident of cultural suppression. After the riot the petitioners themselves became objects of popular wrath, and "for at least one agonizing night," Dennis Berthold speculates, "Melville and his family," who lived within blocks of the Opera House, "must have slept uneasily, dreading a workers' assault on their homes" (Berthold 438).

For Berthold, the Astor Place Riot marks "a turning point" in Melville's "literary and political consciousness" as he evolved from what Berthold calls a "youthful enthusiast for a democratic literature to [a] cool critic of popular excess and creator of literary esoterica" (Berthold 431, 432). In truth, Melville had never been the naïve nationalist Berthold supposes—his natural affinities, as Lawrence Buell observed, had always been with "the larger Anglophone literary tradition"[51]—nor did his protest in behalf of Macready indicate anything more than a disgust at thuggish censorship of the cultural marketplace. What the riot probably did make clear to Melville was that in the polarization of urban cultural politics the moderate democratic middle could not hold; the *Democratic Review*, for example, defended the attack on Macready as within the common law rights of audiences and severely criticized the "most injudicious epistle" of the petitioners.[52] In arguing that Melville found himself in the "political bed" of patrician Whigs (Berthold 435), Berthold echoes the divisive rhetoric of the extremists. From the time of *Mardi* Melville had gradually been fashioning his own political bed, and in "Hawthorne and His Mosses," under the contrary pulls of democratic optimism and tragic pessimism, nativism and universalism, egalitarianism and elitism, he came as near as he ever would to articulating an ideology of democratic literature.

Estimates of Melville's politics have suffered severely from the politics of the estimators. Melville is not above ideology or without it; he is simply subtler and more capacious than most of his ideological readers. His experience as a déclassé patrician and later as a shipboard underling led him to sympathize with the oppressed both practically in their physical suffering and theoretically from his conviction of the inherent rights and essential dignity of all human beings. But Melville lived too long and intimately among the working class to romanticize it as a group. His judgments were of individuals, not of classes, though nautical discipline had shown him the tendency of social stratification to corrupt. His politics are closest to the surface in *White-Jacket*, an anatomy of power relations aboard a warship that becomes, through its allegorical subtitle (*The World in a Man-of-War*), a vehicle for exploring class society at large. Melville's allegiance is openly with the common sailors (whom he calls "the people") against the officers (likened to aristocrats), but in a chapter allegorically titled "'The People' are given 'Liberty'" he has White-Jacket describe "the lamentable effects of suddenly and completely releasing 'the people' of a man-of-war from arbitrary discipline" (*WJ* 227). Melville's ethical and political position is that human rights are absolute, that "the general ignorance or depravity of any race of men [is not] to be alleged as an apology for tyrannizing over them" (*WJ* 304), and that most sailor vices are the result of "the morally debasing effects of the unjust, despotic, and degrading laws under which" sailors live (*WJ* 304). At the same time, he is aware that liberty aboard ship and, by analogy, to some degree in society "at first, must be administered in small and moderate quantities, increasing with the patient's capacity to make good use of it" (*WJ* 227).

A political egalitarian by conviction, Melville, like most literary intellectuals, was a cultural aristocrat by temperament and taste. While believing in the need for order and restraint, he differed from patrician Whigs in his skepticism toward the self-anointed custodians of order, the justice of class-based institutions, and the sanctity of the social and religious traditions used to legitimate them. Melville cannot be called a conservative for the simple reason that there was little in established society he wanted to "conserve" beyond the freedoms and civilities of public life and the right of souls to select their own society. Like White-Jacket, who calls himself "A Man-of-War Hermit in a Mob" (*WJ* 50), each of Melville's early narrators remains aloof from the run of his shipmates, choosing his companions from a small circle of congenial spirits characterized not so much by "the class-oriented standards of birth, breeding, manners, education, and social condition,"[53] as Larry J. Reynolds claimed, as by intellect, literary bent, or transfiguring sorrow. Melville's "aristocracy" was never the factitious one of class and wealth but, like Emerson's in "Natural Aristocracy" (a lecture Melville seems to have heard in Boston in 1849, three months before Astor Place),[54] "a real aristocracy" that "sit[s] indifferently in all climates and under the shadow of all institutions" and whose "basis" is "truth."[55]

The chief significance of Astor Place for Melville would not have been its conflict of classes or political parties but its opposition of leveling democracy and culture. Throughout this period, historian Rush Welter observed, "democratic efforts to put an end to 'aristocratic' distinctions in American society often took shape in what seemed to be an effort to put an end even to learning, to distinction, to prudence, and to competence."[56] In the case of Astor Place, the silencing of Macready, an actor of "inward passion and outward restraint" (Shattuck 70), in favor of Forrest, "a brawny, massive, passionate" theatrical presence who "narrowed himself into a symbol of American nationalism—self-consciously parochial, belligerent, and at worst downright bullying" (Shattuck xii)—seemed to encapsulate the anti-intellectualism and xenophobia that had come to disfigure cultural nationalism at its extreme.

The problem of establishing intellectual and aesthetic standards in an egalitarian society was and remains a difficult and politically volatile one in American culture. George Bancroft voiced the radical democratic position when he argued that "if it be true that the gifts of mind and heart are universally diffused, . . . then it follows, as a necessary consequence, that the common judgment in taste, politics, and religion is the highest authority on earth and the nearest possible approach to an infallible decision."[57] Was it possible to be an egalitarian democrat without acceding to Bancroft's cultural majoritarianism? Fresh from the popular failure of *Mardi*, Melville answered this question in *White-Jacket* when he had the shipboard poet Lemsford distinguish between "the public" (an "addle-pated mob and rabble") and "the people" (the Commons as portrayed in natural rights theory and idealizations of the American freeman). "The public and the people!" Jack Chase adds in confirmation: "Ay, ay, my lads, let us hate the one and cleave to the other" (*WJ* 192). In the "Mosses" essay Hawthorne is presented as a casualty of the democratic "public" ("perhaps too deserving of popularity to be popular" [*PT* 240]), while even a "great genius" like Shakespeare suffers from the fact that "few men have time, or patience, or palate, for [his] spiritual truth" (*PT* 245).

Melville's distinction between the public and the people resembles that of other nineteenth-century literary progressives who, as Daniel Aaron said, "held forth the possibility of human development while noting the appalling evidences of human mediocrity."[58] By the mid-1840s Emerson's faith in the latent capacities of the common man had evolved into a reverence for the "great man who inhabits a higher sphere of thought, into which other men rise with labor and difficulty."[59] In Melville the trope of ascending becomes one of *descending*; Emerson himself, for example, is praised as belonging to the "corps of thought-divers, that have been diving & coming up again with blood-shot eyes since the world began" (*Corr* 121). The difference between Melville's thinkers and Emerson's is that Melville's are marked by the stigmata of *dark* knowledge. As Stanley Geist long ago remarked, "the isolation of Melville was, at bottom, and in his maturity, neither the aristocrat's scorn of the mob, nor the snob's vanity, nor . . . the rugged individualist's confident self-reliance. It derived, rather, from a consciousness of tragedy so acute and deep-seated, that true kinship with any man but one who shared his tragic vision was a grotesque mockery."[60] The political problem was that in identifying greatness with tragic depth Melville, in Geist's view, "overstepped the bounds of a strictly democratic art" since "the capacity for profound self-scrutiny belonged to the spiritual nobleman alone, and not to Everyman."[61]

The Tragedian as Democrat

Two factors return Melville's tragedian to democracy; the first is the inherent nature of the tragic vision, the second the still unforeclosed possibilities of America as they represent latent possibilities for humanity. What established Hawthorne as a democratic writer was not his party affiliation or scorn for the arrogance of class. His democracy stemmed rather from the very skepticism that Whigs identified with a conservative distrust of reform but that Melville understood as a distrust of life itself. Far from precluding egalitarian democracy or opposing it in spirit, a tragic view of experience made democracy all the more imperative, the very indifference of nature and absence or silence of God obliging human beings to huddle together for mutual protection and support. This is what Ishmael means in "Loomings" when he asks "Who ain't a slave?" and goes on to imagine "the universal thump" being "passed around," so that "all hands should rub each other's shoulder-blades, and be content" (*MD* 6). By virtue of their deeper insight, the blackest tragedians were almost necessarily the greatest philanthropists, "full of sermons-on-the-mount, and gentle, aye, almost as Jesus," as Melville characterized Shakespeare in an 1849 letter to Evert Duyckinck. "I take such men to be inspired," he added: "I fancy that this moment Shakspeare in heaven ranks with Gabriel Raphael and Michael. And if another Messiah ever comes twill be in Shakespere's person" (*Corr* 119). The Lear who "tears off the mask, and speaks the sane madness of vital truth" (*PT* 244) is also, as A. C. Bradley wrote in a Melvillean spirit, a man who "comes in his affliction to think of others first . . . ; to pierce below the differences of rank and raiment to the common humanity beneath; [and] whose sight is so purged by scalding tears that it sees at last how power and place and all things in the world are vanity except love."[62]

Compassion for others, as much as loftiness in oneself, was for Melville the very mark and measure of the tragic vision. This is the significance of his account of "the hither side of Hawthorne's soul" (*PT* 243) with its "depth of tenderness," "boundless sympathy with all forms of being," and "omnipresent love" (*PT* 242), all leavened by "a humor so spiritually gentle, so high, so deep, and yet so richly relishable, that it were hardly inappropriate in an angel" (*PT* 241). Not only was love "compatible with universal wisdom,"[63] as Emerson wrote in his own essay on Shakespeare, it was the natural consequence of wisdom, and wisdom the precondition for the highest love. And both of these things emanated from sorrow. Thus the tenderness and sympathy in Hawthorne's work could furnish "clews" for Melville of an "intricate, profound heart" deeply touched by suffering, for only "this only can enable a man to depict it in others" (*PT* 242).

In joining sorrow, compassion, and laughter, Melville was responding to Carlyle's imaginative synthesis of these things in his portrait of Shakespeare in "The Hero as Poet," still fresh in his mind as he wrote: "Doubt it not, [Shakespeare] had his own sorrows. . . . How could a man delineate a Hamlet, a Coriolanus, a Macbeth, so many suffering heroic hearts, if his own heroic heart had never suffered?—And now, in contrast with all this, observe his mirthfulness, his genuine overflowing love of laughter. . . . It is always a genial laughter. . . . Laughter means sympathy" (Carlyle, *HHW* 929–23).

Another phrase from Carlyle's chapter would also have struck Melville: "the courage to stand by the dangerous-true" (Carlyle, *HHW* 91). Like Hawthorne, Carlyle was not an instructor for Melville so much as a reagent who quickened and developed tendencies within him. Pondering the two sides of Hawthorne's nature and joining his thoughts with elements from "The Hero as Poet"—Shakespeare as "the greatest of Intellects" (Carlyle, *HHW* 91), the "dangerous-true," private sorrow, laughter and sympathy, the "universal Psalm" rising out of Shakespeare (Carlyle, *HHW* 94), the "sacredness in the fact of such a man being sent into this Earth" (Carlyle, *HHW* 95), and the reverence for such a man as a spiritual hero, even a messiah of sorts—Melville seems suddenly to have grasped a vital relationship between blackness and democratic love: "there is no man in whom humor and love are developed in that high form called genius; no such man can exist without also possessing, as the indispensable complement of these, a great deep intellect, which drops down into the universe like a plummet. Or, love and humor are only the eyes, through which such an intellect views this world" (*PT* 242). The discoveries of the intellect activate and give sinew to the compassion of the heart, for what the intellect perceives is the underlying blackness of life that makes human beings common sufferers.

The basis for egalitarian brotherhood in "Hawthorne and His Mosses" is not "humility before God," as F. O. Matthiessen claimed of Melville (Matthiessen 446); it is vulnerability before apparent godlessness. Ontologically, democracy rests on what Melville called "the tragicalness of human thought in its own unbiassed, native and profounder workings" (*Corr* 186). From this it draws the ethical and political corollary that a shared victimhood communalizes us beyond differences of wealth, class, race, gender, education, and taste. The idea had been germinating in Melville at least since the late chapters of *White-Jacket*, in which the ruling trope of a world-ship turns metaphysically grim. Sailing "with sealed orders" from a port "forever astern" and "our last destination . . . a secret to ourselves and our officers" (*WJ* 398), "oppressed by illiberal laws" (*WJ* 399) and subject to all the terrors of sickness and death, "let us never train our murderous guns inboard," Melville writes; "let us not mutiny with bloody pikes in our hands" (*WJ* 400). Behind these words is a sober recognition that human beings must attend to themselves and each other since "what we call Fate [read: Providence; God in history] is even, heartless, and impartial" (*WJ* 320). *White-Jacket* stops short of an openly tragic metaphysics because Melville, obliged to write a marketable book and still smarting from the reception of *Mardi*, was not prepared to break publicly with orthodox religion. Instead he tacitly separates Christian metaphysics (God the sovereign) from Christian ethics (Jesus the teacher), depicting a naturalistic universe while holding to the ideals of the Sermon on the Mount and empowering human beings to "mold the whole world's hereafters" (*WJ* 320). The "Mosses" essay brings this idea to fruition. The "unshackled, democratic spirit of Christianity in all things" (*PT* 248) that it commends as genuinely American—a Christianity of brotherhood without a superintending Father or an atoning Son—stands beside a vision of unmitigated cosmic blackness, the latter the existential background of life, the former the ethical and political foreground.

Emerson defined "the true Christianity" as "a faith like Christ's in the infinitude of Man."[64] Matthiessen saw Melville as "responsive" to this liberal nineteenth-century movement "from belief in the salvation of man through the mercy and grace of a sovereign God, to belief in the potential divinity in every man" (Matthiessen 446), but he presented him as criticizing it through his portrait of Ahab as a self-reliant individualist run amok (Matthiessen 447). In the "Mosses" essay Melville is close to Emerson in his liberal humanism, save that the test for "infinitude" is now one's capacity to know and endure a thoroughly non-Emersonian and un-Christian body of ontological truths. When Melville writes that "Shakespeares are this day being born on the banks of the Ohio" (*PT* 245), he is clearing space for himself as an aspiring writer, but he is also claiming a Shakespearean depth for all human beings provided they remove the lenses of convention and regard life directly and fearlessly as all great thinkers do.

What distinguished America as a scene for the realization of human capacities was the independence of thought inspired by American newness and physical space and encouraged by American political principles. While in America as elsewhere in "this world of lies" (*PT* 244) the subversiveness of truth forced the writer into indirection and prudent concealment, the experimental nature of America allowed him the freedom, and imposed on him the duty, to address that part of his audience that could rise to face the revelation of blackness. No society was entirely free of the "muzzle" of censorship that Melville believed "intercepted Shakspere's full articulations." "Who in this intolerant Universe is, or can be," a "frank man to the uttermost"? he asked Evert Duyckinck. Nonetheless, he insisted, "the Declaration of Independence makes a difference" (*Corr* 122). How small a difference it made Melville would discover with the reviews of *Pierre*, which confirmed Tocqueville's contention that in "no country" was there "so little independence of mind and real freedom of discussion as in America."[65] At some level Melville understood this even as he wrote "Hawthorne and His Mosses." His subject, however, like Emerson's or Whitman's, was the potential rather than the actual America, and his claims for the American citizenry are probably best understood as an enabling fiction meant to underwrite his nascent ambitions for *Moby-Dick*. For a brief time, it was at least Melville's avowed faith that the American writer had unprecedented leave and opportunity to forge a bold, independent native literature founded upon "the great Art of Telling the Truth" (*PT* 244).

A Three-Stranded Lesson

"'You really feel belittled when you're reading Melville,'" an undergraduate told Paul Lauter, who noted that his "students seemed actively to dislike Melville, to feel humiliated by the prose and ignorant before the dense web of Melville's allusive, syntactically intricate style and his convoluted plotting."[66] More than any other nineteenth-century American novelist, Melville raises the problem of cultural "representativeness" because of the demands his work makes on the common reader. *Mardi* was the first serious check to his popularity, and yet, as William Charvat noted, a "hostility" to the reading public was inscribed in *Mardi* and was "antecedent to its failure."[67] In contrast to Whitman's ideal of a native "culture . . . eligible to the uses of the high average of men—and *not* restricted by conditions ineligible to the masses,"[68] the culture exalted in "Hawthorne and His Mosses" is that of a confraternity of thinkers distinct from social class yet constituting a freemasonic elite. Hawthorne's blackness, Melville writes, "is, mostly, insinuated to those who may best understand it, and account for it; it is not obtruded on every one alike" (*PT* 245). Without being *of* or *from* the people, as Whitman's writing purports to be, Melville's truth-telling literature is democratic in being *for* the people in the sense of being ethically and politically on their behalf.[69]

In his distance from the democratic populace Melville was more typical than not of contemporary writer/intellectuals. Far from insisting on the writer's participation in popular life or sharing of popular standards, "most ante-bellum critics," as Benjamin T. Spencer observed, "seem rather to have been of the mind of Theodore Parker, whose faith in the people went only so far as to suppose them capable of being instructed, of being elevated through a high-minded literature written by "scholars" who had extrapopular sources of insight and who formed a vanguard of truth."[70] Even here, the "Mosses" essay is democratic in a singular fashion. The role of the writer, Parker maintained, was to "'represent the higher facts of human consciousness to the people'"[71]—in Emerson's words, to "occupy the whole space between God or pure mind, and the multitude of uneducated men."[72] But what if the "higher facts" of consciousness were unbearable by the mass of human beings? Solomon was "the truest man who ever spoke," Melville remarked, yet even "he a little *managed* the truth with a view to popular conservatism" (*Corr* 193). So, in Melville's view, did Hawthorne and Shakespeare, whose work addressed two audiences, one middlebrow, one more select. Hawthorne and Shakespeare were thus writers of what Leo Strauss called "exoteric" (or publicly accessible) texts, which combine "a popular teaching of an edifying character, which is the foreground; and a philosophic teaching concerning the most important object, which is indicated only between the lines."[73] (Interestingly, this is how Frederick C. Crews presented Hawthorne in his revisionist work *The Sins of the Fathers* [1966].)[74] Strauss believed "that there are basic truths which would not be pronounced in public by any decent man"[75]—in Melville's words, "the things, which we feel to be so terrifically true, that it were all but madness for any good man, in his own proper character, to utter, or even hint of them" (*PT* 244). For Strauss these truths needed to be hidden "immediately because they would harm others, ultimately because those others would turn and harm" the writer.[76] Melville believed this as well, until *Pierre* when recklessness took charge: "Let any clergyman try to preach the Truth from its very stronghold, the pulpit, and they would ride him out of his church on his own pulpit bannister" (*Corr* 191). "In this world of lies," he wrote in the "Moses" essay, the truth had to be told "covertly, and by snatches" (*PT* 244), even in democratic America.

"Instructing the people" was therefore a matter of crafting a "two-stranded lesson" (*MD* 119). A "bearer" (conveyor) of truth to the strong, the democratic tragedian was also a "bearer" (sufferer) of truth for the weak, to whom he preached the fruits of knowledge (love and humor) without inflicting the pain of knowing. Like Shakespeare, the tragic writer was greatest "not so much for what he did do, as for what he did not do, or refrained from doing" (*PT* 244). Quite apart from prudence, there was a magnanimity to this strategem of reticence and disguise. The hero of Shakespeare's works was Shakespeare, of Hawthorne's works Hawthorne, and nothing evinced their heroism more fully than the tenderness they bestowed upon the world in an almost Christlike assumption of common grief. The third and choicest strand of Melville's lesson in the "Mosses" essay is that of the writer's own literary self-apotheosis. Standing high to receive the lightning bolts of truth and mediating them for a popular audience while delivering a gospel of equality and love, the writer became, as Carlyle had said, a "hero," perhaps the greatest hero the modern world could supply now that the races of gods and prophets were extinct.

Like other literary manifestoes, "Hawthorne and His Mosses" is ultimately a work of idealized self-proclamation, or so it became as Melville worked on it. The initial reference to Shakespeare is introduced casually, not for purposes of sustained comparison to Hawthorne but as an illustration of the quality of blackness in both writers. From there, driven on by the ramifications of his idea and his own pent-up enthusiasms and ambitions, Melville elaborates on the blackness of Shakespeare, whose plays he presents as ventriloquist devices for the revelation of the terrifying. Only when Melville has exhausted his thought does he seem to catch himself up and realize its significance for a national literature and for his own work-in-progress. "Some may start to read of Shakespeare and Hawthorne on the same page" (*PT* 245), he begins, arguing more systematically now and moving toward that vision of an American Shakespeare that will underlie his performance in *Moby-Dick*. In a volume of Chatterton's works purchased months earlier, he had checked the editor's prefatory remark on the unapproachable greatness of Shakespeare, commenting in the margin, "Cant. No man 'must ever remain unapproachable.'"[77] The discovery that "Shakespeare has been approached" (*PT* 245), and by a countryman and a contemporary, implied that he might be approached again or even be "surpassed by an American born now or yet to be born" (*PT* 246). Why not by himself?

The closing pages of the "Mosses" essay bring forward its self-reference with an almost disarming transparency. Melville's quotation of a passage from "The Intelligence Office" on the "brawny," "rough-hewn" truth-seeker, offered as a portrait of "the temper of [Hawthorne's] mind" and that of "all true, candid men" (*PT* 250), is more accurately a portrait of his own aspect and temper.[78] In praising Hawthorne, Melville had good reason to feel, as he archly confessed, that he had "more served and honored myself, than him" (*PT* 249). His remarks on Hawthorne's conceit of the "'Master Genius'" of the age (from "A Select Party") develop Hawthorne's opinion "that this great fullness and overflowing may be, or may be destined to be, shared by a plurality of men" (*PT* 252), of whom Hawthorne may be only the first—the Marlowe, perhaps, to some Shakespeare to come. Hawthorne, he is careful to say, is "the American, who *up to the present day*, has evinced, in Literature, the largest brain with the largest heart" (*PT* 253; my emphasis). That Hawthorne will not be not the crowning American author is hinted by Melville's judgment that *Mosses from an Old Manse* signals the "culmination" of Hawthorne's "developable" powers and "will ultimately be accounted his masterpiece" (*PT* 253). Privately, Melville came to imagine an even less flattering trajectory; the *Mosses*, he wrote Evert Duyckinck in February 1851, were inferior to "an earlier vintage from [Hawthorne's] vine," *Twice-told Tales* (*Corr* 181). Even at his best, Melville added, "there is something lacking—a good deal lacking—to the plump sphericity of the man. . . . He does'nt patronise the butcher—he needs roast-beef done rare" (*Corr* 181). The want of masculine vigor in Hawthorne had earlier been noted by critics like Charles Fenno Hoffman, who saw Hawthorne as a kind of literary John the Baptist whose "use" was to "smooth and prepare the path for nobler (but not better) visitants" ahead.[79] Hoffman's view of Hawthorne was a familiar one, and Melville evokes its substance to Duyckinck, a friend and literary sponsor of both Hawthorne and himself, as if inviting Duyckinck to judge between them. If Hawthorne was an inspiration, a paradigm for democratic tragedy, and by February 1851 an intimate friend, he was also, for those very reasons, a rival. The constellation of American luminaries could have only one brightest star.

The wagon to which Melville hitched his own star in 1850s–51 was democratic tragedy. American literature for Melville was not primarily a literature about America but one in which the writer, as representative self and in accordance with the experimental nature of America, "drop[ped] down into the universe like a plummet" (*PT* 242) and surfaced with a vision of life's blackness and concomitantly of democratic love. For those in his audience capable of rising to meet and endure his intimations of truth, the writer provided a stimulus for, and example of, the self-transfiguration that realized the democratic ideal of human greatness. A spiritual aristocrat himself, the writer sought through his text to extend aristocracy as far as it might reach: why *not* a nation of Shakespeares? There were powerful reasons why not, as Melville knew, yet for some Americans—enough, perhaps, to make a cultural difference—democracy needn't be founded on a shallow optimism bound to collide with experience or to leave the nation puerile in its collective evasions. Years later Melville would come to see the "terrible historic tragedy" of the Civil War as potentially "instructing our whole beloved country though pity and fear" (*BP* 202). In 1850 he imagined that literature itself might perform this function, and, impelled by an idea of democratic tragedy, he set out in *Moby-Dick* to do it.

4

The Theory and Practice of Democratic Tragedy (2): Ishmael's Grand Erections

Oh man! admire and model thyself after the whale! Do thou, too, remain warm among ice. Do thou, too, live in this world without being of it. Be cool at the equator; keep thy blood fluid at the Pole. Like the great dome of St. Peter's, and like the great whale, retain, O man! in all seasons a temperature of thine own. But how easy and how hopeless to teach these fine things! Of erections, how few are domed like St. Peter's! of creatures how few vast as the whale!

—Melville, *Moby-Dick*

HM had a mind rare of men, capable of founding a new humanitas. Which I say he did. . . .

—Charles Olson, letter to Merton M. Sealts, Jr.

A Rationale of Narrative Form

First-time readers of *Moby-Dick* approaching it through the tradition of the novel are often surprised and disconcerted by chapter 29, "Enter Ahab, to Him Stubb"; they thought they had been reading a retrospective first-person narrative and suddenly find themselves in what presents itself as a stage play. Chapter 30 ("The Pipe") goes on to feature a dramatic soliloquy, chapter 31 ("Queen Mab") a conversation between Stubb and Flask that Ishmael does not even pretend to have overheard. With chapter 32 ("Cetology") the book returns to Ishmael's point of view until chapter 36 ("The Quarter-Deck") introduces a new set of stage directions and a ubiquitous perspective unavailable to sailor Ishmael. Chapters 37–39 are soliloquies by Ahab, Starbuck, and Stubb, chapter 40 a theatrical crowd scene. All of these chapters are framed by stage directions; nowhere is character or narrator Ishmael in sight or in mind.

Since Walter E. Bezanson's landmark essay "*Moby-Dick*: Work of Art" (1953), criticism has tended to regard Ishmael as "the enfolding sensibility of the novel, the hand that writes the tale, the imagination through which all matters of the book pass."[1] "If Ishmael can give us conjectural material in expository form," Robert Zoellner reasoned, following Bezanson, "he can also give us conjectural material in dramatic form."[2] For Zoellner, "every word of *Moby-Dick*, including even the footnotes, comes from Ishmael rather than Melville;"[3] for Harrison Hayford, "the mind of Ishmael" is the very "ground and cause" of *Moby-Dick*.[4] "Ishmael's vast symbolic prose-poem in a free organic form,"[5] Bezanson called the book in celebration of its endogenously idiosyncratic blending of styles and modes.

Written in the heyday of New Criticism, Bezanson's essay helped establish Melville's book as art by bringing it into line with the post-Jamesian assumptions about unity of point of view that governed New Critical thinking about the novel. After Bakhtin, *Moby-Dick* looks rather different; if anything, it looks more like the polyphonic book Melville might actually have intended at a time when fictive practice was still largely uncodified and generic heterogeneity reigned in the sprawling German romances Melville admired.[6] Literary history aside, the Ishmael-as-author theory poorly corresponds to audiences' temporal experience of the book. The real question is not whether Ishmael or Melville is the "author" of *Moby-Dick* but whether readers of the dramatic chapters are asked to regard them as filtered through the consciousness of Ishmael or as having the quasi-objective immediacy of stage presentation. There are thirteen dramatic chapters in *Moby-Dick* (chaps. 29, 36–40, 108, 119–22, 127, 129) if we count only those that use stage directions, more if we include chapters in which an opening passage prefaces a soliloquy, a series of parallel soliloquies, or a play of voices that imitates the exchange of characters on stage. Common to all of these is the suppression of an Ishmaelean perspective on the action. In chapters like "Sunset," "The Quarter-Deck," and "The Candles" Melville's form dissolves the mimetic distance fiction establishes between character and reader and places its audience as directly in Ahab's presence as the conventions of printed literature allow. Attention is focused wholly upon Ahab, whose size increases with proximity and whose power readers are left to confront as best they can without the interpretive guardianship of the narrator.

I admire Bezanson's essay enormously, but I find its account of form the kind of question begging that Northrop Frye had in mind when he likened interpreters of *Moby-Dick* to "the doctors of Brobdingnag, who after great wrangling finally pronounced Gulliver a *lusus naturae*."[7] If *Moby-Dick* is an "organic" book, why not try to discover the principle of its organicism, specifically the relationship between Ishmael's quest for "the ungraspable phantom of life" (*MD* 5), cast in the form of fictional narrative, and Ahab's hunt for Moby Dick, presented largely as dramatic tragedy?

There are several reasons why Melville might have taken liberties with point of view. A sense of generic decorum may have led him to conceive Ahab in the high mimetic mode of heroic drama rather than the characteristically low mimetic mode of the novel or its somewhat rarefied cousin, the romance. Or, as Charles Olson and others have argued, it may be that the influence of Shakespeare "caused Melville to approach tragedy in terms of the drama."[8] There is much about Ahab that Ishmael simply cannot know, and in presenting Ahab's "intellectual and spiritual exasperations" (*MD* 184) Melville may have found it desirable to bring Ahab forward to soliloquize on his own rather than confine himself to Ishmael's speculations, which inevitably reflect back upon the speculator. As matters of conscious authorial choice, generic elements should be considered functionally in light of their consequences. R. S. Crane saw the form of literary texts as arising from and pointing back to the writer's determination "to affect our opinions and emotions in a certain definite way such as would not have been possible had the synthesizing principle" of the work "been of a different kind."[9] It makes an enormous practical difference that readers should experience Ahab apart from the mediation of Ishmael, but what "synthesizing principle" might Melville's choice imply?

One principle might be simple juxtaposition, as R. W. B. Lewis suggested when he called *Moby-Dick* "the supreme instance of a dialectical novel—a novel of tension without resolution."[10] Like Bezanson, Lewis wrote during the ascendancy of New Criticism, for which "tension" (Allen Tate's special term)[11] was a prime literary virtue. The dialectic might also reflect what Murray Krieger called the "unending tension between the ethical and the tragic," which Krieger saw as illustrative of modern skepticism toward universals and as manifesting itself in doubly heroed books like *Heart of Darkness* and *Moby-Dick*.[12] More recently John Bryant gave another turn to the idea of dialectical tension when he described *Moby-Dick* as "most like revolution when it places the reader in the condition of one caught between two deeply felt but conflicting ideologies."[13]

Moby-Dick does mean to be revolutionary, but its structural principle is not that of ideological conflict (Ahab's worldview is never an exemplary possibility) but of exorcism: the purgation of an outworn mindset to make way for a modern one. Like Whitman, Melville saw "the forming of a great aggregate Nation"[14] as dependent on sloughing off a traditional theocentric consciousness that shaped the perceived coordinates of experience and governed assignments of energy and value within them. "Take God out of the dictionary," Melville told Hawthorne, "and you would have Him in the street" (*Corr* 186); that is to say, dissolve the established categories of thought with their reification of experience and you would find reality, truth, a new foundation for being, perhaps even Divinity itself, omnipresent in the living moment. "I hear and behold God in every object," Whitman wrote: "I find letters from God dropt in the street" ("Song of Myself," ll. 1281, 1286).

Whitman conceived his own literary enterprise as prophetic—the creation of a "New Bible."[15] What he meant by that was the kind of communal scripture, at once fictive and philosophical, that Northrop Frye denoted by the term "epic": "a narrative poem of heroic action, but a special kind of narrative" with "an encyclopaedic quality to it, distilling the essence of all the religious, philosophical, political, even scientific learning of its time, and, if completely successful, the definitive poem for its age."[16] "Song of Myself" and *Moby-Dick* are consciously epics of this kind, with the difference that Ishmael's encyclopaedic voyage into the universe encloses the tragedy of Ahab. Where Whitman fashioned his scripture by writing as if a revolution of mind had already occurred and he were the Adam of a post-Christian age, *Moby-Dick* *enacts* the process of revolution by staging the death throes of an old civilization and the birth of a new. M. H. Abrams titled a section of *Natural Supernaturalism* "Apocalypse by Revolution," referring to the faith of some Romantics in a paradise to be regained through political action. *Moby-Dick* envisions the reverse, revolution by apocalypse, as an exhausted cultural order presses its discourse to the point of extremity where it shatters against the obdurateness of naturalistic fact and leaves the mind naked and illusionless, like Ishmael alone on the ocean clinging to Queequeg's coffin.

Behind the structure of *Moby-Dick* seems a determination on Melville's part to engage his readers vitally with Ahab's quest and self-immolation, which is the immolation of their own culture's constricting theism. "The job" Melville undertook, Charles Olson said, "was a giant's, to make a new god. To do it, it was necessary for Melville, because Christianity surrounded him as it surrounds us, to be an Anti-Christ as Ahab was"[17]—and then to destroy Ahab himself. The ending of *Moby-Dick* is not its final word "orphan" uttered in an ethical and cosmological void. The ending is its opening chapter, "Loomings," whose "Call me Ishmael" (*MD* 3) introduces the reader to an outcast destined like his biblical prototype to be the progenitor of a new race. Ahab and Ishmael; residual and emergent; drama and narrative/discursive prose: *Moby-Dick* is a heroic tragedy enclosed within a foundational American epic, itself tragic in its vision of experience but drawing from tragedy the instructed democrat's humor and love.

Killing Crazy Ahab

The Ishmael who goes to sea in "Loomings" is a descendant of the morose young Redburn, toughened by experience and leavened by a waggish sense of humor but still a dropout from what Robert Zoellner aptly called "Jehovah's Winter World," a flinty-hearted mix of Calvinist theology and predatory capitalism.[18] Ishmael is initially an "Ishmael" for socio-economic reasons (his name will later come to have ontological reference); he is fallen in class, empty in pocket, and embittered by the "civilized hypocrisies and bland deceits" of self-professed Christians on land (*MD* 51). But Ishmael is also engaged in a quest identified with the sea, with the "portentous and mysterious" figure of the whale, and with the prevision of a "grand hooded phantom, like a snow hill in the air" (*MD* 7), a quest that he quickly makes the reader's quest. "We are going a-whaling" (*MD* 11), Ishmael announces in "The Carpet-Bag," seizing us by the arm and leading us through the door of the Spouter-Inn, then dropping suddenly into the second person ("Entering that gable-ended Spouter-Inn, you found yourself . . . "), telling us what we would have seen, how we would have felt (*MD* 12).

"The writer's audience is always a fiction," Walter J. Ong remarked; the writer imagines "an audience cast in some sort of role" and by rhetorical means tries to ensure that the audience will "correspondingly fictionalize itself."[19] The audience of "Loomings" is cast in the role of would-be adventurers: respectable landsmen "tied to counters, nailed to benches, clinched to desks" (*MD* 4) who secretly yearn for the sea and who realize (once Ishmael shows them) that what they are seeking is nothing less than the meaning of life itself. Ishmael is their (our) surrogate, who, having gone to sea and returned, spirits us away with him as he retraces his course, assuming, like the speaker in so many of Whitman's poems, the dual part of companion-in-discovery and tutor. He carries us over traveled ground, making his past impressions our present ones and filling us as we go with *his* story, but he is also a voice speaking in our ear, commenting, explaining, interpreting, speculating, seriocomically moralizing, besieging us writer-to-reader in the book's temporal present even as he enlists our imaginative participation in the reenacted whaling voyage.

In its double structure—a past-tense journey to the frontier "encased in a rhetorical appeal to the reader,"[20] as Lawrence Buell described *Walden*— *Moby-Dick* ranges itself with other writings of the American Renaissance, particularly Whitman's and Thoreau's. In each case, a character-narrator repudiates the mindset of the community, takes the measure of life and of himself as a representative human being, and returns to the community with a new vision conveyed dramatically through the lines of his rehearsed action and philosophically through the overlay of his discursive talk. The speaker begins as an outsider from society, but through the organization of his work he implicates his readers in its action, instructs them with his running commentary, and lays the foundation for a new cultural order on the basis of what he and his audience have come to learn. Works so constructed are not simply "about" experience in the common mimetic sense; they are efforts to *provide* and collectively digest experience and radically alter the terms of perception and judgment. They are acts on behalf of a new civilization.

The difference between *Moby-Dick* and *Walden* or "Song of Myself" is that beyond pursuing his own quest Melville's narrator is centrally engaged in telling the story of someone else's. As early as chapter 16 when Peleg's description of Ahab evokes in Ishmael "a strange awe" (*MD* 80), *Moby-Dick* departs from Melville's earlier books and looks ahead to a class of fictions (*Heart of Darkness, The Great Gatsby, All the King's Men, Absalom! Absalom!*) alternatively called "observer-hero narratives" or "meditations on the hero," novels in which the fate of a mythically proportioned hero is presented through the consciousness of a realistic first-person narrator and assimilated to the story of the narrator's education.[21] The double action in such books is part of a single action, as the hero in his extremity plays out latent tendencies within the narrator and serves as both a vehicle for the revelation of truth and a cautionary example of the dangers of obsession.

Through its dramatic chapters, *Moby-Dick* creates a unique subspecies of this form by circumventing the narrator's filtering mind and ushering the reader directly into Ahab's presence. The role of Ishmael vis-à-vis Ahab and the reader is to act as a go-between who frames the dramatic chapters in an interpretive context and helps Melville shape the reader's relationship to the quest. Down to the resonance of its alliterative poetry ("an infinity of firmest fortitude, a determinate, unsurrenderable wilfulness, in the fixed and fearless, forward dedication of [his] glance" [*MD* 134]), Ishmael's first descriptions of Ahab elevate him into a figure ravaged by suffering and of transcendent spiritual heroism. However diabolized Ahab may become during the course of the book, it is important to remember that Ishmael's early allusions associate him with heroes and redeemers (Christ, Prometheus, Perseus) and establish his revenge as a collective one drawing upon "the sum of all the general rage and hate felt by his whole race from Adam down" (*MD* 184). In "The Quarter-Deck" Ahab stands forth as if on stage and magnetizes the reader as he does the crew, yet the significance of his hunt— what it means for *us* in *our* world—remains unclear until we are cued by Ishmael in the chapter "Moby Dick." The "intellectual and spiritual exasperations" Ishmael ascribes to Ahab (*MD* 184) turn out to be the common exasperations of being-in-the-world: the silence of the universe in the face of human needs for justice and order ("The Sphynx"); the tauntingly indecipherable meaningfulness of experience ("Queequeg in His Coffin," "The Doubloon"); the want of assurances in nature for human hopes of immortality ("The Dying Whale"). Ahab will declaim against all of these things in his soliloquies and staged encounters with various foils, but it is essential that Ishmael vouch for Ahab at the outset, as Nick Carraway vouches for Gatsby and Marlow for Kurtz, and that he identify Ahab's grievances as latently his own ("my shouts had gone up with the rest" [*MD* 179]) and universal humanity's.

It has been suggested that Melville's naming of Ahab may have been prompted "by Milton's use of Job as the prototype of Christ and Ahab as the counter-type in *Paradise Regained*."[22] If so, prototype and countertype converge in *Moby-Dick* in the figure of a long-suffering Job unreconciled by God's answer from the whirlwind and directing his wrath against the putative source of evil embodied in the "agent" or "principal" of the white whale (*MD* 164). Ahab is Job, a sufferer; he is Christ, a deliverer of humanity from suffering; and he is an anti-Christ "chasing with curses a Job's whale round the world" (*MD* 186). A symbol of unapproachable power who rules as "a king over all the children of pride" (Job 41: 34), the leviathan of Job is glossed in the Oxford Bible as "the sea-monster . . . which was associated with chaos,"[23] and whose origins lie in the myths and religions that preceded and were absorbed into Judeo-Christianity. "In the Bible," Northrop Frye writes,

> we have a sea-monster usually named leviathan, who is described as
> the enemy of the Messiah, and whom the Messiah is destined to kill
> in the "day of the Lord." The leviathan is the source of social sterility
> . . . and is described in the Book of Job as "king over all the children
> of pride." It also seems closely associated with the natural sterility of
> the fallen world, with the blasted world of struggle and poverty and
> disease into which Job is hurled by Satan and Adam by the serpent
> in Eden. . . . In the Book of Revelation the leviathan, Satan, and the
> Edenic serpent are all identified. This identification is the basis for an
> elaborate dragon-killing metaphor in Christian symbolism in which
> the hero is Christ (often represented in art standing on a prostrate
> monster), the dragon Satan. . . .
>
> Now if the leviathan is the whole fallen world of sin and death
> and tyranny into which Adam fell, it follows that Adam's children are
> born, live, and die inside his belly. Hence if the Messiah is to deliver
> us by killing the leviathan, he releases us.[24]

As myth, Ahab's hunt is a reenactment of the "dragon-killing theme" Frye sees as rooted in biblical typology and as constituting the "central form of quest romance."[25] That Melville himself was thinking along these lines is suggested by the fifth of his prefatory Extracts, from Isaiah, traditionally read as a prophecy of the advent of Christ: "In that day, the Lord with his sore, and great, and strong sword, shall punish leviathan the piercing serpent, even Leviathan that crooked serpent; and he shall slay the dragon that is in the sea" (*MD* xviii). Melville underscores the theme in "The Lee Shore" when he has Ishmael describe the *Pequod* as embarking on Christmas Day and "thrust[ing] her vindictive bows into the cold malicious waves" (*MD* 106). Ahab is not simply tragedy's "great man" marred by a character flaw or singled out for catastrophe by fate; he is a scapegoat-hero who enacts humanity's common fantasy of slaying the dragon or father or tyrannical god who has dispossessed the race of its title to earthly paradise.

An action like this is of a different mimetic order from actions in the novel or even in Shakespearean tragedy. It is what Henry A. Murray called "a mythic event," or an essentially symbolic occurrence "represented in sensory terms" that enlists the reader's imagination because it appeals to "emotions, wants, and actions" that "are present as potential tendencies in virtually all men and women of all societies and times."[26] Resurrected from the delirium that followed the loss of his leg, Ahab is like Lear returned to strength but not to serenity, and his pursuit of "an audacious, immitigable, and supernatural revenge" (*MD* 186) is a response to the hitherto unthinkable question "What next?"

It is not known by what route Melville came to Ahab, but an early adumbration appears in an April 1849 letter to Evert Duyckinck in which Melville expressed "shock" at the derangement of their common acquaintance Charles Fenno Hoffman. "What sort of sensation permanent madness is," Melville wrote, "may be very well imagined—just as we imagine how we felt when we were infants, tho' we can not recall it. In both conditions we are irresponsible & riot like gods without fear of fate. —It is the climax of a mad night of revelry when the blood has been transmuted into brandy" (*Corr* 128). As Melville presents it, the "permanent madness" that overtook Hoffman was something other than "the sane madness of vital truth" (*PT* 244) he would describe in the "Mosses" essay; it was that condition of psychic license in which the inhibitions of the ego and the moral sense, indeed of the reality principle itself, gave way to the urgencies of buried desire, which played themselves out oblivious to the judgments of man and God. "Sane" (or tragic) madness, as in Lear or *Mardi*'s Azzageddi, was the blindness that came from too much light, that is, from a full, unmediated, and potentially annihilating apprehension of the nothingness of things. By contrast, "permanent" (or pathological) madness was a peculiarly exhilarating form of insanity which, mentally freeing the sufferer from inner and outer restraint, allowed a cathartic enactment of the impossible.

Written at a time when Melville was struggling to press beyond the dramatic impasse of *Mardi*'s ending, the Hoffman passage represents one of those rare surfacings that signals the direction of a mind. So long as the philosopher and the madman remained opposite poles of human development, Melville could only divide his allegiance, as he had in *Mardi*, between a profound but nondramatic exploration of life's blackness (Babbalanja) and a willful but callow defiance (Taji). The imaginative breakthrough that enabled Ahab was Melville's realization that tragic madness and permanent madness might be synthesized in a single character, made to involve a separation from reality so acute as to border on metaphysical hallucination, and directed toward an apocalyptic action beyond the boundaries of experience. The discovery and articulation of dark truth that *Mardi* took for one of its principal themes *Moby-Dick* assumes as a given and proceeds to imagine a "post-tragic" action in which the hero, formerly cast down by knowledge, rises again in uncompromising defiance. Insanity, as Ahab knows, is the very condition for such an action; "For this hunt," he tells Pip, rejecting his "curing" influence, "my malady becomes my most desired health" (*MD* 534).

Ahab needed to be mad in order to act at all, yet for his hunt to signify more than a lurid derangement his madness had to be related to the reader's sanity. Melville pre-empts audience objections to Ahab by having Starbuck voice them openly: "Vengeance on a dumb brute . . . that simply smote thee from blindest instinct! Madness! To be enraged with a dumb thing, Captain Ahab, seems blasphemous" (*MD* 163–64). Throughout *Moby-Dick* Melville will work to counter the objections of common sense by "giv[ing] Ahab's sense of the whale a qualified plausibility,"[27] as Richard H. Brodhead said, and by reinforcing Ahab's quarrel with God with testimonies like Queequeg's in "The Shark Massacre" ("de god wat made shark must be one dam Ingin" [*MD* 302]) and Stubb's in his comically blasphemous rendering of the Book of Job with its scornful "There's a governor!" (*MD* 327). But Melville's chief instrument for connecting the reader to Ahab is Ishmael, who keys reader reaction to the hunt in "Moby Dick" and "The Whiteness of the Whale" when he makes "Ahab's quenchless feud" his own (*MD* 179). The Aristotelian emotions of pity and fear—the former drawing us toward the tragic hero, the latter warning us to keep our distance—become, with Ishmael, "a wild, mystical, sympathetical feeling" joining him to Ahab's quest and a profound "dread" making for rational and moral distance (*MD* 179). The balance of these feelings will shift as the book unfolds, but initially Melville needs to unite readers with Ishmael in yielding to "the abandonment" of the moment even though they, too, can foresee "naught" in the hunt "but the deadliest ill" (*MD* 187).

Philosophically, Melville's challenge in managing the reader was how to establish a relationship between the impassively naturalistic world Ishmael encounters at sea and the malignantly supernatural one predicated by Ahab's hunt. Life in *Moby-Dick*, as Warner Berthoff observed, is "displayed . . . as harsh, violent, laborious, chancy, long, inequitable, fate-ridden, overwhelming; it appears profoundly disrespectful of persons and indifferent to private fortune or sorrow; it is tragic, and it is disinheriting";[28] it is not, however, malevolent, for it betrays no definite signs of conscious agency or purpose. To the Ishmael of "Moby Dick," Ahab is "crazy Ahab" (*MD* 184), his hatred of Creation morbid, his monomania insane. Yet having dissociated himself from Ahab's view of the universe and the white whale and having offered in its place a world of whiteness, empty and indifferent, Ishmael gives voice to that remarkably Ahabian phrase "the instinct of the knowledge of the demonism in the world" (*MD* 194). Although Ishmael professes to believe, and in most chapters does believe, in a naturalistic universe "malignant" to us only when we measure it by our human needs, in "The Whiteness of the Whale" he falls into language that reveals a latently Ahabian outrage and abhorrence: "invisible spheres . . . formed in fright"; "all deified nature . . . paint[ed] like the harlot, whose allurements cover nothing but the charnel-house within"; the "palsied universe" lying before us like "a leper" (*MD* 195). Confronted with the dread, soul-extinguishing prospect of whiteness, Ishmael projects his revulsion outward upon the universe and posits a stimulus causing his response; like the Vermont colt terror-struck at the shaking of a buffalo robe, he, too, intuits that "somewhere" the terrifying thing "must exist" (*MD* 195). It hardly matters that there is no place for "demonism" in the icy universe he has evoked. Overwhelmed by a visceral sense of loathing, Ishmael reverts to the anthropocentrism of Ahab and locates the prompt for his feeling in Creation itself. "Wonder ye then at the fiery hunt?" (*MD* 195), he concludes "The Whiteness of the Whale," as though the appalling truth of nothingness justified one's going mad and joining with Ahab in personifying a fiery hostile world one might set out to defy.

The achievement of "The Whiteness of the Whale" is to ground Ahab's hunt in shared experience by showing how fluidly naturalism can pass into paranoid supernaturalism when we cease to regard the indifferent universe intellectually and begin to register it on our pulses. Melville was able to represent this process because he lived it himself, his intellect and experience inclining him toward an open-minded agnosticism, his temperament and emotions toward an apocalyptic theism. His oscillation between these poles shows itself most openly in his mock review of *The House of the Seven Gables* from an April 1851 letter to Hawthorne:

> There is a certain tragic phase of humanity which, in our opinion, was never more powerfully embodied than by Hawthorne. We mean

the tragicalness of human thought in its own unbiassed, native, and profounder workings. We think that into no recorded mind has the intense feeling of the visible truth ever entered more deeply than into this man's. By visible truth, we mean the apprehension of the absolute condition of present things as they strike the eye of the man who fears them not,—the man who, like Russia or the British Empire, declares himself a sovereign nature (in himself) amid the powers of heaven, hell, and earth. He may perish; but so long as he exists he insists upon treating with all Powers upon an equal basis. If any of those other Powers choose to withhold certain secrets, let them; that does not impair my sovereignty in myself; that does not make me tributary. (*Corr* 186)

Writing ostensibly of Hawthorne, Melville is speaking of himself, and the reference of the passage quickly shades from "Hawthorne" to the "sovereign nature" to the first-person singular. The world of the passage undergoes a concurrent change. Phrase by phrase, the "visible truth" is transformed first into a set of "present things" that may "do their worst" to the man of courage, then into the quasi-objective "powers of heaven, hell, and earth" amid which the "sovereign nature" stands, and finally into a conclave of haughty, personified "Powers" with whom (not which) the "sovereign nature" treats "upon an equal basis." Never mind that this refractory, animated world is a non sequitur or that Melville's bravado has little in common with the ironic self-deprecation of Hawthorne. The passage is driven by the needs of a temperament that cannot sustain itself continuously on the scanty emotional fare of naturalism but must recast the world's emptiness as a conspiracy of antagonistic Powers against which the soul affirms itself in the act of resistance. As the urgencies of Melville's nature play themselves out in rhetoric, his mind tips back toward sanity and the universe again appears an empty collection of things. "And perhaps, after all, there is *no* secret," Melville continues: "We incline to think that the Problem of the Universe is like the Freemason's mighty secret, so terrible to all children. It turns out, at last, to consist in a triangle, a mallet, and an apron,—nothing more!" (*Corr* 186).

In the space of less than a paragraph, Melville has traversed the spectrum of belief from Ishmael to Ahab and back again. What makes the passage so compelling is the ontological slippage that makes the world of *Moby-Dick* so compelling. Beginning with experiential facts that cannot be denied (the "visible truth"), both passage and book lead us by degrees into empathy with a defiance we intellectually know is fantastic, egotistical, and self-destructive. Melville knows this himself—his rhetoric is posture, not proposition—yet only by following the logic of emotion to tantrum pitch can he can purge himself of anger and frustration at the condition of things. By the end of the passage he has arrived at a provisional serenity and can look wryly upon Omnipotence: "We incline to think that God cannot explain His own secrets, and that He would like a little more information upon certain points Himself. We astonish Him as much as He us" (*Corr* 186). Yet no sooner does Melville say this than the old vocabulary reasserts itself and detachment breaks down: "But it is this *Being* of the matter; there lies the knot with which we choke ourselves. As soon as you say *Me*, a *God*, a *Nature*, so soon you jump off from your stool and hang yourself from the beam" (*Corr* 186). The words themselves are the conceptual trap, and yet they have a tenacity beyond the influence even of nurture and tradition; they persist as frames of discourse because they are the only language the self has available to express its hunger for the Father.

Moby-Dick is the "visable truth" passage writ large and projected outward onto mid-nineteenth-century Western civilization as a diagnosis of, and proffered cure for, its spiritual crisis. If the "knot" of theistic discourse could never be untied, it might at least be decisively cut. *Moby-Dick* is Melville's attempt to do precisely that by exorcising a religious consciousness that under the pressure of science and liberal thought had begun to recoil upon itself and arraign the God of traditional theology. The book is Melville's act of spiritual purgation, performed for himself but also for his audience, which stands for America at large. The implied reader of *Moby-Dick* is a member of what Melville called the "*yes*-gentry," burdened with "heaps of baggage" from the cultural and religious past (*Corr* 186). By going to sea with Ishmael the reader leaves behind the prejudices of the land and ventures forth into a "wonder-world" (*MD* 7) under Ishmael's guidance. The introduction of Ahab—first obliquely in "The Ship" and the Elijah chapters, then in full—reveals a different kind of book, and one the reader might never have begun at all had it announced itself at the start. It is not until "Moby Dick" and "The Whiteness of the Whale," however, that Ahab's "quenchless feud" (*MD* 179) is made to seem the reader's own. Angers and frustrations that had been repressed are raised to consciousness, then licensed by Ishmael's own exhilaration at the hunt and mobilized in a vicarious revenge that promises all the gratification of a sudden unleashing of buried impulse and all the safety of fantasy and daydream. The artifice of the Ahabian chapters, whether cast as drama or presented narratively in elevated prose, adds to this sense of moral holiday. It exempts the hunt from a guilt-ridden comparison to reality and invites readers to give it what I. A. Richards called "emotional belief," or a belief that arises from and fulfills a psychological need without requiring intellectual assent or making claims on practical behavior.[29]

A work that evokes feelings as primal as humanity's fear and resentment at Creation has an enormous potential for conversion, or fastening its loose fish of a reader to whatever vision or belief the rhetoric of the book artfully provides. In this respect, too, *Moby-Dick* operates like myth, which, in Henry A. Murray's words, "presents a model" that may "excite and orient certain valued actional dispositions" or "weaken or suppress certain disvalued actional dispositions."[30] "If," Murray continues, "the aim or action of an otherwise admirable hero is extravagant, vainglorious, shameful, or immoral, and its outcome tragic, the story should produce, in susceptible receptors, an emphatic discharge and a subsequent reduction of . . . comparable, latent dispositions. . . . But if the aim and action of the hero or heroic group is admirable and the outcome happy (or even tragic), a potent myth will serve to encourage or sometimes impose comparable behavior."[31]

There are numerous ways in which Melville might have managed the reader's engagement with Ahab, depending upon his thematic and affective purposes. He might have presented Ahab, a rebel against God, as a champion of oppressed humanity (Aeschylus's Prometheus), as an earnest but blaspheming seeker (Byron's Cain), or as a prideful villain (Milton's Satan, who nonetheless seemed a hero to Romantics like Blake and Shelley). "Shaped in an unalterable mould, like Cellini's cast Perseus" (*MD* 123), Ahab has sealed off his mental life before the narrative begins and is fixed, static, and immune to the pull of other characters, who are at most dramatic foils, like Starbuck and the carpenter, or symbolic accessories, like Fedallah. Ahab's development has taken place before the book begins, and he is now defined entirely in relation to his purpose. Yet if Ahab does not change other than to grow more furious as he approaches Moby Dick, the allusions surrounding him change considerably. Likened in early chapters to heroes and redeemers, Ahab is increasingly associated with demonic overreachers like Macbeth, Faust, and Satan. In chapters like "The Forge," "The Quadrant," "The Candles," and "The Needle," the would-be deliverer of humanity becomes in "his fatal pride" (*MD* 519) a source of tyranny and inhumaneness who must himself be purged for the well-being of the community. Fedallah is Melville's Gothic symbol for the inner darkness Ahab has summoned up and ceded himself to. Early on, Peleg told Ishmael that "stricken, blasted, if he be, Ahab has his humanities!" (*MD* 79). Ahab retains his humanities to the last, but he forcibly suppresses them, spurning Pip, rejecting Starbuck's appeals, and refusing to help Captain Gardiner of the *Rachel* search for his lost son.

For the reader, drawn imaginatively into the hunt by Ishmael, Meville's darkening presentation of Ahab has the rhetorical effect of an ad hominem argument, discrediting the hunt by diabolizing the hunter even as he makes us sensibly aware of Ahab's pain. With chapter 106 Ishmael disappears from the narrative, not to return until the epilogue, and an omniscient third-person voice directs a series of lurid tableaux of almost Shakespearean amplitude and intensity. Formerly the reader's surrogate, Ahab has devolved into a scapegoat-hero, or what Kenneth Burke called "a 'suppurating' device,"[32] who absorbs the reader's cosmic anger and who is repudiated, expelled from the moral community, and finally slain, though not without performing the act of symbolic defiance the reader delegated him to perform. When Ahab thrusts his harpoon into Moby Dick—"'*Thus*, I give up the spear!'" (*MD* 572)—the reader is at once with him and apart from him, sharing emotionally in the act of god-defiance, then consenting to the death of Ahab, the offending deicide in himself or herself.

Always an inventor of forms, Melville in *Moby-Dick* reinvented tragedy's pattern of audience involvement and turned it to his rhetorical purposes. Toward the end of a tragedy, Simon O. Lesser argued, the audience abandons the hero as "his doom becomes certain" and in some measure appears just.[33] Where previously we had been both "spectators and actors in the fiction" (Lesser 248), "err[ing] with the characters and vicariously secur[ing] the instinctual gratifications their errors entail" (Lesser 249), "we now act like a person who has narrowly escaped some catastrophe and is still in grave danger. To reassure and safeguard ourself we emphasize our *separateness* from the tragic protagonist. . . . We dissociate ourself from [him] and to some extent even repudiate him. Pharisaically, we congratulate ourself that *we* have not yielded to the impulses which have brought him to disaster" (Lesser 249). But the dissociation is never complete; we have shared too intensely in the wishes of the hero to disavow them entirely, and our lingering identification makes for a catharsis that is moral as well as emotional. "At the conclusion of a great Greek or Shakespearean tragedy," Lesser writes, "we feel purged not only of pity and fear but of the desires to which the tragic hero has yielded and whose gratification is responsible for his suffering. The feeling is explicable only on the assumption that we, too, have vicariously satisfied those desires. Having done so, we now feel relieved and fulfilled, momentarily free of tension and anxiety" (Lesser 249–50).[34] To paraphrase Melville's words about the composition of *Moby-Dick*, we have done a "wicked" thing and "feel spotless as the lamb" (*Corr* 212).

The catharsis tragedy effects needn't simply be a factitious one confined to temporary identification with imaginary characters in an imaginary situation; so far as the desires the hero enacts are representative ones, tragedy can involve the evocation, management, and purgation of psychic elements the audience brings to the work, both as private selves and as members of a culture. What dies with Ahab is more than a morbid, defiant strain within the individual reader; it is a mode of consciousness and an established cultural order. The Ahab who is compounded of Pro-

metheus, Job, Christ, Lear, Satan, Faust, Manfred, Cain, and Teufelsdröckh, among others, is the legitimate heir of these mythic and literary figures who sails toward his encounter with Moby Dick bearing the
entire legacy of Western thought with its monotheism, its preoccupation
with the problem of evil, and its hope for redemption from a fallen world
through the mediation of a savior. In his magnitude and grandiloquence
Ahab is a throwback to Renaissance drama, but the problems that afflict
him are those of the mid-nineteenth-century reader, who inherits a system of belief that can no longer answer or evade the questions put to it
but that nonetheless tyrannizes over the terms of thought.[35] Ahab is the
last and fullest flowering of the Christian tradition, which now, in its
death rattle, turns against itself and in the name of Christian values calls
God to account for not behaving like God and destroys itself in a furious
act of immolation.

"The work of the hero," Joseph Campbell has said, "is to slay the tena-
cious aspect of the father (dragon, tester, ogre, king) and release from its
ban the vital energies that feed the universe."[36] In *Moby-Dick* there are
two "fathers," only one of whom can be slain. Just as Moby Dick (the
dragon) represents the forces of chaos that preside over the fallen world,
so Ahab represents a way of conceiving and responding to experience that
has governed the Western world for nearly two millennia and stamped its
repressed theocentric consciousness on the institutions of social and political life as well as on traditions of mind. The climactic confrontation of
"father" with "father" resembles another cultural Armageddon familiar to
Melville—the Norse "*Twilight of the Gods*" described by Carlyle in "The
Hero as Divinity":

> the divine Powers [or heroes] and the chaotic brute ones . . . meet at
> last in universal world-embracing wrestle and duel; World-Serpent
> against Thor, strength against strength; mutually extinctive; and ruin,
> "twilight" sinking into darkness, swallows the created Universe. The
> old Universe with its Gods is sunk; but it is not a final death: there is
> to be a new Heaven and a new Earth; a higher supreme God, and Jus-
> tice to reign among men.[37]

In *Moby-Dick*'s world-embracing duel the whale swims away, invincible;
but insofar as the "universe" is a human construction—a naming and order-
ing of experience brought into being by categories of thought—it, too, per-
ishes with Ahab. The "work of the hero" is accomplished in *Moby-Dick* by
the hero's own sacrificial death. Ahab has freed us, not from the prison of
a fallen universe but from the imprisoning mind-set that is himself, that is
*our*self.

The Jackal and the Hyena

The sea that closes around the sinking *Pequod* engulfs the world in emptiness, but as in Norse myth the death of the old order "is not a final death." Up pops Ishmael clinging to Queequeg's coffin-lifebuoy, the lone survivor of this nineteenth-century Twilight of the Gods. Larzer Ziff described the resurrected Ishmael as "a lowly figure squatting on the hatches in intense talk with those of us who will squat with him and recognize that the most recent thump we received is not the last that will be dealt us."[38] This may be Captain George Pollard of the stove whaleship *Essex*, but it is not Ishmael, whose jaunty readiness finds delight in the endless vicissitudes of experience, thumps included. If Ahab signifies the end of a cultural epoch, Ishmael signifies the beginning. His is a new voice in Western literature and a new stance toward experience; he is Melville's avatar of the American-to-be and of the emerging mind and sensibility of post–Judeo-Christian humanity.

Ishmael's deliverance from a watery near-death in the epilogue is the narrative representation of what he has thematically done several times before. The prospect of drowning is *Moby-Dick*'s ubiquitous *memento mori* and the chief occasion for Ishmael to reconsider "this matter of Life and Death" (*MD* 37). Ishmael's defining moments are typically skull soliloquies in which thoughts of a sudden and violent death recoil upon themselves and engender a giddy creative despair—giddy from relief at having fronted the worst, creative for having divested itself of the numbing palliatives society uses to hide the worst. In "The Chapel," brooding on the cenotaphs to lost whalemen, Ishmael executes a characteristic psycho-philosophical "turn": "But Faith, like a jackal, feeds among the tombs, and even from these dead doubts she gathers her most vital hope" (*MD* 37). After bottoming out, Ishmael "somehow" grows "merry again" (*MD* 37) and rushes headlong toward what seems a testament of belief:

> Methinks that what they call my shadow here on earth is my true substance. Methinks that in looking at things spiritual, we are too much like oysters observing the sun through the water, and thinking that thick water the thinnest of air. Methinks my body is but the lees of my better being. . . . And therefore three cheers for Nantucket; and come a stove boat and stove body when they will, for stave my soul, Jove himself cannot. (*MD* 37)

As Merton M. Sealts, Jr., noted, Ishmael's words conflate two passages from Plato, one describing the heavens as viewed through the dense but unapparent medium of water, the other drawing on Socrates' remark that we are "fettered to [the body] like an *oyster* to its shell."[39] In combining the passages in a single image ("oysters observing the sun"), Ishmael confounds his idea even as he presents it, since oysters (having no eyes) see nothing at all, nor, so far as we resemble them, do we. Ishmael builds meaning, then coyly subverts it, constructing and deconstructing grand erections as he will do throughout *Moby-Dick*. What is vital and characteristic in "The Chapel" is not Ishmael's declared faith in immortality, which cannot survive the telling; it is his metamorphosis of despair into devil-may-care exuberance, his delight in linguistic play, and his affirmation of the spirit against all powers of fate and circumstance, divinity included—"for stave my soul, Jove himself cannot."

In "The Dying Whale" Ahab reflects bitterly on this same theme, nature's failure to lend support to human hopes for immortality. By contrast, disillusion is oddly exhilarating for Ishmael, for it frees him from the supplicatory position of dependence on the universe and its unreliable governing powers. In "The Hyena," whaler Ishmael's first encounter with the indifference of the sea, the "thump" delivered in "Loomings" by "some old hunks of a sea-captain" (*MD* 6) is metamorphosed into the "sly, good-natured hits, and jolly punches in the side bestowed by [an] unseen and unaccountable joker" (*MD* 226), whose ultimate joke may be not to exist at all. All-important to himself, Ishmael is brought to recognize his signal unimportance to the universe, which may casually dispatch him at any moment. Yet rather than turn angrily against the source or sourcelessness of his grievance, as Ahab does, Ishmael chooses to take the "universe for a vast practical joke," most likely on himself, and to laugh (*MD* 226). Like Camus's absurdist hero, Ishmael lives with and from a lucid awareness of the "divorce between the mind that desires and the world that disappoints."[40] He is a scavenger "among the tombs," jackal or hyena, who draws strength and psychic health from the very proximity of death, and hope about temporal life from the apparent groundlessness of hope for eternal life. His "free and easy sort of genial, desperado philosophy" (*MD* 226) is desperate (a pun on despair) because, like all humanity, he is an outlaw from Creation, disinherited and left to fend for himself in the world like the biblical Ishmael in the desert; and it is "genial" because in outlawry he can be happily irresponsible toward God and the universe and indulge a disinterested curiosity in all things, his own moods, perceptions, fancies, and verbal flights above all.[41] Stubb has something of Ishmael's wry appreciativeness, but Stubb takes refuge from knowledge in a happy-go-lucky fatalism that waives the problematic with "that one little sufficient word queer" (*MD* 472);[42] "think not" is Stubb's "eleventh commandment, and sleep when you can" his "twelfth" (*MD* 128). "Everything begins with consciousness and nothing is worth anything except through it," Camus wrote.[43] The distinction of Ishmael is that he is able to *remain* an Ishmael and inhabit the limbo of universal exile without leaping toward faith like Starbuck, cultivating indifference like Stubb, or (save in moments of existential terror, as in "The Whiteness of the Whale") descending into demonism like Ahab.

In his conjoined outlawry and openness to experience Ishmael resembles nothing so much as a kind of metaphysical picaro whose road is the sea and whose society is the universe itself. Robert Alter characterized the picaresque hero as at once "an image of human solitude in the world" and "an image of human solidarity in the world."[44] In *Moby-Dick* the solitude is ontological, the solidarity social and political: democratic tragedy. "The Monkey-Rope" draws out the social implications of "The Hyena" by making the indifference of nature the backdrop for a compensatory human solicitude. The "interregnum in Providence" that would allow guiltless Ishmael to suffer for Queequeg's "mistake or misfortune" (*MD* 320) is, Ishmael comes to feel, the chronic condition of things. Two chapters earlier in "The Sphynx" Ahab had fretted at the Jobian problem of God's silence at the sufferings of the innocent; "The Monkey-Rope" is Ishmael's absurdist answer to Job: against the imminent prospect of "unmerited disaster and death," we must become each other's keepers and comforters, for the "even-handed equity" of Providence is not to be relied on (*MD* 320).

Like other diptychs in *Moby-Dick*, "The Sphynx" and "The Monkey-Rope" pair a philosophically stated grievance of Ahab's with a concretely rendered discovery of Ishmael's. Both characters look upon the same universe, but Ahab measures it anthropocentrically against human needs while Ishmael adopts a seriocomic humility before its unfathomable mysteries. Second only to the problem of immortality for Ahab is the problem of knowledge. Gazing on the tattooed body of Queequeg, inscribed by a Polynesian seer with "a complete theory of the heavens and the earth, and a mystical treatise on the art of attaining truth," all written in indecipherable hieroglyphics, Ahab exclaims, "Oh, devilish tantalization of the gods!" (*MD* 480, 481). In making Queequeg "a wondrous work in one volume; but whose mysteries not even himself could read" (*MD* 481), Melville is playing off Emerson's blithe assurance in *Nature*: "Undoubtedly we have no questions to ask which are unanswerable. We must trust the perfection of the creation so far, as to believe that whatever curiosity the order of things has awakened in our minds, the order of things can satisfy. Every man's condition is a solution in hieroglyphic to those inquiries he would put."[45]

Ishmael, too, attempts to read nature when, as a retrospective narrator who has "swam through libraries and sailed through oceans" (*MD* 136), he undertakes his own project to command Job's whale, not by physical force but by comprehension.[46] In a series of linked chapters beginning with three on whales in art and culminating in "The Fountain" and "The Tail," Ishmael marshals the range of human arts, sciences, and pseudosciences as he tries to understand the whale both as a piece of living nature (as Thoreau tries to know beans) and as a symbol for the universe and the powers that govern it. Dumb, blind, majestic, powerful, stolid, riddling, and mute—these are the qualities he attaches to a creature who progressively comes to represent an image of divinity. "The Tail" is Ishmael's *reductio ad absurdum* of his entire epistemological enterprise. Echoing Jehovah's words to Moses in Exodus 33 ("And I will take away mine hand, and thou shalt see my back parts: but my face shall not be seen"), Ishmael throws up his own hands in mock despair:

> Dissect him how I may, then, I go but skin deep. I know him not, and never will. But if I know not even the tail of this whale, how understand his head? much more, how comprehend his face, when face he has none? Thou shalt see my back parts, my tail, he seems to say, but my face shall not be seen. But I cannot completely make out his back parts; and hint what he will about his face, I say again he has no face. (*MD* 379)

As Ishmael ponders the whale, the "inscrutable thing" that enraged Ahab (*MD* 164) prompts a virtuosic literary performance in the face (or facelessness) of nature's opacity. Borrowing Keats's term, Warner Berthoff spoke of the Melvillean narrator's "'negative capability'"—"that is [Keats's words], when a man is capable of being in uncertainties, mysteries, doubts, without any irritable reaching after fact and reason."[47] Unlike Ahab, Ishmael can live and thrive with indetermimacy as it invites the mind to speculation and the imagination to creative wordplay. Negative capability becomes positive capability. The quality is at once epistemological, psychological, moral, and aesthetic. In "The Fountain," unable to determine whether the whale's spout is "really water, or nothing but vapor" (*MD* 370) even after having been showered by it himself, Ishmael is content to "hypothesize, even if we cannot prove and establish" (*MD* 373). His stance toward experience, freed earlier from systematizing "thunder-heads" like Locke and Kant (*MD* 327), is pyrrhonistic but receptive: "Doubts of all things earthly, and intuitions of some things heavenly; this combination makes neither believer nor infidel, but makes a man who regards them both with equal eye" (*MD* 374).[48]

In place of the binaries of water and vapor, Understanding and Reason, materialism and idealism, denial and asserveration, the Everlasting No and the Everlasting Yea, Ishmael develops a third position, agnosticism—the Everlasting Maybe. The "oysters observing the sun through the water" in "The Chapel" (*MD* 37) become in "The Fountain" Ishmael himself (a creature with eyes) receiving "divine intuitions" through the "fog" of "dim doubts" clouding his mind (*MD* 374). His illustrative image of a rainbow—the invisibility of the heavens refracted through vapor to form a variegated show of light—also suggests a possible mediation of the dualities of "The Whiteness of the Whale": color and whiteness, surface and depth, earthly beauty and cosmic emptiness, belief and atheism. Through the prism of the whale's spout, an apparent discordance is brought into harmony; opposites are made to correspond. Ishmael makes no grand claim to have reconciled heaven and earth; he only speculates and analogizes with comic exaggeration and with the Missourian Pitch's awareness that analogy ain't argument (*CM* 124). Down through the execution scene in *Billy Budd*, Melville's suggestions of divinity in nature—the sun breaking through the mist—will always carry this equivocalness. Is it heaven or only meteorology? We cannot tell. For Ishmael, analogy and hypothesis are enough. Like Emily Dickinson, Ishmael dwells in possibility; toward the divine, his soul always stands ajar.[49]

Melville sets "The Fountain" and "The Tail" immediately before "The Grand Armada" the last chapter of this epistemological triad. Here Ishmael figuratively enters the heart of nature as he penetrates the chaotic outer circles of a whale herd under attack. "The Grand Armada" is Ishmael's answer to "Brit," his earlier rendering of the Romantic myth of the lapse from "peace and joy" into "all the horrors of the half known life" (*MD* 274). In "The Grand Armada," Ishmael seems to complete the Romantic quest. He has arrived at the region of "enchanted calm which they say lurks at the very heart of every commotion" (*MD* 387)—the generative core of Creation, ostensibly benign. Yet the harmony Ishmael describes does not reside in the outer world, nor is it created by that world; it lies within himself, in the "mute calms" and "deep inland joy" he manages to preserve even "while ponderous planets of unwaning woe revolve around me" (*MD* 389). Melville himself had such moments of oneness with nature—the "'all' feeling" he called these experiences in a letter to Hawthorne, anticipating Freud's "oceanic feeling."[50] "You must often have felt it, lying on the grass on a warm summer's day," he wrote: "Your legs seem to send out shoots into the earth. Your hair feels like leaves upon your head. But what plays the mischief with the truth," he quickly added, "is that men will insist upon the universal application of a temporary feeling or opinion" (*Corr* 194). A mood was not the basis for a metaphysics. Unlike Whitman's epiphany in "Song of Myself"—"Swiftly arose and spread around me the peace and knowledge that pass all the argument of the earth / And I know . . . that a kelson of the creation is love" ("Song of Myself," ll. 91–92, 95)—Ishmael's "eternal mildness of joy" (*MD* 389) is a purely psychic phenomenon in which body, mind, imagination, and emotion happily conjoin. Far from arising from or mirroring nature's order, it is a compensatory human refuge against its *dis*order.

Samuel Johnson felt that "a system of social duty [might] be selected" from Shakespeare's works.[51] So perhaps might a system of conduct and belief be selected from *Moby-Dick*, for, casual and mood-dependent as they are, Ishmael's reflections do cohere in a stance toward experience: skeptical, unillusioned, absurdist, humanitarian, democratic. But codifying an "Ishmael philosophy" would betray its life principle—that thought is an activity, not a set of conclusions, and one that "at last returns," as Camus said of abstract thought, "to its prop of flesh."[52] "Flesh," indeed, whether of the literal body or the body of lived experience, is what repeatedly qualifies or undercuts Ishmael's philosophizings with a situational contradiction (dropping "the ball of free will" in "The Mat-Maker" [*MD* 215]), a double-edged metaphor, or a subversive play on words. Exhorting us in "The Blanket" to be temperate in all climes "like the great dome of St. Peter's, and like the great whale," Ishmael undoes his work with a countersermon capped by a phallic pun: "But how easy and how hopeless to teach these fine things! Of erections, how few are domed like St. Peter's! of creatures, how few vast as the whale!" (*MD* 307). Ishmael is continually raising grand erections only to dismast them. His thinking is not a pathway to settled truth but a process of taking the world provisionally and by pieces, squeezing it for what it will yield while knowing always that there are other moods and other angles of vision, none of them adequate to experience in its rich multiplicity yet each productive of its own passing meditation or verbal flight, and each to be explored as a temporary intellectual and imaginative habitation.

Ishmaelean Romantic Irony

In the absence of transcendent belief, the expansion and refinement of the self through sallies of intellectual and verbal inventiveness is what constitutes Ishmaelean spiritual life. Borrowing a phrase from "Cetology," Warwick Wadlington called this play "godly gamesomeness"—"the savor of one's private being" as "a primary register of reality."[53] While anticipating modernism and postmodernism, Ishmaelean gamesomeness has its closest analogue in the vision of the universe, the self, and the literary work advanced by Friedrich Schlegel at the turn of the nineteenth century and later denominated German Romantic irony. For Schlegel (I draw on accounts by Anne K. Mellor, Ernst Behler, and G. R. Thompson as well as on Schlegel himself), Romantic irony was both philosophical and aesthetic. Its first premise was that the world was "fundamentally chaotic" and "abundantly fertile, always throwing up new forms, new creations," with "no specifiable direction, no telos, no comprehensible pattern or purpose."[54] As truth was fragmentary and conditional, so necessarily were literary attempts to represent it. Human beings, poets especially, had an impulse toward order and coherence (*Selbstschöpfung* or "self-creation"), which prompted them to synthesize disparate parts of experience through wit, and an impulse toward anarchic freedom (*Selbstbeschränkung* or "self-destruction"), which led them to dissolve established ideas and forms, including those of their own creation, also through wit.[55] The artist responding to a dynamic universe needed, in Mellor's words, to "acknowledge the inevitable limitations of his finite consciousness and of

all man-made structures or myths. But even as he denies the absolute validity of his own perceptions and structuring conceptions of the universe, even
as he consciously deconstructs his mystifications of the self and the world,
he must affirm and celebrate the process of life by creating new images and
ideas" (Mellor 4).

So imagined, Romantic irony is the ludic counterpart to what Paul de Man
saw as the Romantic's angst-ridden nostalgia for a coincidence of mind and
world.[56] Schlegel and de Man address a common representational situation—
the fictiveness of all attempts to order and interpret experience—but what
de Man regards as an intellectual and spiritual exasperation Schlegel takes as
occasion for a self-generating play of mind upon phantasmagoric reality. Ahab
is a demonized de Man, Ishmael a colloquialized Schlegel. In *Mardi* the elusiveness of truth had been a source of irony in de Man's sense of intellectual
dizziness;[57] earnest in his own initial journeyings of mind, Melville lacked the
seasoned traveler's companionable ease with thought. At some point between
Mardi and *Moby-Dick*—perhaps through the agency of Friedrich Schlegel,
whom he apparently discussed with German-American scholar George J.
Adler during their travels to and on the Continent in 1849;[58] perhaps through
the mediation of Carlyle and Jean Paul Richter, who read Schlegel and whom
Melville read by the summer of 1850; perhaps through immersion in the several of the same authors who influenced Schlegel (Plato, Cervantes, Rabelais,
Sterne, Goethe); or perhaps simply by homology: Mellor notes that many
of the English Romantics "did not know Schlegel's work but were responding similarly to the same intellectual, sociological, economic, and political
milieu" (Mellor 6)—Melville came to appreciate, *conceptually as the basis for a
new mode of being*, the pleasures of cognitive and linguistic invention that had
marked his more naïve writings from the start. It is as if, through a conversion no less epochal than his discovery of the word "blackness," he realized
how the picaresque irreverence of Tommo and White-Jacket might be joined
to the philosophical exploration of Babbalanja to produce the disaffiliated
picaresque intellectual, Ishmael. Traveling light, carpetbag in hand, Ishmael
is a type of what Schlegel called "the energetic man [who] always makes use
of only the moment, and is always ready and infinitely flexible" (in Mellor
16). Like Whitman's author-hero, Ishmael "tramp[s] a perpetual journey,"
with "no church, no philosophy" ("Song of Myself," ll. 1202, 1205), taking pleasure in the ongoing adventure, unconcerned about its destination. As
Schlegel put it, "Never will the mind that knows the orgies of the true Muse
journey on this road to the very end, nor will he presume to have reached it;
for never will he be able to quench a longing which is eternally regenerated
out of the abundance of gratifications."[59]

The special condition of Ishmaelean Romantic irony is that its rhythm
of self-creation and self-destruction takes place in a universe as terrifying
as it is wondrous, and as spiritually vacant as it is phenomenologically full.

Sharing Schlegel's delight in the fabricating powers of the mind, Ishmael is also subject to feelings of terror and dread, whether provoked by some outward experience or welling up from within. The irony Schlegel admired in Socrates and took for his model was "both playful and serious, both frank and obvious and deeply dissimulated" (Schlegel, in Behler 52). Ishmaelean irony is comparably double-sided, but its seriousness has a grim cast and its dissimulation is rooted in the belief that truth is unutterable for its darkness as well as for its multiplicity. Ishmael's metaphysical humor is a gallows humor, behind which looms a real gallows.

In his mixture of ironic wit and ontological dread, Ishmael stands midway between Schlegel and his darker Romantic successors, for whom "the initial optimism of joyous freedom" shaded into "sadness, melancholy, and despair . . . from the contradictory experience of infinite longing in the face of the finitude of life," and from a feeling that "immeasurable sadness permeates every form of life, since the absolute can only appear in limited, finite, and transitory form" (Behler 45). This last idea is remarkably like *Mardi*'s vision of the sadness of angels in heaven, shut out from the complete knowledge of God and Creation that alone can provide happiness. Schlegel's ironist *thinks*; Ishmael also *feels*, and in his feeling lie the roots of his fundamentally tragic measure of experience and his latent empathy with Ahabism, which will always contend with his mind's sense of the sufficiency of intellectual and aesthetic play. To be Ishmael is to live in a precariously balanced state between comedy and tragedy, straddling their midpoint without tipping too far toward the former (like Stubb) or the latter (like Ahab). The quality of "self-restraint"—for Schlegel a disciplined suspension between the impulse to discover patterns in nature and the impulse to dissolve them (Behler 61)—thus assumes an additional meaning with Ishmael. It signifies a conjoining of the traditional tragic and comic masks, not as complementary faces gazing in opposite directions but as elements of a single ludic grimace held in permanent, indissoluble union.

Ernst Behler notes that Schlegel's concept of irony belongs to his early period of "progressive republicanism, emancipatory liberalism, and optimistic messianism with its futuristic belief in infinite perfectibility" (Behler 44). Liberationist and prophetic, Romantic irony was not so much a substantive ideology as a promise of freedom from *all* ideology save what emanated from the celebration of nature's fullness and of humanity's potential for growth through creative response to it. In the fixity of his thinking, Ahab is the antithesis of the Romantic ironist and a darkly inverted image of the fixity of all theocentric thinking (Father Mapple's, Starbuck's), which can preserve its categories only by denying, evading, or attempting to transcend whatever life testimony runs counter to them. All thinkers who function within a received idiom, whether to affirm it or to contest it, are "conservatives," as are all philosophers whose methods and vocabularies reify the flux of experience. "Throw all these thunder-heads overboard," Ishmael says, "and then you will float light and right" (*MD* 327). In its appeal to experience over tradition and authority, and to the private, vitalistic, and contingent over the systematic and absolute, Ishmael's spirited iconoclasm resembles what Tocqueville identified as "the philosophical method of the Americans,"[60] and it looks ahead to the present- and future-oriented pragmatism of William James. It is a philosophy admirably suited to a democratic "New World," or at least to a visionary's ideal of what the mind and sensibility of such a world might fittingly be.

The literary mode commensurate with the Romantic ironist's vision of happy chaos was, generically, happily chaotic, as art strove, in A. O. Lovejoy's words, "to match the abundance and diversity and complexity of Nature."[61] Schlegel refers to the literary work as an "artfully ordered confusion,"[62] Ishmael to "the true method" as "a careful disorderliness" (*MD* 361). Schlegel felt that novels were "the Socratic dialogues of our time,"[63] but by the "novel" (German: *Roman*) he meant a Roman(-)tic literature that crossed formal boundaries to include "poetry, song, prose, dramatic exchanges, epic, pastoral, satire, mock-heroic, and so on" (Mellor 19) and whose "mission," like that of the epic in earlier times, was to "become a mirror of the entire surrounding world, a picture of its age."[64] In *Mardi*, Melville had crudely attempted to imitate Socratic dialogue; in *Moby-Dick* he came to understand, as Schlegel did, that a "progressive universal poetry"[65] of epic intent needs to be both vitally polyphonic in character and unabashedly subjective, constituting the "more or less veiled confession of the author" and displaying "the quintessence of his originality."[66]

"'QUITE AN ORIGINAL'" (*CM* 238) Melville begins a chapter of *The Confidence-Man*. Originals are rare, he argues; they go back to origins, illuminating experience by a light "akin to that which in Genesis attends upon the beginning of things" (*CM* 239). Originals may also origin*ate* by causing others to regard the world as they do. Emerson called such paradigm-makers "mind[s] of uncommon activity and power"; Foucault called them "initiators of discursive practices."[67] "For much the same reason that there is but one planet to one orbit," Melville wrote, "so can there be but one such original character to one work of invention" (*CM* 239). Ishmael, Melville's home-grown Romantic ironist and sometime alter ego, is the "original" in *Moby-Dick*, a new voice in literature and a paradigm-maker. The sinking of the *Pequod* is Melville's rendering of a cultural apocalypse, represented by the death and birth of an avatar, or center of cultural energy, or "god." The old god (Ahab) had defined himself by his relation to God; the new god (Ishmael) is humanity itself as it assumes the task of reconstituting social and spiritual life in the wreckage of the Christian promise.

"Every good man progressively becomes God," Schlegel wrote: "To become God, to be man, and to educate oneself, are expressions that are synomous."[68] Such an idea had special pertinence to antebellum America, whose prophetic writers—Emerson, Thoreau, Melville, Whitman, Fuller—centered New World democracy in what Emerson called "the gradual domestication of the idea of Culture,"[69] by which he meant *self*-culture. Emerson saw human beings "becoming God" by progressively unlocking their powers as they fathomed the laws of nature; Melville saw them "becoming God" through a spiraling play of mind and imagination upon nature's *un*fathomability, even as they recognized such play as whistling in the tragic dark. Where in former ages the "grand, ungodly, godlike man" (*MD* 79) of tragedy exulted in a consciousness of sublimity, the modern hero—less grand but still more ungodly, or god-bereft, and in an undemonstrative way godlike—had only his candor, wit, resilience, and democratic humaneness to sustain him, along with the intuition that though he will never "arrive" anywhere in this world or possibly the next, the journey itself was (almost) a sufficient compensation.

If, as Whitman said, "the proof of a poet is that his country absorbs him as affectionately as he has absorbed it,"[70] then Melville fared only marginally better than Whitman did. In setting out "to produce a mighty book" (*MD* 456), Melville had also set out to refashion his readers and, through them, America itself. Melville would have been particularly stung by the unsigned review in the *Literary World*, usually attributed to Evert Duyckinck, which attacked Ishmael's "piratical running down of creeds and opinions" as "out of place and uncomfortable. We do not like to see what . . . must to the world be the most sacred associations of life violated and defaced."[71] If a democrat and literary nationalist like Duyckinck could not rise to the jaunty irreverence and innovation of *Moby-Dick*, who could? Melville's mistake, as William Charvat pointed out, was to involve his reader "in exploratory, speculative thinking which is concerned not with commitment but with possibility" and which was "the one kind of thinking that the general reader [would] not tolerate" and that "the nineteenth-century critic . . . declared . . . subversive."[72] Melville had offered his countrymen "God in the street," but his hopes for a New World consciousness foundered, as Whitman's would, on middle-class gentility, fastidiousness, sentimentality, and moral and religious conventionalism. In the end Melville might well have said with Ishmael and Job, "'And I only am escaped alone to tell thee'" (*MD* 573).

5

Exiled Royalties

It is not to taste sweet things, but to do noble and true
things, and vindicate himself under God's Heaven as
a god-made Man, that the poorest son of Adam dimly
longs.

> —Carlyle, *On Heroes, Hero-Worship,*
> *and the Heroic in History*

And slowly I began to understand that father-wounded
sons never recover, never confess, never remember; slowly,
I began to understand why women can never satisfy the
longing of boys who are love-starved for their fathers; why
women can never exorcise the grief of men, lured by their
fathers into wanting the impossible: revenge, reunion,
redemption.

> —Phyllis Chesler, *About Men*

Enceladus

In the chapter "Moby Dick," having established Ahab's hunt as a surrogate action drawing on "the general rage and hate" of the human race "from Adam down" (*MD* 184), having speculated, too, on the process of development that generated and sustains Ahab's monomania, Ishmael reaches the limits of all but his most searching imagination. "This is much," he says, "yet Ahab's larger, darker, deeper part remains unhinted" (*MD* 185). What follows is as close as Ishmael will come to excavating the lowest layer of Ahab's hunt:

> Winding far down from within the very heart of this spiked Hotel de Cluny where we stand—however grand and wonderful, now quit it;—and take your way, ye nobler, sadder souls, to those vast Roman halls of Thermes; where far beneath the fantastic towers of man's upper earth, his root of grandeur, his whole awful essence sits in bearded state; an antique buried beneath antiquities, and throned on torsoes! So with a broken throne, the great gods mock that captive king; so like a Caryatid, he patient sits, upholding on his frozen brow the piled entablature of ages. Wind ye down there, ye prouder, sadder souls! question that proud, sad king! a family likeness! aye, he did beget ye, ye young exiled royalties; and from your grim sire only will the old State-secret come. (*MD* 185–86)

Ishmael's "nobler, sadder souls"—"exiled royalties"—are a spiritual aristocracy descended from the "captive king" and marked by a consciousness of divine disinheritance. The "spiked Hotel de Cluny" is the edifice of human achievement reared up from a phallic "root of grandeur" buried deep in the self. Carlyle had broached a similar idea in *Sartor Resartus* when he declared that "in every the wisest Soul lies a whole world of internal Madness, an authentic Demon-Empire; out of which, indeed, his whole world of Wisdom has been creatively built together, and now rests there, as on its dark foundations does a habitable flowery Earth-rind."[1] What Ishmael and Carlyle are figuratively describing is the sublimation of obscure psychic needs into cognitive structures of thought and art. Throughout *Moby-Dick* the questions that preoccupy Ahab—questions of meaning, order, cosmic purpose, divine existence and character, and eternal life—are clothed in intellectual language, yet Ahab's deepest impulse is not toward knowledge of reality but toward knowledge of "the old State-secret," the origin and mystery of his own being. Ultimately, it is not even knowledge that Ahab seeks so much as *acknowledgment*. Like his ancestral archetype, the captive king whose spiritual exile he shares, Ahab craves recognition that he is heaven-born and, if not heaven-destined, then at least, by nature and bearing, heaven-worthy. For this he requires a gesture of kinship from the source. His "bearded state" is his manhood, even in symbolically emasculated captivity, but it is also—since "beard" can mean "confront and oppose with boldness, resolution, and often effrontery: DEFY"[2]—the posture he takes toward withholding divinity. If God will not condescend to him by word or sign, Ahab will extort the sign, if only by forcing God to kill him.

Moby-Dick is a reader's book that openly addresses its audience, implicates it in Ishmael's and Ahab's quests, rhetorically manages its responses, and attempts to reshape its vision, and thereby reshape contemporary America. But in places like the "captive king" passage—"The Candles" is another, Ahab's "foundling's father" speech in "The Gilder" a third—*Moby-Dick* seems to depart from any effort at intelligible communication. What F. O. Matthiessen called Ahab's "staggering indifference to anything outside himself"[3] applies in these sections to the author of *Moby-Dick* as well. It was not simply that Ahab's charismatic literary force led Melville into obscurity as he tried to find mythic objective correlatives for it; it was that Ahab's God-relation derived from urgencies in Melville himself that he only partly understood and that he was content to express without requiring he be understood by others. In *Pierre* Melville would make these drives his open subject and probe them with analytical detachment; in *Moby-Dick* he can only follow where they lead, even if that means upstaging Ishmael and impairing his power to enclose Ahab ethically and imaginatively.

This chapter will be a counterstatement to the previous two, just as the myth of the "captive king" is itself a counterforce to Melville's vision of democratic tragedy. If Ishmael is the expression of Melville's experience in the world and of his naturalist's intellect and his ironic Schlegelian sensibility, Ahab is the expression of his ineradicable Father-hunger. The sources of Melville's need date to his childhood, as he would show with Pierre, but they were also representative culturally. For the Romantics, who felt themselves "abandoned by God," as J. Hillis Miller said, the burden of the artist was "to re-establish communication" through "the 'unheard of work'" (Shelley's phrase) of creating "a marvelous harmony of words which will integrate man, nature, and God."[4] Yet the most urgent impulse behind Romantic writing was not to find a transcendent God or reunify the broken world; it was to fashion a replacement for the spiritual life forfeited by their lapse from traditional Christianity and threatened by an empirical psychology that reduced the soul to corporeal consciousness, or "clay." T. E. Hulme once described Romanticism as "spilt religion."[5] The Romantics themselves might well have agreed. For visionary Romantics like Wordsworth in *The Prelude* or Emerson in *Nature*, retaining the content of the vessel without the vessel itself meant affirming a spiritually congenial universe designed to nourish and educate the soul. By contrast, for histrionic Romantics like Byron or Carlyle, "spilt religion" involved *performing* the spiritual self by living grandiloquently in the rarefied air of God-aspiration, independent of definite belief. For the latter writers, literature was not a mimesis of reality; it was the creation of an alternative reality in which to enact—dramatically for the fictive hero, rhetorically for themselves—a spirituality dissevered from church and creed yet no less subjectively vital for its want of theological conviction.

The "captive king" passage is Melville's metaphorical statement of the problem; Pierre's dream of the heaven-storming Enceladus is his mythologized answer. Indeed, Ahab's hunt *is* the Enceladus myth projected on one level into a metaphysical revenge tragedy, on another into the psychodrama of an outcast son's quest for the Father. In both cases the image for exile is burial—in *Moby-Dick* burial in a subterranean ruin; in *Pierre* burial in "the imprisoning earth" (*P* 345). "Earth" carries a double reference: the earth we inhabit (the conditions of our outer being) and the earth we contain inside us as terrestrial clay incongruously mixed with our divine fire. In Pierre's dream, Enceladus is the multiply incestuous descendent of Coelus (Heaven) and Terra (Earth), with a predominance of Earth. This is our common human genealogy and human character, Melville implies, "an organic blended heavenliness and earthliness" (*P* 347) that leaves us dissatisfied with the sublunary world yet unable to transcend it. As Byron put it in *Manfred*, a text that stands beind *Moby-Dick*:

> We,
> Half dust, half deity, alike unfit
> To sink or soar, with our mix'd essence make
> A conflict of its elements, and breathe
> The breath of degradation and of pride,
> Contending with low wants and lofty will
> Till our mortality predominates.[6]

The challenge for Romantics like Byron was how to live as a god in one's state of continuing exile from God. Leslie A. Marchand sees *Manfred* illustrating "the dual thesis . . . of the spirit's inevitable slavery to the limited human condition, and the defiant Promethean invincibility of the mind and will."[7] Flawed as they are and rooted inescapably in earth, Melville writes in *Pierre*, it is "according to eternal fitness" that human beings should "still seek to regain [their] paternal birthright, even by fierce escalade" (*P* 347). The aspiration is itself deifying, for "whoso storms the sky gives best proof he came from thither! But whatso crawls contented in the moat before that crystal fort, shows it was born within that slime, and there forever will abide" (*P* 347).

The myth of Enceladus has a twofold movement, downward from heaven to earth (exile) and upward from earth toward heaven (escalade). In Melville's writings, as in other Romantics', "Ishmael" is the figure of exile condemned like Cain and the Wandering Jew to eternal homelessness. The achievement of *Moby-Dick*'s Ishmael is to convert that wandering into (for the most part) a genial picaresque adventure. Ahab is the prouder, tragic side of the Enceladus myth: the outcast Ishmael refusing anything less than his birthright and returning to press his claim upon the Father, overtly in defiance, covertly from a need to ratify his spiritual worth and elicit a sign of paternal love. Psychological critics like Edwin H. Miller and Philip Young trace the roots of Melville's myth to the family romance, with Allan Melvill, dying early, as the abandoning father (later transposed into the Father) whom Melville was never able to please. "In all the holy fire" of 'The Candles,'" Young remarks, "what is hardest to measure is how far [Melville's] Quarrel with God was an unextinguished quarrel with Allan Melville [sic]."[8] This is a question more properly reserved for *Pierre*. In *Moby-Dick* the "larger, darker, deeper part" of Ahab (*MD* 185) is still only hinted at, but the hints are powerful enough to suggest layers of motive and meaning beyond the cognitive.

The Foundling's Father

When asked who his father is, Billy Budd, who was "found in a pretty silk-lined basket hanging one morning from the knocker of a good man's door in Bristol," replies, "God knows, sir" (*BB* 51). Like Carlyle's Diogenes Teufelsdröckh, left on a doorstep in a basket "overhung with green Persian silk" (*Sartor* 64), Billy is a foundling of visibly "noble descent" (*BB* 52). The foundling was a favorite Romantic image for humanity, children of high lineage abandoned on the threshold of the world. Ahab's mother was a widow who died when Ahab was barely a year old, leaving him virtually a foundling and burdening him with a name that, like his white scar, prophesies a fate. The scar may be a birthmark connecting him to Moby Dick in advance of experience. Compared to the "seam" lightning makes in a "great tree" (*MD* 123), the scar also links Ahab to the Romantic exiles Cain, who is marked, and the Wandering Jew of Shelley's *Queen Mab* ("Thus have I stood,—through a wild waste of years / . . . Even as a giant oak, which Heaven's fierce flame / Had scathèd in the wilderness, to stand / A monument of fadeless ruin there").[9]

Unless he can establish paternity and thereby identity, the Romantic foundling is condemned to be a wanderer. In his "distresses" and "loneliness," Teufelsdröckh turns in imagination to "'that unknown [biological] Father'" who "'might have taken [him] to his paternal bosom'" and "'screened [him] from many a woe. . . . And yet, O Man born of Woman,'" he adds "'wherein is my case peculiar? Hadst thou, any more than I, a Father whom thou knowest? . . . thy true Beginning and Father is in Heaven, whom with the bodily eye thou shalt never behold but only with the spiritual'" (*Sartor* 66). Ahab shares Teufelsdröckh's exile, but he cannot behold God even with his spiritual eye, except in childlike moments of belief fated to pass with the onset of rational intelligence in a cycle endlessly repeated. "There is no steady unretracing progress in this life," he soliloquizes in "The Gilder":

> we do not advance through fixed gradations, and at the last one
> pause;—through infancy's unconscious spell, boyhood's thoughtless
> faith, adolescence' doubt (the common doom), then scepticism, then
> disbelief, resting at last in manhood's pondering repose of If. But once
> gone through, we trace the round again; and are infants, boys, and
> men, and Ifs eternally. Where lies the final harbor, whence we unmoor
> no more? In what rapt ether sails the world, of which the weariest will
> never weary? Where is the foundling's father hidden? Our souls are
> like those orphans whose unwedded mothers die in bearing them: the
> secret of their paternity lies in their grave, and we must there to learn
> it. (*MD* 492)

Lapsed from early belief, human beings not only search for a new belief but are destined to pass recurrently through all the phases of relationship to belief. As first printed, the speech lacked quotation marks and was long taken for Ishmael's. The Northwestern-Newberry edition (1988) reassigned it to Ahab, yet John Bryant is right to observe that in this meditation on cyclicality Ahab "sound[s] more like Ishmael" than like himself.[10] At moments Ahab can doubt his premises—"Sometimes I think there's naught behind" (*MD* 164)—but concessions like this are incidental footnotes to a mindset of remarkable fixity. In the foundling's father passage Ahab is Ishmaelizing, just as Ishmael sometimes Ahabizes; Ahab's role here is to scrutinize a pattern of life that Ishmael is aware of but does not stand back to conceptualize and examine. When Ishmael begins his explanation for going to sea in "Loomings," with "*Whenever*" (*MD* 3; my emphasis), he is confessing a cyclicality that belies critical interpretations of his narrative as a definitively progressive story of education. The Ishmael who takes to ship is ridden by the hypos; they have seized him before and will seize him again. The will Ishmael writes in "The Hyena" is the fourth of his "nautical life" (*MD* 227), as if the fact of life's chanciness had to be rediscovered with each voyage. "Despite his various bits of advice to the reader to embrace the land values of marriage, stability, and so on," Paul Brodtkorb, Jr., observes, Ishmael "never follows that advice himself" but "remains a sailor."[11] The allure of "the ungraspable phantom of life" (*MD* 5) is not so easily exorcised; the land turns out not to be the soul-comforting habitation Ishmael imagines it at sea.

Brodtkorb sees Ishmael caught in a recurrent oscillation between "boredom" and "meaninglessness" at one extreme (the tedium of life on land drives him to sea) and "horror and dread" at the other (the alienness of the sea throws him back upon the community of the land).[12] Ishmael's pendulum swings are projections of Melville's own, just as Ahab's foundling's father speech seems Melville's displaced metaphysical confession. The psychological import of Ahab's hunt is to put an end to an otherwise endless periodicity. "There is a way to disclose paternity," Charles Olson said of *Moby-Dick*: "declare yourself the rival of earth, air, fire, and water."[13] Like Job and Byron's Cain, both of whom interrogate God and provoke an answer through a whirlwind, Ahab, in pursuing a Job's whale to the point where he must either kill or be killed, succeeds in cornering divinity and obliging notice. Father Mapple is content to know God "chiefly . . . by [His] rod" (*MD* 48), and Stubb, kicked by Ahab (a god to *him*), tells Flask "it's an honor" to be "kicked by a great man" (*MD* 132). Ahab is kicked by the greatest of beings. If "the secret of [the foundling's] paternity lies in [the] grave," Ahab is willing to go "there to learn it" (*MD* 492). He will not submit to "the circularity of human consciousness" that John Bryant calls "Ishmael's salvation"[14] but that even for Ishmael is sometimes more like a permanent spiritual limbo.

Making Converse

When in "The Candles" Ahab grasps the lightning chains that put him in touch with the heavens, he is trying to "strike through the mask" even more intimately than by assaulting God's "agent" or "principal," Moby Dick (*MD* 164). A likely source for "The Candles," the imaginative donnée or touchstone for Ahab's hunt, is a passage Melville inscribed on a blank leaf of volume 7 of his edition of Shakespeare, which Charles Olson, who first discovered the lines, called "rough notes for *Moby-Dick*":[15]

> Ego non baptizo te in nominee Patris et
> Filii at Spiritus Sancti—sed in nomine
> Diaboli.— Madness is undefinable—
> It & right reasons extremes of one.
> —Not the [*inserted later above the line with caret below*
> (black art)] Goetic
> but Theurgic magic—
> seeks converse with the Intelligence, Power, the
> Angel.[16]

Olson was mistaken in assuming the originality of the lines—as Geoffrey Sanborn has shown, they were extracted "from various parts of an essay called 'Superstition and Knowledge'" published anonymously by Sir Francis Palgrave in an 1823 issue of the *Quarterly Review*—but even Sanborn feels that Olson "was right to insist" on their close connection to *Moby-Dick*.[17] The subject of Palgrave's remarks is witchcraft and witch-hunting, but Melville drew from them only what spoke to him, detaching Palgrave's ideas from their context and inserting them into an associational context of his own. Other notations on the flyleaf include "Goethe's Autobiography" and "Eschylus Tragedies"; an allusion to Cain appears on a preceding leaf.[18] The Aeschylean tragedy Melville most likely had in mind was *Prometheus Bound*, which he may have connected with Goethe's remark in the *Autobiography* that "the Titans are the foil of polytheism, as the devil may be considered the foil of monotheism."[19] Goethe goes on to address Prometheus specifically, a discussion that Mansfield and Vincent link with his theory of the Demonic, which so impressed Melville that he used its closing Latinity, "Nemo contra Deum nisi Deus ipse" (No one against God but God himself), as an epigraph to the career of his would-be P(p)arricidal hero Pierre.[20] Melville's line on madness—"It & right reasons extremes of one"—significantly alters Palgrave's thought that right reason and insanity are poles on a spectrum; as Sanborn says, Melville's words seem to imply their "underlying identity" (Sanborn 219) or perhaps their status as opposite paths toward the same end. Sanborn reasons that the notes probably date from the summer of 1849 when Melville was writing *White-Jacket* (Sanborn 222), a few months after he had empathetically commented on the "going mad of a friend or acquaintance" in letter to Evert Duyckinck (*Corr* 128). The practice of theurgical magic is described by Palgrave with reference to the Gnostics (Sanborn 219), whom Melville knew from Pierre Bayle and to whom he alluded in *White-Jacket*. Altogether, it is as though in the act of reading and paraphrasing Palgrave, Melville imaginatively fused disparate strands from his reading and thinking—Prometheus, Cain, Goethe's Demonic, diabolism, reason and madness, and Gnosticism—in the vision of a heroic/demonic madman striving to make "converse" with the Father through an act of transcendent defiance.

The overt (intellectual) and covert (psychological) levels of Ahab's hunt are intertwined in the tangled rhetoric of "The Candles":

"Oh! thou clear spirit of clear fire, whom on these seas I as Persian once did worship, till in the sacramental act so burned by thee, that to this hour I bear the scar; I now know thee, thou clear spirit, and I now know that thy right worship is defiance. To neither love nor reverence wilt thou be kind; and e'en for hate thou canst but kill; and all are killed. . . . But war is pain, and hate is woe. Come in thy lowest form of love, and I will kneel and kiss thee; but at thy highest, come as mere supernal power, and though thou launchest navies of full-freighted worlds, there's that in here that remains indifferent. Oh, thou clear spirit, of thy fire thou madest me, and like a true child of fire, I breathe it back to thee!" (*MD* 507)

"I as Persian" is an allusion to the Zoroastrian worship of Ormuzd, a beneficent god associated with fire; "so burned by thee" recalls Ahab's white scar, likened earlier to the mark lightning makes when it sears a large tree. Literally, Ahab is saying that he used to worship a god of light and goodness until he was struck by the heavens during an act of prayer;[21] figuratively, through the displacing idiom of Zoroastrianism, he is measuring the ascribed character of the biblical God against the forces that preside over experience. He is holding God to his announced promise (justice, love, mercy, benign superintendence of the universe) and, finding him wanting, is protesting in the name of those values against a tyrant's unsanctified power.

Culturally, Ahab's position is far less extreme than his blasphemous rhetoric makes it seem. "The gods we stand by are the gods we need and can use,"[22] William James remarked. An age of political absolutism produced an absolutist God who by the mid–nineteenth century had become unusable. Robin Gilmour notes that the crisis of faith that surfaced among early Victorian intellectuals was rooted in "objections to Christianity [that] were overwhelmingly *moral* rather than scientific. . . . The Atonement, chiefly, hell, everlasting punishment, original sin—a God who required the obedience of his creatures on those terms was a God who did not deserve worshipping, a primitive, barbaric Deity."[23] This was the position of William Ellery Channing in his manifestoes of liberal religion, "Unitarian Christianity" and "The Moral Argument Against Calvinism": "We cannot bow before a being, however great and powerful, who governs tyrannically. We respect nothing but excellence, whether on earth or in heaven. We venerate not the loftiness of God's throne, but the equity and goodness on which it is established."[24] It is not far from Channing's "We cannot bow" to Ahab's "but . . . come as mere supernal power." Channing rescued God from Calvinist unaccountability by binding him to human reason and conscience and emphasizing his "parental character."[25] God for Ahab is also parental, but he is a remote, uncaring parent whose theological origins reach back beyond Reformation exegesis to the Old Testament but whose nature is more immediately inferable from the harsh indifference of Creation—a God not of awesome presence like Jehovah, but of stark absence.

Within the fictively realized world of *Moby-Dick*, it is hard to condemn Ahab as morally or spiritually wrong. Though an arch-blasphemer in Father Mapple's terms, Ahab is as faithful to his conception of God as Mapple is to *his*. If commitment to "anything with absolute passion" is the measure of religious heroism, as W. H. Auden said, then the "negative religious hero"—the person passionately committed to the *un*ethical, even to the demonstrably false—can be rejected only on the ground that he is "mad."[26] Madness in fiction, however, is a matter chiefly of textual, not extratextual context, and the presentation of life in *Moby-Dick* does more to vindicate Ahab than it does Mapple. Throughout the book, as Henry Nash Smith observed, "we are given various hints which amount to the declaration that the universe is not controlled by an all-powerful and loving God, but by an omnipotent power resembling the Devil of Calvinist theology."[27] Smith has Ishmael and Melville ultimately retreating from this view "by declaring that Ahab is mad," but his phrase "Devil of Calvinist theology" misrepresents the case.[28] What Ishmael feels and *Moby-Dick* illustrates is that, contrary to Christian belief, no benign intelligence is perceptibly at work in Creation. Ahab's "madness" is not in his protest against a naturalistic universe, which is essentially a Christian protest against an un-Christian world, but in his hallucination of a "personified impersonal" against which his "queenly personality" can assert itself (*MD* 507). If Ahab is mad, it is in much the way that Melville was mad when he wrote Hawthorne of "the man who, like Russia or the British Empire, declares himself a sovereign nature (in himself) amid the powers of heaven, hell, and earth. He may perish; but so long as he exists he insists upon treating with all Powers upon an equal basis" (*Corr* 186). Melville's "madness" was a rhetorical posture fed by the exhilaration of a mood; Ahab's is a chronic condition, but it is one, as Ahab knows, that is partly self-induced and willfully sustained.

The deeper motive behind Ahab's cosmic "No!" is to evoke from the Father-God an answering "Yes! " The "Sudden, repeated flashes of lightning" (*MD* 507) that follow Ahab's words of defiance in "The Candles" are not the answer he sought.but they do, in his mind, constitute a recognition. "Oh, thou magnanimous!" he hails the lightning-sender:

> now do I glory in my genealogy. But thou art but my fiery father; my sweet mother, I know not. Oh, cruel! what hast thou done with her? There lies my puzzle; but thine is greater. Thou knowest not how came ye, hence callest thyself unbegotten; certainly knowest not thy beginning, hence callest thyself unbegun. I know that of me, which thou knowest not of thyself, oh, thou omnipotent. There is some unsuffusing thing beyond thee, thou clear spirit, to whom all thy eternity is but time, all thy creativeness mechanical. Through thee, thy flaming self, my scorched eyes do dimly see it. Oh, thou foundling fire, thou hermit immemorial, thou too hast thy incommunicable riddle, thy unparticipated grief. Here again with haughty agony, I read my sire. (*MD* 508)

The mythic context for Ahab's speech is Gnosticism, which Melville knew from Pierre Bayle's *Historical and Critical Dictionary* and probably from

Andrews Norton's magisterial *The Evidences of the Genuineness of the Gospels* (1844).[29] "The scheme of the Gnostics," as Norton observed, was in part "a crude attempt to solve the existence of evil in the world."[30] What separated the Gnostics from other heretical sects was their fierce opposition to the Old Testament, whose God they found morally repugnant and at odds with the spirit of the Gospels. Rejecting orthodox Christian explanations of evil, the Gnostics developed an elaborate cosmology that distinguished the spiritual principle in the universe, or Supreme Being, from the Creator, or Demiurge, a blind, mechanical power who tyrannized over the spiritual life of humanity. Ahab's reference to the fiery spirit as a "foundling" recalls the Gnostic Creator's maternal descent from the heavenly Sophia, whose fall from the spiritual world (or Pleroma) occasioned the birth of the Creator, who made and governed the material world "ignorant of the Pleroma above him" and in the "belief that he is himself the Supreme God."[31] The leviathan of Job, who ruled "as a king over the children of pride" (Job 41:34), was an agent of the Gnostic Creator; the Old Testament Jehovah was the Creator himself; and Jesus was an emissary from the Supreme Being commissioned to slay the leviathan and announce the advent of the higher God. Ahab's hints about his genealogy echo the Gnostic creation myth, in which (according to Norton) the Demiurge imbued man with a "rational (or psychical) soul of the same essence with himself," only to have Sophia, "unknown to him" and in quasi-incestuous fashion, infuse into this "a portion of the spiritual substance which she had produced, a leaven of immortality."[32] The Gnostic Creator, then, is Ahab's "fiery father," and the missing Sophia is his "sweet mother" and the source of that "queenly personality" in him that scorns "mere supernal power."

Regarded as metaphor, Gnosticism spoke intimately to Melville's sense of the tragic gulf between Christian ethics and the world. Years later in *Clarel* Melville would cite the Gnostic belief that "Jehovah was . . . / Author of evil, yea, its god; / And Christ divine his contrary: / A god was held against a god" (*C* 3, 5: 41–44). Elements of Gnostic myth are prefigured in Aeschylus' *Prometheus Bound*, whose hero teaches humanity reason and the arts of civilization against the prohibition of Zeus. An echo of Gnosticism also appears in Goethe's *Autobiography* in his character Egmont's notion of the Demonic, an intermediate force between divinity and empty chaos. Both Aeschylus and Goethe, along with Gnostic theurgy, are mentioned in Melville's notes on Palgrave. In *Moby-Dick* hints of the Gnostic Creator show themselves in the blank front of the whale ("one broad firmament of a forehead, pleated with riddles; dumbly lowering with the doom of boats, and ships, and men" [*MD* 346]); in the giant squid ("an unearthly, formless, chance-like apparition of life" with "no perceptible face or front" and "no conceivable token of either sensation or instinct" [*MD* 276]); and in the figure of the ship's carpenter, whose "impersonal stolidity . . . so shaded off into the surrounding infinite of things, that it seemed one with the general stolidity discernible in the whole visible world" [*MD* 467]).

The Gnostic Creator is the metaphoric divinity that corresponds to Melville's sense of the "visable truth": "the apprehension of the absolute condition of present things as they strike the eye of the man who fear them not" (*Corr* 186). These "things" are "absolute" because they constitute empirical reality and cannot be mitigated or denied; they are "present" because they are provisional and refer only to temporal, not to ultimate reality, which is unknowable. In "The Candles" Ahab has a momentary sense of ultimate reality, of a higher God than the Creator: "There is some unsuffusing thing beyond thee, thou clear spirit, to whom all thy eternity is but time, all thy creativeness mechanical. Through thee, thy flaming self, my scorched eyes do dimly see it" (*MD* 508). Ahab's burden is that he must strike through *two* masks—through the mask of Moby Dick to reach and defy the Creator, his "sire," and through the mask of the Creator to make converse with the Supreme Being, the source (via Sophia) of spirit in himself and the Father whom he would know, love, and be loved by.

Within the framework of Gnosticism, Ahab's "Ego non baptizo . . ." (*MD* 489) is not diabolical in the ordinary sense; it is an invocation of "deviltry" as a counterforce to the reigning God, the Creator, and therefore, by a kind of double negative, it is an act of fealty to the Supreme Being. Since the Gnostics regarded Old Testament injunctions as "founded on [the] arbitrary will" of the Creator and aimed "at the subjection of man's free spirit to the yoke of necessity," to "defy the ordinances of the law, and thereby throw off all allegiances to the inferior god" became "a duty obligatory on the true Gnostic."[33] Among the Gnostic sects who inverted the moral compass in this way were two that Melville would have encountered in Norton and Bayle, the Ophites (alluded to in "Moby Dick") and the Cainites. "Maintaining the common opinion that the Creator was *not spiritual*, and regarding him as being opposed to the manifestation and development of the spiritual principle in man," Norton commented, the Ophites "honored the serpent for having thwarted his narrow purpose, withdrawn our first parents from allegiance to him, induced them to eat the fruit of the tree of knowledge, and thus brought them the knowledge of that Power which is over All."[34] The Cainites went further still; according to Bayle, "they carried their Presumption to such a Height, as to condemn the Law of *Moses*, and look upon the GOD of the Old Testament, as a Being who had sown Discord in the World, and subjected our Nature to a thousand Calamities; so that, in order to be revenged on him, they, in every thing, acted contrary to his Commandments."[35]

The Cainites would have linked themselves in Melville's imagination with Byron's *Cain*, whose climactic altar scene (the killing of Abel later is almost incidental) is the closest literary analogue to "The Candles." In

Manfred Byron's hero, in refusing to bow down to the god Arimanes, senses, as Ahab does, a higher God to whom both he and Arimanes should defer. In Cain's Old Testament world there are few such glimmerings of a spiritual realm beyond Jehovah's. Cain's drive, like Ahab's, is toward knowledge, most of all toward a revelation of his origins and nature ("Let me but / Be taught the mystery of my being" [*Cain* I, 1: 322–23]) and an explanation for the evil that afflicts the guiltless descendants of Adam. In the altar scene, standing erect, Cain pays God a homage that is consistent with human reason and conscience but scornful of the propitiatory rites of blood sacrifice and prayer. Cain forces God either to prove himself a benign parent by accepting an innocent offering ("the sweet and blooming fruits of earth" [*Cain* III, 1: 259] in contrast to Abel's slaughtered lamb) and or else to smite him and confirm Cain's sense of a jealous tyrant. Byron has God answer Cain by destroying his altar through a whirlwind, as God would answer Job. Though rebuked by "mere supernal power," Cain has taken his stand on the human right to inquire and morally judge, prerogatives that Unitarians like Channing made requisite for religious belief. Beyond that, Cain has compelled a distant, impersonal God to descend and take cognizance of him; he has made converse.

In "The Candles" Ahab makes converse when his words to the fiery spirit—"I leap with thee; I burn with thee; would fain be welded with thee: defyingly I worship thee!" (*MD* 508)—are met with a "flame of pale, forked fire . . . like a serpent's tongue" (*MD* 508) that engulfs the barb of his harpoon. It hardly matters here which of the antagonists, if either, is "diabolical"; the subject of the chapter, beyond its idiom of ethico-religious protest and its language of blasphemy, is the child's hunger for love and recognition from the withdrawn parent. Father Mapple's sermon ends with a vision of the "eternal delight and deliciousness [that] will be his, who coming to lay him down, can say with his final breath—O Father!—chiefly known to me by Thy rod— . . . I have striven to be Thine, more than to be this world's, or mine own" (*MD* 48). Ahab can say this, down to knowing God chiefly by his rod, though for Ahab "Thine" and "mine" are not oppositional. Ahab is most his own *and* most God's when, "like a true child of fire" (*MD* 507), he breathes the Creator's fire back to him in a defiance that fuses love and hate in an almost eroticized desire for union with the Father.[36]

Primogenitures of the Gods

If not beyond good and evil, "The Candles" seems largely apart from it. In nearby chapters like "The Forge," "The Quadrant," "The Needle," and "The Log and Line" Melville adopts a moral stance and shows Ahab's egocentrism in all its destructive fury, but in "The Candles" ethical and social questions pale before the spiritual pageant of Ahab's God-relation. "Tragic heroes," Northrop Frye observed, "are wrapped in the mystery of their communion with that something beyond which we can see only through them." They "are so much the highest points in their human landscape that they seem the inevitable conductors of the power about them, great trees more likely to be struck by lightning than a clump of grass,"[37] and liable to convey the charge fatally to those around them. In the high mimetic world of tragedy, which is not our lived world, these victims barely seem to matter. It is greatness, not goodness, that tragedy invites us to marvel at and commend.

Melville brings forward the distinction between the ethical and the spiritual in Ahab's late colloquy with Starbuck in "The Symphony." Denied more than fleeting converse with the divine, Ahab is drawn momentarily toward the compensatory life of the "green land" (*MD* 544). "Let me look into a human eye," he tells Starbuck: "it is better than to gaze into sea or sky; better than to gaze upon God" (*MD* 544). The chapter illustrates a special form of tragedy's *anagnorisis*, or illumination—not the "adequate moral recognition" that Matthiessen found wanting in the unrepentant Ahab but the hero's understanding of what Frye called "the determined shape of the life he has created for himself, with a implicit comparison with the uncreated potential life he has forsaken."[38] In baring Ahab's pain Melville heightens the pathos of the final catastrophe, but he also pointedly contrasts two modes of being, the God-centered (even when ungodly) and the humane. Encouraged by Starbuck, Ahab reveals his long-suppressed "humanities" (*MD* 79) until the sight of an albicore chasing a flying-fish recalls for him the cannibalism of nature and therefore the reason for the quest, and until his own Hamlet-like process of association leads him to pass from "sleep" to death, and from death to thoughts of nothingness ("'Sleep? Aye, and rust amid greenness; as last year's scythes flung down, and left in the half-cut swaths'" [*MD* 545]). The scene ends with Starbuck stealing off, "blanched to a corpse's hue with despair" (*MD* 545). Starbuck retreats because he knows he can't contend with Ahab on the levels of language and passion but also because he feels in Ahab a depth of suffering beyond his own capacity to bear or even to witness.

"Suffering" in tragedy, Frye observed, "has something subdivine about it": "the tragic hero has normally an extraordinary, often a nearly divine, destiny within his grasp, and the glory of his original vision never quite fades out of tragedy."[39] Ahab's "nearly divine" destiny is to come close to fulfilling the prophecy of Isaiah and slaying "the dragon that is in the sea" (*MD* xviii). In his death speech—"to the last I grapple with thee; from hell's heart I stab at thee; for hate's sake I spit my last breath at thee" (*MD* 571–72)—Ahab recalls Milton's Satan, but for Melville, as for Blake and

Shelley, "Satanism" was less a moral vice than a political and theological virtue. As Robin Grey observes, Melville's marginalia in *Paradise Lost* show him responding to "depictions of wrathful power and belligerent remonstrations against tyranny"[40] and to what he described as Milton's "many profound atheistical hits" and covert heresy in "mak[ing] the Devil himself a Teacher & Messiah."[41]

What vindicates Ahab, finally, is not what he does, or nearly does; it is what, through the arduousness and pain of attempting it, he becomes. In *Moby-Dick*'s imaginative world there is an aristocratic spiritual truth—the counterforce to Ishmael's democratic truth—to Ahab's dismissal of Starbuck and Stubb, the moral man and the hedonist, as "opposite poles of one thing," with Ahab "alone, among the millions of the peopled earth, nor gods nor men his neighbors" (*MD* 533). As the *Pequod* sinks before his eyes, all hope gone, Ahab exclaims, "Oh, now do I feel my topmost greatness lies in my topmost grief" (*MD* 571). This is Ahab's own self-apotheosis, but it has been anticipated and underwritten two chapters earlier by Melville's omniscient voice. "Dragged into Stubb's boat with blood-shot, blinded eyes" after the first day's chase (*MD* 551), Ahab is transfigured by the intensity of his suffering into an image of human godlikeness:

> In an instant's compass, great hearts sometimes condense to one deep pang, the sum total of those shallow pains kindly diffused through feebler men's lives. And so, such hearts, though summary in each one suffering; still, if the gods decree it, in their life-time aggregate a whole age of woe, wholly made up of instantaneous intensities; for even in their pointless centres, those noble natures contain the entire circumference of inferior souls. (*MD* 551–52)

In his extremity, Ahab is the culmination of that fascination with grief that characterized Melville's writing from the time of *Typee* and that he found elevated to the status of a religion in the writers who counted most for him in 1850–51: Shakespeare, Hawthorne, Byron, Carlyle, and the authors of Ecclesiastes and Job. In *Mardi*, Melville had made sadness the token of spiritual life and the tenor of heaven; in *Moby-Dick*, he gives "heart-woes an archangelic grandeur":

> To trail the genealogies of these high mortal miseries, carries us at last among the sourceless primogenitures of the gods; so that, in the face of all the glad, hay-making suns, and soft-cymballing, round harvest-moons, we must give in to this: that the gods themselves are not for ever glad. The ineffaceable, sad birth-mark in the brow of man, is but the stamp of sorrow in the signers. (*MD* 464)

To be sorrowful at this depth and pitch is to be kin to royalty but only, so far as the sorrow is passively borne, to prostrate exiled royalty like the "patient" captive king of "Moby Dick" whom "the great gods mock" (*MD* 185). The "primogenitures" passage appears in "Ahab's Leg," shortly after Melville describes the "agonizing wound" Ahab suffers when his ivory leg shatters and "stakewise . . . all but pierce[s] his groin" (*MD* 463). The image of symbolic and near-literal emasculation links Ahab to the figuratively emasculated captive king and, looking ahead, to the mutilated, earth-imprisoned Enceladus in *Pierre*. Mutilation, however, is not the focus of heroic tragedy but of ironic tragedy or pathos.[42] "*There is no tragedy without transcendence*," Karl Jaspers remarked: "Even defiance unto death in a hopeless battle against the gods and fate is an act of transcending; it is a movement toward man's proper essence, which he comes to know as his own in the presence of his doom."[43] Ahab's mad, impossible pursuit of the "all-destroying but unconquering" whale (*MD* 571) is a "hopeless battle" but one that nonetheless calls forth and evinces his "proper essence." The "old State-secret" of the exiled royalty's lineage can be revealed only through a forced interrogation of his "grim sire" (*MD* 186). It is not necessary that the interrogator receive an outward answer to his question; the act of pressing the question against all temptations is itself his transcendence, confirmed by the inward answer of spiritual self-recognition: "Oh, now I feel my topmost greatness lies in my topmost grief" (*MD* 571). In the absence or silence of the Father, the patent of spirituality becomes the mirror image beheld by the ennobled son.

"The Life We Imagine"

When Melville told Hawthorne he had "written a wicked book" and felt "spotless as the lamb" (*Corr* 212), he was acknowledging that *Moby-Dick* was preeminently Ahab's book, whatever his previous intentions might have been.[44] He was also confessing that *Moby-Dick* was not simply a literary artifact but a symbolic personal act. In creating Ahab and investing his own urgencies in the hunt—cosmic anger, intellectual and emotional frustration, F/father-resentment, F/father-yearning, a half-religious, half-narcissistic impulse toward grandeur—Melville was staging a drama of spiritual self-proclamation denied him by the terms of actual life.

"The life we imagine." The phrase is Byron's. Returning to *Childe Harold's Pilgrimage* after a hiatus of several years, Byron poses the question of why the mind "seeks refuge" from ordinary life in acts of imagination: "'Tis to create, and in creating live / A being more intense, that we endow / With form our fancy, *gaining as we give / The life we imagine, even as I do now*" (*Childe Harold* III, 43, 46–49; my emphasis). To write, for Byron, is not merely to escape from or compensate for unsatisfying reality, as Freud theorized;[45] it is to fabricate an idealized self inhabiting a more glorious reality, and, by dwelling in that self and publicizing it in literature, to *become* that self in his own eyes and in the ratifying eyes of the world. Former generations found a framework for heightened living in the cosmic morality play of Christian eschatology; lapsed Christians like Byron had to construct their own spiritual framework and arena or do without.

"Religion . . . is man's appeal from fellow-clay" (*C* 3, 3: 54–55) Melville wrote in *Clarel*. So, for Byron and Melville, in the absence of religion, was literature. "The beings of the mind are not of clay," Byron wrote:

> Essentially immortal, they create
> And multiply in us a brighter ray
> And more beloved existence: that which Fate
> Prohibits to dull life, in this our state
> Of mortal bondage, by these spirits supplied,
> First exiles, then replaces what we hate;
> Watering the heart whose early flowers have died,
> And with a fresher growth replenishing the void.
>   (*Childe Harold* IV, 37–45)

The void for Byron was the turbid confusion of his private life from his abandonment by his father and unstable childhood to his disastrous marriage, but these things and others—his Calvinist upbringing, his overbearing and capricious mother, the genteel poverty of his youth, his lameness and its attendant social ridicule, his ambiguous sexual identity, the meteoric rise and fall of his literary and political career—were interwoven with a feeling of ontological void, or the insufficiency of life to the demands of the imagination. This was the life "we hate." The psychological achievement of Byron's writing from the juvenile *Hours of Idleness*, published at the same age (nineteen) that Melville published "Fragments from a Writing Desk" and Pierre began his Byronic inward journey, was to transform an experience of grief-as-passive-suffering into a myth of grief-as-greatness. The miseries that "others would have bowed to, as misfortunes," his friend and biographer Thomas Moore observed, Byron's "proud spirit rose up against, as wrongs."[46] And because of "those sceptical views of religion, which clouded . . . his boyish thoughts" without freeing him emotionally from the categories of Scotch Calvinism (Moore 1:184), his temperamental melancholy and feeling of injury assumed a metaphysical cast at once rebellious and suppliant. In its indictment of God the Father for his responsibility for evil, "Cain" was the poem Byron seems to have been destined to write; and yet, as Moore says of Byron's early freethinking, "there is a fervour of adoration mingled with his defiance of creeds, through which the piety implanted in his nature . . . unequivocally shows itself" (Moore 1:124).

Deprived of his father, repulsed by his mother, and lacking "the sympathy of a sister's love" (Moore 1:177)—his half-sister Augusta (later his lover) was raised apart from him, as Isabel was from her half-brother/lover Pierre—Byron redirected his "yearning desire for affection" toward an absent Father in whom he half-disbelieved and, at the same time (like Pierre with Glen Stanly), toward those "boyish [i.e., homoerotic] friendships" he cultivated with "passionate enthusiasm" (Moore 1:177). Central to the myth Byron developed was the figure of the disinherited youth seeking a knowledge that must remain incomplete and whose partial achievement could only intensify his suffering. This was his curse—the curse of Cain, the Wandering Jew, and Ishmael, all figures in Byron's poetry or journals—but it was also his badge of allegiance to the F/father who deserted him. Guinn Batten described Byron's F/filial ambivalence as a state of "preterition, a terrifying inversion of Calvinist election in which sons are damned as a consequence not of paternal rejection but of paternal neglect."[47] To convert the wound of abandonment into heroic defiance—to *will* damnation, if it came to that—was "better," Batten argues, "than to be the in-between 'nothing' called preterite. It [was] to *do* something, rather than to *be* the nothing evoked by ennui."[48]

For Melville, Byron was more than a source or analogue; he was an "influence" in the most literal sense of a tributary stream flowing into Melville's mind and sensibility at an age when literary works can take hold of an impressionable character singularly prepared for them and can be assimilated on levels beyond the reach of analytic intelligence. "When Melville read a book that absorbed him," Henry A. Murray remarked, "he *became* the hero and lived through his adventures as if they were his own."[49] Byron, Murray feels, was the greatest of the young Melville's heroes and the "most potent" literary influence on his character and writing.[50] For a youth forced "to think much and bitterly before [his] time" (*R* 10), as Melville said of *Redburn*, Byronic melancholy and defiance served as a ground for self-reconception much as they had for Byron himself, in whose life, familiar to him through Moore's biography, Melville found a glamorized image of many of his own trials and their accompanying emotional, spiritual, filial, and perhaps sexual conflicts. Above all, Byron supplied a structure of feeling that valorized the pain of father-loss and exile, clothed it in the idiom of philosophy, and eroticized melancholy as a posture for idealized self-contemplation. To some degree, the emotions of Byronism would remain with Melville throughout his life, down to his late enthusiasm for Scottish poet James Thomson, a melancholic of Calvinist background and a self-described "outcast and Ishmael"[51] whose "City of Dreadful Night" impressed Melville as "Massive and mighty" in the "sublimity" of "its gloom" (*Corr* 514) and "looming with the same aboriginal verities" as the Book of Job (*Corr* 522).

The challenge for the Byronic hero and later for the Melvillean one was how to vault himself out of his terrestrial condition, spurn "the clay-cold bonds which round our being cling," and "remount" the spiritual heights from which he feels himself exiled (*Childe Harold* III, 697, 693). In its main lines Melville's development from *Mardi* to *Moby-Dick* recapitulates Byron's from *Childe Harold* through *Manfred* to *Cain*. As the predicament of Childe Harold evolved from the boredom and satiety of cantos 1 and 2 to the *Weltschmerz* of cantos 3 and 4, Byron increasingly addressed the division within human nature (spirit/clay) and between human beings and the world (alienation) that Romantics from Schiller onward saw as the modern condition—a fruit of knowledge—and whose cure seemed to lie in a reunification of experience through greater knowledge. "Let us ponder boldly—'tis a base / Abandonment of reason to resign / Our right of thought" (*Childe Harold* IV, 1135–37), Byron proclaims late in *Childe Harold*. Cain believes that "knowledge is good" (*Cain* I, 1: 37) and craves more of it, but the lesson of Lucifer, whose knowledge extends across time and space (though not to the ultimate mysteries of God's design), is substantially the one that Byron had announced earlier in "Manfred" and that Melville would illustrate in *Mardi*: "Sorrow is knowledge: they who know the most/ Must mourn the deepest o'er the fatal truth,/ The Tree of Knowledge is not that of life" (*Manfred* I, 1: 10–12).

Mardi is Melville's *Childe Harold* and *Manfred* in one, beginning in quest-travelogue and ending with an act of will testifying to the spirit's proud indomitableness but to little else. The earlier Byron and Melville were confined to declamation because they could not conceive a literary action commensurate with their need to enact and inscribe their spiritual lives. Byron would find his ideal vehicle in the story of Cain, Melville in the story of Ishmael as its theme of dispossession—exiled royalty—was completed in the Enceladan myth of attempted return. Set off from "dull life, in this our state / Of mortal bondage," the stories enlisted feelings of frustration, resentment, aspiration, and egotism in an apocalyptic rebellion that each writer with his intellect knew to be fantastical, even mad. In his notations on Palgrave, Melville described madness as a route to divine "converse." Practically what this came to mean for him was that authorial "madness"—the writer's creation and habitation of a literary world of otherwise unrealizable desire—could be a way of spiritually "*gaining as we give* / *The life we imagine.*" What Byron said of Rousseau—in his "desire / . . . to be glorious," he "knew / How to make madness beautiful, and cast / O'er erring deeds and thoughts, a heavenly hue" (*Childe Harold* III, 723–24, 729–31)—might be said of Byron and Melville themselves: in their desire to live and be seen as living exalted spiritual lives, they knew how to invest narcissism with eloquence and give bold, subversive thought the earnestness and intensity of religion.

Melville's "visable truth" letter with its stance of defiance toward "the powers of heaven, hell, and earth" (*Corr* 186) is Melville's *Manfred*, bombastic but actionally wanting; the Ahab sections of *Moby-Dick* are his *Cain*. In contrast to Ishmael and Melville himself, Ahab the Romantic foundling delivers himself from the endless cycle of belief and unbelief by fixing his mind in the phase of malevolent theism and setting out to assault God or his offending agent. As a "being of the mind" inhabiting a fictional universe, Ahab can perform what Melville can only posture at in words: "declare himself a sovereign nature (in himself) amid the powers of heaven, hell, and earth" (*Corr* 186). Yet to create such a figure is itself, in some respect, to rise to his level—vicariously to do what he does, inwardly to *be* what he *is*. As Carlyle said, the poet "could not sing the Heroic warrior, unless he himself were at least a Heroic warrior."[52] The great writer has all the elevation of his hero, whose deeds he imaginatively contains and whose understanding and eloquence he surpasses. As he describes Ahab's "topmost greatness" in "topmost grief" (*MD* 571), Melville is also inscribing himelf as a spirit large enough to imagine, gauge, and record such a greatness. Melville is *with* Ahab, cathartically, as he darts the harpoon into Job's whale, but the deeper significance of this and kindred passages is in its status as writing. I am not referring simply to the dramatic power of the text but to what Eliot calls "the intensity of the artistic process, the pressure, so to speak, under which the fusion" of elements must have "take[n] place."[53] In Eliot this fusion is impersonal; in Melville it is deeply personal—the artist, in his passion, making prose, and the prose in turn crystallizing feelings of would-be loftiness in the artist. For Melville, the "artistic process" is not a mysticism of craftsmanship; in lieu of religious belief, it has become the site and substance of a spiritual life that realizes itself most intensely in the literary telling.

I do not believe *Moby-Dick* is a "wicked" book any more than *Cain* is a "wicked" poem. Both are fantasies of protest and paternal "converse" by writers who morally and metaphysically knew better and who in other moods could make light of their own histrionics. For Melville to "live a being more intense" it was necessary for him to override common sense, the moral sense, and his extraordinary sense of humor and irony, qualities that helped create Ishmael but could never have created Babbalanja, Ahab, Pierre, or several of the characters in *Clarel*. Beneath the posturings of his heroes—cries of protest; claims of injury and usurped rights; flights of self-assertion—Melville did not hate God. He wanted to be, and to receive divine recognition as being, God's servant. The divinity that Ahab dimly perceived behind the god of "The Candles" Melville may also at times have dimly perceived, or at least aspired toward, beyond the world of the "visable truth." Melville could not live honestly without acknowledging the darkly chaotic in experience, but neither could he live without hoping that the royalty he felt in himself answered to something Paternal in the universe. If there is a calm identic center beyond the excesses of Melville's metaphysical mood swings, it is evidenced by a passage from his letter to Hawthorne of June 29, 1851:

> This most persuasive season has now for weeks recalled me from certain crotchetty and over doleful chimaeras, the like of which men like you and me and some others, forming a chain of God's posts round the world, must be content to encounter now and then, and fight them the best way we can. But come they will, —for, in the boundless, trackless, but still glorious wild wilderness through which these outposts run, the Indians do sorely abound, as well as insignificant but still stinging mosquitoes. (*Corr* 195)

"God's posts." However attractive Ishmael was for him as a character, a locus of values, and an example of being for himself and America, Melville could not rest content with a secular humanitarianism even of the most inventive, exploratory sort. With Carlyle, he believed "it is not to taste sweet things, but to do noble and true things, and vindicate himself under God's Heaven as a god-made Man, that the poorest son of Adam dimly longs."[54] And like Carlyle and Byron, he felt that this "doing" and "vindicating" came best, for the writer without definite belief, through a literary performance of spiritual life. If the universe were truly godless, performance might be all there was. In the end, like Father Mapple, Melville wished to be able to say, "I have striven to be Thine, more than to be this world's, or mine own" (*MD* 48), though like Ahab he would have amended the words to read, "I have striven to be Thine *by* most nobly being mine own." His stance toward God was like Job's in a passage he marked in a Bible inscribed March 1850: "Though he slay me, yet will I trust in him: but I will maintain mine own ways before him" (the underlining is Melville's).[55]

6

"The Ugly Socrates": Melville, Hawthorne, and the Varieties of Homoerotic Experience

Man is an animal organism with (like others) an unmistakably bisexual disposition. The individual corresponds to a fusion of two symmetrical halves, of which, according to some investigators, one is purely male and the other female. It is equally possible that each half was originally hermaphroditic.

—Freud, *Civilization and Its Discontents*

What Cosmic jest or Anarch blunder
The human integral clove asunder.

—Melville, "After the Pleasure Party"

Homosocial, Homoerotic, Homosexual, Homotextual

"The Ugly Socrates," an echo of Alcibiades' words in Plato's *Symposium*,[1] is drawn from a letter Melville wrote to Hawthorne on or around November 17, 1851, in response to Hawthorne's "joy-giving and exultation-breeding letter" of praise for *Moby-Dick* (*Corr* 212). What we know of Melville's feelings toward Hawthorne is largely contained in such letters, along with "Hawthorne and His Mosses," which Edwin H. Miller called "a love letter" in the guise of a book review.[2] Hawthorne's letters to Melville do not survive, and his journal entries on Melville, while respectful, even admiring, tend to hide rather than reveal his private feelings and to hint very little about Melville's.

"Our intellectual and active powers increase with our affection," Emerson observed in "Friendship": "the scholar sits down to write, and all his years of meditation do not furnish him with one good thought or happy expression; but it is necessary to write a letter to a friend,—and, forthwith, troops of gentle thoughts invest themselves, on every hand, with chosen words."[3] Emerson was speaking generally, but the content and language of his essay borrow from his sometimes ardent letters of the period to twenty-one-year-old Caroline Sturgis. What was Emerson, married and in his late thirties, thinking when he told Sturgis he "could spend 'the remainder of [his] days' in her 'holy society,'" or when he wrote erotically in "Friendship" of those "jets of affection which make a young world for me again"?[4] What is the spectrum of relationship between sexuality and textuality, or genital desire and an overheated rhetoric that may be anything from metaphor to fantasy to a form of emotional masturbation? How may we determine where on that spectrum a particular textual utterance lies? Could Emerson himself have said what he thought, felt, fantasized, and intended vis-à-vis Sturgis? And with what confidence and on what evidential grounds may interpreters write of these things? When so much is suggested but so little determinably known—the meaning of a text, the relationship of text to consciousness, the relationship of consciousness to subconsciousness, the ambiguity of marginally erotic feelings generally—questions and provisional speculations seem the most proper discursive mode. To claim more is to mythologize or ideologize.

Melville's letters to Hawthorne of 1850–51 show him at his happiest and most fertile. With what sort of affection—fraternal, filial, homoerotic; all of these in some combination?—did Melville write to Hawthorne? How conscious was he of the nature of his affection? What did this affection signify within the context of mid-nineteenth nineteenth-century male friendships as they were understood by the participants themselves and as they have variously come to be characterized by modern interpreters? And how did this affection figure in his writing, especially in *Pierre*, written immediately after the height of their relationship?

These are difficult questions to answer, not only for want of biographical evidence but also because cultural changes have created a chasm of idiom and ideology between Melville's time and the present while politicizing the issue in ways that occlude discussion of the singular relationship at hand. To say flatly that Melville was homosexual, latently homosexual, or not homosexual is not simply to overread the evidence; it is to neglect the problematizing work of recent cultural historians which suggests, in Eve Kosofsky Sedgwick's words, "that the differences between the homosexuality 'we know today' and previous arrangements of same-sex relations may be so profound and so integrally rooted in other cultural differences that there may be no continuous, defining essence of 'homosexuality' to *be* known."[5]

If styles of sexuality have changed, so have categories for thinking about sex, often because of the changes in styles and with radical consequences for interpreting past behaviors. Before the later nineteenth century, shades of homosociality and homosexuality ranged themselves along a spectrum. The twentieth century replaced this gradational sexuality with what Carroll Smith-Rosenberg calls a "dichotomized universe of deviance and normality, genitality and platonic love,"[6] a universe we continue to inhabit and can only with difficulty extricate ourselves from as we try to understand creatures from a very different universe.

The challenge in thinking historically about homosexuality, as David M. Halperin said, "is, first of all, how to recover the terms in which the experiences of individuals belonging to past societies were actually constituted and, second, how to measure and assess the differences between those terms and the ones we currently employ."[7] What languages did historical actors have or not have available to them and how did that (un)availability affect their understanding of themselves? In her autobiographical essay "A Sketch of the Past," Virginia Woolf speaks of reading Freud "only the other day" (1940) and "for the first time . . . discover[ing] that [her] violently disturbing conflict of love and hate [toward her father] is a common feeling; and is called ambivalence."[8] Thirteen years after she published *To the Lighthouse*, one of the subtlest treatments of filial love/hate in the English novel, Woolf finds that simply having the word "ambivalence" has brought together a constellation of feelings in a sudden epiphany. For most of her life Woolf did not have the word "lesbian" available to her; as late as 1925 she writes (of Vita Sackville-West) as if observing a new phenomenon, "These Sapphists *love* women; friendship is never untinged with amorosity."[9] It seems only dawningly to occur to Woolf at age forty-three that she herself may be a "Sapphist," though for years she has been aware of her strong emotional and imaginative preference for women and soon she would sexually experiment with Vita.

The word and concept "homosexual" was not current in England and America until Melville was past fifty, when his active sexual life was long behind him; he certainly had no term or idea analogous to the modern "sexual orientation." "Homosexuality" for him would have meant certain acts people performed. It might have extended to a class of people who enjoyed or preferred those acts. It did not constitute a psychosexual identity, if only because few nineteenth-century Americans defined themselves in terms of "psychosexual identity." In the absence of primary materials like letters and journals, it is difficult to determine how actors before Freud's or Havelock Ellis's time understood their feelings and intentions. Perhaps they would have been naïvely unsuspicious of them, in many cases with good reason—the "strict interdiction against full genital sexuality" permitting, as Robert K. Martin has suggested, "a much fuller expression of male friendship" precisely because it "in no way threatened to spill over into genitality."[10] If present-day distinctions such "as an absolute split between homo- and heterosexual based on genital sexuality were nascent and fluid" in mid-nineteenth-century America, as Martin contends, then it is highly probable that the rise of the term "homosexual" later in the century came to preclude "many spontaneous forms of open affection that had previously seemed normal"[11] and that seem "abnormal" to us largely because we live on the hither side of the threshold of suspicion. The same is true for language. It was one thing for Melville as "Virginian" to speak of Hawthorne "shoot[ing] his strong New-England roots into the hot soil of my Southern soul" (*PT* 230) in the decorous *Literary World* in 1850; it would be quite another for him to publish the words in the *New York Times Book Review* in 2005.

As a matter of vocabulary, I will be using "homosexuality" to refer to same-sex relationships that demonstrably involve genitality or at least a pronounced and persistent pattern of genital fantasy, "homosociality" to refer to same-sex friendship, and "homeroticism" to suggest the broad middle range from intermittent sexual desire unaccompanied by characteristic adult behavior, on one side, to feelings of extraordinary warmth, delight, and personal intimacy, on the other.[12] To these terms, I would add a neologism of my own in response to Martin's 1986 differentiation between statements about books and statements about authors—"homo-*text*uality": a pattern of same-sex eroticism in a work or body of work that has no necessary implications for the author's life.[13] I mention this idea chiefly to acknowledge and discount it; I am not concerned with "Melville" simply as a body of texts.

In sifting these terms, the alienness and frequent inscrutability of mid-nineteenth-century psychoerotic experience should always be kept in mind. In a world of gradation, ambiguity, and cultural otherness, signs and behaviors that today would be taken as proclamations or hints of homoeroticism could seem sufficiently innocuous to pass muster even among the conventional. Melville admired busts of Antinous, the emperor Hadrian's lover, and late in life he owned one himself; but so did Sophia Hawthorne, who furnished the red cottage in Lenox with a bust of Antinous, "a favorite nineteenth-century subject, considered an emblem of ideal friendship,"[14] James R. Mellow notes—and of whatever other complex of feelings we can only surmise. *Pierre* devotes several pages to its hero's youthful friendship with Glen Stanly, but while reviewers censured the book's many offenses against religion and morality, none seem to have objected to its florid celebration of "boy-love" (*P* 216).[15] Was this embarrassment? obtuseness? a journalistic conspiracy of silence? Or was the mock-heroic overtness of the eroticism a signal to contemporary readers that it was not transgressively sexual at all but a form of giddy preadolescent masculine chivalry, benign because soon to be transferred to heterosexual love? We don't know.

"Platonic Love"

Within the spectrum of cultural possibilities, problematic in itself, Melville occupies an anomalous position thanks to his youthful experience aboard ship, where homosexual practices were not uncommon even among otherwise heterosexual men, and in Polynesia, whose sexual customs may have bred in him an erotic latitudinarianism that John Bryant calls "'pansexual'"[16] and that Freud would likely have viewed as polymorphously perverse. Even within Melville's "sexual orientation" (if so homogenizing a term can be applied to his relationships to individuals), his feeling for Hawthorne would have been a special case of his attraction to male beauty and male character, just as his feeling for Jack Chase of the frigate *United States*—"that great heart" (*BB* 42) to whom he dedicated *Billy Budd, Sailor* nearly half a century later—was a special case of a different sort. With Hawthorne, the legacy of South Seas eroticism was less important for Melville than the masculine rituals of feasting, drinking, smoking, and genial conversation, which Melville enjoyed even in their lighter forms and which, when combined with heady speculation, were among his greatest pleasures. The difference between talking "ontological heroics" with Hawthorne (*Corr* 196) and "high German metaphysics" with George J. Adler (*Journals* 19), his companion during part of his 1849–50 journey to England and the Continent, was that Hawthorne was darkly handsome with a spellbinding air of mystery almost universally remarked on by contemporaries. In Hawthorne, Melville found an unmatched union of the four things that most attracted him to men: physical beauty, an air of natural aristocracy, a taste for (modest) festivity and frank conversation, and a brooding melancholy suggestive of deep sorrow. Hawthorne was also a fellow writer.

Possibly no other man, through a combination of these qualities, could have affected Melville as Hawthorne did. Could a woman? Probably not any woman of his acquaintance. If "there was . . . something in Herman Melville's life that caused him to dissociate woman from an account of man's deepest experience," as Lewis Mumford observed, that "something" may have been his want of opportunities for knowing an intellectual yet distinctively feminine woman.[17] When Melville finally did come upon such a woman in his reading of Mme. de Staël's *Germany* in 1862, it was with a sense of wonder that "such penetration of understanding" could coexist with "so femininely emotional a nature."[18] The lines that prompted Melville's admiration were those remarking on Goethe's "profound" but "discouraging knowledge of the human heart,"[19] an echo of "that Calvinistic sense of Innate Depravity and Original Sin" that Melville had found in Hawthorne and ascribed to all "deeply thinking minds" (*PT* 243) but seems surprised to have encountered in a woman.

This was not misogyny on Melville's part, nor was he alone in first discovering an intellectual woman abroad. Reading George Sand through the lens of her own cultural acquaintance with gender differences, Margaret Fuller professed "astonishment" at Sand's "insight into the life of thought," which Fuller believed must have come to her "through some man." "Women, under any circumstances, can scarce do more than dip the foot in this broad and deep river," Fuller added: "they have not strength to contend with the current. . . . It is easy for women to be heroic in action, but when it comes to interrogating God, the universe, the soul, and, above all, trying to live above their own hearts, they dart down to their nests like so many larks."[20] The Melvill(e), Gansevoort, and Shaw women, though intelligent and sometimes gifted, were conventionally religious; there was no Mary Moody Emerson in Melville's life; Pittsfield neighbor Sarah Morewood, lively and acute, was of a social rather than an intellectual disposition; even Sophia Hawthorne, with her artistic tastes and "spiritualizing nature" (*Corr* 219), was sunny-minded and Christocentric. One wonders how Melville might have reacted to a woman with the intellect of Mme. de Staël and the vibrant sexuality of, say, Hawthorne's Zenobia. But Melville never met such a woman—the Duyckinck circle he frequented in New York was a masculine one—and looking for a soul-mate, or a recipient for the superabundance he felt in himself, it was both serendipitous and biographically appropriate that he should have discovered one in Zenobia's creator.[21]

"Superabundance" seems the right word for the prodigal outpouring of self that distinguishes Melville's letters to Hawthorne through the fall of 1851. Their conversations during visits seem to have been largely one-sided, with Melville (in Sophia Hawthorne's words) "dash[ing] his tumultuous waves of thought against Mr. Hawthorne's great, genial, comprehending silences," broken occasionally by "a wonderful smile or one powerful word" that would change Melville's "foam and fury into a peaceful booming calm" or "murmuring expostulation."[22] As his letters bound forward from subject to subject—nearly all of them connected to *his* book-in-progress, *his* career, *his* opinions on God, man, and truth—Melville senses that his grandiose self-display may tax Hawthorne's patience or demand a requital Hawthorne is unwilling to give. "Don't trouble yourself, though, about writing; and don't trouble yourself about visiting; and when you *do* visit, don't trouble yourself about talking. I will do all the writing and visiting and talking myself" (*Corr* 192).

There is an aptness to Melville's offer of unilateral egotism, for what is of greatest interest to him is not Hawthorne but himself as he emerges in his relation to Hawthorne. His performance, as he says, is done "incidentally and without premeditation" (*Corr* 195–96), like that of a jazz musician improvising on a tune, intoxicated by his own virtuosity yet conscious of a special listener whose approval would be the measure and vindication of his enterprise. "You did not care a penny for the book [*Moby-Dick*]," he wrote Hawthorne in November 1851 in response to just such a vindication: "But, now and then as you read it, you understood the pervading thought that impelled the book—and that you praised. Was it not so? You were archangel enough to despise the imperfect body, and embrace the soul. Once you hugged the ugly Socrates because you saw the flame in his mouth, and heard the rushing of the demon,—the familiar—and recognized the sound; for you heard it in your own solitude" (*Corr* 213).

Melville alludes naturally to Plato's *Symposium* because the dialogue "was fresh in [his] mind in November of 1851."[23] In Book 1 of *Pierre*, composed close to this time, he invokes the *Symposium* when he cites Aristophanes' myth of the parts of the divided self "roaming in quest of each other" as they seek completion.[24] Aristophanes' purpose is to explain the origin and significance of Eros, or the desire "implanted in us" of "reuniting our original nature, making one of two, and healing the division in man" (*Symposium* 32). Originally there were three sexes, Aristophanes explains, each with a pair of genitals: one (the noblest) was doubly male, another doubly female, and the third male and female. Cut in two by the gods for their assault upon heaven, the severed halves searched for their complement, whether of the same or of the opposite sex; and so, ever since, human beings have been driven by "the desire and the pursuit of the whole [which] is called love" (*Symposium* 33). When aboriginal selves meet, "the pair are lost in an amazement of love and friendship and intimacy" and overwhelmed with an "intense yearning which . . . does not appear to be the desire of lover's intercourse, but of something else which the soul of either evidently desires and cannot tell, and of which she has only a dark and doubtful presentiment" (*Symposium* 33). The elusiveness of this "something else" survives in the ambiguous contemporary definition of "Platonic love": "a close relationship between two persons in which sexual desire is *nonexistent* or has been *suppressed* or *sublimated*,"[25] a definition that implies nothing about the erotic character of such a relationship except that it is not overt.

In mid-nineteenth-century America "Platonic love" functioned as a screen behind which a complex and virtually indecipherable set of emotions might lurk. "It is so true that a woman may be in love with a woman and a man with a man," Margaret Fuller wrote, adding immediately, as if to deny the erotic, that "undoubtedly it is the same love we shall feel when we are angels." Quoting Goethe—"'Sie fragen nicht nach Mann und Weib'" (It is not a question of man and woman)—Fuller described such love as "purely intellectual and spiritual, unprofaned by any mixture of lower instincts," and motivated by "the desire of the spirit to realize a whole, which makes it seek in another being what it finds not in itself."[26] It would be naïve to take such words at face value, but it would also be unwarranted to assume they necessarily mask conscious or unconscious sexual desire. Speakers like Fuller were often themselves confused about their impulses, and the idiom of Platonic soul-completion provided a language in which ardent feelings could be expressed without having to be examined or acted upon. Whether or not these feelings were truly asexual in the most literal sense of nongenital, the invocation of Platonism could allow the speakers to think they were.

What Melville *was* conscious of finding in and through Hawthorne was the figurative "other" who drew forth and completed his fragmented self as dark characters in Melville's fiction had given promise of doing for his heroes since *Typee*. "Whence come you, Hawthorne?" the "ugly Socrates" passage begins: "By what right do you drink from the flagon of my life? And when I put it to my lips—lo, they are yours and not mine. I feel that the Godhead is broken up like the bread of the Supper, and that we are the pieces. Hence this infinite fraternity of feeling" (*Corr* 212). Freud appeals to a similar idea in *Beyond the Pleasure Principle* when he alludes to Aristophanes' myth as a metaphor for psychic reintegration: "Shall we follow the hint given us by the poet-philosopher, and venture upon the hypothesis that living substance at the time of its coming to life was torn apart into small particles, which have ever since endeavoured to reunite through the sexual instinct?"[27] Through one vocabulary or another, Christian mystery or Platonic myth, Melville is laboring to express his wonder at finding his ideal self-image reflected back to him from the pages of his letters to Hawthorne, then ratified by an appreciation of *Moby-Dick* so penetrating and sympathetic it might almost have been written by the author himself. "If our loves were perfectly accomplished, and each one returning to his primeval nature had his original true love," Aristophanes says, "then our race would be happy," by which he means rescued from the urgencies of seeking and harmoniously at rest (*Symposium* 34). Melville implies just such a harmony when he refers to the "sense of unspeakable security . . . in me this moment, on account of your having understood the book" (*Corr* 212). "It is a strange feeling," he adds: "no hopefulness in it, no despair. Content—that is it; and irresponsibility; but without licentious inclination" (*Corr* 212). Eros in this context is not a desire for sexual consummation but an impulse toward integration of being that drives Aristophanes' lovers and that Melville makes an attraction of preappointed souls: "The divine magnet is in you, and my magnet responds. Which is the biggest? A foolish question—they are *One*" (*Corr* 212).

Jonathan Lear sees Aristophanes' myth as directing psychic energies away "from any tendency to strive for the transcendent" toward a search for "human completion" in "the socio-political realm."[28] This is how Eros functions for Ishmael in "A Squeeze of the Hand," as he "lower[s], or at least shift[s], his conceit of attainable felicity" from "the intellect or the fancy" to the satisfactions (sexual and otherwise) of the human community (*MD* 416). In Melville's letters to Hawthorne, the intellect and the fancy—the spirit's quest for truth—comprise the very basis for community, or at least for an elite kind of male bonding. Rather than a social counterforce to aspiration, the (homo)erotic becomes its affective stimulus and reinforcing accompaniment. For once in Melville's life, the twin foci of his nature—"land" and "sea," senses and intellect, the ethico-political realm and the realm of metaphysics—are in full harmony as he fronts the present and imagines the spiritual journey ahead. "Ah! it's a long stage, and no inn in sight, and night coming, and the body cold," Melville writes Hawthorne: "But with you for a passenger, I am content and can be happy" (*Corr* 213).

In the bower scene by the Jordan in *Clarel* that Edwin H. Miller and others have read as an emotional projection of the Melville-Hawthorne relationship, Clarel silently implores Vine, "Give me thyself!" (*C* 2, 27: 70). What Melville implicitly asked of the actual Hawthorne seems rather to have been "Give me *my*self!" Having enlisted Hawthorne as a comrade in an adventure à deux, Melville transforms the prospective colloquy into an epistolary soliloquy, with Hawthorne as catalyst for and recipient of Melville's boundless self-enthusiasm: "I'll tell you what I should do. I should have a paper-mill established at one end of the house, and so have an endless riband of foolscap rolling in upon my desk; and upon that endless riband I should write a thousand—a million—billion thoughts, all under the form of a letter to you" (*Corr* 213).[29]

It was Melville's narcissistic delight in himself that gave his relationship to Hawthorne its special ardor and, with Hawthorne's departure from the Berkshires in late November 1851, its special devastation. There is no evidentiary basis for Edwin H. Miller's conjecture that Melville overstepped the bounds and at some point made what was intended or received as a homoerotic "'advance,'" a word even Miller chooses to render in quotation marks.[30] Given Hawthorne's reserve and almost abnormal fastidiousness on matters of touch, together with his uneasiness about sexuality of any sort other than heterosexual monogamy, Melville would have known better than to try. If he did transgress by word or deed, it is extremely unlikely that Hawthorne would have invited him to visit Concord in 1852 or found himself "on pretty much our former terms of sociability and confidence" when Melville stayed with him in Liverpool four years later.[31] Even in *Clarel* the intimacy Vine rejects in the bower scene is not a homosexual but a homosocial one—"the *soul's* caress," for which "the negatives of flesh" imply "*analogies* of non-cordialness in spirit" (*C* 2, 27: 125–28; my emphasis). Hawthorne had more than enough reasons to leave the Berkshires—he disliked the isolation and the climate; he missed the ocean; the little red cottage was too small for his family, soon to receive a third child; he quarreled with his landlords[32]—and when the opportunity to rent his sister-in law's house in West Newton presented itself, he seized it quickly, with no apparent change in his relationship to Melville. The probable truth of the friendship during their months together in the Berkshires is that "Hawthorne responded" to "Melville's reckless emotional attachment" with as much openness and "warmth" as his native reserve allowed but with considerably less than could satisfy Melville's accumulated need.[33] If an "estrangement" did occur—and like Walter E. Bezanson and others, I read "Monody" as an elegy for Hawthorne: "To have known him, to have loved him / After loneness long; / And then to be estranged in life, / And neither in the wrong" (*Poems* 319)—it was almost certainly one of gradual attenuation, undramatic and, as "Monody" suggests, with no fault on either side.[34]

Mourning and Melancholia in *Pierre*

To the degree that Hawthorne had become essential to Melville's ideal of himself as well as to his emotional life, his removal was felt as a profound deprivation second only to the loss of Melville's father years before, an event whose feeling of abandonment it rekindled. There is a ring of truth to Newton Arvin's conjecture that "a sense of having been somehow rejected, unreasonable and egoistic though it was, festered in Melville's consciousness."[35] Hawthorne's withdrawal (so it would have seemed to Melville) was like a defection or a death. And taking place amid a Berkshire landscape haunted with familial associations, it would have linked itself with the emotions and reversal of fortune consequent upon Allan Melvill's death in 1832. Already susceptible to remembrances of his father, Melville all but came upon him in spirit on July 7, 1851, when he "first detected [Allan's] pencil signature" in an edition of Robert Burton's *Anatomy of Melancholy* he chanced to purchase in a New York bookstore four years earlier. "Strange!" he mused; strange, too, that of all Allan Melvill's books, probably "sold at auction, at least twenty-five years ago,"[36] Melville should have found the inscription in Burton's *Anatomy*, a work he had cherished since his teenage years and whose title evoked feelings of "enduring grief and melancholy" left in him by Allan's death.[37] "Never again can such blights be made good," Melville has Redburn say of his own father's bankruptcy and death: "they strike in too deep, and leave such a scar that the air of paradise might not erase it" (*R* 11). Melville would return to the subject of father-loss in *Pierre*, close to the time Hawthorne left Lenox. "Tranced grief" he would call such "coffined" but still vital suffering, capable of reawakening at any moment in response to a prompting situation (*P* 286).

Long before Freud's classic essay "Mourning and Melancholia," Melville seems to have grasped the affinity and relational etiology between the mourner's chronic, unresolved grief and the depression of the melancholic with his sense, in Freud's words, of "being slighted, neglected, or disappointed" by a loved object he cannot abandon.[38] In his memoir of depression, *Darkness Visible*, William Styron remarks that "loss in all of its manifestations is the touchstone of depression" (Styron traces the "probable genesis" of his own suicidal crisis to the death of his mother when he was thirteen).[39] British psychologist John Bowlby argued the point exhaustively: the importance of "childhood experiences" in "predispos[ing] an individual towards a pathological response to loss."[40] Developing Freud's notion of ambivalence toward the lost object, Bowlby finds that a child "at risk of developing chronic mourning" will "almost always" have, on one side, "a model of his parents as above criticism and a complementary one of himself as a more or less worthless person," and, on the other side, a view of his parents "as grudging in their affection and attention and too often unavailable" and of himself as neglected, underappreciated, and justified in his resentments of them (Bowlby 234)—the Ishmael/Abraham syndrome. As the third of eight children, Melville had reason to feel neglected, particularly as he was outshone by his older, more aggressive, and outwardly more brilliant brother, Gansevoort, the favorite of both parents and the bearer of family ambitions as well as of the maternal surname. Herman was "an uncommon good Boy" but "more sedate" and "less bouyant [*sic*] in mind" than Gansevoort, Allan wrote in one of several such judgments.[41] It is a measure of the tenacity of Allan's undervaluation that even the achievements of his second son, such as proving "the best speaker in the introductory Department of the High School,"[42] came as a surprise to him. Nothing seems to have occurred in later years to revise the father's opinion, so that when Allan died in 1832 Herman was left not only with vastly reduced expectations but with no possibility of ever vindicating himself in his father's eyes.

The mourning theories of Freud and Bowlby help explain Melville's lifelong preoccupation with the quest for the father, both human and divine. Still more directly pertinent may be Heinz Kohut's account of narcissistic personality disorders. According to Kohut, a child responds to "the unavoidable shortcomings of maternal care . . . (a) by establishing a grandiose and exhibitionistic image of the self: the *grandiose self*; and (b) by giving over the previous perfection to an admired omnipotent (transitional) self-object: *the idealized parent imago*,"[43] to be replaced in time by the child's consolidating superego. "Under optimal circumstances," Kohut says, this process occurs gradually as the child discovers the idealized parent's imperfections and is able to wean himself or herself from the need for parental approval and develop an autonomous sense of self-worth (Kohut 45). If, however, "the child suffers the traumatic loss of the idealized object . . . or a traumatic disappointment in it," the "psyche remains fixated on the archaic self-object" and will experience "throughout life . . . an intense form of object hunger" leading it to seek "a union with the idealized object" as represented by various "present-day . . . replicas" (Kohut 45, 55).

In their different idioms, Freud, Bowlby, and Kohut are describing versions of the process by which adult crises of self-esteem build upon and reenact childhood traumas, as investments of the self are shattered by the loss of or rejection by a subsequent loved object. In Kohut's terms, the psychodynamic visibly at work in Melville's letters to Hawthorne through November 1851 is that of the grandiose self performing for and seeking the approval of an idealized parent imago. At once father, brother, and Platonic second self, Hawthorne gave Melville the assurance of being known and valued for what he took himself to be at his best. Correspondingly, the effect of his departure was to deflate Melville and plunge him into a state that might now be diagnosed as depression but for which the older term "melancholia," with its literary resonance and link with mourning, seems more appropriate. The melancholic, Freud speculated, has also lost a loved object (not necessarily by death), but unlike the mourner, whose grief is focused and readily comprehensible, the melancholic "knows *whom* he has lost but not *what* he has lost in him" (*MM* 246). Essentially, what he has lost is himself. The melancholic shares the mourner's profound dejection and reduced energy and affect but differs from the mourner in "an extraordinary diminution in his self-regard. . . . In mourning it is the world which has become poor and empty; in melancholia it is the ego itself" (*MM* 246).

Freud is wary of assigning a single explanation to a phenomenon so various and so rudimentarily understood; Bowlby, however, finds the experience of "feeling abandoned, unwanted and unlovable" to stem "in most forms of depressive disorder" from the sufferer's incapacity "to make and maintain affectional relationships," a failing he traces to the family history, which more often than with other children includes the loss of a parent (Bowlby 246, 247, 248). The sufferer is likely to feel he has disappointed his parents' expectations of him despite his efforts to please, and he is prone "to interpret any loss he may later suffer as yet another of his failures" to relate successfully to others (Bowlby 247). Adults vulnerable to this kind of "narcissistic injury" frequently experienced in childhood a "sudden, unexpected, intolerable disappointment" in or loss of an idealized parent prior to their development of stable structures of identity and value (Kohut 55). It is significant in this regard that Hershel Parker should begin his two-volume biography of Melville with a chapter titled "The Flight of the Patrician Wastrel and His Second Son," which opens with the eleven-year-old Herman helping his father pack up their house and slip away from his creditors at night.[44] Melville intimately witnessed the humiliation of his father; less than sixteen months later he would witness his father's death.

Hawthorne's departure from the Berkshires reawakened the trauma of Allan Melvill's death, not because Melville doubted Hawthorne's regard but because thriving in its felt presence, even through the substantial gaps in their letters and visits, he had become dependent on it for his *self*-regard. Two characteristics of Freudian melancholia are particularly relevant here: first, the proneness of the melancholic to blame himself for "the loss of the loved object" and to join in the other's real or imagined humiliation of him (Freud *MM* 251) and, second, the "remarkable . . . tendency [of melancholia] to change round into mania," its affective opposite (*MM* 253). The portrait of Melville in late 1851 given by granddaughter Eleanor Melville Metcalf shows a "sick man" of "driven and flagging energies" who struck neighbor Sarah Morewood as "'more quiet than usual,'" given to "'irreverent language,'" and writing "'under a state of morbid excitement which will soon injure his health.'"[45] The chronology of late 1851 is uncertain—when did Melville learn of Hawthorne's decision to leave the Berkshires? when did he begin *Pierre*? mid- to late October is a likely date for both events— but the febrile, half-diabolical tone of the opening books of *Pierre*, which Brian Higgins and Hershel Parker take for buoyant confidence,[46] seems rather the splenetic counterfeit of confidence, "a mixed state, in which," as psychiatrist Kay Redfield Jamison describes the phenomenon, "manic and depressive symptoms exist together."[47]

Desolated by Hawthorne's removal, Melville felt himself a monumental fool for having nourished illusions of intimacy. Freud notes that the melancholic, in responding to present loss, "extends his self-criticism back over his past" and "declares that he was never any better" (*MM* 246). So Melville may have believed when he looked back upon the development of mind on which he had progressively come to stake his life since *Mardi*. The long journey with "no inn in sight, and night coming, and the body cold" (*Corr* 213) seemed infinitely less alluring without Hawthorne beside him as companion and witness. It was one thing to boast of stepping from *Moby-Dick* to bigger fish, to "Krakens" (*Corr* 213), with a godlike listener empathetically at hand and quite another when the listener turned *deus absconditus* and one's words echoed mockingly in an empty room. *Pierre* is Melville's ironic deconstruction of the quest, embodied in a hero who at once invites identification with the author and serves as an object for the author's relentless unmasking of self-infatuated idealism. Like the Freudian melancholic, who, far from feeling shame about his imagined failures, displays an "insistent communicativeness which finds satisfaction in self-exposure" (*MM* 247), Melville turned against himself early in *Pierre* through the mocking self-reference of the Glendinning/Gansevoort parallels and the giddy delight his narrator takes in promising to topple Pierre from his "noble pedestal" (*P* 12) and strip him of all inward and outward complacencies.

In directing his formidable powers of analysis against a parodic fictionalization of his younger self, Melville was systematically uprooting his own familial, personal, intellectual, and vocational identity, apparently in response to a profound psychological shock. Was the shock that of discovering that Allan Melvill had an illegitimate daughter? This was the conjecture of Amy Puett Emmers and later of Henry A. Murray and two collaborators working from a letter from Thomas Melvill (Allan's brother) about a claim made against Allan's estate after his death. Judiciously weighing the evidence, Hershel Parker finds it inconclusive even apart from the related problems of how and when Melville might have heard such a story and how it might have affected him twenty years after Allan's death.[48] "A well-constituted individual refrains from blazoning aught amiss or calamitous in his family" (*BB* 55), Melville would write in *Billy Budd*. If Allan did have an illegitimate daughter, why did Melville choose to flaunt it in print? If not, why was he insinuatingly blackening Allan's name and "horrifying his mother and other close relatives"?[49] Perhaps Melville in the fall of 1851 was not "a well-constituted individual." In a letter to Sarah Morewood of mid-September he wrote of "certain silly thoughts and wayward speculations" that "the Fates have plunged me into" (*Corr* 206). Within several weeks these wayward speculations or others would evolve into *Pierre*, in F. O. Matthiessen's words "about the most desperate [book] in our literature."[50]

Matthiessen ascribes *Pierre* to the "surg[ing] up into Melville's mind" of material that "remains unconscious for most authors" and that tapped "Melville's pained awareness of an Oedipus-relation" (with which parent, Matthiessen does not say) and of "the latent homosexuality" he projected into the Pierre–Glen Stanly friendship.[51] Was the putative shock that catalyzed *Pierre* the shock of homoerotic self-recognition? In *Closet Writing/ Gay Reading*, James Creech contends it was when he takes Pierre's "I will write it, I will write it!" (*P* 273)—Pierre's enthusiast response to the discovery of incest-desire—as the author's own veiled declaration of coming out. Creech's argument owes much to two sources, Newton Arvin's theory of father-son incest ("Pierre's unconscious wish is to escape from Lucy and to preserve the incestuous bond with his father by uniting himself" with the father's self-proclaimed illegitimate daughter)[52] and John Seelye's suggestion that the Pierre-Isabel relationship draws upon Melville's "passionate feelings for Hawthorne," substituting one form of proscribed sexuality (incest) for another (homoeroticism).[53] Creech joins these threads in a "camp reading" of *Pierre* as the "transvested" story "of a man who forswears his fiancé [*sic*] and runs away to the city with his homosexual lover."[54]

Arvin and Creech are right to see the initial action of *Pierre* as the rejection of domesticity for an alliance with a darkly erotic being associated with the father, though it is important to note that Pierre is fascinated by Isabel *before* she tells him she is his father's child. Are Arvin and Creech also right to infer a fantasy of homosexual incest? And if so, what can this mean? Was Melville implying literal, genital incest or some form of emotional incest such as Phyllis Chesler suggests when she asks, apropos of the final plate of

William Blake's *Jerusalem*, "Do sons wish to mate with their fathers? Is the shame of abandonment by fathers so great the 'Oedipal dilemma' can only be 'resolved' through prohibited erotic means—and then only in a 'spiritual' sense which excludes woman entirely?"[55] Was it sexual consummation with the father or father-substitute that Melville sought with Hawthorne or was it the loving acknowledgment of worth withheld by the earthly father (Allan) and by the spiritual Father (God)? Was it both at once—the former as a means to and token of the latter? the exiled son reuniting with the exiling F/father through the vehicle of sexual consummation?

In *The Analysis of the Self* Kohut discusses the case of a Mr. A., whose history and condition bear notable resemblances to Melville's. Though intelligent and professionally accomplished, Mr A. was "forever in search of guidance and approval" from his "elders or superiors," whose praise was crucial to his self-esteem (Kohut 57). The immediate cause of his entering analysis was anxiety over homosexual fantasies extending back to his adolescence. These fantasies, Kohut came to believe, were only subordinately related to a wider tendency to depression that surfaced whenever Mr. A felt his seniors' indifference to him. Mr A.'s father, like Melville's, had been a successful businessman whose financial collapse was accompanied by "emotional and physical deterioration" and "hypochrondriacal complaints," witnessed intimately by his son at an impressionable age (Kohut 59). His mother, also like Melville's, had been an erratic caregiver whose fluctuations of attention and empathy caused him to overidealize the father imago and thereby expose himself to later traumatic injury in response to the father's humiliation.[56] Mr. A.'s homosexual fantasies, in Kohut's view, were "sexualizations" of his father imago—that is, by-products and "means for the discharge of intense narcissistic tensions" rather than symptoms of genuine incestuous desire or deep-seated homosexuality (Kohut 70). As the analysis proceeded, Kohut reports, these fantasies and their associated fears "disappeared almost entirely" (Kohut 70).

Was Melville like or unlike Mr. A? Did he harbor incestuous feelings toward his father that were displaced onto Hawthorne, as Arvin and Creech maintain, or did his feelings for Hawthorne involve the sexualization or quasi-sexualization of a narcissistic trauma asexual in itself? With respect to Melville the man, we can only speculate; with respect to *Pierre* as a literary text and the fictive site containing "the most evident traces of the interaction of Hawthorne and Melville,"[57] the weakness of Creech's argument is all that it leaves out: virtually the entire philosophical content of the book, which Creech dismisses as an "alibi" on Pierre's part and an obfuscation on Melville's (Creech 167). Arvin had also foundered on the difficulty of reconciling the book's sexual interest and presumptive roots in "the accumulation of emotional strains" dating back to Melville's childhood with its dominant concern with the "ambiguity of idealistic absolutism."[58] Arvin's response was the Freudian one of separating manifest content (intellectual and conscious) from latent content (sexual and unconscious), a division Creech replicates when he argues that "a literary text can wink at us about its homoerotic content without, as it were, knowing what it is doing" (Creech 113).

The indications are, however, that, through Book XIV at least ("The Journey and the Pamphlet") *Pierre* knows perfectly well what it is doing and that the distinction between manifest and latent, intellectual and erotic, is precisely what it sets out to contest: this is the terra incognita to which Melville's relationship with Hawthorne has led him. The "spiritual" in *Pierre* is not a mere superstructure of illusions reared up from the desires of the unconscious; spiritual drives in the form of impulses toward an enigmatic wonder-world in the self and the universe are *part* of the unconscious, entangled with other drives (the sexual included) but by no means reducible to them. For Pierre, who has "never known" grief (*P* 41) or been deeply "initiated into that darker, though truer aspect of things" (*P* 69), the mournfulness of Isabel's face unlocks depths in himself and discloses "one infinite, dumb, beseeching countenance of mystery, underlying all surfaces of visible time and space" (*P* 51–52), which previously "had seemed but too common and prosaic to him" (*P* 128). Incantatory words like "mournful," "mystical," "melancholy," "sadness," "anguish," and "grief," smokescreens within Creech's reading, invest Isabel with a transcendent woefulness reminiscent of *Mardi*'s heaven, an "extraordinary atmospheric spell" so interpenetratingly "physical and spiritual" (*P* 151) that one quality is barely distinguishable from the other. In *Moby-Dick* Ishmael's pursuit of "the ungraspable phantom of life" (*MD* 5) had been associated with the sea, the whale, and "one grand hooded phantom, like a snow hill in the air" (*MD* 7) In *Pierre* Isabel assumes the function of spiritual magnet as Pierre, seized by "the divine beauty and imploring sufferings of [her] face" (*P* 49), feels his sense of "the solid land of veritable reality . . . audaciously encroached upon by bannered armies of *hooded phantoms*, disembarking in his soul, as from flotillas of specter-boats" (*P* 49; my emphasis). Melville's "phantoms" have been relocated from the outer world to the mind of the hero and have taken on an aspect of compulsion. It is as though Melville suddenly realized the meaning and psychic origin of the dark Other he had been creating in book after book. What fascinates Pierre is not so much "the mournful person as the olive girl" as what she evokes in "his own soul. *There*, lurked the subtler secret" (*P* 51). Isabel is the epitome of what Milton R. Stern called the "lure" in Melville's writings, a figure or idea that directs the hero "toward God's ideal realm of other-world" but that at bottom is "an external objectification of the quester's own predisposition."[59] As Henry A. Murray put it, "the 'ungraspable phantom of life' is not in Isabel but in [Pierre]. He is Narcissus plunging to embrace his own image."[60]

I am not trying to explain away the eroticism and cryptic homoeroticism of *Pierre* but to understand it in its own fictive and psychobiographical context. Since Henry A. Murray's 1949 introduction to *Pierre*, it has been common to see Isabel as "the personification of Pierre's unconscious," particularly of his "aroused soul-image, or [Jungian] anima," which Murray goes on to give an atypically Freudian character.[61] On the Jungian side, Isabel points ahead to a fuller self to be realized through the ego's integration with "the as-yet-unformulated components" of the personality usually projected by a male upon a female but sometimes (as in Aristophanes' myth) upon another male; on the Freudian side, Isabel leads Pierre backward to "the child in him who felt unloved" and to "the grief and self-pity which have been bottled up."[62] Though Murray draws on two conflicting notions of the unconscious—as a reservoir of mature intellectual and creative possibilities (Jung); as a labyrinth of repressed childhood desires (Freud)—his eclecticism is apt, for the object of Melville's investigation in *Pierre* is precisely this relationship between the developmental and the fixational, the intellectual quest and its buried psychic determinants.

What does Melville mean by intertwining the drive toward individuation with the regressive pull of the archaic, and by representing both of these things in the alluring Janus-faced melancholy of Isabel? To pursue this question is to dive into the Melvillean self and speculate on "subtile causations" that "defy all analytical insight" (*P* 67). Through some process that can only be fitfully reconstructed, the sadness of father-loss to which *Redburn* testifies was transmuted beginning in Melville's teens into a proto-metaphysical stance at once defiant of God, hungry for God, and enamored of melancholy as an affective surrogate for the emotions of filial and religious devotion. Allusions to *Childe Harold's Pilgrimage* and Burton's *Anatomy of Melancholy* in "Fragments from a Writing Desk" (1839) suggest a literary acquaintance with melancholy that helped Melville cope with depression and blight by elevating sadness into a noble malaise. As Murray argued, the life and writings of Byron as mediated through Thomas Moore were instrumental in shaping the adolescent Melville who was father of the man.[63] From the similarities between Byron's situation and his own—a dead father, a "supremely bossy" mother,[64] a Calvinist heritage they could neither accept nor wholly discard, economic privation and social slights, sexual ambiguity—and from the glorious way in which Byron turned suffering and exile into dark heroism, Melville came to assimilate, on some level of consciousness, a nexus involving P/paternal abandonment, intellectual aspiration, pervasive *Weltschmerz*, an alternating sense of grandiosity and worthlessness, an open or insinuated eroticism (including homoeroticism), and a fixation on metaphysics as the idiom in which these combined things were played out. Through the medium of Byron, Melville converted narcissistic father-loss and father-hunger into God-loss and God-hunger, which later, as a writer, he came to embody in a series of mournfully dark anima figures through whom his hero affirms his identity as a noble sufferer and spiritual son of God.

One might term this process the homoeroticization of father-loss into quasi-religion. It was not unique to Melville. In his early journal written in college, Emerson, who himself lost his father in youth and was an ardent admirer of Byron, confides his fascination with a dark, brooding classmate aptly named Martin Gay. Emerson never spoke to Gay or seems to have attempted to; they only exchanged what Emerson described as piercing glances, as Clarel would with his imagined soul-brother, the dark Celio. Gay was not a distinct individual for Emerson so much as an externalization of the mysterious, romantic self Emerson wished himself to be but knew he was not. In fact, Emerson's idea of "Gay" preceded the actual encounter. "Before I ever saw him, I wished my *friend* to be different from any individual I had seen. I invested him with a solemn cast of mind, full of poetic feeling, . . . & possessing a vein of rich sober thought. When I saw —'s pale face & large eye, I instantly invested him with the complete character which my fancy had formed."[65] As a same-sex anima figure, Gay is an idealizing mirror for Emerson as he contemplates and imaginatively reaches out toward a fantasized self.

In homoerotic relationships like Emerson's with Gay or, more profoundly, Melville's with Hawthorne, the sexual element is part of a larger constellation of factors—psychological, intellectual, spiritual—of almost unanalyzable intricacy: the love that defies being named. In *Pierre*, Isabel becomes the object of that love. Darkly mournful, Isabel takes her place with earlier figures in Melville's writings as the representative of a larger, more exhilarating, God-infused world of suffering and knowledge, with the difference that Isabel is female, which allows the libidinal attraction of melancholy to surface as an explicit theme (brother/sister incest was a staple of Gothic and Byronic romance as well as a fact of Byron's actual life). John Seelye is right, I think, in associating Isabel with Hawthorne as a figure pointing away from the ordinariness of domesticity toward "the darkness and suffering of Truth."[66] If Pierre's early behavior reveals "a man whose unconscious is lying in wait for the first plausible opportunity to desert"[67] (Isabel providing the opportunity), a similar lurking receptivity might be ascribed to Melville on the eve of meeting Hawthorne— "Mr. Noble Melancholy," as Cornelius Mathews called him in his literary account of the Monument Mountain expedition that brought the two men together.[68] Though Melville sometimes "took comfort (and perhaps even inspiration) from domesticity,"[69] he could also, when writing, feel himself besieged by it. Ensconced now in a Berkshire farmhouse with his wife, two children, his mother, and three unmarried sisters, Melville must have felt, as Arvin says, "the smothering network of family relations and family responsibilities [pulled] tighter than ever about his head."[70] His visits, even his epistolary visits, to Hawthorne were a deliverance from this life and a reimmersion in the world of intellect and frank, genial conversation that was his greatest pleasure but that found no satisfying outlet in his life at Arrowhead. Other feelings may have surfaced as well: nostalgia for his bachelor days, with their youthful sexual opportunities aboard ship and in Polynesia; responsiveness to male beauty; the narcissist's yearning for an approving father and soul-brother; his fascination with dark, mysterious introverts; his effort to know, articulate, and ratify himself through dedication to his journey of mind. All of these things combined to draw him powerfully toward Hawthorne and away from the confining, if supportive, domesticity of his household.[71] Like his fictive heroes, Melville impulsively fled the land for the sea and, in a kind of emotional adultery, made his relationship with Hawthorne the identic center of his life even as the Pittsfield farmhouse remained its practical center.

Pierre's spiritual fortunes turn in the moment of "terrible self-revelation" (*P* 192) in which he realizes the erotic underpinnings of his devotion to Isabel. A comparably shattering self-revelation overtook Melville, I would suggest, as his feeling of bereftness at Hawthorne's departure made him aware that in some fashion, for reasons buried deeply in his life history, he had been "in love" with another man. Intimations of the crisis go back several months, as if Melville's emotions had already begun to make for uneasiness even as his intimacy with Hawthorne was at its height. Early in June 1851, he confided to Hawthorne that strange premonition of decay so crucial to an understanding of his self-conception and so prophetic of *Pierre*. Adapting the Romantic metaphor of growth as the unfolding of a plant from a principle contained in the seed, he characterized himself, not yet thirty-two and at the height of his imaginative powers, as having "come to the inmost leaf of the bulb" and "shortly" to "fall to the mould" (*Corr* 193). Perhaps Melville was simply exhausted by the imaginative strain of writing *Moby-Dick*, yet even as he "cooked" the "tail" of his book (*Corr* 196) he may already have been looking beyond or beneath Ahab to the psychic underpinnings of the quest that his heroic purposes required him to suppress. In *Pierre* he would write that no man ever arrives at "the Ultimate of Human Speculative Knowledge," there to "abide": "Sudden onsets of new truth will assail him, and overturn him as the Tartars did China; for there is no China wall that man can build in his soul, which stay permanently stay the irruptions of those barbarous hordes which Truth ever nourishes in the loins of her frozen, yet teeming North" (*P* 167). The image joins two literary sources: Emerson's phrase "a Chinese wall that any nimble Tartar can leap over" and Milton's description of the throng of fallen angels in *Paradise Lost* ("a multitude, like which the populous North / Pour'd never from her frozen loins").[72] The implication is that truth, formerly the hunted, has now become the hunter and turned upon the quester in the unwelcome revelation of something primitive, chaotic, and deeply subversive of the structures of the self.

The truth that overturned Melville I take to be his realization that the quest for a knowledge associated with otherworldly sadness and divinity was fueled by a F/father-hunger rooted in the child's need for love and approbation. Writing of Ahab's drive to "make converse" led Melville to investigate his own need for converse and to glimpse how his attachment to Hawthorne was somehow connected to it. It was not, however, until the euphoria of writing *Moby-Dick* waned and Melville, like Pierre after his Enceladus dream, "woke from that ideal horror to all his actual grief" (*P* 346) that he turned inward "to penetrate into [his] heart, and memory, and inmost life, and nature" (*P* 67) and began to excavate the foundations of his personality.[73] In a letter to Sarah Morewood from mid-September 1851, he spoke of "certain silly thoughts and wayward speculations" that "the Fates have plunged me into" (*Corr* 206). By late October or early November, the time he most likely began *Pierre*, Melville knew of Hawthorne's impending departure from the Berkshires,[74] and the shock of an abrupt termination to a relationship he had come to live in caused a heartsickness that, in the mind's analysis of its nature and sources, led to a "terrible self-revelation."

"Why this strife of the chase?" (*MD* 544) Ahab asks toward the end of *Moby-Dick*, thinking of the ordinary comforts of the land he forsook for the transcendent. In the fall of 1851 Melville was asking that question of himself. Reacting to the new wound of Hawthorne's departure as it reopened and compounded the old wound of his father's humiliation and death, he began to drop "his angle into the well of his childhood, to find what fish might be there" (*P* 284). Instead of a selfless aspiration toward God and truth, the quest now seemed obscurely grounded in his feelings toward his father and father-surrogates—the male love-objects that drew him toward an eroticized otherworld of "Gloom and Grief" (*P* 169) associated with the divine Father who had replaced the earthly one as his idealized parent imago. In his earlier writings Melville had taken this attraction to melancholy unquestioningly as the mark of intellectual depth and spiritual heroism; in *Pierre* he anatomizes it virtually as a narcissistic personality disorder. In his new mood, the values and commitments to which he had mortgaged his domestic life seemed tainted by unconscious compulsion. The "infinite fraternity of feeling" (*P* 212) he had felt in Hawthorne's presence now appeared to him a symptom of psychic dependence; even the quest itself, so far as he imagined it occurring under the gaze of an approving Parent, seemed to derive from a baffled father-love and father-resentment—the child's ambivalence writ large in the adult's mythopoesis. Reacting to the discovery of incest-desire, Pierre cries, "I will write it, I will write it!" (*P* 273); reacting to the uncovered tangle of feelings for which incest-desire was a literary symbol, Melville did write it:

> There is a dark, mad mystery in some human hearts, which, some-times, during the tyranny of a usurper mood, leads them to be all eagerness to cast off the most beloved bond, as a hindrance to the attainment of whatever transcendental object that usurper mood so tyrannically suggests. . . .
> Weary with the inevitable earth, the restless sailor breaks from every enfolding arm, and puts to sea in height of tempest that blows off shore. But in long night-watches at the antipodes, how heavily that ocean gloom lies in vast bales upon the deck; thinking that that very moment in his deserted hamlet-home the household sun is high, and many a sun-eyed maiden meridian as the sun. He curses Fate; himself he curses; his senseless madness, which is himself. For whoso once has known this sweet knowledge, and then fled it; in absence, to him is the avenging dream. (*P* 267)

The "avenging dream" is to *Pierre* what "The Lee Shore" is to *Moby-Dick*, but with a complete reversal of mood and idea. With the recognition of the trauma-based origins of his spiritual life—symbolized in Isabel, whose lineaments of grief seem to beckon Pierre onward to God, truth, and his own deepest self but whose fascination is sourced in her transgendered resemblance to the father—Melville recoiled against himself and his family with proselytic zeal. Allan Melvill was the special focus of his anger as undervaluing father, as stand-in for the current father-image, Hawthorne, who just deserted him, and as source or scapegoat for his present crisis of self-esteem. Bowlby notes that when a child has been divided in his attitude toward a lost parent—on the dominant side admiring the parent and blaming himself for failures in the relationship, on the subordinate side blaming the parent and feeling himself misunderstood or wronged—a "change of cognitive balance" may occur some time in later life in which "the individual's latent resentment breaks through and . . . he rebels."[75] Whether or not Allan Melvill had to Herman's knowledge an illegitimate child, the significant fact is that Melville chose to found his plot on the discrediting insinuation that he did. "I will no more have a father" (*P* 87) Pierre exclaims, as he replaces fidelity to an earthly father with allegiance to a divine one, symbolized in his devotion to Isabel. In some wordless sub-terranean fashion, Melville seems to have recognized that he himself had done the same years earlier when he came to terms with Allan's bankruptcy and death by supplanting him with the image of an idealized father-sur-rogate/quasi-lover/divinity, now crowningly realized in Hawthorne. To lose Hawthorne was to lose what had become the emotional prop of his self-definition and of his justification vis-à-vis his family for the domestic derelictions of his life. It was as if instead of being one of "God's posts" (*Corr* 195), Melville suddenly found himself what he would make Pierre—God's fool. The "hardest" lesson Pierre is brought to confront is the one Melville seems to have confronted as he set out to write his book: that the quester who has renounced common happiness for truth finds himself not only spurned by the social world, the mother (and Melville's own mother was always harshly critical of his failure to make a living as a writer), but "likewise despise[d]" by the gods, the father, who "own him not of their clan" (*P* 296).

From its own time through the present, *Pierre* has been called a morbid book. It may also be morbid in the clinical sense of arising from and illustrating what Kohut describes as the regressive phases of a narcissistic personality disorder, figured in the following diagram:

DIAGRAM 1

Development and regression in the realm of the grandiose self	*Development and regression in the realm of the omnipotent object*	
(1) Mature form of positive self-esteem; self-confidence.	(1) Mature form of admiration for others; ability for enthusiasm.	Normalcy
(2) Solipsistic claims for attention: stage of the grandiose self.	(2) Compelling need for merger with powerful object: stage of the idealized parent imago.	Narcissistic Personality Disorders
(3) Nuclei (fragments) of the grandiose self: hypochondria.	(3) Nuclei (fragments) of the idealized omnipotent object: disjointed mystical religious feelings; vague awe.	
(4) Delusional reconstitution of the grandiose self: cold paranoid grandiosity.	(4) Delusional reconstitution of the omnipotent object: the powerful persecutor, the influencing machine.	Psychosis

The solid arrow indicates the oscillations of the narcissistic configurations in the course of the psychoanalytic treatment of the narcissistic personality disorders (see Diagram 2 in Chapter 4); the dotted arrow indicates the direction of the process of cure in the analysis of these disorders. The alternatingly dotted and interrupted part of the long arrow indicates the still reversible depth of the regression toward psychosis; the interrupted part signifies that depth of the regression toward psychosis at which the psychotic regression has become irreversible.

(Kohut 9)

In their exhibitionism and drive toward an intimacy bordering on psychic merger, Melville's letters to Hawthorne through November 1851 belong to Kohut's phase (2). The opening books of *Pierre*, from the hero's first glimpse of Isabel's face to his utter bewitchment by her dark mystery, exemplify phase (3) with its "hypochrondria" and "disjointed mystical feelings; vague awe." The narrative tone of *Pierre*'s early books (manic melancholy) suggests authorial morbidity as well, though in a form that heightens rather than impairs Melville's capacity for analysis. Originating in the melancholia of object-loss, *Pierre* is not a mad book but a keenly insightful book about madness that projects a catastrophic version of the author's situation in the downward course of its hero toward dissolution. In its closing sections, Pierre oscillates wildly between belligerent grandiosity and masochistic self-abasement ("there was nothing he more spurned, than his own aspirations; nothing he more abhorred than the loftiest part of himself" [*P* 339]), accompanied by paranoid feelings of persecution by society and the fates. This is Kohut's phase (4), irreversible psychosis: Melville's prophecy of his own fate, perhaps, should he succumb to the feelings of anger, betrayal, and self-betrayal roiling within him, which the act of writing allows him to objectify and control. His affinities of background, character, and condition with Pierre allow him to psychoanalyze himself under the cover of fiction while his differences of knowledge and self-knowledge enable him to transfer his self-castigation onto his naïve hero and stage a purgational melodrama of overreaction, excess, and self-destruction.

Do the sexual themes of *Pierre* pertain to the melodrama of character Pierre or to the self-analysis of the author as well? To both, it seems to me, but with a perplexity on Melville's part that leaves their erotic significance unclear. Kohut observes that "the regressive psychic structures, the patient's perception of them, and his relationship to them, may become sexualized both in the psychoses [Pierre's condition] and in the narcissistic personality disorders [Melville's]. In the psychoses the sexualization may involve *not only the archaic grandiose self and the idealized parent imago . . . but also the restitutively built-up delusional replicas of these structures which form the content of the overt psychosis*" (Kohut 9–10). In some respect, Melville may have arrived at a comparable distinction between "psychotic" and "narcissist" in ascribing to Pierre a sexualization of Isabel as "delusional replica" that may only have problematically applied to himself in his relationship to Hawthorne. The child's desire for the father and, with his loss, for the father-surrogate, is profound and compelling, Melville realized, but he seems genuinely unsure whether the feelings attached to the father and transferred to the father-surrogate are literally sexual (as in Creech's supposition of the young Melville's homosexual incest fantasy) or transformational and metaphoric—the eroticization, years later, of emotions that were not sexual in the original relationship and *may* not, in any genital sense, be sexual in the present relationship enlisted to replace it. Melville knew that Hawthorne had touched his center of being, or helped *him* to touch it, as no other person had, and he sensed that his feeling of completion and self-worth under Hawthorne's eye was obscurely linked to a complex of emotional and spiritual needs rooted in his father's underappreciation of him and solidified by his father's premature death. Beyond that, and in the face of the fundamental mysteriousness of "the strongest and fieriest emotions of life" (*P* 67), everything was dim and uncertain. The terrible insight behind *Pierre* was not Melville's suspicion of homoeroticism, which could remain only a suspicion and seems not in any case to have been either a spur for self-redefinition or a ground for shame, but his recognition of the incontrovertible truth (so he saw it) that the entire enterprise of his intellectual and spiritual life was connected, in ways he could hardly begin to measure, with the unmet needs of the child. Written in the wake of Hawthorne's departure and with the "self-reproaches and self-revilings" of the melancholic (*MM* 244), *Pierre* was Melville's act of autopsychoanalyis, of self-exposure, of self-laceration, and, he may have hoped, of therapeutic cure.

After Great Pain

That *Pierre* was, in the end, an exorcism and partial cure was owing largely to the circumstance of Melville bottoming out and arriving at a center of indifference beyond love and devastation alike. Depression has its life cycle—this is its "only grudging favor," William Styron remarked[76]—and, as with Emerson in "Experience" or Whitman in "As I Ebb'd With the Ocean of Life," the very act of self-humiliation, of shedding illusion and taking one's stand on the bedrock of a diminished self, can become a source of strength and potential renewal. For the melancholic, even the gesture of self-punishment—joining with the world or the wounding love-object in heaping scorn upon oneself—may be cathartic. Pelted by "hate the Censor," the speaker in "Shelley's Vision" (from *Timoleon*) decides that he "too would pelt the pelted one." He casts a stone at his shadow,

> When lo, upon that sun-lit ground
> I saw the quivering phantom take
> The likeness of St. Stephen crowned:
> Then did self-reverence awake.
>
> (*Poems* 323)

In anatomizing his F/father-dependence, Melville may also have acted as his own psychotherapist. The conditions for resolving a narcissistic personality disorder, according to Kohut, are, first, "analytic penetration of the

defensive structures" of the self, resulting in "cognitive and affective mastery" of its "*primary defect*," and, second, the creation of reliable "compensatory structures" that allow for successful functioning.[77] In *Pierre* Melville
was both analyst and analysand. By probing Pierre's unconscious and being
"more frank with [him] than the best men are with themselves" (*P* 108),
Melville was able, through the displacements of plot and stylized characterization, to be frank with himself and explore the "defensive structures"—
rationalizations, denials, metonymic substitutions, fictions of the self—that
masked his affective dependencies and motivating needs. The "compensatory structures" emerged later, after the impulses that incited the book
expended themselves and left him in the narrative and tonal slackwater evidenced by most of the early New York sections (*P* Books XV, XVII-XX). As
he began to describe Pierre as a truth-telling author beset by the "Imbecility,
Ignorance, Blockheadedness, Self-Complacency, and the universal Bleared-
ness and Besottedness" around him (*P* 338–39), his aggression turned outward from himself and his family to the social world (including the reviewers of *Moby-Dick*), and, in bitter opposition to it, he came to rehabilitate
himself on new grounds. For a man who had inscribed a fantasy of converse
with the divine, it was humbling to acknowledge that, in addition to bearing
society's contempt, he must allow that the heavens were indifferent to his
trials. Yet unlike the "little soul-toddler Pierre" (*P* 296), Melville was able
to negotiate his exile by "wrest[ing] some comfort" from the myth of Enceladus (*P* 346)—namely, however tainted by clay the seeker's drive toward
the transcendent might be, it still raised him above the creatures of clay
who lived only for clay. When narrator Melville commends the thwarted,
aspiring Enceladus ("Wherefore whoso storms the sky gives best proof he
came from thither!" [*P* 347]), he is assuming the emptied role of vindicating
father-surrogate and royally commending himself.

Years later Melville would return to this theme in "Timoleon," whose
hero, "estranged" from the citizenry of Corinth through the "transcendent
deed" (*Poems* 308) of slaying of his tyrant-brother Timophanes, finds himself ignored by the silent gods and left "fatherless" (*Poems* 309). With time,
Timoleon comes to discover his justification in himself, independent of the
acclaim of Corinth (his mother and the social world) and the approval of
the gods. By the end of *Pierre* Melville had only a tentative grasp of this
idea, but it was enough to serve as the foundation for a new "compensatory
structure" on which to build an identity and further a career. The measure
of Melville's new stability is the character of his work after *Pierre*, which,
though "wary of the naked attack upon unspeakable truths,"[78] shows him
objectifying emotions and points of view that were formerly part of his psychological and ideational constitution. Instead of writing *from* melancholia,
Melville can now, in tales like "The Fiddler," "Bartleby, the Scrivener,"
"Cock-a-Doodle-Doo!," and "I and My Chimney" write seriocomically

about it. The contrast between "dark" and "bright" views of life, a matter of dire personal importance in *Pierre*, has become part of the writer's free exploration of the relationship between temperament, life history, and philosophical worldview as he works to consolidate his own renascent sense of how to live.

This is not to say that Melville put Hawthorne and homoeroticism behind him. If the tone of his 1852 letters can be trusted, Melville bore himself with the dejection of an abandoned lover resigned to his condition and adopting a stoic reserve but not above subtly parading his injury when occasion allowed. Hawthorne had not merely deserted him; he had bartered friendship for celebrity and advanced to better or at least worldlier things. Melville's letter declining Hawthorne's invitation to visit Concord during the summer of 1852 is notable for its tacit acknowledgment of the personal and professional distance between them. Hawthorne is now the triumphant author of *The Blithedale Romance*, and, borrowing a hint from the stationery on which he wrote (embossed with a crown and two garlands), Melville offers Hawthorne a crown: "Significant this. Pray, allow me to place it on your head in victorious token of your 'Blithedale' success" (*P* 230). Crowning Hawthorne meant one thing in "Hawthorne and His Mosses" when Melville himself was bestowing the acclaim and his own career seemed meteorically on the rise and quite another when Hawthorne was reveling in praise and *Pierre* had just been deposited for publication, its prospects dubious. (Melville knew what his audience could abide; he could not have been in his senses if he anticipated anything but disaster.) The vanquished's sigh of acquiescence breathes through Melville's final words on the subject: "Well, Hawthorne is a sweet flower; may it flourish in every hedge" (*P* 230). The letter is signed "H Melville" (*P* 231), in contrast to the "Herman" of nine months earlier (*P* 213). Melville will no longer presume on intimacy.

When Melville wrote Hawthorne again the following month, it was to call attention to the story of Agatha Hatch Robertson, which he had recently heard in Nantucket while traveling with his father-in-law, Judge Shaw. Melville probably did feel that the "great patience, & endurance, & resignedness" (*Corr* 234) of women like Agatha, herself an abandoned lover, was more naturally suited to Hawthorne's talent than to his own, but in hinting that the appeal of the story for him came from "very different considerations" than literary ones (*Corr* 234) he was inviting Hawthorne to look beyond the emotional reserve of his letter to the writer's unspoken feelings. "Perhaps this great interest of mine," he resumes, as if unwilling to let the subject drop, "may have been largely helped by some accidental circumstances or other; so that, possibly, to you the story may not seem to possess so much of pathos, & so much of depth" (Corr 234). In effect Melville is telling Hawthorne that he himself has private reason to be moved by a story of desertion and patient waiting as Hawthorne does not. In embellishing the account of Agatha that he later received from its teller (lawyer John H. Clifford) and that he now forwards to Hawthorne, Melville adds the picture of Agatha "feverishly expecting a letter" from Robertson, of her daily trek to the mail-post, and of the post eventually rotting away (*Corr* 236; for Clifford's narrative of Agatha, see *Corr* 621–24). Like the Freudian melancholic, Melville is obliquely "taking revenge" on the loved object by "tormenting" him with a display of his pain (*MM* 251).

A like impulse may underlie Melville's otherwise gratuitous postscript to the Agatha letter of October 25, 1852: "If you find any *sand* in this letter, regard it as so many sands of my life, which run out as I was writing it" (*Corr* 240). Kohut sees "pervasive feelings of emptiness and depression" as "indicative of the ego's depletion because it has to wall itself off against the unrealistic claims of an archaic grandiose self, or against the intense hunger for a powerful external supplier of self-esteem" (Kohut 16–17). Both conditions apply to Melville in 1852. Having formerly imagined himself filling "an endless riband of foolscap" with thoughts addressed to Hawthorne (*Corr* 213)—the grandiose self performing for the idealized self-object—Melville now feels on the brink of exhaustion and, with the melancholic's accusatory self-humiliation, he wants Hawthorne to know it. The two men met again in Concord on December 2, a visit Melville "greatly enjoyed," he wrote in acknowledgment, and from which he hoped, in an oddly formal phrasing, that Hawthorne had "reaped some corresponding pleasure" (*Corr* 242). The effusive, self-dramatizing persona of the 1851 letters has become laconic and guarded, not because his affection has diminished but because, wounded by casual neglect, he has learned to armor himself against further hurt.

The armor would be lifelong. "Monody" expresses no bitterness toward Hawthorne, only sadness and regret, and *Clarel*, though keenly analytic, even critical, in its treatment of Vine, is tonally remote. Nonetheless, when Julian Hawthorne visited him in 1883 to inquire about letters from his father, Melville replied "with agitation" that "if any such letters had existed, he had scrupulously destroyed them," and when Julian pressed further for "memories in him of the red-cottage days—red-letter days too for him—he merely shook his head," as if the entire subject were still too painful to recall.[79] As time, distance, and Hawthorne's death in 1864 made their relationship seem almost to belong to another life, Melville achieved a measure of emotive control—but only in art, not in life, and even in art he remained uncertain of the character of his feelings for Hawthorne.

In *Clarel*, where he "brood[s] privately and at length over the man who had meant most in his own life,"[80] the question is not whether the title character is homoerotic (he is) but what his homoeroticism signifies as an ambiguous middle ground between homosociality and homosexuality and to what extent his feelings are a projection of what Melville's had been. "Possessing

Ruth," Clarel is "still, in deeper part, / Unsatisfied" (C 3, 30: 48–49), and he imagines an intimacy, like David's with Jonathan, "passing the love of woman fond" (C, 3, 30: 152).[81] What Clarel seems to want, consciously at least, is a "solacement of mate" (C, 2, 2: 12) founded in the other's spiritual and intellectual strength, such as he might have with Vine or Celio but not, he feels, with the domestic Ruth and her mother, Agar, his models for womanhood. Moreover, virginal in temper as well as in body, Clarel requires a love free of the earthliness of sexuality, which woman, whose very appeal he regards as sexual, cannot provide:

> Can Eve be riven
> From sex, and disengaged retain
> Its charm? Think this—then may ye feign
> The perfumed rose may keep its bloom,
> Cut off from the sustenance of loam.
> But if Eve's charm be not supernal,
> Enduring not divine transplanting—
> Love kindled thence, is that eternal?
> Here, here's the hollow—here the haunting!
> Ah, love, ah wherefore thus unsure?
> Linked art thou—locked, with Self impure?
> (C 3, 31: 38–48)

Young and sexually squeamish with the hypersensitivity of the innocent, Clarel is not Melville as he was in 1851–52, much less at the time he wrote the poem, yet the issue remains of whether a manly love would also be entwined with fleshliness, Clarel's "Self impure." Here Melville returns to the central ambiguity of Platonic homoeroticism and of his own relationship to Hawthorne: is "Uranian" or "heavenly" love, as idealized male friendship is called by Pausanias in the *Symposium* (*Symposium* 22–23), higher than heterosexual love because exempt from carnality or is the language of heavenliness a (self-)deception meant to gild homosexual passion or, at the other extreme, to deny passion altogether from a Manichaean repugnance to the flesh?

Melville's answer in the poem is inconclusive: Clarel may be a Platonic idealist; he may be a latent homosexual; he may be a naïf or a fastidious ascetic; or in some proportion he may be and probably is all of these things, as when he responds to Derwent's enthusiasm for the "warm soft outline" of the Lyonese Jew with a "stare of incredulity" that may suggest prudish shock, unwelcome self-recognition, or both at once (C 4, 47: 19–12). The sexuality of *Clarel* exists in such lacunae, which readers fill as they like. In Clarel's dream in "The Prodigal" (C 4, 26), the Lyonese is set against the Franciscan monk Salvaterra, one symbolizing the fleshpots of the East, the other a desert asceticism, yet neither is as unambiguous as he seems. The attraction of the Lyonese may be homoerotic—the Russian, his cell-mate for a night, calls him "a juicy little fellow" (*C*, 4, 28: 102)—or, as a sensualist indifferent to Judea, he may be a stand-in for Ruth and the "Fruit of the tree of life" (*C*, 4, 47: 57), which supplant him in Clarel's thoughts as a counterforce to the transcendent—or is it as heterosexual displacement of the homosexual? On the other side, the St. Francis–like Salvaterra, "slender . . . and young / With curls that ringed [his] shaven crown," and "under quietude . . . Excitable" (*C* 4, 13: 15–16), may have erotic leanings of his own, as well as distinct homoerotic appeal. The boundary between the sexual and the spiritual in *Clarel* is bewilderingly indefinite and permeable. The blithesome Cypriote is a beguiling figure of "homoerotic fantasy,"[82] according to Edwin H. Miller, but so, in an opposing way, is the hair-shirted Syrian monk, whose otherworldliness radiates a kind of tumescence of the spirit that enthralls his listeners, the Melvillean Rolfe in particular, more completely than any physical magnetism could.

Melville was not alone in struggling with the indeterminacies of Uranian love. Under the aegis of Platonist Benjamin Jowett, as Linda Dowling has shown, students at Victorian Oxford developed a "counterdiscourse of spiritual procreancy" that celebrated an "innocent or asexual" homoeroticism as "superior to the blind urgencies" of both heterosexual reproduction and homosexual sodomy.[83] For students of Jowett like John Addington Symonds, however, the sublimations of Uranian love proved an unsatisfying, hypocritical compromise that denied the claims of the body in favor of a rarefied mysticism.[84] Looking back thirty years, Symonds berated Jowett for revealing, then morally curbing the truth that men like himself "had been blindly groping after"—that homosexuality was "once an admitted possibility" within a high civilization and a stimulus to its "great achievements and . . . arduous pursuit of truth."[85]

If Melville himself never reached such a conclusion, it was partly because his "characteristic gravity and reserve of manner,"[86] as Hawthorne called it, was accompanied by a strong inner check on behavior and, progressively, on attitude and emotion as well. In his poem "After the Pleasure Party" (from *Timoleon*) the astronomer-heroine Urania, lured by love from study of the heavens and subsequently betrayed, complains bitterly against the power of sex to usurp allegiances of mind and spirit. Urania, too, cites Aristophanes' myth of the divided self, but her words are in protest against the urgencies of Eros rather than in praise:

> For, Nature, in no shallow surge
> Against thee either sex may urge,
> Why has thou made us but in halves—
> Co-relatives? This makes us slaves.

If these co-relatives never meet
Self-hood itself seems incomplete.
And such the dicing of blind fate
Few matching halves here meet and mate.
What cosmic jest or Anarch blunder
The human integral clove asunder
And shied the fractions through life's gate?

(*Poems* 312–13)

Urania's tragedy is that she *has* met her other half but has been deserted by him, tasting completion, then losing it. Since her lover is male, the line "against thee either sex may urge" is oddly inapplicable to her situation, but it does apply to Melville's if one reads the poem with Robert K. Martin as Melville's projection of his relationship to Hawthorne.[87] "Urania" is the muse of astronomy, but the name also recalls the distinction Pausanias makes in the *Symposium* between the "'heavenly'" Aphrodite, daughter of Uranus and patron of an ennobling love between "intelligent" males, and the "'common'" Aphrodite, daughter of Zeus and goddess of those who seek the love "of the body rather than of the soul" (*Symposium* 22, 23). Urania's example confounds the supposed split, along with the illusory notion that the "intelligent" are lifted above physical passion. "One's sex asserts itself," Urania says ambiguously, referring either to one's sexual nature or to the sexual claims of one's own gender. Martin views the poem as "a defense of homosexuality" and a "warning against the consequences of repression,"[88] but the thrust of the poem is in quite the opposite direction. Urania's monologue is an outcry against the disturbances wrought by *any* form of sexuality, which "clogs the aspirant life" (*Poems* 314) and overwhelms self-conceived "heavenly" commitment to intellect and art.

To read "After the Pleasure Party" as figurative autobiography is not to imply that Melville lusted after and was rejected by Hawthorne but to suggest that in the wake of Hawthorne's departure from the Berkshires, Melville was overcome by feelings of emptiness and self-accusation that obliged him to ask what Hawthorne had meant to him and that left him questioning the erotic underpinnings of spiritual life for the next forty years. At first, like Urania, he felt angry and ashamed at the power of his emotions to overthrow him ("And kept I long heaven's watch for this?" [*Poems* 311]) and bitter at life for so constituting human nature. However, as Hawthorne retreated as a presence in his life, with no remotely comparable figure to replace him, the subject of homoeroticism increasingly became one for remembrance and, in *Clarel* and later in *Billy Budd, Sailor*, for absorbed and largely (though not entirely) disinterested exploration.

The speaker of "After the Pleasure Party" claims not to know if Urania ever forgot the party or "lived down the strain / Of turbulent heart and rebel brain" (*Poems* 313). Did Melville live down the turbulence? It is fitting that "After the Pleasure Party" immediately follows the title poem in *Timoleon*, for the two narratives are complementary recastings of *Pierre*. The first is concerned with transcendent virtue and the indifference of the remote father-gods, the second with psychosexual impulses that avenge themselves on the aspiring spirit for its slighting of the flesh. Melville has not forgotten the pleasure party, if so his months of intimacy with Hawthorne can be called, but neither does he seem to agonize over its legacy. Hawthorne is long dead, and the question of "sexual orientation" was not a critical one for the older Melville; wanting opportunity, incentive, boldness, and probably even desire to act upon his homoerotic feelings, he was content to relegate them to the closed episode of "Hawthorne" and channel his natural sensuousness into aesthetic appreciation and creation. Given his interest in art, history, and a refined epicureanism, it is surprising that the late Melville seems not to have read Walter Pater's work *The Renaissance*, which grew out of Oxford Platonism and whose synthesis of the intellectual, the spiritual, the aesthetic, and the ambiguously erotic might have spoken to matters that remained a tangle in him till the last.

7

An Arch between Two Lives: Melville and the Mediterranean, 1856–57

> I once thought there were no second acts in American lives.
>
> —F. Scott Fitzgerald, "My Lost City"

Bottoming Out

Perhaps nothing is more remarkable in Melville's remarkable career than that an intellectual and imaginative life lived intensely and, as it seemed, leading to a literary and philosophical cul-de-sac should have had its creative sequel, its "afterlife," to use John Updike's resonant term.[1] The gateway between Melville's lives was the trip he took to Europe and the Levant in 1856–57, a journey funded by his father-in-law, Judge Shaw, in response to family concern over physical and psychological ailments that seemed to threaten outright collapse. The Mediterranean had fascinated Melville as early as 1849, when, having barely set foot in England on a journey nominally to arrange for the English publication of *White-Jacket*, he sketched a plan for traveling across Europe for the Levant. "I am full (just now) of this glorious *Eastern* jaunt. Think of it! —Jerusalem & the Pyramids—Constantinople, the Egean, & old Athens!" (*J* 7). A light purse and "the cursed state of the copyright" (*J* 20) put an end to his daydream, and when he returned to England en route to the Holy Land seven years and five books later, he was an altered man. Meeting him in Liverpool, Hawthorne, now consul there, found him "much overshadowed since I saw him last,"[2] as well he might be, having lost his novelistic audience in *Pierre* and written himself into a labyrinth of skepticism in *The Confidence-Man*. "He said that he already felt much better than in America," Hawthorne reported, "but observed that he did not anticipate much pleasure in his rambles, for that the spirit of adventure is gone out of him."[3]

Hawthorne noted that Melville journeyed light, "taking only a carpet-bag to hold all his travelling-gear."[4] So Melville figuratively liked to imagine himself in his life journey, a "judicious, unincumbered" traveler responding to impressions of time and place (*Corr* 186). But Melville in 1856–57 was hardly a tabula rasa. He was laden with the weight of an irresolvable spiritual crisis and of a quarrel with his American audience, and therefore with contemporary America itself, that had led him to question man, society, and the course of history as for years he had been questioning God. He also bore with him patterns of thought and imagination, clusters of feeling, and tangles of psychic need, as well as the attitudes and images inscribed in his writing and now, reflexively, a part of himself. Before he ever saw it, Egypt evoked for him the pyramids, hieroglyphics, Sphinxes, and mummies he had used as symbols in *Moby-Dick* and *Pierre*; Palestine stood forth in the landscape of the Old Testament and the dread image of Jehovah; and Rome lived in the classics and in the acquaintance with ancient history he absorbed from his irregular education and ecletic reading, "brought to a focus," as Merton M. Sealts, Jr., said, by Gibbon's *Decline and Fall*.[5] Indeed, declension seems to have been the paradigm through which he approached and experienced the Mediterranean world just as it seemed the demonstrable truth of his life and literary career.

So far as Melville carried with him the accumulated baggage of a decade—it was just over ten years since he had published *Typee*—Dorothee Metlisky Finkelstein had reason to call his travels "an end, not a beginning." "In spite of the restoring effect on his health," Finkelstein argued, "the journey to the Mediterranean did not influence Melville's idea of man and God."[6] Of God, no, beyond the incalculably significant effect of making vivid to his senses and imagination what he already apprehended with his intellect; of man, yes, so far as the East presented him with a spectacle of polyglot humanity in the mass he had not witnessed to a comparable degree either in America or in Europe. But the great legacy of Melville's travels was to deepen and revise his idea of history and America's place in history, and consequently to modify his stance as a writer as he worked to redefine his subject matter and his relationship to his audience. Beyond "furnish[ing] him with probably the most important pool of experiences for his later career,"[7] as William H. Shurr remarked, the Orient dis-oriented Melville, then, with time, helped re-orient him as the lessons of the East joined with his readings of the 1860s and 1870s to recontextualize his age and nation within 2,500 years of Western civilization.

In the absence of surviving letters and of literary texts other than the lecture "Statues in Rome" (1857) and the poems (of uncertain date) grouped in *Timoleon* under the title "Fruit of Travel Long Ago," we know Melville at this nadir of his career chiefly through the journal he kept on his travels. Melville was not a habitual or an especially eloquent journalizer. The conditions for journal-keeping were not optimal through exhausting days of sightseeing and nights in shabby Mediterranean hotels, and Melville, in any case, seems to have preferred a spare, elliptical style to the artfulness of Hawthorne and Thoreau in their journals. Emerson called his journal a "Savings Bank" for intellectual coin, deposited with thought to later use.[8] Though more impromptu, and written in a crabbed handwriting that grew still worse under the combined irritants of bad weather, the hypos, and fleas, Melville's journal not only has interest as "a kind of barograph for the weather of his mind"[9] but also, like Emerson's, it would accumulate interest as he returned years later to draw upon it for *Clarel*. By the later 1850s travel writing on the Middle East had become an Anglo-American subgenre with set pieces of its own. The distinction of Melville's journal is its bluff idiosyncrasy and the insight it offers into the *process* of his thinking as observations begin to crystallize into attitudes, and attitudes into conscious ideas. Like the trip itself, the journal is thus transitional. What counts most as one reads it is the life and writing ahead of Melville, not the life and writing behind. For all its expressions of weariness and disillusion, the journal is the work of a man of immense curiosity who knows he has put one phase of life behind him and is moving forward, haltingly, toward another.

Governed by the logic of Melville's itinerary, the journal reads inadvertently like the working outline for a Melvillean quest narrative: a pilgrimage backward in time through layers of civilization to confront the existential core of life and explore the ways in which various cultures have responded to it. At times circumstances seemed to cooperate with the imagination to give the terse notations a mythic resonance. As if by a preordained irony, the steamer that carried Melville from Constantinople to Alexandria was the *Arcadia*, commanded by a Captain Orpheus. It was the only Arcadia Melville was to see in the Levant and the only Orpheus, but they sounded the controlling note of Attic glory long past. Flanked on one side by the dignity of classical Greece, on the other by his recollections of the freshness of Polynesia, the legendary Greek islands seemed to Melville "worn" and "meagre, like life after enthusiasm is gone" (*J* 72). "They look like the isles of absentees— / Gone whither?" he would later ask in the poem "The Archipelago" (*Poems* 335). Sometimes the classical absentees seemed all the more conspicuous for their descendants' physical presence. Visiting Syra, a bustling nautical hub, Melville was struck in the "New Town" by dock workers and merchants with "fine forms" and "noble faces" garbed with a quaint "theatrical" impracticality, as if trade were new and still an innocent pastime, and in the "Old Town" by "a union of [the] picturesque & poverty stricken," with some of the "old men look[ing] like Pericles reduced to a chiffonier" (*J* 53, 54).

This was Arcadian Greece for Melville, dessicated and crumbling in the background, colorful but spiritually diminished in the foreground, the lineaments of the past surviving chiefly as a reminder of descent. Physical ruin was everywhere, the casualty of neglect and plunder. In Salonica Melville noted a delapidated Roman arch and a mosque with pieces of ceiling mosaic raining down upon the floor; "brought away several" (*J* 55), he confessed, joining in the plunder himself. But it was the delapidation of Greek moral and imaginative life that seems to have troubled Melville most. In *Clarel* he would have his bookish divinity student ask the Smyrniote Glaucon about Homer, "a man / With Smyrna linked, born there, 'twas said" (*C* 2, 5: 14–15). "'Homer? Yes, I remember me; / Saw note-of-hand once with his name: / A fig for him, fig-dealer he, / The veriest old nobody'" (*C* 2, 5: 19–22). Against this backdrop of former grandeur was present-day teeming humanity—"an immense accumulation of the rags of all nations" (*J* 56), Melville described the crowd debarking from a Salonica steamer, a world-ship of the Middle East as the *Fidèle* in *The Confidence-Man* had been of the American West.

Constantinople was the modern Levant in extremis and the inmost circle of this alien, intriguing hell, if anything so conspicuously non-Christian can be called Dantesque. Ill-equipped to appreciate the intricacies of Islamic culture, Melville saw what any casual Western traveler would see—poverty, filth, and the ubiquitous "swarms," "crowds," and "mobs," dizzying in their numbers and babel of tongues and all but oblivious to the ruins of a monumental past.[10] "In these lofty arches, ivied & weatherbeaten, & still grand," he wrote of an ancient aqueduct, "the ghost of Rome seems to stride with disdain of the hovels of this part of Stamboul" (*J* 62). Melville rarely meditates at length, he simply notes; but his notations mount to significance as he marks the contrast between classical order and beauty and contemporary disrepair—statues with their "Heads broken off," masonry "Leaning over & frittered away" (*J* 59), a Roman arch with "fine sculpture" about the base and "miserable buildings of wood" around it (*J* 55). The chaos is replicated for Melville in the human world of the Bazaar, "a wilderness of traffic" where "You loose [*sic*] yourself & are bewildered & confounded with the labyrinth, the din, the barbaric confusion of the whole" (*J* 60). Throughout the *Journal*, whether in Constantinople, Syra, or Egypt, Melville struggles with an almost panicked sense of physical and psychological suffocation, trying repeatedly "to get *up* aloft," "see [his] way out," and "Soar out of the maze" (*J* 58). From the top of the Serasker Tower, "my God, what a view! Surpasses everything" (*J* 60), he exclaims, as though the antidotes to the oppressiveness of the East were oxygen and panoramic perspective.

The strangeness of Eastern culture might have been cause enough for anxiety—"Curious to stand amid these millions of fellow beings . . . with one consent rejecting much of our morality & all of our religion" (*J* 65)—but Melville had been tolerant of other peoples since his sailor days and was relatively free of the kind of racial and imperial mythmaking that

Edward W. Said in *Orientalism* associated with nineteenth-century Anglo-French colonialism. There were simply *too many* Easterners to be taken in; they dizzied Melville, used to the physical and spiritual space of republican America where the individual was paramount within the mild but containing rule of law (the white male individual, at any rate). What appalled Melville in Salonica and still more in Constantinople was not squalor so much as a clamorous disharmony (so it seemed to the outsider) amid the vestiges of toppled Roman order, as if it were structures alone, physical and civil *walls*, that kept humanity from lapsing into a Hobbesian state of nature, like the packs of wild dogs that roamed the streets "in bands like prairie wolves" (*J* 67). Revisiting the Serasker Tower, Melville remarked on "An immense column of the Saracenic order. Colossal Saracens. Saw drill of Turkish troops there. Disciplining the barbarians" (*J* 64). In the absence of an organizing cultural hegemony represented by the ancient column, unruly humanity was now regulated by a column of soldiers; the moral and civil checks of civilization had been replaced by anarchic instinct on one side (the barbarians) and vigilant suppression on the other (the Turkish troops).

Without necessarily intending meaning, Melville's language suggests an imagination at work joining impressions into what will later coalesce into ideas—specifically, into the theme of order that will counterbalance his commitment to natural rights and lend an increasingly skeptical cast to his reflections on politics. In *Battle-Pieces* the speaker of "The House-Top" goes aloft to survey and moralize upon the destructiveness of the New York draft riots of 1863, an anti-Federal, anti-Negro uprising of the Irish quelled, after arson, looting, and racial murder, by harsh military force: "All civil charms / And priestly spells which late held hearts in awe— / Fear-bound, subjected to a better sway / Than sway of self; these like a dream dissolve / And man rebounds whole eons back in nature" (*BP* 89). Melville is writing about the temporary abrogation of two forms of Roman rule (republican citizenship and Catholic authority), but his deeper subject is the impulse to violence sourced in human nature and contained for a time by law and convention but liable always to erupt anew.

The relationship between human nature and salutary or oppressive institutions would become a major concern in Melville's writing beginning with *Battle-Pieces*. Vere's "forms, measured forms" (*BB* 128), though hardly Melville's in substance or application, reflect his late belief that human beings need to be persuaded, charmed, or coerced by structures of *some* sort that can have no transcendent authority. The private root of his reaction against popular democracy was his disenchantment with his American audience, inscribed in *Pierre* and aggravated by the critical response to the book. The contribution of his Mediterranean experience was to confirm and conceptually broaden his feeling by displaying the problem of civilization upon a visible socio-historical canvas. In this, the Mediterranean served Melville as it had earlier served the painter Thomas Cole. Frustrated by the conditions of artistic production in America, Cole gradually came to question not the ideal of republican government but its actualization in 1820s–1830s America.[11] His five-painting series "The Course of Empire" was "conceived during his first visit to Italy in 1829–32,"[12] where his vocational and political anxieties coalesced in a cyclical view of history patterned upon Italian experience but taken to apply to all civilizations, America's included, or perhaps America's in particular. Cole never entirely lost his feeling of American exceptionalism if "exceptionalism" means a belief in the uniqueness and prototypal importance of the American experiment; yet America's status as "'the hope of the wise and the good'"[13] by no means exempted it in Cole's eyes from the perils of empire, the most dangerous of which came from its lurking susceptibility to corruption and tyranny.

Melville also saw America as "the world's fairest hope" ("Misgivings," *BP* 37), but drawing upon the example of Rome, as Cole had, he would frame the problem of America in *Battle-Pieces* within a vision of the precariousness of empire. The uncompleted iron dome of the Capitol is Melville's symbol of imperial ambition analogous to the classical buildings and monuments in Cole's painting "The Consummation of Empire." The denuded Greek islands, corresponding to Cole's fifth canvas, "Desolation," spoke to Melville of a level of civilization that *had been* but no longer *was*—a *memento mori* for millenarian America to ponder. Gibbon was an important source for Melville's reflections on empire, but the experience of moving physically among evidences of decline, especially as they answered to grievances about America related to his vocational decline, reinforced and helped pattern structures of feeling that would evolve into articulate thought. Cultures were not linear but cyclical, Melville saw in the Middle East—as, it seemed, were lives.

The juxtaposition of classical rubble and human rabble in Constantinople struck Melville as tangible proof of both the necessity and the impermanence of civilizing forms. The more ruinous sections of Cairo reinforced the lesson, but the striking "contiguity of desert & verdure, splendor & squalor, gloom & gayety" (*J* 74) also raised metaphysical questions of the sort Melville had explored through the opposition of sea and land in *Moby-Dick* and of mountain and plain in *Pierre*. Seen from a distance, the pyramids were "purple like mountains" (*J* 75), recalling the beckoning sterility of the purplish Titanic mountain's near Pierre's Saddle Meadows; up close, they were desert-colored, barren, and seemed ageless, coeval almost with Creation itself and belonging neither to nature nor to man (*J* 76). "Vast, indefinite, incomprehensible, and awful" (*J* 76), the pyramids struck Melville as an emanation of the spirit of Egyptian priestcraft, which, by way of Moses' immersion "in all the lore of the Egyptians" (*J* 75; see Acts 7:22), formatively influenced the Hebraic idea of Jehovah. A "Terrible mixture of the cunning and awful," Melville called this pyramid-"born" deity (J 75), voicing one strain of his lifelong attitude toward the Judeo-Christian God.

In contrast to the stark otherworldliness of the pyramids, areas of Cairo were a natural and human oasis, tropically lush:

> Avenues of acac[i]as & other trees. Shrubs. Seems country. No fences. The booth & cafes. Leapers, tumblers, jugglers, smokers, dancers, horses, swings, (with bells) sherbert, &c. Lovely at evening. In morning, golden sun through foliage. Soft luxurious splendor of mornings. Dewy. Paridise [*sic*] melted & poured into the air. Soft intoxication; no wonder these people never drink wine. (J 76–77)

In Cairo it was "hard to believe you are near the pyramids" (J 76), Melville reflected, yet the two stood juxtaposed almost as a diptych of Creation: "Line of desert & verdure, plain as line between good & evil. An instant collision of the two elements. A long billow of desert forever hovers as in act of breaking, upon the verdure of Egypt" (J 76). Oceanic desert and fertile land, the realm of divinity and the sensuous realm of humanity: so Melville inscribed the landscape of Egypt with the antimonies of *Moby-Dick* and *Pierre*. But which was "good" and which "evil"? Was the "soft luxuriousness" of Cairo a deliverance from the desert as place and cosmic symbol or an enervating evasion of it?

The possibility of a carnivalesque hedonism in the face of physical and metaphysical blight fascinated Melville and left him deeply ambivalent. "May one be gay upon the Encantadas?" (*PT* 130) he had recently asked of another blighted world, the Galapagos Islands. May one be gay living beside the pyramids, he now wondered of Cairo. Evidently one could. The whole city seemed to him "one booth and Bartholomew Fair—a grand masquerade of mortality" (J 73) with only its "multitudes of blind men—worst city in the world for them. . . . Too much light & no defence against it" (J 74) to serve as a reminder of the awfulness of unmediated truth; even the Sphinx turned its "back to the desert & face to verdure" (J 76). Melville would soon find another "masquerade of mortality" among the Neapolitans dwelling under the shadow of Vesuvius; "skaters on ice" (J 105) he called them with mingled appreciation and disdain. Some time later he would return to this theme in his poem "Naples in the Time of Bomba," asking whether the "careless pleasure" he saw in the citizenry was "mirth's true elation" or "a patched despair, / Bravery in tatters debonair, / True devil-may-care delapidation"[14]—Ishmael's "genial, desperado philosophy" (*MD* 226) but without philosophy. What he remarked of Naples—"The beauty of the place, in connection with its perilousness" (J 105)—might be said ontologically, he knew, of virtually any place. Could a life of epicurean delight be fashioned honestly from a confrontation with the terrifying rather than in studied avoidance of it? Or did modernity—as in the Greek islands, in Egypt, in Naples—characteristically involve a suppression of the tragic, the effect of which was to flatten and trivialize human life?

In even the barest of the journal entries Melville seems to be revolving moral and metaphysical questions about how to live. He had done so in the stories of 1853–56 and *The Confidence-Man*, but now it was under new provocations that gave the matter a broad cultural and historical reference to humanity at large. The Mediterranean took Melville out of himself, or rather it led him deeper into himself by way of extroverted yet personally charged speculation. On the issue of religious belief, Egypt awoke in him a kind of deconstructive historicism. From "the rude elements of the insignificant [i.e., unsignifying] thoughts that are in all men" (*J* 78) and the "diabolical landscapes" of Judea, the Egyptian priests and later the Jewish prophets shaped a "ghastly theology" (*J* 89), which events combined to establish in the West as hegemonic truth. Yet understanding the historical contingency of religion, as he imagined it, did not enable Melville to free himself from its sway. In its "unleavened nakedness of desolation" (*J* 83), the desert remained for him (like oceans, mountains, and prairies, but more intimately) a mirror of the divine. It was the substratal reality on which all viable philosophies had to rest and against which they needed to erect whatever human order, whatever "green myths,"[15] they could.

Clarel would begin his pilgrimage in Jerusalem, then venture out to the Judean wilderness to confront this stark reality. Melville's own journey through the Holy Land followed the opposite course, recapitulating biblical history as it traced a circuit through the lands of the Old Testament before substantially exploring Jerusalem, the climactic site of the New. John W. Davis argues that nineteenth-century Americans in Palestine brought with them a "special relationship with the lands of the Bible" predicated on their notion of "the United States as a new Israel."[16] So Melville might have felt had he visited the Holy Land in 1850. By 1856–57 he was closer to the position of William Bradford, who, perplexed by the ungodly direction his new Israel had taken, set out to learn Hebrew in his old age so that he might read the Old Testament in the original and see something of "the Laws and Oracles of God" with "mine owne eyes."[17] In a like fashion Melville's questers in *Clarel*—Celio, Nathan, Rolfe, Mortmain, Clarel himself—gravitate toward the Holy Land to find meaning in origins: "Some lurking thing [Rolfe] hoped to gain— / Slip quite behind the parrot-lore / Conventional, and——what attain?" (*C* 1, 31: 36–38).

Rolfe's question had probably been Melville's own, and while Melville found no more definite answer to it than Rolfe would, the mere fact of treading biblical ground may have brought matters to an emotional head. Except perhaps by climbing Mount Sinai, Melville could scarcely have come nearer

the Old Testament Jehovah than he did at the Dead Sea, a barren landscape
1,300 feet below sea level and the legendary site of God's destruction of
Sodom and Gomorrah. Yet most of Judea was blighted for Melville, as it
was for other travelers. "Palestine is desolate and unlovely," Mark Twain
observed: "And why should it be otherwise? Can the *curse* of the Deity beautify a land?"[18] Melville posed the opposite question: "Is the desolation of the
land the result of the fatal *embrace* of the Deity? Hapless are the favorites of
heaven" (*J* 91; my emphasis). Melville may have been thinking of the fate
of Pip in *Moby-Dick* or of Ishmael's "wilful travellers in Lapland" who gaze
themselves blind at the whiteness of Creation (*MD* 414, 195). His language,
in any case, is only rhetorical and emotive. Melville knows he is melodra-
matizing—personifying the impersonal—but postures like this in letters,
journal entries, reading marginalia, and books were a periodic necessity for
a temperament that needed to relieve the ongoing strains of agnosticism
through symbolic ventings of blasphemy. The entry follows upon a confession of utter disillusion—"No country will more quickly dissipate romantic
expectations than Palestine" (*J* 91)—and its effect is to convert despon-
dency into cathartic aggression. The mere fact of registering his protest
unburdens Melville temporarily of its weight and restores him to common
sense and proportion. Hunting God on his own "direful yet holy" ground
(*C* 2, 12: 89), Melville occasionally thrusts a rhetorical harpoon into him.
Having done so in Palestine, however, what could be left for him to do in
America? All subsequent verbal gestures would be anticlimactic.

Returning to Jerusalem, Melville shifted his attention from the Father
to the Son. He visited the Church of the Holy Sepulchre "almost every
day" (*J* 87), though repelled by the surrounding filth, the contempt of the
Turkish guards, the venality of the local peddlers, and the sectarian squab-
bling of the devout, and though finding the tomb itself "a sickening cheat"
(*J* 88). Melville's experience was common among Protestant travelers, who
"were almost always skeptical about holy shrines" and "almost always disappointed" if "they expected these shrines to evoke a religious response in
their hearts."[19] The greatest threat to Christian belief, as traveler J. Ross
Browne noted, was the historical site of Christendom itself.[20] Faced with
the discordance between ancient and modern Jerusalem, Mark Twain consigned the sacred Palestine of "poetry and tradition" to "dream-land."[21]
His friend Charles Dudley Warner was even tempted to wish that Jerusalem
had gone the way of Carthage so that "the modern pilgrim" might "choose
a seat upon a fallen wall or mossy rock, and reconstruct for himself the pageant of the past, and recall that Living Presence, undisturbed by the impertinences which belittle the name of religion."[22]

For Melville, the impertinences were not so easily dismissed, for they
belonged as much to historical reality as the reduced state of the Greek
islands belonged to reality. The "belittling" of Christianity across 1,900

years—its incongruence with actual life—spoke volumes about its practical meaning in the world of power, though not about its sublimity as an ideal. By returning daily to the Church of the Holy Sepulchre despite its tawdry affronts to faith, Melville fanned the spirit of belief even as he distanced himself from its trappings and creeds. His emotional tie to Christianity would never be broken—"The wrong / Of carpings never may undo / The nerves that clasp about the plea / Tingling with kinship through and through" (*C* 1, 3: 114–17) he would write of the Church in *Clarel*—but having fronted God (or God's absence) in the desert and having detached theological and institutional Christianity from the person of Jesus, he would increasingly make religion an inward matter whose sign was not doctrinal belief but an agnostic earnestness of questioning. In focusing on the futility of Melville's metaphysical speculations—"It is strange how he persists . . . in wandering to-and-fro over these deserts, as dismal and monotonous as the sand hills amid which we were sitting"[23]—Hawthorne missed what Melville came to regard as the essential point. One didn't need to *get* anywhere in terms of settled belief. To live honestly and courageously under the manifold pressures of spiritual life, resisting the temptation of spurious certainty on one side and of atheistic materialism, shallow sensualism, or simple indifference on the other, was itself to demonstrate one's fitness for immortality, whether or not immortality proved to be a fact.

Recovering

Newton Arvin spoke eloquently and wisely when he referred to "the slow, uncertain, irregular, and always precarious, but nonetheless effectual process of healing that took place in the years" after *The Confidence-Man* and that "somehow" had its "curative" beginning in Melville's trip to the Middle East.[24] The journal is too spotty and elliptical to serve as spiritual autobiography, but if there was anything like a bottoming out for Melville in the Holy Land, its symbolic sites would likely have been the Dead Sea and the Church of the Holy Sepulchre. Melville did not solve the problems of Jehovah and Jesus; instead, as his travels took him to Greece and Italy, he found new interests that weaned him away from them, for a time at least, and set him thinking in other directions.

If Palestine was the otherworld of religion, Greece and Italy were the humanistic world of classical and Renaissance culture. The museum pieces Melville viewed were discrete works of art to which he often had his own idiosyncratic responses, but they were also for him expressions and indices of a rich civilization to be set against modernity's. The topography of the Mediterranean also impressed him, especially as it seemed related to culture. Perhaps the most distinctive quality of the Greek landscape was that, though arid like Palestine's, it was not harsh and forbidding. Nor was the aura of ancient Greece, embodied for him in the Parthenon, darkened by a grim, supernatural theology, or by any serious theology at all. The relationship between Egypt and Greece was and still is a matter of contention,[25] but for amateurs like Melville the issues were sufficiently unsettled to leave ample room for speculation and philosophical bias. For traveler George William Curtis, whom Melville knew, "Greece fulfilled Egypt," adding grace and refinement to "the austere grandeur of simple natural forms," as a flower succeeds to foliage.[26] Curtis was sensitive to the alienness of Egyptian culture to Western sympathies (Curtis 214), his own included, but within his model of civilization taking its origin from nature and evolving organically from the rude to the harmonious, there was no room for antithetical cultures, only for ancestral ones (Curtis 61, 216). "The whole art [of Egypt], in its feeling and form, seems to symbolize foundation" for subsequent Western cultures (Curtis 218) yet not so as to transmit to them its "somber" theocentrism (Curtis 62). So conceived, Egypt became a severe but benignly remote progenitor for Curtis, who even professed to find "something essentially cheerful . . . in an Eyptian ruin" (Curtis 214).

To Melville, Greece was not the heir to Egypt and Palestine but the humanistic counterpoint, as Hellenism (mediated partly through Matthew Arnold) would later represent for him the counterpoint to Hebraism.[27] By contrast to his reflections on Egypt and the Holy Land, Melville's journal entries on Greece and Italy are little more than a list of things seen and done (a function largely of fatigue); nonetheless, his jottings on the Acropolis are revealing: "Parthenon elevated like cross of Constantine. Strange contrast of rugged rock with polished temple. At Stirling [in Scotland]— art & nature correspond. Not so at Acropolis" (J 99). Melville's reference is to the flaming cross in the sky seen by Constantine before the epochal battle at the Milvian Bridge. The Parthenon analogously seemed to Melville the marshaling symbol of a triumphant order, but one founded on neither the divine (Melville never regarded Greek religion seriously) nor the natural, but on artifice. Nature was "rugged," the polis "polished"; civilization was a human construct wrought in "contrast" to nature, even against nature.

When he came to poeticize his impressions of Greece and the Parthenon, perhaps as early as the late 1850s, Melville reversed himself and described an architecture at one with nature. As he wrote in "The Attic Landscape,"

> The clear-cut hills carved temples face,
> Respond, and share their cultural grace.
>
> 'Tis Art and Nature lodged together,
> Sister by sister, cheek to cheek;

Such Art, such Nature, and such weather
The All-in-All seems here a Greek
(*Poems* 332)

Melville has already begun to transform his travel experience and put it
to thematic use within an emerging theory of civic life. Greece in "The Attic
Landscape" is not the fount of Western civilization but a splendid exception
of natural, moral, and metaphysical harmony located at the beginnings of it.
Greek nature is only "such Nature," as Greek weather is "such weather"—a
felicitous local manifestation, not a normative reality. "The All-in-All" may
seem "here a Greek," but everywhere else in Melville's Western world it has
the Hebraic face of Jehovah, in Melville's theological moods, or the blank
face of desert, ocean, or prairie, in his naturalistic moods. With Greece as
with Egypt, Melville seems to have recognized how climate and topography
contributed to shape a culture and evoke its presiding gods, and how culture
in turn projected itself back upon the landscape until even natural forms
seemed to assume culture's aspect. In Greece this process made for clarity
and grace, in Egypt for otherworldly dread. Greece was admirable precisely
because (contra Curtis) it *wasn't* like Egypt or descended from it, yet the
conjunction of circumstances that generated Greek life and art also rendered them anomalous in their own age and inimitable by later ones. Melville's sense of Greece as a cultural and civic sui generis helps explain why
he never became a neo-Hellenist, as did so many of his alienated contemporaries. Like the German Romantics, Melville saw Greece as belonging to
the fortunate childhood of humanity, which Christianity ended, irrecover-
ably, by defining experience morally and spiritually in relation to eternal
life. Modern Americans could not be Greeks; modern Athenians could not
even be Greeks.

In another travel poem, "The Apparition" (published in *Timoleon* and not
to be confused with "The Apparition" of *Battle-Pieces*), Melville returns
to his analogy of the Parthenon to Constantine's cross. Both symbols are
elevated on a height, but the cross points upward to a "supernatural" source
and directs the "soul's allegiance there" (*Poems* 338), while the Parthenon "with other power appeal[s] down" to the city at its base. A "trophy
of Adam's best!" the Parthenon represents a triumph of the harmoniously
rational over the anarchic in nature, the remote or terrifying in God, and
the ungovernable in man. And yet as symbol of civic order, the Parthenon
has not endured except in the "long after-shine" of art. "The ancients of
the ideal description," Melville would write in "Statues in Rome," "instead
of trying to turn their impracticable chimeras, as does the modern dreamer,
into social and political prodigies, deposited them in great works of art,
which still live while states and constitutions have perished" (*PT* 409). But

the Greeks, as Melville knew, *had* tried to realize their ideal of civic life in institutional form. It was the permanence of their aesthetic success together with the *im*permanence of their political success—both symbolized by the Parthenon—that forcibly struck Melville in 1857, disposed as he was by his disaffections with America to deprecate the public world and transfer the ideal inwardly to thought and art.

Melville's education in classical civilization continued in Italy, rarely without some filtration through his quarrel with America. For Melville, as for Hawthorne in *The Marble Faun*, Rome was a layered city: classical Rome, historical Christian Rome, modern Rome. It was the first of these that counted most for Melville in the late winter of 1857 when he spent nearly a month in Rome, along with briefer stays in Naples, Florence, and other cities. By the time he reached Rome and Florence, his eyes were bothering him severely, and the museums, whose initial effect was "stunning" (*J* 108), eventually began to stun him in other ways. "'It's as bad as too much pain; it gets to be pain at last'" (*J* 114), he quoted a weary sightseer fresh (or stale) from the Uffizi. The bust of Tiberius in the Capitol Museum prompted him to moralize on the union of refinement and wickedness as the bust of Nero would prompt Hawthorne. But unlike Hawthorne, Melville typically viewed statuary and painting with an eye less to character than to history and the progress or regress of civilization. What impressed him most about ancient Rome was the scale of life its remains evidenced. Words like "massive" (*J* 106), "majestic" (*J* 106), "colossal" (*J* 107), "gigantic" (*J* 107), and "grandeur" (*J* 107) suggest an awe for the life-that-was, against which even Christian Rome (the exterior of St. Peter's) seemed a diminishment and contemporary Rome (the parade of "fashion & Rank" on the Pincian Hill) a "Preposterous posturing" (*J* 106).

Returning to America in May 1857, Melville would never again regard the New World provincially, nor would his faith in "that free unshackled, democratic spirit of Christianity in all things" (*PT* 248) he associated with America at its best go unchallenged by the pre-Christian, non-democratic glories he had seen in Egypt, Greece, and Italy. Against the meliorism he had maintained with increasing reservations through most of his fictive career, his travels intimated a cyclical or even a degenerative view of history. The Mediterranean had provoked him as perhaps nothing had done since his reading of Hawthorne and Carlyle during the composition of *Moby-Dick*, and in time even those literary enthusiasms would pale beside the perspective opened out for him by his travels. *Clarel* would become the repository for his mature thoughts about history, expressed dramatically by the poem's characters yet seldom without a large degree of authorial investment—in Rolfe's elegy for lost innocence, for example ("The rank world prospers; but alack! / Eden nor Athens shall come back:— / And what's become of

Arcady?" [*C* 2, 8: 35–37]), or in Ungar's scornful comparison of past and present ("the Phidian marbles prove / The graces of the Grecian prime" and "declare / A Magnanimity which our time / Would envy, were it great enough / To comprehend" [*C* 4, 10: 142–44, 146–49]).

Laocoön in Clarksville

Clarel would take a good part of a decade to write and, as Melville must have known at the time, was "eminently adapted for unpopularity" (*Corr* 483), if publishable at all. More immediately, a volume of ruminative travel sketches like Curtis's "Howadji" books might have seemed the natural vehicle for Melville to shape his impression into ideas and begin to reclaim his literary audience. Having determined, however, like Bartleby, that he was "not going to write any more at present,"[28] as his brother-in-law Lemuel Shaw reported, Melville decided to try his fortunes as a popular lecturer and began casting about for what he sardonically described to Curtis as "a good, earnest subject: *Daily progress of man toward a state of intellectual and moral perfection, as evidenced in the history of 5th Avenue & 5 Points*" (*Corr* 314)—"5 points" being a notorious New York slum.

"Progress" is indeed the subtext of his first season's lecture, "Statues in Rome," delivered "between November of 1857 and February of 1858 . . . in sixteen cities and towns,"[29] as Melville set out to sift both his impressions of classical art and the various metanarratives of history—progressive, cyclical, declensional—suggested by his travels. The Vatican and Capitol museums had impressed him as more than repositories for the treasures of the past; they were time capsules through which one might imaginatively reenter the life of former civilizations and measure it against the life of one's own. As a record of "ancient personages" (*PT* 400), the busts of emperors, statesmen, and philosophers showed the permanence of "the component parts of human character" (*PT* 402) and the continuity of human types; Julius Caesar, for example, resembled a railroad magnate or other modern-day corporate president (*PT* 401). "And yet," Melville adds, "there was about all the Romans a heroic tone peculiar to ancient life" (*PT* 402). Secular pride—a virtue before it was "swallowed . . . up" in the "humility" of Christian times—contributed largely to this "natural majesty" (*PT* 402), but so did the Romans' forthrightness about the essentials of human experience: "It was not at all unusual for them at their feasts to talk about the subject of death and other like mournful themes forbidden to modern ears at such scenes. Such topics were not considered irrelevant to the occasions" but "rather added to it a temperate zest" (*PT* 407). In "The Age of the Antonines" Melville would celebrate these Romans and contrast them to the philosophical and political palterers of his own time: "We sham, we shuffle while faith declines— / They were frank in the Age of the Anto-nines" (*Poems* 325). Melville had ample ground for his contempt for Ameri-can public life, but what fueled his vision of a nobler past were recollections of similar evenings of earnestness and geniality with Hawthorne or Evert Duyckinck, seldom to be repeated in the more than thirty years of life that remained to him.

On some level Melville understood that his ancient Rome was an ide-alization, but frustrated in his own life and despairing of 1850s America in its materialism, sentimentality, political mediocrity, and sectional strife, he had come to feel that the ideal was a firmer stay than the actual. Thus, among the classical statues favored by tourists he preferred the Apollo Bel-vedere in Rome to the Venus de Medici in Florence. "In the Venus the ideal and actual are blended," he argued in "Statues in Rome," "yet only repre-senting nature in her perfection, a fair woman startled by some intrusion when leaving the bath" (*PT* 403); in his journal he was more critical: "Not pleased with the Venus de Medici" (*J* 115). Unlike the Venus, which was "of the earth," the Apollo was "divine" (*PT* 403); it appealed to "that class of human aspirations of beauty and perfection that, according to Faith, cannot be truly gratified except in another world" (*PT* 402). Viewing the statues a year later, Hawthorne had similar reactions but put an altogether different valuation upon them: the Apollo was "ethereal and godlike" but too supernal to be apprehended steadily, while the earthliness of the Venus evoked "tenderness" and "affection" as if she were "all womankind in one."[30] It seems odd that the man whom Melville described as "need[ing] roast-beef, done rare" (*Corr* 181) should have shown a far livelier appre-ciation of the natural—or was it simply Hawthorne's preference for the domestically female (Venus' "tenderness" and "affection") and Melville's for the nobly male? Melville's aesthetic idealism resembles Schiller's in *Poems and Ballads* (acquired by Melville in 1849), which, according to Shir-ley M. Dettlaff, held that "art allows the mind to soar beyond the natural world to catch a glimpse of an ideal, a perfect one," in whose presence it feels "a sense of joy and well-being."[31] Such a position was atypical of Mel-ville until now, and it is a measure of the disenchantment with which he regarded his countrymen, the modern age, and all present or prospective beliefs that for a time in the late 1850s he should have embraced it as virtu-ally the only refuge available to him.

That Melville was indeed thinking historically becomes apparent when, with the Laocoön in mind, he ascribes "the ideal statuary of Rome" to "the doubt and the dark groping of speculation in that age when the old mythol-ogy was passing away and men's minds had not yet reposed in the new faith" (*PT* 403–4). In *Clarel* Rolfe would describe the latter days of the Roman republic as an age "'much like ours: doubt ran, / Faith flagged'" (*C* 1, 31: 237–38), as if history were an alternation of epochs of belief and epochs of skepticism. In "the sculpted monuments of the early Christians" Melville finds evidence of the renovating effect of belief, but the glow of the founders has not perpetuated itself in their latter-day descendants, as witnessed by "the somber mementoes of modern times" (*PT* 405). Even before he read Matthew Arnold in the early 1860s, Melville felt himself and his contemporaries "wandering between two worlds, one dead / The other powerless to be born."[32] The question Melville would ask in *Clarel* and was already beginning to frame in 1857 was whether the present age of doubt was an age of religious transition or of religious termination—and, if the latter, "what shapeless birth" (the words are Melville's own, not Yeats's or Henry Adams's [*C* 3, 5: 81]) would replace Jesus on the cross as the focus of human energies.

In "Statues in Rome" the shapeless birth is materialistic science—the Washington Patent Office as the "index" of the modern world as the Vatican Museum "is the index of the ancient" (*PT* 408). Established as points on a line like the "Virgin" and "dynamo" in *The Education of Henry Adams*, the Museum and the Patent Office become instruments for gauging the direction (or directionlessness) of history from Pericles' Athens to the newly elected Buchanan's America. "The world has taken a practical turn, and we boast much of our progress, of our energy, of our scientific achievements," Melville writes toward the close of the lecture: "Do all our modern triumphs equal those of the heroes and divinities that stand there silent, the incarnation of grandeur and of beauty?" (*PT* 408) Reluctant openly to play the Juvenalian satirist (he cites Juvenal and Dickens as examples of satire's past magnitude and present diminution [*PT* 408–9]), Melville leaves his indictment of the modern in the form of rhetorical questions. It will be left for Ungar in *Clarel* to sketch the full horror of the portending "Dark Ages of Democracy" (*C* 4, 21: 139):

> . . . Sequel may ensue,
> Indeed, whose germs one now may view:
> Myriads playing pygmy parts—
> Debased into equality:
> In glut of all material arts
> A civic barbarism may be:
> Man disennobled—brutalized
> By popular science—Atheized
> Into a smatterer———
> (*C* 4, 21: 125–33)

If "Statues in Rome" is "the product of a mind grown alien to mid-century America,"[33] it also reflects Melville's conflation of his sense of personal obsolescence with the marks of cultural decline he saw throughout the Mediterranean. The possibilities for a dignified private and civic life seemed everywhere to be contracting, and, like authors before him faced similarly with the betrayals of history and the vicissitudes of reputation, Melville retreated, temporarily, from the public world and relocated the ideal inwardly. By closing his lecture with Byron's lines from *Childe Harold's Pilgrimage*—"'While stands the Coliseum, Rome shall stand; / When falls the Coliseum, Rome shall fall; / And when Rome falls, the world'" (*PT* 409; *Childe Harold's Pilgrimage* IV, 1297-99)—he invoked a monument at once synonymous with Roman aesthetic achievement and notorious as a site of organized brutality. He was not eulogizing political Greece and Rome so much as he was celebrating its artists and visionaries who looked beyond the barbarities of even the most admirable times to an elevation of being unsusceptible of embodiment in any institutional state. "Governments have changed," he wrote: "empires have fallen; nations have passed away; but these mute marbles remain. . . . Can art, not life, make the ideal?" (*PT* 408).

Melville would outgrow his stance of aesthetic withdrawal as the Civil War recalled him to history and the possibilities for contemporary heroism, not least the heroism of the national bard who shaped the meaning of events even as he commemorated them. What he needed most in 1857 was an ideal to sustain him within an inhospitable American world. In this respect "Statues in Rome" served as a transitional private ideology. It may also have provided an aesthetic credo as he moved from the mimesis of fiction to experiments in the more crafted and rarefied art of poetry. In its chief capacity, as a marketplace performance, it was less successful, as it must have been so far as its theme of cultural degradation was utterly at odds with national assumptions, not to mention with the lecturer's tacit obligation to flatter his audience. Although most newspaper accounts commended "Statues in Rome" as a literary effort, they found it ill-adapted for a popular audience used to more contemporary themes and more energetic performances. Melville was bookish, it was said, and spoke in a "subdued tone" and with a "general want of animation."[35] In delivering such a lecture in such a style in places like Auburn, New York, Chillicothe, Ohio, and Clarksville, Tennessee, Melville seems almost to have been courting rejection, not so much from defiance or a perverse will to failure as from a desire to exemplify, for himself and others, a standard of intellectual seriousness and an undemonstrative dignity he must have known would meet with indifference. The demeanor audiences found so unsatisfying in Melville was precisely the one he admired in Roman statuary: "a tranquil, subdued air such as men have when under the influence of no passion" (*PT* 407). The reporter for the Cincinnati *Enquirer* paid grudging tribute to this stance when he remarked that Melville's delivery, though "monotonous and often indistinct," was "not devoid of impressiveness, which sometimes approached the ministerially solemn."[36]

Beyond the lecture platform Melville was hard-pressed to maintain his stoic reserve. Although his travels had the immediate effect of improving his spirits along with his health, the decade between his return from the Mediterranean and the death of his son Malcolm in 1867 was the most difficult in his life. Visiting him in Pittsfield in 1859, Williams College student John Gulick found him "a disappointed man, soured by criticism and disgusted with the civilized world and with our Christendom in general and in particular. The ancient dignity of Homeric times afforded the only state of humanity, individual or social, to which he could turn with any complacency."[37] Gulick seems almost to be describing "Statues in Rome," though neither he nor Melville could have imagined how the contempt for modernity inscribed in that lecture would develop, through the combined influences of the Civil War, Melville's reading, and the mellowing effects of family tragedy and age, into the ruminative historicism that distinguishes *Clarel* from *Moby-Dick*.

Melville's irascibility should never be forgotten in considering these years, if only because others were made to suffer for it. But neither should one forget what Melville, describing the Laocoön, called the "semblance of a great and powerful man writhing with the inevitable destiny which he cannot throw off" (*PT* 403). It may well have been with an image of himself in mind that Melville scored the lines on the Laocoön from Schiller's poem "The Ideal and the Actual Life": "Here, suffering's self is made divine, and shows / The brave resolve of the firm soul alone."[38] The words are like a prophecy of the stance Melville would cultivate through the remainder of his life. Scorned by society and "likewise despise[d]" by the gods, Pierre "the little soul-toddler" never develops beyond the orphan's initial "shriek" and "wail" (*P* 296) while Melville himself seems fixed in the grim defiance of Enceladus. By 1857 Melville had put both Pierre and Enceladus behind him, and though he would continue to fashion tormented questers and God-upbraiders like Celio in *Clarel*, he was no longer one himself, even in fantasy. He resided on earth now with the undramatic spiritual trials of the religionist manqué, among them the ones implied for him by Schiller's title: how to live for the ideal amid the actual; how to *be* a god without believing in God.

In March 1858, a month after Melville's final delivery of "Statues in Rome," Hawthorne recorded his own response to the Laocoön, which Melville would read in *Passages from the French and Italian Note-Books* in 1872: "The Laocoön, on this visit, impressed me not less than before; there was such a type of human beings struggling with an inexplicable trouble, and entangled in a complication which they can never free themselves from by their own efforts, and out of which Heaven will not help them."[39] The agony Hawthorne finds in the physical sufferings of the Laocoön recalls the agony he earlier ascribed to Melville in his metaphysical sufferings. In both cases, the victims are, as Schiller says, "alone" in their agony and "divine" in the "resolve" with which they bear it, as Hawthorne came very near to saying of Melville in his religious plight: "He has a very high and noble nature, and better worth immortality than most of us."[40] It was Melville's achievement that, with time, he learned to live in the coils that threatened to strangle him and, in the Mediterreanean-inspired *Clarel*, came to fashion a restrained but magisterial art out of what in 1856–57 was still a muffled cry of pain.

8

Uncivil Wars

... so that He said and not in grief either Who had made

them and so could know no more of grief than He could

of pride or hope: *Apparently they can learn nothing save*

through suffering, remember nothing save when underlined in

blood—

—William Faulkner, *Go Down, Moses*

So, then, Solidity's a crust—

—Melville, "The Apparition (A Retrospect)"

The Rhetoric of *Battle-Pieces*

As Melville's first published book of poetry and first published book of any kind since *The Confidence-Man* nine years earlier, *Battle-Pieces and Aspects of the War* (1866) marks a watershed in his career, much as the Civil War itself marks a watershed in American experience. Henry James invoked the terms in which antebellum Americans liked to think of the nation when he referred to "the broad morning sunshine" in which "the immense, uninterrupted material development of the young Republic" took place and to the "kind of superstitious faith" this progress engendered "in the grandeur of the country, its duration, its immunity from the usual troubles of earthly empires."[1] Among writers and intellectuals of the period, the faith James describes as "simple and uncritical" was in truth neither;[2] yet writers critical of the actualities of national life seldom doubted the ideal, and in taxing their countrymen with unworthiness or apostasy, they commonly bore witness to their own version of the popular belief "that the great American state," as James said, "was not as other human institutions are, that a special

Providence watched over it."[3] The Civil War, James added, put an end to American exceptionalism: "It introduced into the national consciousness a certain sense of proportion and relation, of the world being a more complicated place than it had hitherto seemed, the future more treacherous, success more difficult. . . . The good American, in days to come, will be a more critical person than his complacent and confident grandfather. He has eaten of the tree of knowledge."[4]

Battle-Pieces takes its thematic origin from America's fall into history and sets itself the task of re-creating the "good American" according to a pattern that promises spiritual redemption to the nation and vocational redemption to Melville, its neglected man of letters. The focus of the book is the "terrible historic tragedy of our time" (*BP* 202)—the Civil War—whose lesson for America was yet to be evolved; its deeper subject is the failure of an America given to shallow optimism and naïvely unaware of or resistant to the dark undercurrents of experience that Melville saw as the philosophical foundation for democracy. As a crisis that threatened to dissolve the American order, the Civil War was also potentially an occasion for national renewal. Like the Panic of 1837 as Emerson saw it or the Great Depression for Edmund Wilson and others, it was a historical breach that the writer might enter to help refound America upon a worthier ideal of character and citizenship than selfish individualism. The prose Supplement to *Battle-Pieces*, composed as an afterthought barely a month before the book's publication, is openly hortatory in its plea for Northern forbearance and national reconciliation, but its argument is only the overt political expression of an intention that operates throughout the volume.[5] Where the Supplement reasons with its audience on matters of policy, the poetry undertakes the subtler work of converting its readers to the prospect of a wise and magnanimous America reestablished on the bedrock of tragic vision. As a collection of occasional poems, *Battle-Pieces* is uneven; its achievement lies in the artfulness of design by which Melville, writing at a distance from events and mindful of the nation's future as much as of its recent past, patterns his readers' shared experience of the war into national myth and leads his audience, without proclaiming it, toward his own special vision of democracy.

"An author," Peter J. Rabinowitz remarked, "cannot make artistic decisions (conscious or unconconscious) without making some assumptions about his or her readers' knowledge and beliefs: their ethical values, their historical knowledge, their political attitudes, their familiarity with conventions."[6] The readers that *Battle-Pieces* implicitly assumes are Northern, white, middle-class, and chiefly male; educated but not necessarily intellectual; patriotic to the Union (overzealously at times) yet fundamentally humane; and "empowered" in the sense that they and their like will define the moral and political character of the postwar America-to-be.

This figure—the "inscribed reader"—is neither the "ideal reader" thoroughly versed in literary conventions and subtly responsive to the author's management of technique nor the "actual historical reader" who bought (or ignored) Melville's books. Rather, he or she is the authorial construct toward which the rhetoric of *Battle-Pieces* is perceptibly aimed: a conventional, moderately literary person of affairs, "ideal" enough to be counted upon to recognize a Miltonic allusion and respond appropriately to the large thematic effects of the text yet "actual" enough to support Melville in the enabling belief that he is addressing a sample of his countrymen whose minds and hearts may be open.

Whether or not Melville had a specific design upon his audience when he began assembling Civil War poems in April 1865 (his initial poetic efforts date back about a year),[7] the volume he published sixteen months later shows a scrupulous attention to the phases of the reader's engagement, though crucial to its effect is the appearance of having virtually no design at all. "I seem, in most of these verses, to have but placed a harp in the window, and noted the contrasted airs which wayward winds have played upon the strings" (*BP* 33) Melville announces in his brief prologue to the book, which indicates more properly how he wants his book to be read than how it was written and organized or what it means to achieve. "With few exceptions" (*BP* 33), he acknowledges, the poems were written after the fall of Richmond at the close of the war and therefore with the advantage of hindsight, yet the illusion the prologue would have us accept is one of memory untinctured by knowledge or instructional purpose. The reader is invited to relive the war through what disingenuously offers itself as but is not a spontaneous and nearly random poetic journal.

The volume begins starkly with an image of lost innocence—the shadow of John Brown's body darkening America's "green" ("The Portent," *BP* 35)—then widens out into three meditations set in the winter of 1860–61 ("Misgivings," "The Conflict of Convictions," "Apathy and Enthusiasm") that establish the interpretive frame for events. "The Portent" is written in the present tense from the perspective of 1859, but for the postwar reader looking backward through the conflict but also ahead to the uncertainties of reunification, its details function trebly as description, foreshadowing, and symbol of continued anxiety. "The cut . . . on the crown" and "the stabs [that] shall heal no more" (*BP* 35)—literal references to Brown's wounds—are signs of both the fratricidal war to come and the permanent injury suffered by the nation, while the cap covering Brown's face suggests a veiled future that even in Northern victory remains problematic.

In the poems that follow, images of natural cataclysm forbode civil disorder, as in Shakespeare's plays, but with the impending war figured as a fall: politically, as a lapse from confidence in America as a providentially guarded nation; philosophically, as an initiation into "Nature's dark side," unheeded in tranquil times and alien to Americans' "optimist-cheer" ("Misgivings," *BP* 37). Late in *Battle-Pieces* Melville will unite these themes and make a recognition of darkness the condition for a new national covenant, but at first, cautious before Americans' aversion to the tragic, he leaves their relationship ambiguous. When he writes in "Misgivings" of "The tempest bursting from the waste of Time / On the world's fairest hope linked with man's foulest crime" (*BP* 37), it is unclear whether the storm about to break upon America is (as abolitionists would have it) a consequence of the sin of slavery, in which case America might be restored to innocence once the evil is purged, or whether slavery is but the most flagrant example of humanity's historical liability to wickedness and folly, in which case innocence would be a dangerous illusion. We cannot even be sure of a causal relation between between "crime" and "tempest": the storms that shake societies may come independently of human behavior and be generated *by* as well as *from* "the waste of Time," a Shakespearean metaphor for dissolution that Melville's capital tends to objectify into a chaotic historical womb, if not a malignant, extraprovidential agent.[8]

The issues adumbrated in "Misgivings" are, first, whether evil is sociopolitical (and centered on slavery) or moral and existential (emanating from the human heart and/or some perverse irrationality in Creation) and, second, whether America is a covenanted nation with a special relationship to God or a nation among others subject to the common historical lot. The uncertainties of "Misgivings" are recast in Miltonic terms in "The Conflict of Convictions," in which Melville introduces two versions of the fall that will operate on different levels throughout *Battle-Pieces*, to be joined at the last. In the more explicit version, the fall is that of the rebel angels (the traitorous South), the moral lines of the ensuing action are clear, and the outcome, though externally in doubt, is assured in advance by the divinely backed potency of Right. This is the context in which Melville would have expected Northern readers to understand the war. Allusions to *Paradise Lost*, as Daniel Aaron notes, were common among Americans "who viewed secession as a 'foul conspiracy' against a God-ordained Union,"[9] especially in New England where the war reawakened an ancestral Puritan Manichaeanism that tended to regard threats to America unity as Satanic. To liken the Civil War to the war in heaven was to deny Southern claims about the legitimacy of secesssion founded on the "free consent" theory of government enunciated in the Declaration of Independence; it was also to identify the Union aim as, in James Russell Lowell's words, "the reëstablishment of order, the reaffirmation of national unity, and the settling once and for all whether there can be such a thing as a government without the right to use its power in self-defense."[10] Melville chose his framework advisedly. Despite his abhorrence of slavery as "the systematic degradation of man" (*BP* 197), it is Unionism, not abolition, that *Batttle-Pieces* presents as the

Northern cause, as indeed it was for most Northern moderates, Lincoln included, at least through the Emancipation Proclamation. But Unionism for Melville involved more than national interest; as for Lincoln, it "was based squarely on the idea of an American mission," which identified "the advance of democracy in the world" with "the preservation of the American nation" (Fredrickson 66).

Alongside this first Miltonic context, righteously sectional in application, "The Conflict of Convictions" sets another, the fall of man, which Melville associates macrohistorically with the collapse of American promise:

> On starry heights
> A bugle wails the long recall;
> Derision stirs the deep abyss
> Heaven's ominous silence over all.
> Return, return, O eager Hope,
> And face man's latter fall.
> (*BP* 37)

A prefatory note to the poem situates and helps gloss the lines:

The gloomy lull of the early part of the winter of 1860–1, seeming big with final disaster to our institutions, affected some minds that believed them to constitute one of the great hopes of mankind, much as the eclipse whioch came over the promise of the first French Revolution affected kindred natures, throwing them for the first time in doubts and misgivings universal. (*BP* 207)

Like most of his contemporaries, Melville saw America as "engaged in a profound national 'experiment,'" the subject of which was not so much the value of democratic institutions as the capacity of human beings to meet their requirements.[11] Within this context, "man's latter fall" was an eruption of violence and disorder that threatened not only to destroy the model American republic but to confute the Enlightenment/Romantic faith in human nature on which dreams of social regeneration had been made to rest. The impending war was thus a transnational as well as a specifically American event. It was also, Melville intimates, a metaphysical event (or nonevent), his phrase "Heaven's ominous silence over all" implying a divine laissez-faire in contrast to Northerners' certainty of providential support. "Man's latter fall" was political (the division of the American republic); it was ideological (the betrayal of democratic hopes for humanity); and it was philosophical (the revelation of an ethically impartial universe).

Since notions of an epochal lapse from innocence were unthinkable for victorious Northerners of 1865–66, Melville is careful to present "The

Conflict of Convictions" dramatically as a debate between two antiphonal voices, a hopeful but troubled idealist increasingly taxed to maintain his faith in God's America (and America's God) and a mocking skeptic who points to the persistence of evil and the flounderings of history. Like Starbuck in *Moby-Dick*, the idealist would look deep down and believe, even against the testimony of experience: "What if the gulfs their slimed foundations bare? / So deep must the stones be hurled / Whereon the throes of ages rear / The final empire and the happier world." There is irony even in the idealist's hope, for "empire"—a new imperial America supplanting the old republic, as happened with Rome—is precisely what Melville most fears. Its symbol in *Battle-Pieces* is the Capitol's unfinished iron dome:

> Power unanointed may come—
> Dominion (unsought by the free)
> And the Iron Dome,
> Stronger for stress and strain,
> Fling her huge shadow athwart the main;
> But the Founders' dream shall flee.
> Age after age shall be
> As age after age has been,
> (From man's changeless heart their way they win);
> And death be busy with all who strive—
> Death, with silent negative.
>
> (*BP* 40)

The statist nightmare Melville imagines may reflect his fear of the brutalization wrought by the war, less among the participants, perhaps, than among zealous civilians intent on punishing the defeated South, writers and intellectuals no less than politicians; but it may also have been fueled by the revival during the war of the "conservative idea of American nationality and patriotism," derived from Alexander Hamilton, which held "that America should be judged by the traditional standards of national power, not as the embodiment of an Enlightenment theory of government" (Fredrickson 149). Convinced by recent events that millennialist notions of America were in retreat, conservatives argued "with some effect that the ultimate America to which allegiance was due was not some vague and improbable democratic utopia but the organized and disciplined North that was going to war before their eyes" (Fredrickson 150). As a political Democrat, Melville would have had serious qualms about the direction he saw America taking during the war as the Republican administration suppressed civil rights, persecuted critics, and equated loyalty to its policies and conduct of the war with patriotism. "Power unanointed" is Melville's phrase for the authority of the Hamiltonian state unconsecrated by social idealism and devoted to the *Realpolitik* of national interest. The ugliness of the skeptic's jeer shows the withering effect of such cynicism, yet the skeptic's estimate of humanity and history rings truer within the poem than the God-reliant idealist's. The question Melville implicitly raises is the one later explored by progressives like V. L. Parrington: how to reconcile Right and Power, Jeffersonian idealism and Hamiltonian realism, American destiny and the teleological anarchy of history—in short, how to create a godly society in a world ungoverned by God. Speaking to and for its Northern readership, *Battle-Pieces* will sometimes cultivate a sectionalist rhetoric of divine favor, but the reading of history that presides over it is the one Melville proclaims in capital letters in "The Conflict of Convictions": "YEA AND NAY— / EACH HAS HIS SAY; / BUT GOD HE KEEPS THE MIDDLE WAY" (*BP* 40–41).

The poems that complete the introductory frame, "Apathy and Enthusiasm" and "The March into Virginia," are transitions to the battle-pieces themselves and announce the themes that will govern the body of the collection—the halting wisdom of age versus the enthusiasm of youth; the passage from innocence to experience; the sacrifice of a generation; the horrors of even a "just" war—while the enclosing issues of America's character and future are held in abeyance. "Apathy and Enthusiasm" divides itself stanzaically between an evocation of what Melville later called "the dolorous winter ere the war" (*C* 4, 5: 76) and the "elation" among the young that followed the bombardment of Fort Sumter and the Northern call to arms. In truth, the elders of the North were as exhilarated by the beginning of hostilities as their children; as George M. Fredrickson observes, "even the most cautious and conservative intellectuals were ready by 1860 to welcome a great national catastrophe" as an instrument for spiritual as well as civic renewal.[12] Melville distinguishes parents from children not as a matter of historical fact but in preparation for two voices, those of the "enthusiast" and the "meditator," that will coexist within the battle-pieces themselves. "All wars are boyish, and are fought by boys, / The champions and enthusiasts of the state," he writes in "The March into Virginia" (*BP* 43). The Civil War made boys out of many otherwise staid Northerners (Emerson, for one), and, unlike the children who grew to adulthood through the trial of battle, the parents remained all the more vociferous and ideological for their distance from the conflict. Melville's lines *"Grief to every graybeard / When young Indians lead the war"* ("Apathy and Enthusiasm," *BP* 42) apply to more than glory-seeking naïfs; they apply to fire-eaters on both sides, who lack the wisdom that comes with an immersion in the horrors of history.

With its picture of callow Northern youths filing "in Bacchic glee" toward Manassas (*BP* 44), "The March into Virginia" is a miniature of each soldier's experience of the war and a foreshadowing of the collective initiation that will prepare Americans for the difficult future ahead. For Northern intellectuals who approached the war as a purifying crusade, the carnage of early routs like Manassas and Ball's Bluff was acceptable, even perversely welcome, as a means (in Charles Eliot Norton's words) for "quicken[ing] our consciences and cleans[ing] our hearts."[13] To conservatives like Norton, "filial sacrifice . . . restored patriarchal power"[14] by promising an America purged by the bloodletting and redeemed from vulgar, materialistic ways but otherwise unchanged. In "The March into Virginia," the sacrifice is not to God but to Moloch—a useless, revolting sacrifice with no conscience-quickening capacity at all. The weight of the poem, however, is upon those who will survive and come to stamp their battle-tempered image upon an emergent America, possibly in ways unanticipated by and inimical to conservatives like Norton: "Turbid ardors and vain joys / Not barrenly abate— / Stimulants to the power mature, / Preparatives of fate" (*BP* 43). In place of the Northern rhetoric of national atonement—the sons dying to redeem the political order of the fathers—Melville's context for the battles ahead will be one of trial and growth through suffering, with the sons attaining to a tragic wisdom denied the innocent, righteous fathers.

The wealth of intimation in these opening poems casts doubt on William H. Shurr's contention that Melville began *Battle-Pieces* "as a patriotic citizen fully believing in the righteousness of the Northern cause"[15] and only later came to see in events the chronic moral and metaphysical evil he had explored in his fiction. From the outset Unionism and blackness control the volume as an overtone and insistent undertone. The rising awareness of a horror beyond the throes of war and civil dissolution belongs to the experience of the reader as it unfolds in response to the text, not to the putative development of the writer.

From "The March into Virginia" through "The Surrender at Appomattox," Melville orders his poems to follow the course of the war, but the subtler movement of *Battle-Pieces* resides in its orchestration of voices and points of view. With the sixth poem, "Lyon," the meditative speaker of the opening gives way to a new persona, the Laureate, who will celebrate Northern victories and heroes in a tone of righteous jubilation.[16] Through the Laureate, the Northern reader's spokesman in *Battle-Pieces*, Melville voices his moral and political support for the Union cause and his admiration for valor in any uniform, but he repeatedly qualifies the Laureate's assurance of divine favor toward the North by his juxtaposition of poems, by ironies within the celebratory poems themselves, by poems assigned to alternative speakers, by paired poems that contrast Northern and Southern attitudes toward the same event, and by recurrent motifs like the "night-fight," a circumstance exploited by Melville (as by Arnold in "Dover Beach") as an emblem of moral as well as military chaos. Thus a poem like "The Battle for the Mississippi," which compares the triumphant North to Israel delivered from the pharaoh, is placed between two elegies, "Shiloh" and "Malvern

Hill," that set the slaughter of holy war against the soothing but neutral backdrop of nature's renewal. The rhetoric of the poem is further undercut by the proximity of "Battle of Stone River, Tennessee. A View from Oxford Cloisters," in which a British speaker likens North and South not to Roundhead and Cavalier (the expected analogy) but to York and Lancaster, who "warred for Sway— / For Sway, but named the name of Right" (*BP* 80). In a similar fashion, the righteous exultation in "Gettysburg. The Check" ("When before the ark of our holy cause / Fell Dagon down" [*BP* 88]) and "Look-out Mountain" (in which "Wrong" and "Right" contend and "the Anarch" is routed [*BP* 91]) is tempered by the portrait of Northern lawlessness in the intervening poem, "The House-Top," a response to the mob violence of the New York draft riots of July 1863 that voices Melville's distrust of ungoverned human nature, Northern and Southern alike.

By far the greatest counterweight to the zeal of the Laureate is the presentation of suffering and death that runs through the collection. Though "Melville gives entire trust to the significance of the battles he recounts, and to the heroism of the combatants," as Richard Harter Fogle remarks,

> his great and brooding intelligence impels him to look on every side of his subject, and thus the epic strain in him in complicated and deepened by his painful awareness of lurking doom and the abyss he senses underneath life's surface; by his correspondingly keen *memoria mori*, his mindfulness of death; and by his sympathy with the anonymous mass of common soldiers, the "nameless followers" who fill the background of the portrait of war.[17]

The combination of epic and pathetic strains that Fogle ascribes to Melville's complexity of attitude should also be understood as purposively controlled. In poems like "The Battle for the Mississippi," "Gettysburg," and "The Armies of the Wilderness," a three-part pattern governs the arrangement of particulars: a biblically resonant prologue identifies the North with God's party, the South with Satan's; an agon marked by clamor and confusion dissolves the certainties of the prologue even as the Northern armies emerge victorious; and a closing eulogy, muted rather than triumphant, lingers on the dead and the mystery of death and reflects backward on the fight with an awed respect for human valor. The movement in each of the poems is from righteousness through tragic ambiguity to compassion, as the reader is engaged on the ground of ideological assurance and led through "the maze of war" ("The Armies of the Wilderness," *BP* 101) till the hubris of abstraction yields to a chastening fullness of knowledge.

The journey of the reader in these battle-pieces parallels the education of the young soldiers themselves from "The March into Virginia" through

"The College Colonel." The latter poem is based on the career of Massachusetts officer William Francis Bartlett, who was honored in Melville's Pittsfield on August 27, 1863, before returning to the war in which he had already lost a leg.[18] Unlike most of the heroes Melville eulogizes, Bartlett is left unnamed to widen the reference of the poem, and the Pittsfield event is transposed to 1864 to include Bartlett's later experience (a wound in the Battle of the Wilderness, a term of captivity in a Richmond prison) and render his distilled knowledge more complete. Ravaged by suffering but inwardly strengthened, the college colonel is a type of all those youths from Manassas onward whose lessons have been both physical and metaphysical, and who now stand as instructors to the uninitiated reader in the realities of war and life:

> It is not that a leg is lost,
> It is not that an arm is maimed,
> It is not that the fever has racked—
> Self he has long disclaimed.
>
> But all through the Seven Days' Fight,
> And deep in the Wilderness grim,
> And in the field-hospital tent,
> And Petersburg crater, and dim
> Lean brooding in Libby, there came—
> Ah heaven!—what *truth* to him.
>
> (*BP* 114)

The cumulative effect of the battle poems is outwardly to confirm Northern readers in their commitments while laying the groundwork for a tragic sense of experience that later poems will consolidate and direct toward a new political faith. Before that can be done, the passions of the war need to be allayed. Writing after the surrender, Melville understood that the threat to political reconciliation came less from the bitterness of the defeated South than from the retributive zeal of the victorious North. Two poems on Sherman's march through Georgia dramatize the problem, along with the difficulties Melville faced in trying to moderate Northern readers without alienating them. "The March to the Sea" metrically evokes the high-spiritedness of Sherman's troops as they sweep across the land, "brush[ing] the foe before them" and liberating slaves but also (as the poem unfolds) plundering the countryside and devastating crops in what Sherman understood as total war. Was this "Treason's retribution— / Necessity the plea?" the poem asks (*BP* 123), echoing *Paradise Lost*: "So spake the Fiend, and with necessity, / The Tyrant's plea, excus'd his devilish deeds."[19] The appeal to *Paradise Lost against* the North is striking. God had consigned the rebel angels to eternal damnation, as many Northerners wished figuratively to do with the South. Now, however, it is the flushed North, not the prostrate South, that is shown as playing the Satanic part. The allusion belongs to Melville's larger effort to refocus the Miltonic context from the fall in heaven to "man's latter fall" into common sin and tragic knowledge and to move from an Old Testament context of righteousness and divine wrath (as reflected, for example, in Julia Ward Howe's "Battle Hymn of the Republic") to a New Testament context of forgiveness. To show the legacy of wrath, Melville assigns the second Sherman poem, "The Frenzy in the Wake," to a defeated South Carolinian for whom humiliation and despair breed unrelenting hate. He underscores the theme by directing the reader to an endnote that contrasts the severity of Sherman with the generous restraint of Pompey during the Roman civil war, though even in the obscurity of an appendix he must write cautiously; Sherman was a hero in the North.

As the war draws toward a close and Northern sentiment grows shrill, Melville gives voice to the victors' hymns of celebration but distances himself from them through subtitles assigning the poems to the excesses of popular feeling ("The Fall of Richmond. The tidings received in the Northern Metropolis," "A Canticle: Significant of the national exaltation of enthusiasm at the close of the War," and "The Martyr. Indicative of the passion of the people on the 15th Day of April, 1865"). The last of these poems, on Lincoln, is notable for its point that those who wailed loudest at Lincoln's death were those least disposed to follow his example of "clemency and calm" ("The Martyr," *BP* 130). The death of Lincoln on Good Friday seemed an almost providentially ordained conclusion to what Northerners took as a providential plot, yet their association of Lincoln "the Forgiver" with Christ, Melville shows, served chiefly to reinforce hatred for the Southern Christ-killers and call forth an anti-Christ, "the Avenger" (*BP* 130), in themselves. "The Martyr" mourns for Lincoln and for the tragic inopportuneness of his death ("when with yearning he was filled / To redeem the evil-willed / and, though conqueror, be kind" [*BP* 130]), but its deepest emotion is anxiety about the future, as Northern vengefulness threatens to compromise the deeper lessons of the war and evoke a righteous authoritarianism:

> There is sobbing of the strong,
> And a pall upon the land;
> But the People in their weeping
> Bare the iron hand:
> Beware the People weeping
> When they bear the iron hand.
> (*BP* 130)

After "The Martyr," the persona of the Laureate disappears and a more sober, reflective voice, that of the Reconciler (heir to Lincoln), comes to govern the collection. For this final persona the issues that prompted the war have been settled at Appomattox or, with respect to the freed slaves, will be settled by legislation in the months and years ahead. The immediate challenge for America is reunification, which for Melville required distinguishing the Southern people from the Southern cause and beginning the process of healing, without which any political reintegration could only be mechanical and inwardly foredoomed. "Perish their Cause! but mark the men" (*BP* 132), Melville writes in "Rebel Color-bearers at Shiloh," pointedly subtitled "A plea against the vindictive cry raised by civilians shortly after the surrender at Appomattox." In "On the Slain Collegians" Melville reaches further to curb Northern righteousness by showing how "lavish hearts" on both sides "caught / The Maxims in [their] temples taught." "Warred one for Right, and one for Wrong?" he asks without recrimination: "So put it; but they both were young— / Each grape to his cluster clung. / All their elegies are sung" (*BP* 143). Singing the elegies—all of them—is Melville's purpose in the ensuing "Verses Inscriptive and Memorial," a solemn, if repetitive battlefield tour with sixteen stops, at each of which the poet sounds his literary version of "Taps." For readers assembled by the graves of sacrificed youth like Shakespeare's warring families around the bodies of Romeo and Juliet, the elegies are meant to induce a feeling of emotional closure, the Northern reader grieving not only with the Southerner but *for* the Southerner in a recognition of common sorrow that dissolves regional and political differences.

It remains for Melville to shape this communicated experience into knowledge—philosophical closure—and direct it toward America's future. He sets out to do this in two brief but powerful poems, "'The Coming Storm'" and "The Apparition. (A Retrospect.)." The former, subtitled "A Picture by S. R. Gifford, and owned by E. B., Included in the N. A. Exhibition, April 1865," originated in a series of coincidences uncannily fitted to join public history and private vision and help Melville synthesize his disparate thoughts on the war, on America, and on tragic experience generally. The painting was owned by Shakespearean actor Edwin Booth, brother of John Wilkes Booth, and exhibited the same month as Lincoln's assassination. Booth at the time had been playing Hamlet, one of four characters cited by Melville in "Hawthorne and His Mosses" as vehicles through which Shakespeare "craftily says, or sometimes insinuates" the "terrifically true" (*PT* 244). Stanton Garner suggests that Melville "may have known Gifford, . . . may have attended one of Booth's performances of *Hamlet*," and may even "have known Booth" himself."[20] Gifford's painting was of a storm cloud encroaching upon the placid landscape of a mountain lake, much as "Misgivings" had pictured the tempest of the war about to break upon America. The poem's wealth of allusion initially obscures its logic, even its subject—is it about the war? the assassination? Edwin Booth? Shakespeare?—but its final stanza unifies these elements by enclosing the calamities of Booth (personal tragedy) and the nation (collective tragedy) within the full, unillusioned measure of life found in Shakespeare. To one who "reaches Shakespeare's core," specific evils like the assassination or the war itself come as "no utter surprise" (*BP* 132), for they appear as surfacings of a darkness always lurkingly present in human affairs. The lesson is more pointedly drawn in "The Apparition":

> Convulsions came; and where the field
> Long slept in pastoral green,
> A goblin-mountain was upheaved
> (Sure the scared sense was all deceived),
> Marl-glen and slag-ravine.
>
> The unreserve of Ill was there,
> The clinkers in her last retreat;
> But, ere the eye could take it in,
> Or mind could comprehension win,
> It sunk!—and at our feet,
>
> So, then, Solidity's a crust—
> The core of fire below;
> All may go well for many a year,
> But who can think without a fear
> Of horrors that happen so?
>
> (*BP* 140–41)

With their imagery of massive natural forces intruding upon a pastoral calm, "'The Coming Storm'" and "The Apparition" are mirror images of "The Portent" and "Misgivings" that evolve the lesson intimated in the earlier poems. What seemed America's idyllic serenity—in James's words, its "immunity from the usual troubles of earthly empires"—is now shown to have been only a historical sleep.[21] The Civil War was not a divine judgment on America or a prelude to the millennium; it was a "terrible historic tragedy" (*BP* 202) of a kind that periodically convulses nations and peoples, and the restoration of outward peace is no more than a temporary stay against convulsions to come. To regard the Civil War in this macrohistorical light is not to remove it from time and context; it is to situate its particular horror within the larger sweep of events in the hope that tragedy's "terror and pity" (*BP* 202) may relieve Americans of their national innocence and instruct them in the moral and existential truths that other suffering peoples have come to know. The "terror" is at the appalling carnage of the war, at the human heart that could generate it, and at the indifferent processes of nature and history that could placidly absorb it. The "pity" is for human beings as victims of these inward and outward forces yet capable in their suffering of extraordinary feats of heroism, sacrifice, and endurance.

The aim of classical tragedy is catharsis, a purging of the emotions of pity and fear raised by the work; the aim of *Battle-Pieces* is persuasion, or the conversion of these emotions into knowledge and action. Melville concludes the main body of the volume with the allegory "America," which in recapitulating the moral phases of the conflict—sunny innocence, horror at the slaughter, horror at the deeper meaning of the slaughter, and chastened wisdom—shapes the confusion of events into an overarching national myth and clarifies the process of growth the poems have meant to occasion in the reader. The question in "America" is how the personified mother nation will deal with the philosophical legacy of the war: its revelation of "earth's foundation bare, / And Gorgon in her hidden place" (*BP* 146). This is the truth that leaves the survivors of Manassas "like to adamant" ("The March into Virginia," *BP* 44) and haunts the college colonel. The third stanza of the poem shows shrouded America in a nightmare-ridden sleep, but in the fourth stanza she breaks free from her "trance" into a higher life, just as her soldier-sons give promise of doing:

> At her feet a shivered yoke,
> And in her aspect turned to heaven
> No trace of passion or of strife—
> A clear calm look. It spake of pain,
> But such as purifies from stain—
> Sharp pangs that never come again—
> And triumph repressed by knowledge meet,
> Power dedicate, and hope grown wise,
> And youth matured for age's seat—
> Law on her brow and empire in her eyes.
>
> (*BP* 146)

With "America," the trauma and national reeducation that began with John Brown's hanging is complete, if only in the poet's idealizing imagination. Slavery has been abolished ("the shivered yoke") and the nation "purifie[d] from stain"; the North has learned forebearance through its trials ("triumph repressed by knowledge meet"); and the generation of participants shocked into truth has been readied to preside over a strengthened, more profound, and more humane America. "Man's latter fall," it now becomes clear, has not been into sin, which was always present, but into an *awareness* of personal and communal sin, the fruit of which is "Power dedicate," Melville's answer to the "Power unanointed" of "The Conflict

of Convictions." There can and should be no return to the illusory innocence of the antebellum republic, whose assumptions about human virtue and divine guidance have been exploded. American will come to be an
"empire," just as its citizens will become sober adults, but the character of
"empire" has shifted, for it now rests upon reasserted Law as tempered by
tragic wisdom. Melville has not relinquished the "Founders' dream" but
reestablished it on the sturdier basis of humanity's fallen but free nature and
its capacity to shape the future through knowledge and choice. If America,
lapsed from its pretensions to innocence and divine favor, can rise to meet
the turbid uncertainties of mature nationhood, its fall, Melville implies, will
have been a fortunate one.

After the Fall

The distinctiveness of Melville's vision in *Battle-Pieces* emerges sharply
when the volume is set against the unwritten "Federal Epic" whose argument Daniel Aaron draws from the collective consciousness of the North:

> In Heaven, a disgruntled Jehovah decides to rebuke the American
> people for whom He has hitherto felt (as Emerson put it) a "sneak-
> ing fondness." Repudiating the commandments of their fathers, they
> have become stiff-necked and luxury-loving. Northerners, besotted by
> materialism, forsake principles for profits and connive with Southern
> defenders of a cursed institution. After repeated warnings from above
> (financial panics, cholera epidemics, civil strife) God finally speaks
> through the pens and voices of His prophets. Harriet Beecher Stowe
> sermonizes under divine dictation; Garrison thunders; John Brown
> is martyred by the Harlot South. Around his gibbet gather principals
> of the cast—among them Lee, Jackson, Stuart, and Booth—who take
> major parts in the drama to come. God blasts the nation with "fratri-
> cidal strife," but solicitous always, sends His servant Abraham to pre-
> side over its redemption. Lincoln frustrates the Satanic plotters of the
> South and preserves the Union just before God translates the Illinois
> Savior on that crucifixion day.[22]

In its main lines Aaron's "Federal Epic" follows the pattern of the American Jeremiad, the Puritan-bequeathed ritual of communal reaffirmation in
which the speaker, assuming God's special covenant with the American people, berates them for their apostasy from the ideals of the founders, prophesies or moralizes upon a divine chastisement, and exhorts his audience
to return to the virtues of the ancestors and resume the work of personal
and collective salvation with an eye toward the millennium.[23] Within the

framework of the national covenant, the Civil War seemed at once a scourge inflicted by God and a purifying crusade intended to restore the nation to divine favor and confirm its status as the vanguard for worldwide political reformation. The role of calamity was thus instructive: to redirect America toward a future that promised the progressive fulfillment of ideals from the past, the sufficiency of which were deemed self-evident.[24]

The thrust of *Battle-Pieces* is counter-Jeremiadic: to reconsecrate America's political mission (which Melville never doubts) on the secular basis of exemplary wisdom, generosity, and metaphysical realism. Not Providence but the enlightened will acting in and upon history gives promise of the millennium (figuratively understood), and enlightenment begins neither in pious optimism nor in romantic benevolism but in a recognition of the experiential facts that confute both, God's aloofness from history and humanity's capacity for evil. In its historical contingency, Melville implies, America is like all other nations. Its special destiny lies in what its democratic traditions of innovation and social idealism may allow its people to become and achieve, provided they assimilate the humanizing lessons of the war. The model of character that *Battle-Pieces* projects is not a post-bellum translation of the virtues of the Founders. The "good Americans" of future days will differ from their forebears because they have "eaten of the tree of knowledge." Their exemplariness will consist in their reaffirmation of American civil ideals but on the solid and newly discovered foundation of tragic naturalism.

It is telling that *Battle-Pieces'* advocate for this new America should not be a victorious Northerner but a defeated Southerner, Robert E. Lee. In "The Irony of Southern History," written two decades before the American experience in Vietnam, C. Vann Woodward pointed out the anomalousness of "the American legend of success and victory, a legend that is not shared by any other people of the civilized world" and that Woodward saw as having "isolated America, . . . rather dangerously, from the common experience of the rest of mankind, all the great peoples of which have without exception known the bitter taste of defeat and humiliation."[25] Melville would have agreed, with the qualification that it was not defeat so much as collective tragedy that deepened a nation. In "Lee in the Capitol" he departs from fact and has his tragic Southerner take the "worthier part" and break his cold silence to help save "the flushed North from her own victory"(*BP* 190). Lee's practical advice—that Northern retribution can only "prolong the evil day" and "infix the hate" *BP* 192)—reflects Melville's own Lincolnesque position in the post-Appomattox poems and in the carefully modulated argument of the prose Supplement, soon to follow. Beyond that, Melville has Lee offer what amounts to a one-sentence handbook for the rulers of the America-to-be: "Where various hazards meet the eyes, / To elect in magnanimity is wise" (*BP* 191).

Lee is respectfully heard by the legislators, but he is not heeded—"His earnestness unforeseen / Moved, but not swayed their former mien" (*BP* 193)—as Melville probably knew he would not be heeded: "Historic reveries their lesson lent, / The Past her shadow through the Future sent" (*BP* 193). For all the instructiveness of its tragedies, is humanity doomed to repeat the folly of the past? The poem tries to argue not: "Instinct disowns each darkening prophecy: / Faith in America never dies; / Heaven shall the end fulfill. / We march with Providence cheery still" (*BP* 193). The poem's "turnabout" is "strange," not only because "instinct" seems a "lame substitute . . . for logic,"[26] as Hennig Cohen remarked, but because Providence has been consistently portrayed as indifferent to the fate of nations. The appeal from human to divine agency is a measure of how deeply, beneath its rhetoric of political self-determination, *Battle-Pieces* is skeptical of humanity's power to "elect in magnanimity," and of how desperately it wants to resist that skepticism. More than a year after the surrender, the most that Melville can do as he looks around and ahead is relate the precariousness of the national situation to the precariousness of life in general, as if walking on the crust of solidity were an art that individuals and nations must learn to master:

> Why is not the cessation of war now at length attended with the settled calm of peace? Wherefore in a clear blue sky do we still turn our eyes toward the South, as the Neapolitan, months after the eruption, turns his toward Vesuvius? Do we dread lest the repose may be deceptive? In the recent convulsion has the crater but shifted? Let us revere that sacred uncertainty which forever impends over men and nations. (*BP* 200)

Revering a sacred uncertainty is a far cry from "march[ing] with Providence cheery still," but it is truer to the vision of postlapsarian life that *Battle-Pieces* dramatizes and exists partly to instill in its readers. Historical and ontological contingency is Melville's basis for the new civil religion that must supplant the exploded idea of a national covenant. This is a brave thought, unmatched in the writing of any of his contemporaries, and brave even in the early twenty-first century in light of the neocovenantal righteousness that has again come to guide or verbally gild national policy.[27] Melville's note of pessimism comes from a feeling that his project is doomed in advance, whether intrinsically because it demands too much of human nature or historically because the generation currently in power is of a lesser breed than the Founders. "Noble was the gesture into which patriotic passion surprised the people in a utilitarian time and country" (*BP* 198), Melville writes in the Supplement. *Battle-Pieces* would solidify this upsurge of idealism in a new, tragically based democratic faith, yet "instead of purging the nation once and for all from self-seeking, materialism, and corruption," as George M. Fredrickson notes, "the war opened the floodgates for the greatest tide of personal and political selfishness the nation had ever seen" (Fredrickson 183). In place of another Washington or Lincoln, "the democratic future belong[ed] to plain-garbed, cigar-smoking Grant," whom Henry Adams would find so troglodytic as to furnish "evidence enough to upset Darwin."[28] The irony that Adams and Melville understood is that while the modern age made new and extraordinary demands upon human beings, its diminished inhabitants were grotesquely unfit to meet them. Melville's obituary for wooden ships in "The Stone Fleet"—"But so they serve the Obsolete" (*PB* 49)—is an obituary as well for the individuals who manned them—relative innocents, it is true, but with more liberality of spirit than their iron descendants and therefore more educable in the moral and political difficulties of modern life.

Given his estimate of human beings as they might be and as they were, it is hard to judge what Melville hoped for from his potential audience. Having failed in two literary genres (novel-writing and lecturing), it is doubtful that Melville anticipated great results in a third, whose readership was more restricted and more conventional. "Unprosperously heroical" (*BP* 76) is the phrase Melville might have applied to his nation-rebuilding efforts in *Battle-Pieces*. The words are from "The Victor at Antietam," his eulogy of McClellan, a great man to Democrat Melville if not to most Americans, and one whose relationship to an ungrateful public may have struck Melville as an analogue to his own:

> Authority called you; then, in mist
> And loom of jeopardy—dismissed.
> But staring peril soon appalled;
> You, the Discarded, she recalled—
> Recalled you, nor endured delay;
> And forth you rode upon a blasted way.
> Arrayed Pope's rout, and routed Lee's array.
> McClellan. . . .
>
> (*BP* 77)

Melville, too, was called (his early fiction), dismissed (*Pierre*), then recalled, or self-recalled, as events of 1859-65 seemed to demand their interpreter and moral guide. In the end, McClellan would be dismissed again, as Melville may have anticipated he would be dismissed by his audience, yet the urgency of the moment was reason enough to write a book of poems that sought to be more for his readers than a book of poems. If the emergence of a wise, magnanimous America was indeed the hope behind *Battle-Pieces*, such hope was quickly shattered by the course of Reconstruction and the popular and critical reception of *Battle-Pieces*, which by February 1868 had sold well under half of the 1,260 copies printed and gone virtually unnoticed by reviewers. During the next ten years the historical vision of *Battle-Pieces* would develop into the more capacious vision of *Clarel*, but by then, following the lead of classical artists as he understood them, Melville would have transferred his ideal of a tragically based democracy from historical time to the imagination, incarnating it in a few extraordinary individuals while despairing of its fulfillment in any modern nation. Withdrawing further from his age, Melville would continue to write and, in privately subsidized editions, to publish, but his "audience" would become largely a sounding board for literary effects rather than a living readership to be influenced or changed. In *Battle-Pieces* he had made an unreserved gesture toward the American world, and it had been ignored. He would not make another.

A House Divided

When *Battle-Pieces* was published in August 1866, Melville had been living at 104 East Twenty-sixth Street in New York City for nearly three years, having transferred his Pittsfield farm to his brother Allan in partial exchange for the Manhattan house. The following December he assumed the position of inspector in the New York Custom House (salary: $4 a day) that he would hold until his retirement in 1885. Family members spoke of his improved spirits, and biographers generally followed their lead until the publication in 1975 of two newly discovered letters to New York Unitarian minister Henry Whitney Bellows—one from Melville's brother-in-law Samuel Shaw, the other from Lizzie Melville, both dated May 1867.[29] According to Shaw, Lizzie believed that Melville was insane, and family members—Gansevoorts and Melvilles, too, it seems, as well as Shaws—were encouraging her to initiate at least a temporary separation. Lizzie's trials were evidently longstanding, but in the end she could not, would not, or at any rate did not elect to leave Melville. Four months later the civil war within the Melville household came to a tragic conclusion when, returning home in the early morning of September 11 after an evening with friends, eighteen-year-old Malcolm locked himself in his bedroom and shot himself in the head.

Was Melville insane? Did he vent his career frustrations in domestic tyranny? Did he abuse Lizzie physically or psychologically? Was he a harsh, distant, or self-preoccupied father, responsible in some fashion for Malcolm's death? No one truly knows. The case for physical abuse rests heavily on a story of "Herman's drinking, coming home smashed on brandy, beating up on Lizzie, throwing her down the back stairs, etc.," which great-grandson Paul Metcalf said he heard from poet Charles Olson, who claimed to have heard it from Metcalf's mother, Eleanor Melville Metcalf, whom Paul Metcalf doubts would have told Olson even if it were true. "All this," Paul Metcalf adds, "has been filtered through so many ears and mouths, and minds of such diverse motivation, it is impossible of verification" (*EWW* 21–22). William Braswell also reported that Eleanor Metcalf told him that Melville "had struck his wife" (*EWW* 19). Braswell is a reliable source, but Metcalf's words might mean anything from "struck her once" to "struck her occasionally when he was drunk" to "struck her regularly." The alleged drinking is also problematic. Elizabeth Renker, whose 1994 article widely publicized the question of abuse, speaks of "indications that [Melville] drank heavily," but her sources are family legends vaguely alluded to in Edwin Haviland Miller's undocumented biography (Miller pointedly adds that Melville was "not an alcoholic") and Eleanor Metcalf's remark that the "closing-in" of her grandfather's life in the 1870s "drove him at times to desperate irascibility and the solace of brandy."[30] The other oft-cited piece of evidence is college student John Gulick's journal observation of 1859 that Melville's "countenance is slightly flushed with whiskey drinking." Gulick met Melville only once, on which occasion Melville was sober enough to impress him as "possess[ing] a mind of an aspiring, ambitious order, full of elastic energy and illumined with rich colors of a poetic fancy," though "soured by criticism and disgusted with the civilized world and with our Christendom in general and in particular."[31] A family "conspiracy of silence" may have muffled stories about Melville's drinking, as Miller suggests, but the dearth of evidence is hardly reason for filling the lack with phrases like Laurie Robertson-Lorant's "excessive drinking" (undocumented in her otherwise well-documented biography) or Stanton Garner's vacuous but insinuating "to an unknown extent he drank" (Garner cites only Gulick).[32]

Because they are unanswerable, questions of Melville's drinking and wife-beating are distractions from the indisputable point: tense and irritable when he was writing, prone to depression when he was not, Melville could be an extraordinarily trying husband and father. Psychiatrist Edwin S. Shneidman put a name to Melville's condition: "'dementia domesticus'—... a tortured syndrome of an individual who shared his deepest self in his written works, who behaved within normal limits before most of the public world, but who at home was something of a tyrant" (*EWW* 40). A classic case of "dementia domesticus" is Leslie Stephen, whom Virginia Woolf described in precisely Shneidman's triadic way—the writerly father, the sociable father, the tyrant father—and whose public and private personalities were so at odds that his friend and biographer F. W. Maitland "resolutely refused to believe" his daughters' accounts of his violent fits of temper.[33] Admiring readers of Melville are a position like Maitland's; they frame a "Melville" from the public literary persona and have difficulty squaring their image with evidence of private impatience, irritability, or worse.

"How badly could [Melville] have mistreated his family?"[34] Hershel Parker asks. Even in the smoothest of times Melville was only fitfully domestic. Although he missed his family deeply when he was away, his most intense life lay in reading and writing books, and except for relationships with an increasingly narrow group of sympathizers (brother-in-law John C. Hoadley, for one), he lived his later life intellectually alone. Sailing home from San Francisco in 1860 after voyaging there for reasons of "health" aboard his brother Tom's ship, the *Meteor*, Melville could enter his profession as "Author," though his only literary production in more than four years (lectures aside) was a slim volume of verse recently submitted to and rejected by New York publishers. By 1867, such a gratifying fiction was no longer possible. With the reception of *Battle-Pieces* Melville was now a failed poet as well as a failed novelist; his profession, had he been required to list one, was "custom house inspector." To a man who habitually dealt in symbols, assuming the badge of office the previous year was as complete and dramatic a self-redefinition as the publication of *Typee* twenty-five years earlier, and one for which the economic burdens of family life might have seemed substantially to blame. Another man might have sought consolation in his wife and children; in Melville's case, it was the family who were made to feel the force of his frustration, if only as the luckless crew who slept below him as he paced his quarter-deck.

I do not believe that Melville was guilty of frequent or deliberate physical abuse. More likely, as Stanton Garner suggested, he and Lizzie "waged psychological warfare against each other,"[35] with Lizzie's of the passive-aggressive sort. On Melville's side, the hostility may have been provoked or aggravated by Lizzie's want of intellectuality and her fretful ordinariness. As Melville's niece Maria Morewood is reported to have said years later, "Herman was always challenging Elizabeth, that she did not understand it."[36] Lizzie probably didn't, whatever "it" was. Kindly, devoted, and "domestic in her tastes without proficiency," as her granddaughter Eleanor characterized her, Lizzie found "much" in her "life with a genius husband . . . that she was emotionally unequal to."[37] "Lizzie had a set of clichés," Hershel Parker remarked: " . . . If you lived with her, you could anticipate phrases coming out of her mouth—as you could *not* anticipate what would come out of Maria's or Helen's mouths. Herman derived his high standards from his mother and his older sister."[38] In their last years together Lizzie came firmly to believe in Melville's writing; but she seems never to have gone far toward comprehending it or, when Melville needed it most, toward supporting him against the adverse judgment of family members and the public.[39]

For the most part, whatever cruelties Melville may have inflicted on Lizzie were probably reflexive, though in time they became part of the marital dynamic. Even Lizzie's goodness might have seemed to Melville a "blank" or "excremental" goodness, less a function of virtue and good sense than of propriety, and maddening in its nervousness (a word often used by relatives for Lizzie) and air of Griselda-like patience. Melville's sense of being in the wrong would have exacerbated matters by pricking his remorse and involving both partners more deeply in a cycle of resentment and sentimental truces that neither could break.[40] Melville truly *was* a man who admired nobility and who attained a great deal of it through native high-mindedness augmented by discipline and reserve—but not in his relationship to Lizzie, the most galling feature of which may have been the self-estimate it forced on him. In the biography of Melville he labored on for decades but never completed, Henry A. Murray, who had access to family intimacies through Eleanor Metcalf, wrote of Melville's "'disastrous'" marriage as "'the incommunicable grief, the ever-gnawing pain that he, apostle of chivalry, could never [*sic*] confess to anyone.'"[41]

Melville's unhappiness does not justify the pain he gave Lizzie, but it does help explain the malign symbiosis through which his irritability and her anxious self-effacement reacted upon one another and made family life tense and unstable. Since the time of *Pierre* at least, relatives had worried about what they euphemistically called Melville's "health." The crisis of 1867 was a climax to what Samuel Shaw told Bellows "has been a cause of anxiety to all of us for years past."[42] Evidently, Melville's condition had worsened to the point where Lizzie, at least, could consider it insanity, though a better diagnosis, as Edwin H. Miller suggested, might be "deep depression" (*EWW* 37). Psychiatrist Kay Redfield Jamison includes a brief section on Melville in *Touched with Fire*, her study of manic-depressive illness and artistic creativity, claiming that Melville "experienced clear and extended periods of both melancholy and manic excitement."[43] This seems probable if "melancholy" and "manic excitement" are understood as pronounced mood swings rather than phases of clinical bipolarity. Bartleby the scrivener is a depressive; Turkey and Nippers, his emotionally unstable coworkers, are manic-depressives, as is the giddily melancholic narrator of "Cock-A-Doodle-Doo!" which takes mood swings and their related philosophy swings as its subject. The opposition of "bright" and "dark" views of life that runs through the magazines pieces of 1853–56 and *The Confidence-Man* seems an effort on Melville's part to objectify the dualities of mild-to-moderate mania and moderate-to-serious depression and, through art and humor, to master psychic states that might otherwise master him. If Melville was manic-depressive, it was never in the devastating form that afflicted Virginia Woolf or Robert Lowell. Few, however, in the Shaw, Gansevoort, and Melville families had the dispassion or empathetic intelligence to distinguish deep depression from "madness." All they knew and practically needed to know was that Melville was behaving erratically and that a temporary separation seemed best for all concerned.

Parker wonders if Melville ever knew or guessed that Lizzie thought him insane and considered leaving him.[44] Certainly he was aware of the general opinion of family and friends, not to mention of hostile reviewers who sometimes openly questioned his sanity. At some point after May 17, 1867, almost exactly the date of Shaw's letter to Bellows, Melville marked a passage from one of Camoen's sonnets: "My senses lost, misjudging men declare, / And Reason banish'd from her mental throne, / Because I shun the crowd, and dwell alone."[45] Coincidentally or not, he also marked another passage in the editor's introduction to Camoens: "Woman was to him [Camoens] as a ministering angel, and for the little joy he tasted in life, he was indebted to her."[46] In his quieter moments, Melville seems to have understood how much he owed Lizzie, both personally for her devotion and domestically for the comforts and financial securities that made his writing career possible. Over time, particularly after he retired from the Custom House late in 1885, this sense of intimacy and deep gratitude—of the two of them having been through the wars together and survived—would become his dominant feeling toward her, though not without continued undertones of resentment.

It was probably the death of Malcolm, less than four months after Shaw's letter, that reconciled husband and wife, subsuming their individual grievances in the kind of the common grief that *Battle-Pieces* envisioned for the North and South. Melvilleans naturally tend to read Malcolm's death as in some way causally related to Melville's behavior, though every parent knows that adolescents have troubles of their own that may have little to do with home life. Still, for the narrrative's sake, we mythologize. Parker sees eighteen-year-old Malcolm caught between his parents and forced to play the role of "his mother's best protector;"[47] Robertson-Lorant imagines Melville diverting domestic anger "from his wife to his older son," partly because (his own father having died prematurely) he had no model for negotiating the conflict "between a maturing son feeling his oats and a father so threatened by the waning of his strength that he cannot gracefully let go."[48] Both these readings are possible; neither has much evidentiary basis. What does seem certain is that if Lizzie had held Melville responsible for Malcolm's death she would not have stayed with him. How could she have?

Robertson-Lorant ends her chapter on Malcolm's death with the closing lines from "The Apparition": "So, then, solidity's a crust . . ."[49] Did the death of Malcolm reawaken Melville to the fact of domestic tragedy, forgotten since Allan Melvill's death in 1832 or Gansevoort's in 1846, as the Civil War awakened America to historical tragedy? Did guilt over Malcolm's death (justified or fancied) constitute for Melville a "latter fall"? Was the young Clarel, close to the age Malcolm would have been circa 1870, an adoptive replacement for Malcolm?[50] And were Billy Budd's final words—"God bless Captain Vere!" (*BB* 123)—Melville's belated effort at self-absolution? Questions like these are only more mythmaking. All we can know, or conjecture, is that the uncivil war in Melville's household ended with an armistice in September 1867, in shared sorrow over one more slain "collegian."

9

Unworldly Yearners:
Agnostic Spirituality in Clarel

If . . . you are desperate about the meaning of life, the
seriousness of your despair is the expression of the meaning in which you are still living. This unconditional seriousness is the expression of the pressure of the divine in
the experience of utter separation from it.

—Paul Tillich, *The Protestant Era*

I know that He exists.
Somewhere—in Silence—
He has hid his rare life
From our gross eyes.

'Tis an instant's play,
'Tis a fond Ambush—
Just to make Bliss
Earn her own surprise!

But—should the play
Prove piercing earnest—
Should the glee—glaze—
In Death's—stiff—stare—

Would not the fun

Look too expensive!

Would not the jest—

Have crawled too far!

—Emily Dickinson, #338 (*Complete Poems*, 1960)

Justification by Doubt

Midway through *Clarel*, at the beginning of part 3 and just after its physical and metaphysical bottoming out at the Dead Sea, Melville asks a question that might be said to govern the poem as a whole:

> What reveries be in yonder heaven
> Whither, if yet faith rule it so,
> The tried and ransomed natures flow?
> If there peace after strife be given
> Shall hearts remember yet and know?
> . . . Do seraphim shed balm
> At last on all of earnest mind,
> Unwordly yearners, nor the palm
> Awarded St. Theresa, ban
> To Leopardi, Obermann?
> (*C* 3, 1: 1–5, 12–16)

At once an epigraph and an epitaph, the passage is curious in several respects. It seems the voice of Melville's narrator and only later is described as the "exhalings . . . of one" (almost certainly Rolfe) standing by "the moundless bed" of the dead Nehemiah (*C* 3, 1: 25, 27). Without undercutting the authority of the lines—the reader's initial response survives largely intact—the belated attribution identifies them with one of the characters to whom they most fittingly apply.[1] What Rolfe asks about others, *Clarel* asks about Rolfe himself and about kindred "yearners," "unworldly" not in their innocence like Nehemiah, a holy fool, but in what the Franciscan monk Salvaterra calls "The pure disdain / Of life, or holding the real, / Still subject to a brave ideal" (*C* 4, 14: 34–36). Fidelity to the ideal is what the poem means by "earnestness," its touchstone for spiritual merit. Situationally, Rolfe's musing looks back to the death of Nehemiah, which ended part 2; figuratively, it looks ahead to the death of Mortmain, the most painfully earnest of *Clarel*'s pilgrims, which will end part 3. "Tried" suggests the probational agony of searching for God and ascertaining a ground for belief: "hard task Thou settest man / To know Thee," the Syrian monk laments (*C* 2, 18: 134–35); "God, my God, / Sorely thou triest me the clod!" Clarel will exclaim (*C* 3, 21: 226–27). "Ransomed" would seem to imply the Atonement, but in *Clarel* the inconclusive process of trial is itself the vehicle for whatever ransoming occurs, if only by raising the sufferer above the profane and certifying a worthiness of immortality. If, as Mortmain says, "Religion . . . / Is man's appeal from fellow-clay" (*C* 3, 3: 54–55), then the idealistic doubter like Leopardi or Obermann may be as much the child of God as the orthodox believer.

The most pregnant phrase in the passage is the nearly parenthetical one "if yet faith rule it so." "Yet" implies waiting: on earth we may be sure of nothing. "Faith" may signify traditional belief in the afterlife and "rule it so" simply mean "control" or "regulate" in the predictive sense of "turn out to be warranted." Or Melville may be implying that faith *causes* the ascent of "tried and ransomed natures." If so, what kind of faith can encompass an unbeliever like Leopardi, who, in William Rounseville Alger's words from *The Solitudes of Nature and of Man* (a book that deeply influenced Melville during the composition of *Clarel*), "accept[ed] in its direst extent that philosophy of despair which denies God, Providence, and Immortality"?[2] The faith that redeems "unworldly yearners" is evidently not a positive faith in God; it is a stance toward experience—Leopardi "dared to think without checks, and to accept as truth whatever he saw as such"[3]—that aspires toward the transcendent without necessarily believing in it, and that God, if He exists, may choose to honor and reward as one form of worship.

"The principle of justification through faith," Paul Tillich wrote,

refers not only to the religious-ethical but also to the religious-intellectual life. Not only he who is in sin but also he who is in doubt is justified through faith. The situation of doubt, even of doubt about God, need not separate us from God. There is faith in every serious doubt, namely, the faith in the truth as such, even if the only truth we can express is our lack of truth. But if this is experienced in its depth and as an ultimate concern, the divine is present; and he who doubts in such an attitude is "justified" in his thinking.[4]

Like Clarel and Celio, who converge from the "poles adverse" of "Belief and unbelief" (*C* 1, 15: 55, 56), Tillich and Melville approach each other as the doubting fideist and the fideistic doubter. The "faith" that *Clarel* testifies to is not in God or immortality (though the poem retains a *hope* of both) but in the sanctifying power of living in a state of intellectual and spiritual aspiration. The seraphim who "shed balm" may turn out to be actual angels in an actual heaven, but in sublunary life they are known, if at all, only as co-seekers whose blessing is the masonic recognition that extraordinary human beings fleetingly accord one another. As to the truth of the Christian promise—a loving Father; a resurrected Son; a benign Providence superintending history; eternal life—*Clarel* is an agnostic poem according to the measure of T. H. Huxley, who coined the word "agnosticism" in 1869 and later described its essential principles: "In matters of the intellect, follow your reason as far as it will take you, without regard to any other consideration"; "do not pretend that conclusions are certain which are not demonstrated or demonstrable."[5] Religion is not of course entirely a matter of intellect, as the life studies in *Clarel* repeatedly show, yet neither does the poem endorse any form of belief at odds with the intellect, beneath it, or self-professedly above it. Agnosticism (not knowing) becomes "spiritual" when its adherents live neither with worldly indifference nor with a passionless deferral of belief but with the continuing interrogation of God and the universe that Tillich called the "state of being ultimately concerned."[6]

Although *Clarel* takes the form of a search for God, its deepest concern is with the nature and destiny of human beings as they define themselves in the God-less interim. The poem is formidable and has a reputation for dryness, based as much on its stony, elliptical style as on its philosophical density. Its extraordinary achievement is how, in cadences removed at once from natural speech and mellifluent epical speech (Milton, Wordsworth), it manages to trace the curve of its characters' thoughts and feelings and the subtle dynamics of their interactions. The characters themselves, as Newton Arvin commented, "are on the whole a remarkable assemblage of distinct and freshly noticed people," many of whom "have the quality of reconciling poetic representativeness with a real sharpness of outline as individuals."[7] Starbuck, Stubb, and Flask are vivid but fixed types whose range of being is established in the thumbnail sketches of "Knights and Squires"; by contrast, Rolfe, Vine, and Derwent are fluid characters who respond to occasions and to each other even as they embody classes of mind and sensibility. Representative, too, are striking cameo figures like the Syrian monk, the Dominican, Margoth, the Cypriote, the Lesbian merchant, Don Hannibal, Salvaterra, and the Lyonese Jew, as well as intensely drawn but narratively aborted characters like Celio and Nathan. Paradoxical as it may seem, *Clarel* is the book in which Melville is most completely the novelist, that is to say, most keenly the observer of *human* affairs with a sustained interest in nuances of personality and the living chemistry of dramatic scenes. At the same time, as Walter E. Bezanson said, *Clarel* is a distinctly "personal" poem with "filaments of self spread through it everywhere."[8] Outwardly, *Clarel* is Melville's attempt to sift the range of intellectual and emotional responses to the later nineteenth-century crisis of belief; inwardly, the poem is his testimonial to unworldly yearners and his effort to inscribe a vindication for their lives and, in the process, for his own.

Faith's Receding Wave

Early in *Clarel* Melville sets his thought-burdened pilgrims against pilgrims of another, simpler sort:

> Unvexed by Europe's grieving doubt
> Which asks *And can the Father be?*
> Those children of the climes devout,
> On festival in fane installed,
> Happily ignorant, make glee,
> Like orphans in the play-ground walled.
>
> (*C* 1, 3: 140)

"Orphan" is the final word of *Moby-Dick* and a favorite Melvillean image for cosmic abandonment. Insulated in their "play-ground walled," these orphans are naïfs whose faith has not been tested through the struggle with doubt that is the mark of modern spiritual life. That this doubt is "Europe's," not Christendom's generally, reflects *Clarel's* participation in a religious crisis as yet more widely felt across the Atlantic than in America. Melville's walled orphans recall another set of children "fenced early in cloistral round / Of reverie, of shade, of prayer," but later forced to "grow in other ground" and "flower in foreign air."[9] The lines are from "Stanzas from the Grande Chartreuse," the Arnold poem that Bezanson feels may have had the "most specific" influence on *Clarel*.[10] Projecting cultural time onto topographical space, Melville invokes Arnold's vision of modern man "wandering between two worlds, one dead, / The other powerless to be born" ("Stanzas from the Grande Chartreuse," ll. 85–86) when he describes the gorge of Kedron as "poised as in a chaos true, / Or throe-lock of transitional earth / When old forms are annulled, and new / Rebel, and pangs suspend the birth" (*C* 3, 21: 16–19). *Clarel* also resonates with "the melancholy, long, withdrawing roar" of Arnold's "Sea of Faith" in "Dover Beach" (ll. 25, 21): Celio is said to contend with "all questions on that primal ground / Laid bare by faith's receding wave" (*C* 1, 19: 28–29); "How far may seas retiring go?" (*C* 3, 5: 83) the pilgrims later ask. The historical backdrop of *Clarel* is that amphibious cultural moment depicted by Arnold that Melville, varying the image but not the idea, calls "that vast eclipse, if slow, / Whose passage yet we undergo, / Emerging on an age untried" (*C* 4, 8: 12–14).

An eclipse may be a brief periodic obscuring of part or all of a celestial body or it may be the passing of something into termless obscurity or decline. A chief concern of *Clarel's* pilgrims is trying to situate the present within a trajectory of history so as to gauge whether the dissolution of faith is temporary or permanent. In one of his first meditations Rolfe, like Arnold in "Obermann Once More," compares contemporary times to Cicero's, an age "much like ours" in which "doubt ran, / Faith flagged" (C 1, 31: 237–38). Soon afterward, Jesus was born, ushering in nearly two millennia of belief, which now appear to be winding down much as classical paganism did in the late Republic. Is history cyclical, with particular religions waxing and waning but religion itself enduring because it is rooted in human needs? Is history progressive, with the world on the verge of a "new hour," as Arnold hopefully prophesies in "Obermann Once More" (l. 301)? Or has religion run its course entirely and, if so, "What interregnum or what reign / Ensues?" (C 3, 5: 101–2)? "What shapeless birth," like Yeats's "rough beast . . . "slouch[ing] toward Bethlehem to be born,"[11] lies "in store" as an organizing center for human energies (C 3, 5: 81)?

High among the many things Melville's agnostic pilgrims cannot know is whether the present age is a religious transition or a slow, demoralizing finale. The practical question is how to bear oneself (in all senses of the phrase) in the meantime. By the Jordan River, "late enamored of the spell / Of rituals olden" (C 2, 24: 21–22), Rolfe invites Derwent and Vine to join him in singing a Latin hymn. The act unites the singers in "concord full, completion fine— / Rapport of souls in harmony of tone" (C 2, 24: 52–53). Without investing belief in the rite, Rolfe is drawn toward it as the speaker in Philip Larkin's "Church-Going" is drawn to old churches as places where, against the diffusions of modern secular experience, people come together in solemn commemoration of the passages of life. This is the defense that the Dominican, overhearing the singers, makes of Catholic ritual: acknowledging human needs, it "'trim[s] them, fit[s] them, make[s] them shine / In structures of fair design'" (C 2, 25: 40–41). But can the psychic and social utility of religion justify a leap of faith? And without such a leap, can spiritual life continue to exist at all? Whatever its referential truth, the merit of religion is that it sacralizes experience and nurtures a feeling of exaltedness no less effectual and morally constitutive for possibly being groundless. "The abdication of Belief / Makes the Behavior small," Emily Dickinson wrote: "Better an ignis fatuus / Than no illume at all—."[12] As if in confirmation of this theme, "The River-Rite" ends with the scoffing of the geologist Margoth, *Clarel's* symbol of the "smallness" of atheistic materialism.

With Margoth at one extreme and Catholicism at the other, "The River-Rite" and its succeeding cantos, "The Dominican" and "Of Rome," establish the boundaries within which agnostic spirituality must define and maintain itself. "Men / Get tired at last of being free" (C 2, 26: 124), Rolfe observes; they want the gnosis of dogmatic religion or the countergnosis of dogmatic irreligion. "Rome and the Atheist . . . shall fight it out," Rolfe continues; "Protestantism being retained / For base of operations sly / By Atheism" (C 2, 26: 140–44). When Derwent objects that this is no way for a

"New-Worlder" to talk (*C* 2, 26: 150), Rolfe answers, "'Tis the New World that mannered me, / Yes, gave me this vile liberty / To reverence naught, not even herself" (*C* 2, 26: 151–54). The bold interrogation of all traditions and ideologies; the hatred of all sham: this is close to Melville's notion of "Americanism" in "Hawthorne and His Mosses," save that time, adversity, and the vulgarization of American life in the decade before the Centennial have made for greater skepticism, as if to be a genuine American were now to be homeless and unaffiliated, dedicated only to truth.

It is apt that *Clarel*'s New Worlders should gravitate toward the very oldest of Western worlds. Pilgrimages are typically undertaken as acts of dedicated belief; in *Clarel* they are venturings back in time and space to the elemental unknown. "'Tis the uprooting of content!" (*C* 1, 1: 105) Clarel says at the outset of the poem, aware that his education will first of all be a divestiture, an "unlearning" (*C* 1, 1: 80; see *C* 2, 14: 52). When Nehemiah asks if he is a pilgrim, Clarel demurs, "'I am a traveler—no more'" (*C* 1, 9: 28). The distinction is part of a taxonomy of character and motive that divides the poem's dramatis personae into four recognizable, if overlapping groups: pilgrims, seekers, wanderers, and travelers. The pilgrim begins with faith (however shaky), purpose (to test or ratify that faith), and destination (a site for definitive trial); the Syrian monk is a pilgrim, Clarel a recently lapsed pilgrim. The seeker (Rolfe) aspires to truth but has no physical or metaphysical end-point in sight; he is a modern descendant of the fabled Magi but without the Magi's guiding star (*C* 4, 1: 1–18). The wanderer (Celio, Mortmain, Ungar) is an embittered seeker, disillusioned with the world and painfully conscious of its incongruence with the Christian promise. The traveler (Derwent, the Greek banker, the Cypriote, and the Lyonese Jew, among others) is precisely that: a tourist in search of diversion, indifferent or hostile to "Judah's mournful sway" (*C* 4, 26: 83).

Clarel is subtitled *A Poem and Pilgrimage in the Holy Land*, as if the pilgrimage were something other than the poem. The poem belongs to its fictional characters; the pilgrimage, like Ishmael's going to sea, is a participatory action that reaches out to involve its audience. Shortly after entering the Judean desert, the Greek banker and Glaucon turn back and Melville addresses the reader: "They fled. And thou? . . . / Part here, then, would ye win release / From ampler dearth; part, and in peace" (*C* 2, 13: 112, 118–19). Melville knows he is writing a difficult poem and can at best "fit audience find, though few"—lines he underscored in his edition of *Paradise Lost*.[13] But he is also deliberately implicating his readers in the poem's testing of souls: How will *you*, reader, bear up in the "ampler dearth" that is figuratively the spiritual habitation of the modern? To read *Clarel* is to be exposed to the range of belief and unbelief its characters themselves confront and be asked to weigh opinions without settling them. As the poem "wilder[s] on / Through vacant halls which faith once kept / With ushers good" (*C* 3, 5: 124–26), the issue it comes to center upon is not what to believe (gnosis) but how to live amid indeterminacy with a suspension of belief (agnosis).

Equivocal

The phrase "faith's receding wave" is used with Celio, "a second self" to Clarel but "stronger" to front the consequences of waning belief (*C* 1, 19: 26–27). Bezanson calls Celio "prelusive" in sounding the poem's themes (Bezanson 590); nowhere is he more so than in his first word, the agnostic's "Equivocal!" (*C* 1, 11: 13). Celio is standing by a group of tombs chiseled out of rock, before one of which lies "a mat of tender turf" (*C* 1, 10: 34). A symbol of life growing out of death? The grass is only "faint green" (*C* 1,10: 34), an intimation but scarcely a promise, like all hints of divinity and eternal life in *Clarel*. More than any other issue, immortality, especially Jesus' immortality, is the linchpin of the poem's religion; in Paul's words, "if Christ be not risen, then is our preaching vain, and your faith also vain" (1 Cor. 15:14). The resurrection is vital in *Clarel* in three respects: it validates Jesus' role as messenger (not necessarily Son) of God; it testifies to God's merciful intentions for humanity; and, by "pledg[ing] indemnifying good / In worlds not known" (*C* 3, 3: 15–16), it answers the problem of evil by crowning the sufferings of the godly. The sticking point for Celio—the cross on which he is crucified—is that Jesus recanted at the last, "crying out in death's eclipse, / When rainbow none his eyes might see, / . . . *My God, my God, forsakest me?*" (*C* 1, 13: 44–45, 47) In pagan times human beings had "lived content— / Content with life's own discontent" (*C* 1, 13: 54–55). By promising what had formerly been unimaginable, then subverting it, Jesus only "enlarged the margin for despair" (*C* 1, 13: 46). "*Thee* we upbraid" (*C* 1, 13: 48), Celio protests. (Later Rolfe will arraign the gospel on similar grounds for "operat[ing] like a perfidy" [*C* 3, 3: 27, 32].) Jesus raised Lazarus from the dead, but did Lazarus rise a second time, Celio asks. Did Jesus himself rise? Celio cannot know; all he has are Jesus' words and stories of an empty tomb: "'Raiser and raised divide one doom: / Both vanished now'" (*C* 1, 14: 115–16).

Like Leopardi, "a young St. Stephen of the doubt" (*C* 1, 14: 4) to whom he is compared, Celio is a hunchback whose deformity is at once a cause and a symbol of his spiritual pain. A Catholic opponent once dismissed Leopardi as "a frog endlessly croaking 'There is no God because I'm a hunchback, there is no God because I'm a hunchback.'"[14] Melville allows as much, yet both Rolfe and the narrator himself will elaborate Celio's main criticisms of Christianity: that Christ's "love" is problematically entangled with the church's "lore" (*C* 1, 13: 66); that Omnipotence is as responsible for the shark as the dove (C 1, 14: 71); that the ethics of Jesus are in conflict with "all else we know" from history and experience (C 1, 13: 79); and that the strife among Christian sects belies the spirit of the founder. These objections are Melville's own, dating back to *Mardi*; in Celio's monologue, delivered near the Ecce Homo gate on the Via Crucis, they become stigmata of the modern doubter and theses tacked to the door of the poem. The real peril for Celio—and his significance as a cautionary example—is not so much intellectual (the substance of his thought) as psychological (how he lives in relation to it). The relentlessness of his questioning throws him back upon himself in morbid self-absorption and exile from the community, symbolized by the night he spends "alone in utter dark" outside the locked city wall (C 1, 14, 16), the first of the poem's Wandering Jews (C 1, 13: 118). Morning readmits him to Jerusalem and even seems to typify a resurrection of sorts, but its "purfled" splendor (C 1, 15: 5) quickly dissipates in the light of "indifferent" day (C 1, 15: 9). Its promise is equivocal.

In Jerusalem Melville has Celio reside at the Franciscan convent. His countertype in *Clarel* is the Franciscan monk Salvaterra, the pilgrims' guide at the manger in Bethlehem and a spiritual heir of St. Francis himself, likened by Rolfe to Jesus. Aglow at once with religious fervor and consumption, Salvaterra in his "Christliness" may be "better—higher" than "carnal manliness" allows (C 4, 14: 106, 105), as Rolfe says, but his faith, whether holy gift or wholly delusion, is peculiarly his own; it cannot be institutionalized in churchly forms, instilled in others, or argued on rational grounds, like the Dominican's. Nor does it seem to have been earned or tempered through the struggle with unbelief that afflicts the pilgrims. The more pertinent example of faith for them is the Syrian monk, who reenacts Christ's forty days in the wilderness in an effort to purge himself of the "sin of doubt" (C 2, 18: 38) and whose reported colloquy with the Devil atop Mt. Quarantania is one of the poem's consummate moments. An urbane master of Socratic argument, the Devil has the best of the debate, and the monk in the end can only appeal to God for assurance or annihilation: "take me back again / To nothing, or make clear my view" (C 2, 18: 135–36). The voice he seems to hear in response does neither; it says, in effect, "Trust Me; all will be revealed in time," which leaves the monk precisely where he was, in need of an act of faith but capable at most of an act of resignation: "His will be done!" (C 2, 18: 145). Rolfe listens transfixed, hanging upon the monk's words, as do we, eager for a resolution, if not a revelation: "'Surely, not all we've heard. / Peace—solace—was in end conferred?'" (C 2, 18: 150–51). But the monk is silent; trial is inconclusive, and the only revelation to be had is of the certainty of indefinite waiting. "Ha, *thou* at peace?" (C 2, 18: 126), the Devil taunts the monk, a stand-in for all unworldly yearners obliged to seek ransom and rest in an afterlife whose equivocal status is the very object of their doubt.

Wandering Jews

Mortmain

Rest-lessness, physical and metaphysical, is the curse laid upon the Wandering Jew, a figure of legend familiar to Melville through Byron, Shelley, and Carlyle and perhaps, as Bernard Rosenthal suggested, through a translation of Eugène Sue's *Wandering Jew*, "widely read in America" after the mid-1840s.[15] The Wandering Jew appears allusively at several points in the poem and centrally in the masque performed for the pilgrims at Mar Saba. Literally, the Jew's offense is a "churlish taunt" hurled at Jesus as he carries the cross (*C* 1, 14: 113); figuratively, it is skepticism, with the Jew a symbol for those in the nineteenth century who have left the comforts of belief and estranged themselves from the community of believers. The fate of the Jew—to "Long live, rove far, and understand / And sum all knowledge for his dower" (*C* 3, 19: 52–53)—exemplifies that striving toward unity of being that Romantics like Schiller saw as the distinction of the modern and that post-Romantics like Arnold saw as its paralyzing burden. Melville's Wandering Jew is Arnoldian. "'His brain shall tingle,'" the Jew's punishment runs, "'but his hand / Shall palsied be in power'" (*C* 3, 19: 55–56).

To one degree or another, all the seekers in *Clarel*—Celio, Nathan, Rolfe, Mortmain, Ungar, Clarel himself—are Wandering Jews. Nathan, the Jew by marriage and conversion whose "tortuous [spiritual] history is an epitome of American experience" (Bezanson 628), least resembles the Wandering Jew, since his adoption of Zionism gives him a geographical and ideological home. The skullcapped Mortmain is the Wandering Jew *in extremis*, cited in his "cragged austerity" at the close of the masque (*C* 3, 19: 179). "Curse on this store / Of knowledge" (*C* 3, 28: 5–6), Mortmain soliloquizes by the palm at Mar Saba, *Clarel*'s emblem of spiritual peace. Mortmain's bitterness is partly an idealist's revulsion at the actual world—"If mad," says Rolfe, "'Tis indignation at the bad" (*C* 2, 37, 54–55)—but Derwent goes deeper (and in doing so betrays his own rose-tinted vision) when he remarks, "God help him, ay, poor realist!" (*C* 2, 16: 137). Derwent's "realist" is like Ishmael's "wretched infidel" in *Moby-Dick* who refuses to "wear [the] colored and coloring glasses" of illusion and "gazes himself blind" at the whiteness of Creation (*MD* 195). Disenchanted with man and unable to believe in God, Mortmain becomes a dogmatist of despair, intent on draining the bitter cup. His obsessiveness is indeed mad, but representatively so; as Rolfe asks, echoing Melville's 1849 comment on the madness of Charles Fenno Hoffman, "Who so secure, / Except his clay be sodden loam, / As never to dream the day may come / When *he* may take [the wild plunge], foul or pure?" (*C* 2, 16: 114–17; see *Corr* 128). Mortmain's death beneath the palm is a deliverance of sorts—"the tried spirit sleeps" (*C* 3, 32: 76)—

but whether his trial is also a ransoming and his deliverance is to anything more than oblivion is left unhinted. Part 3 ends in the question with which it began: may unworldly yearners who live and die with their eyes upon the palm, never attaining belief, win a heavenly palm?

Hawthorne, Once More

If intellectually the Wandering Jew is a type of the modern thinker, socially he illustrates the solitude and misanthropy to which the modern thinker is particularly liable. At least part of the Jew's suffering comes from the willed isolation through which he guards himself against social slights. With time, this isolation becomes a source of perverse pride, down to the Jew's shunning the home of his wife, Esther, and his son, for whom his sympathies yearn. The opposition of the intellectual to the domestic, the latter represented by an "Esther," associates the masque with Hawthorne's "Ethan Brand," whose knowledge-seeking hero exiles himself from common life, psychologically violates a woman named Esther, and is allusively linked to the Wandering Jew. Melville read and remarked on "Ethan Brand" in June 1851 (*Corr* 192), but it was probably not until the writing of *Pierre* that he came to see it as a parable of his own life. In centering his energies upon his inward development, then in late 1851–52 finding that development turn on him with unwelcome revelations, Melville exposed himself to the furies of "the avenging dream" (*P* 180–81), a vision of squandered domestic happiness that rises to mock the folly and pride of the quester.

Melville recognized himself as a Wandering Jew who had transgressed not only against Christ (in withholding belief) but also, like Ethan Brand, against common humanity, represented by his wife and children. Even after the reconciliation with Lizzie that seems to have been effected by Malcolm's death, Melville's primary commitment to his mental life remained unchanged. From early 1870 or so, his "whole searching self," as his granddaughter Eleanor remarked, was "engaged" for the next several years "in writing *Clarel*"—a "dreadful *incubus* of a *book*," Lizzie called it, "because it has undermined all our happiness."[16] Deaths of family members during this period—Melville's mother and his brother Allan in 1872; his sister Augusta in 1876, shortly before *Clarel* was published—increased his isolation and accelerated that withdrawal into himself that would evolve, despite flashes of conviviality and a few enduring friendships, into a protective, almost impenetrable reserve. As the Wandering Jew avoids the gatherings of men, where "'Some wrong / On me is heaped, go where I may'" (*C* 3, 19: 73–74), so Melville increasingly avoided the public world, especially the literary world, even as he celebrated geniality in writings like the unpublished Burgundy Club Sketches, begun during or shortly after the composition of *Clarel*.

Hershel Parker emphasizes Melville's "timidity" during these years in order to highlight the paradox that "the meekest, modestest man you could imagine was writing thousands of lines of poetry a year, and becoming a great poet."[17] But Melville was also a proud man, and insofar as *Clarel* is an obliquely autobiographical poem he may have been using his various Wandering Jews not only to dramatize his intellectual and spiritual situation but to come to terms with his failures as a husband and father and with his simultaneous longing for companionship and aversion to most actual companions. Through his portrait of Rolfe, a footloose intellectual whose "vigorous sallies and withdrawals . . . are those of a thoroughly sociable being" (Bezanson 590), Melville inscribes an idealized image of himself as an earnest but genial seeker, in effect *assuming* the persona of Rolfe against the tendencies of his actual life.

Melville underscores what he is, or how he wants to be seen, by projecting a negative counter-image into the figure of willed isolation in the poem, Vine, who drifts among the pilgrims with "the irrelation of a weed / Detached from vast Sargasso's mead" (*C* 2, 17: 32–33). Like Hawthorne's artist figures and at times Hawthorne himself, Vine is a spectator and *agent provocateur*, "shy prying into men" (*C* 3, 14: 48), his own good-fellowship inhibited by "coyness" (*C* 1, 29: 46) or fear of self-revelation, and rusty with disuse. Vine is the Wandering Jew on the social side, without the redeeming seriousness of the Wandering Jew's intellectuality. During the pilgrims' long debates, Vine typically remains aloof, often picking at a weed or flinging bits of sand or driftwood into the void, "as one / Whose race of thought long since was run" (*C* 2, 33: 109–10). "Barrenness" is a word recurrently used with Vine; "dearth" is another.[18] Like "the rifled *Sepulcher of Kings*," the setting in which Melville chooses to introduce him, Vine is "a waste where beauty clings" (*C* 1, 28: 24, 22). The implication is of great talents dissipated or left fallow for want of earnestness on one side and camaraderie on the other, though Vine's appeal is such that his sterility only makes itself felt to Clarel with time. Where Hawthorne's Wandering Jew, Ethan Brand, suffers from egotism and intellectual pride—heroic faults—Vine as Wandering Jew is marked by intellectual sloth and by a "freakish mockery, elfin light" (*C* 1, 31: 109), an aestheticized version of legendary Jew's debunking.

Through the ongoing "tournament of merits" between Rolfe and Vine (Bezanson 601), staged nominally for Clarel's allegiance, Melville is remythologizing his relationship with Hawthorne and measuring Hawthorne morally and intellectually against himself. Each of them is a Wandering Jew in some respect, yet they are more different from each other, Melville now understands, than alike. By 1876 Hawthorne had been dead for a dozen years, but he was still much on Melville's mind due to a spate of posthumous publications or republications that Melville bought and read between 1868 and 1872: *The Snow-Image* (which included "Ethan Brand"), *Our Old Home, The Scarlet Letter*, Hawthorne's late unfinished romance *Septimius Felton*, and volumes of the selected American, English, and French and Italian notebooks—the English notebook containing Hawthorne's portrait of Melville during his 1856 visit to Liverpool. Melville would probably not have taken offense at Hawthorne's account of him "wandering to-and fro over these deserts [of metaphysics], as dismal and monotonous as the sand hills amid which we were sitting";[19] if anything, he would have admired Hawthorne's insight into his spiritual plight. What would have surprised and pained him was Hawthorne's want of intellectual respect for that plight. It was as if the past had been snatched from him—Hawthorne was *not* the deep-diving intellect and kindred spirit he had imagined—and he were once again forced to say "Fool!" as he had after Hawthorne's departure from the Berkshires late in 1851.

The canto "The High Desert" is Melville's self-apologia and symbolic revenge. Its title has topographical reference, but it also alludes to the high desert of metaphysics, echoing Hawthorne's notebook entry of 1856. As the pilgrims discuss faith and doubt, science, modernity, history, and democracy—the past, present, and future of the human race—Vine sits apart and "pelt[s] his shadow" with crushed rocks (*C* 3, 5: 188). The seekers in *Clarel* are earnest; the poem itself is earnest; Vine/Hawthorne, despite his tendency to moralize, is not.[20] Bezanson sees Melville realizing that "beneath his shy and opulent serenity Hawthorne was scared" (Bezanson 600), perhaps in protection of some "secret" whose existence Melville and others (Hawthorne's friend George Hillard, for one) hypothesized to explain his obsession with buried sin.[21] Reading the published notebooks, however, Melville might have understood that beneath his posture of boredom and irritation at metaphysics Hawthorne was *spiritually* scared as well. In a notebook entry of 1849, standing at his mother's bedside as she lies dying of cancer, Hawthorne looks out the window at his children playing and "seem[s] to see the whole of human existence at once," with himself at middle age poised at its center: "Oh what a mockery, if what I saw were all,—let the interval between extreme youth and dying age be filled up with what happiness it might!"[22] The notebook entry continues:

> But God would not have made the close so dark and wretched, if there were nothing beyond; for then it would have been a fiend that created us, and measured out our existence, and not God. It would be something beyond wrong—it would be insult—to be thrust out of life into

annihilation in this miserable way. So, out of the very bitterness of death, I gather the sweet assurance of a better state of being.[23]

Like Starbuck in "The Gilder" ("Tell me not of thy teeth-tiered sharks, and thy kidnapping cannibal ways . . . I look deep down and do believe" [*MD* 492]), Hawthorne strives to make the terror of experience yield its opposite, hope. Rereading Hawthorne's *Old Manse* sketch "Monsieur du Miroir" in 1865, Melville marked a passage touching on this theme: "He [the narrator's mirror image] will pass to the dark realm of Nothingness, but will not find me there." Melville's comment: "This trenches upon the uncertain and the terrible."[24] In 1850, even in 1865, Melville could fasten on Hawthorne's flirtation with blackness and overlook his effort to contain it ("but will not find me there"), in effect Melvillizing Hawthorne as he read. Melville never read the 1849 notebook entry—Sophia Hawthorne excised it—but he read enough in the expurgated volumes to disabuse him of the idea that Hawthorne was a fearless seer. Hawthorne was a fear*ful* seer, the panicked conventionalist in him reining in the bold intuitional thinker. This process of denial—the very opposite of that "NO! in thunder" (*Corr* 186) he ascribed to Hawthorne in 1851—is what Melville focuses on in Vine's meditation on the palm at Mar Saba. Likening senescent Christianity to the senescent paganism of Roman times, Vine says, in effect, "Well, let it be; religion will last *my* time" ("But braid thy tresses—yet thou'rt fair: / Every age for itself must care" [*C* 3, 26: 55–56]). Vine/Hawthorne's insinuations and twisted mockeries, his curiosities about Mortmain and provocations of Rolfe are products of a nature profoundly divided between a will to know and a fear of what knowledge might disclose. Vine/Hawthone is a Paul Pry of subversive ideas as well as of personalities. This is what Melville must have understood through the notebooks as he looked back upon their intimacy with a shock of recognition and recalled Hawthorne years ago watching *him*—calibrating him to the finest degree, as he did in the 1856 Liverpool passage, but with an artist's dispassion, not with a friend's empathy and love.

By setting Mortmain, the "brotherless" intellectual (*C* 3, 28: 21), against Vine, the brotherless anti-intellectual, and by setting both against the companionable Rolfe, Melville is implying that isolateness, not thought itself, is the corrosive element of the Wandering Jew's malady, and that Mortmain "in gusts of lonely pain / Beating upon the naked brain" (*C* 2, 16: 135–36) has a tragic integrity that Vine lacks. Like the "heap of stones" Vine rears "in the high void waste," Vine/Hawthorne's life, Melville came to feel, was "a monument to barrenness" (*C* 3, 7: 83, 77, 85).[25] Mortmain, the tried soul, has at least a chance of being ransomed; Vine does not. Though knowledge may bring no consolation to Mortmain, he seeks it nonetheless because knowledge is the destiny of human beings, or at least of modern human beings. The Wandering Jew's "perilous outpost of the sane" (*C* 3, 19: 98) is the habitation of all earnest minds; the challenge is to occupy that post without falling into monomania and bitter misanthropy, like Mortmain, or into enervation and arch misanthropy, like Vine.

Clarel

By means of a pun, the curse on the Wandering Jew is also made to bear upon Clarel. "'Ruthless, he [the Wandering Jew] meriteth no ruth. / On him I imprecate the truth'" (*C* 3, 19: 57–58). Though Clarel is not yet permanently Ruth-less, his thoughts during the pilgrimage focus on how to live vis-à-vis knowledge: whether to front it openly, as Rolfe and others do, or to evade its claim through "solacement of mate" (*C* 1, 12: 12). Ruth is for Clarel what Esther is for the Wandering Jew, a proffered escape via Eros from the burdensome task of reuniting the world through knowledge (Logos). "Clarel and Ruth—might it but be," Melville mock-wistfully writes: "And youth and nature's fond accord / Wins Eden back" and makes "tales abstruse / Of Christ, the crucified, Pain's lord / Seem foreign—forged—incongruous" (*C* 1, 28: 1, 8–11). The lines appear in the canto "Tomb and Fountain," which introduces Vine, who will come to displace Ruth as Clarel's object of "personal longing" (*C* 2, 27: 73) and vehicle for redemption from intellectual and spiritual pain. Vine's unspoken rebuke to Clarel in the bower by the Jordan is a rejection not simply of homoerotic bonding but of *all* erotic bonding that seeks to avoid the obligation of the lapsed believer to push forward: "Art thou the first soul tried by doubt? / Shalt prove the last? Go, live it out" (*C* 2, 27: 123–24). It is as if Vine were confuting Matthew Arnold's plea for erotic deliverance in "Dover Beach," "Ah, love, let us be true to one another" (l. 29). Spurned by Vine, Clarel thinks again of Ruth. He is not prepared to accept the fate of the Wandering Jew. He will never be fully prepared, though circumstances (Ruth's death) will decide the issue for him.

The symbolic import of that death, prefigured throughout the poem by allusions to the Armenian bier, is to shatter the myth that Eden can be regained through domesticity. Ruth is the Yillah of *Clarel*, the symbol of a courtship bliss that cannot be maintained against the press of time and truth. From the first, Ruth's promise is hinted to be illusive. The girl who "looked a legate to insure / That Paradise is possible / Now as hereafter" (*C* 1, 16: 161–63) is, "deeper viewed," marked by something "amiss," "impaired," and wanting in "peace" (*C* 1, 16: 170–72), as if she herself doubted the comfort and solidity of what she represents. Melville is not denigrating Ruth as an individual or as a representative of womanhood; like Hawthorne with Faith in "Young Goodman Brown," he is showing how men idealize and thereby dehumanize women by making them instruments for their own salvation, denying them their own private insecurities and needs. As Nathan's child transplanted from pastoral America to an alien, God-fraught world, Ruth has her own pilgrimage to undergo, however much she may wish to escape it through the insulations of home and community.

Except in brief moments of nostalgia, domesticity is not a competing locus of value in *Clarel* any more than the green land is a serious temptation for Ahab. Apropos of art historian Henry T. Tuckerman, a bachelor friend of Melville's, Hershel Parker speculates on Melville's "envy for the respectable, apology-free, semi-monastic life that Melville might himself, after all, have been best fitted for."[26] Rolfe lives that life, as apparently do the other chief pilgrims—Mortmain, Vine, Derwent, Ungar, even the Druse guide Djalea. Reacting perhaps against the tensions and dissatisfactions of his own domestic life, Melville has avenged himself against *Pierre*'s "avenging dream" and valorized the solitariness of the unworldly yearner, on whom, as curse and potential blessing, he imprecates the undomesticated truth.

Of Laxer Mien

As the masque of the Wandering Jew closes, an opposing strain is heard: "Seedsmen of old Saturn's land, / Love and peace went hand in hand, / And sowed the Era Golden!" (*C* 3, 20: 1–3). The singer is the merchant of Lesbos, purveyor to Mar Saba, who led the pilgrims in revelry the previous night and whose festive paganism, set against the Wandering Jew's wail of pain, prompts Clarel to wonder "if in frames of thought / And feeling, there be right and wrong" or whether it is enough for "such counter natures in mankind" to be "true / Each to itself" (*C* 3, 20: 33–34, 39, 41–42). The merchant's song echoes an earlier celebration of the Golden Age by another Greek, the Cypriote, which, delivered "'o'er funeral Siddim'" (*C* 3, 4:2 3) and immediately following a canto on notions of heaven, is bizarrely inappropriate to time and place yet with a power to charm even Mortmain. The pilgrims marvel at the Cypriote's blithe spirits, uncurbed by the shroud he is carrying to immerse in the Jordan for his mother. Modern Greeks, Rolfe explains, "still retain their primal bent, / Nor let grave doctrine intercept / That gay Hellene lightheartedness / Which in the pagan years did twine / The funeral urn with fair caress / Of vintage holiday divine" (*C* 3, 4: 108–13). As if to illustrate the point, the Cypriote's parting song makes light of death, invoking the poem's chief symbol for carefree sensualism, the rose:

> With a rose in thy mouth
> Through the world lightly veer:
> Rose in the mouth
> Makes a rose of the year

. . . . With the Prince of the South
O'er the Styx bravely steer:
Rose in the mouth
And a wreath on the bier!
(*C* 3, 4: 129–32, 135–38)

Immortal gods, whose prime is ever-renewing, can afford to swear by the ephemeral rose. If mortals can also swear by it, cheerfully or stoically accepting the fact of annihilation, then worldly hedonism may represent a humanistic alternative to the pilgrims' obsession with otherworldly religion. It is significant in this respect that Melville's exemplary hedonists (the Lyonese Jew excepted) should be mainly latter-day Greeks. Shirley M. Dettlaff sees Melville following the German Romantics as filtered through Arnold and Mme. de Staël in morally centering *Clarel* upon the distinction between Greco-Roman classicism and Judeo-Christianity[27]— in Arnold's terms, "Hellenism" (marked by "*spontaneity of consciousness*") and "Hebraism" (identified with "*strictness of conscience*").[28] Arnold proposed his idealized Hellenism as an antidote to sectarian British philistinism, as Melville had proposed his classicism to American philistinism in "Statues in Rome" and might have done again in *Clarel*. Instead, he joins the Germanic notion of classical Greeks as "completely the children of nature"[29] (Mme. de Staël's words) with his travel impressions of contemporary Greeks. In doing so he denies *Clarel*'s Greeks both the intellectual and aesthetic contemplativeness of Arnold's Hellenes and the "refined and ennobled sensuality" conceded even by A. W. Schlegel.[30] The Cypriote in his youth is a prepossessing, if callow figure, but at middle age the Lesbian merchant, inhabitant of a "lax Paradise, / . . . Fruitful in all that can entice" (*C* 3, 11: 28, 30), is merely coarse, a reveler like Hawthorne's Merry Mounters, who, "after losing the heart's fresh gaiety, imagined a wild philosophy of pleasure" in flight from wisdom and responsibility.[31] The defect of *Clarel*'s Greeks is not that they are practical pagans (whatever their nominal belief) but that they are trivializing pagans whose "spontaneity of consciousness" amounts to little more than a lively instinct for the gratifications at hand. As Rolfe says of the Lesbian merchant,

Holding to *now*, swearing by *here*,
His course conducting by no keen
Observance of the stellar sphere—
He coasteth under sail latteen:
Then let him laugh, enjoy his dinner,
He's an excusable poor sinner.
(*C* 3, 13: 40–44)

In light of the Greek-inspired aestheticism that was emerging in contemporary England, it is surprising that neopaganism in *Clarel* should be presented so uniformly as vacuous and degrading. The connoisseurly Rolfe might have served as the model for a union of intellect with the pleasures of sense, yet even as Melville praises good-fellowship in *Clarel* he seems insistent (contrary to his stance in earlier works) on separating it from sensualism. After partaking very moderately in the revel at Mar Saba, Rolfe awakens with the spiritual equivalent of a hangover—"that refluence of disquiet dealt / In sequel to redundant joy"—and looks upon his fellow celebrants with "vague annoy" (*C* 3, 15: 7–8, 9). Melville had abruptly terminated the revel by a cry from outside: "*Lord, have mercy / Christ, have mercy. / Intercede for me*" (*C* 3, 14: 128–30). *Memento mori* are never far offstage in *Clarel*, and while death may not make cowards of the pilgrims, it does tend to situate their lives *sub specie aeternitatis* in a way that precludes moral naturalism of any sort.

In later years Melville would show himself responsive to a refined epicureanism. *Clarel* is more austere, otherworldly, and Manichaean, reflecting the disciplined inwardness Melville cultivated during this period, partly against the venality and tedium of life in the New York Custom House and the emotional strains and petty irritations of life at East Twenty-sixth Street. It would take retirement to set Melville at relative ease with himself and the sensuous world, though bonhomie still figured largely in the compensatory life he imagined. It is hard to say why more of the spirit of the near-contemporaneous Burgundy Club sketches failed to find its way into *Clarel*. The aura of Palestine, as Melville remembered it, may have imprinted itself upon the poem, but more likely Melville's spiritual priorities simply swept everything else before them. He meant the poem to bring matters to a head for himself as it did for his characters, if only in a series of unanswerable questions for which the condition of the Wandering Jew was his emblem. Like George Herbert in his seventeenth-century lyric "The Pulley," Melville seems to have felt that dissatisfaction with the blessings of the world—"repining restlesnesse"[32]—was necessary to bring human beings, if not to God's breast, then inwardly to their own. Although uncertain about the "stellar sphere," *Clarel* is fixedly oriented toward it, and its moral scheme cannot afford to include a sophisticated hedonism even if Melville in the 1870s had been able to conceive one. The foil to "earnest" needed to be "lax."

The Confidence Man

Early in the poem Clarel had longed for a guide figure who would "expound and prove, / And make [his] heart to burn with love" (*C* 1, 8: 50–51). The climax of this hope is his colloquy with Derwent in the canto "In Confidence," whose title resonates ambiguously of the intimacy of the priestly confessional and the fatuousness of philosophical optimism in *The Confidence-Man*. Derwent had earlier given Clarel a look that intimated "some saving truth" (*C* 2, 22: 139) to be communicated when the time was ripe. "In Confidence" is Derwent's occasion to make good on his promise and to justify his anti-intellectual response to the condition of agnosis: "let me live but by the heart!" (*C* 3, 6: 69). "Hast proved thy heart? first prove it" (*C* 3, 6: 70), Mortmain retorts. The interview with Clarel is Derwent's moment of personal trial and, synecdochically, of liberal religion's intellectual trial. Is meliorist belief a usable adaptation of Christianity to the modern age or, as Rolfe says, is Derwent's idol—a reconciliation of science and faith—"an hermaphrodite" (*C* 3, 16: 174)?

The portrait of Derwent in "The Cavalcade" is the most engaging of Melville's Chaucerian prefatory sketches but also, in substance, the least adequate to its subject. As Newton Arvin observed, Derwent is a dynamic character who "grows in grace as the poem proceeds, developing lights and shadows of personal quality one had not suspected."[33] Grows in everything *except* grace, it might be truer to say, if grace refers to a spiritual quality rather than simply gracefulness of manner. "I like you" (*C* 2, 33: 93) Rolfe tells Derwent after one of their good-humored but exasperating debates. The reader likes Derwent, too, even while recognizing the code-words ("skim," "trim," "rosy") that identify this worshipper of sunrises as another of Melville's sanguine, prosperous males who "urbanely disengage / Sadness and doubt from all things sad / And dubious deemed" (*C* 2, 1: 48–50). Derwent might almost be parodic or sinister if his avoidance of darkness were not a deep necessity of temperament. Derwent recoils at the unpleasant as an aesthete does at the deformed, with an instinctive shudder of his entire being.

"In Confidence" opens with Derwent exulting in the beauty of the dawn, which rises, significantly (but not for Derwent), over an Arnoldian "throe-lock of transitional earth / When old forms are annulled, and new / Rebel, and pangs suspend the birth" (*C* 3, 21: 17–19). The ensuing scene movingly personalizes the pain of unknowing that, except in Celio, the poem has hitherto presented chiefly as an abstraction. Clarel begins by questioning Derwent about the confusion of sects that had bewildered Celio and that compounds the problem of belief with the subsidiary problem, "Belief in *what?*" Derwent's answer—an appeal to the mythic truth inhering in diverse outward forms—is an effort to save Christianity from its own divisiveness and rigid theology, as Arnold tried to do in the four books on Christianity and the Bible he published in the 1870s. The name "Derwent" recalls the river of Wordsworth's Lake Country, and it may be that in sketching his benevolist priest Melville was thinking of the lines from "Stanzas in Memory of the Author of 'Obermann'" he marked in his copy of Arnold's *Poems*: "But Wordsworth's eyes avert their ken / From half of human fate."[34] The river Derwent is also associated with Arnold himself, whose father, a friend of Wordsworth, purchased a summer house near the poet in the 1830s. Bezanson compares Derwent's liberal progressivism with the Broad Church movement championed by Thomas Arnold in the 1820s and 1830s and renovated (after his fashion) by Matthew in his later prose. Melville's surviving copy of Arnold's *Literature and Dogma* (1873) is dated 1881, but even as he wrote *Clarel* Melville may have been aware of Arnold's controversial argument that to remain viable Christianity had to be relieved of its "mechanical and materialising theology, with its insane licence of affirmation about God, its insane licence of affirmation about a future state."[35]

Whether or not Meville had Arnold specifically in mind, Derwent is an Arnoldian revisionist convinced of the worldly value of Christianity but not of its otherworldly truth. Likening the years just before Jesus to his own century, as Arnold had in "Obermann Once More," Derwent asks, "What [for the priest of Apollo to do] but to temporize . . . , / Stranded upon an interim / Between the ebb and flood?" (*C* 3, 21: 214–16) "Temporize" may represent the sagacity of a broadly cyclical view of history or it may be the kind of metaphysical paltering Melville satirized in *The Confidence-Man*. For Derwent, in any case, cyclicalism is only a tactic, for the real issue is the pragmatic one posed earlier by Rolfe and the Dominican: can human beings live *without* Christianity:

> Christ built a hearth: the flame is dead
> We'll say, extinct; but lingers yet,
> Enlodged in stone, the hoarded heat.
> Why not nurse that? Would rive the door
> And let the sleet in? But, once o'er,
> This tarrying glow, never to man,
> Methinks, shall come the like again.
> What if some camp on crags austere
> The Stoic held ere Gospel cheer?
> *There* may the common herd abide.
> Having dreamed of heaven? Nay, and can you?
> You shun that; what shall needier do?
> Think, think!
>
> (*C* 3, 21: 245–57)

To this general appeal Derwent adds a note of personal history that mirrors Arnold's evolution from introverted laureate of doubt to extroverted cultural sage: "All your ado / In youth was mine; your swarm I knew / Of buzzing doubts. But is it good / Such gnats to fight? or well to brood / In selfish introverted search, / Leaving the poor world in the lurch?" (*C* 3, 21: 260–65). The lines seem almost a recasting of "Rugby Chapel," with Derwent asking Clarel what Arnold's God-figure asks the "storm-beat" pilgrims arrived at the end of their journey: "Whom in our party [do] we bring? / Whom we have left in the snow?" (ll. 114, 115–16). Through Derwent, Melville is representing the mid-Victorian position articulated by Arnold that Christianity, however vulnerable as doctrine, can and must be salvaged as metaphoric truth because it ministers to human psychological and social needs. The weakness of Derwent's argument is the weakness of Arnold's; as Leon Gottfried put it, "the louder it is asserted, 'Religious truth is proved by its adequacy to man's needs; try it and see,' the more surely the critical response is likely to become, 'All that such adequacy really proves is that the religious view of life is manufactured out of those very needs.'"[36] In answer to Derwent's casuistry, Clarel asks the naïf's stubborn yet all-important question: But is Christianity *true*? "A rite they solemnize—" he stammeringly begins, referring to the passion and resurrection that establish Christianity as a religion rather than merely an admirable system of ethics. Derwent equivocates; "Betwixt rejection and belief, / Shadings there are" (*C* 3, 21: 281–82), he tells Clarel, underscoring the poem's vision of Christianity as in doctrinal retreat, with Rome upholding orthodoxy, scientific materialism eroding it, and Derwent's Protestantism left to occupy the slippery slope of concession and compromise.

Melville might have resolved this pivotal canto in any number of ways, depending on how persuasive a hearing he wished to give liberal religion and how urgently he wanted to reason himself into religious stability. The notable fact, in light of his own Unitarian affinities, is the want of sympathy and intellectual respect he chose to give the liberal argument. As Clarel grows more earnest, Derwent becomes more shallow, his final plea consisting in an appeal to cultural fashion: Byron and Shelley are dead, pained introspection is "no more the mode," and "e'ven Hamlet's sigh" would now seem "perverse" —worse yet, "indecorous" (*C* 3, 21: 285, 295, 296). The lines echo Arnold's complaint in "Stanzas from the Grande Chartreuse" that the melancholy of Byron and Shelley "is a pass'd mode, an outworn theme" (l. 100). The difference between "Stanzas" and *Clarel* is in how they react to post-Romantic spiritual alienation. Where Arnold the poet (prior to his transformation into the moralist-critic of the 1860s and later) luxuriates in self-pity, convinced that "the nobleness of grief is gone" (l. 107) and with it the appreciative audience for his suffering, Melville finds the nobility of the seeker *enhanced* by the circumstance of unmodish isolation and private trial. Listening to Derwent, Clarel feels stirrings of this nobility in himself, and for the first and only time in the poem he grows heated: "Forbear! / Ah, wherefore not at once name Job,

/ In whom these Hamlets all conglobe. / Own, own with me, and spare to feign, / Doubt bleeds, nor Faith is free from pain!" (*C* 3, 21: 300–304). This is Paul Tillich's doubt-riddled faith, or, as *Clarel* presents it, faith-riddled doubt. Derwent wants none of it; "Alas, too deep you dive" (*C* 3, 21: 307) he says, in abject confession of what the poem has intimated all along: that Derwent is a "skimmer" whose claim to have modernized Christianity is a confidence-trick delusive to the intellect and perilous for the soul. The canto ends with the wedge between mind and spirit driven deeper than ever and a dismayed Clarel wondering if the only belief may not be one like Nehemiah's, below reason or beyond reason but in either case unavailable to the thought-burdened modern.

Living Like a God

"We sham, we shuffle while faith declines— / They were frank in the Age of the Antonines," Melville wrote ("The Age of the Antonines," *Poems* 325). The countertype to Derwent the shuffler is Rolfe the modern Antonine, who "too frank, too unreserved, may be, / And indiscreet in honesty" (*C* 1, 31: 24–25), as if this could be anything but a virtue in a world of intellectual sleight of hand and guarded gentility. With "a genial heart, a brain austere" (*C* 1, 31: 14), Rolfe is an earnest figure saved from overearnestness by his leaven of humor and self-irony and by a free inquisitiveness that, joined to his broad comparativist knowledge of religion and myth, keeps him alive to the possibility of belief even as he interrogates its claims of referential truth. A descendant of Babbalanja and Ishmael, Rolfe is differenced from them by a ripe maturity. In this respect, though he is sometimes described as an idealized version of the midcentury Melville, he is more accurately a synthesis of Melville-now and Melville-then, the mellowed intellect of the older man refracted through the sensibility of the younger.

The contradiction in Rolfe that most baffles Clarel is his peculiar combination of reverence and irreverence. His visit to the manger recalls for him stories of the "Greeks show[ing] the place where Argo landed" and "the goddess suckled Hercules" (*C* 4, 18: 87–88, 92). The holy sites of Palestine typically have a demystifying effect on Rolfe, as they did on Melville and countless other nineteenth-century pilgrims. Yet Rolfe's skepticism never extends to sneering at holiness itself, whether represented by Jesus, the Syrian monk, the "seraphic" St. Francis (*C* 4, 14: 71), or the Franciscan Salvaterra. As Lawrence Buell observed, Rolfe "is both outspoken in his exposure of religious and ritual formulas and respectful of real religious sincerity."[37] It is precisely because his ideal of Christianity is so high—Derwent dismisses his vision of the early church as mere poetry (*C* 2, 21: 111–14)—that Rolfe objects to its theology, which he can square neither metaphysically with the testimony of experience nor morally with human ethics and the practice of avowed Christians.

Beyond mature self-poise, what distinguishes Rolfe from his predecessors is what distinguishes *Clarel* itself: his (and his creator's) willingness to explore the psychological foundations of belief. "Long as children feel affright / In Darkness, men shall fear a God," Rolfe says, "And long as daisies yield delight / Shall see His footprints in the sod" (*C* 1, 31: 187–90).[38] Aside from terror and wonder, *Clarel* posits a third inducement to belief: the hunger for a paternal presence more intimate than the Supreme Mechanic of deistic science; in the Dominican's words, "'Tis Abba Father that we seek, / Not the Artificer" (*C* 2, 25: 158–59). To approach religion by way of its psychic origins is to add another layer of indeterminacy to the problem of its truth; it is to consider religion as what Freud called an "illusion," by which he meant not necessarily an untruth but a fiction "derived from human wishes" and equally unsusceptible of proof and disproof.[39] The "teachings" of religion, Freud remarked in an argument resembling Rolfe's,

> are illusions, fulfillments of the oldest, strongest, and most urgent wishes of mankind. The secret of their strength lies in the strength of those wishes. As we already know, the terrifying impression of helplessness in childhood aroused the need for protection through love— which was provided by the father; and the recognition that this helplessness lasts throughout life made it necessary to cling to the existence of a father, but this time a more powerful one. Thus the benevolent rule of a divine Providence allays our fear of the dangers of life; the establishment of a moral world-order ensures the fulfillment of the demands of justice which have so often remained unfulfilled in human civilization; and the prolongation of earthly existence in a future life provides the local and temporal framework in which these wish-fulfillments shall take place.[40]

Melville understands this, but he also knows that to deconstruct the religious impulse is not ipso facto to discredit it, much less to uproot it. The question, nonetheless, is one of the legitimacy of belief. Emotionally, "The wrong / Of carpings [e.g., Niebuhr and Strauss] never may undo / The nerves that clasp the plea / Tingling with kinship through and through" (*C* 1, 3: 114–17). But is "tingling" enough to justify a metaphysics? Melville's seekers in *Clarel* are in precisely the position Hawthorne ascribed to Melville himself: they "can neither believe, nor be comfortable in [their] unbelief; and [they are] too honest and courageous not to try to do one or the other."[41] Or rather, they are too honest and courageous not to try to *refrain from doing* one or the other. Resisting the lure of belief and unbelief alike, Melville's modern spiritual heroes live strenuously in the unending tension between them.

Had Melville lived another few years he might have engaged himself with William James's argument in "The Will to Believe" that "*our passional nature not only lawfully may, but must, decide an option between propositions, whenever it is a genuine option that cannot by its nature be decided on intellectual grounds,*" and whenever it is a "*forced* option" that we practically decide in the negative (losing the advantages of belief) when we defer decision indefinitely.[42] Without citing James, Freud dismissed such reasoning summarily: "Ignorance is ignorance; no right to believe anything can be derived from it."[43] Melville might have raised a more Jamesian objection to James: that belief is always belief in *something*—in religion's case, a set of propositions about the world—and that, as James argued in "Pragmatism's Conception of Truth," "our ideas must agree with realities, be such realities concrete or abstract, be they facts or be they principles, under penalty of endless inconsistency and frustration."[44] The test of belief for Melville was always congruence with "the visable truth": "the apprehension of the absolute condition of present things as they strike the eye of the man who fears them not" (*Corr* 186). In these terms, Celio's indictment of the disparity between Jesus' gospel and worldly experience seems Melville's own: "What isolation lones thy state / That all else we know cannot mate / With what thou teachest?" (*C* 1, 13: 78–80). And yet the "tingling" of "kinship" precluded outright denial. If Starbuck was unwarranted in "let[ting] faith oust fact" (*MD* 492), so was Ahab in allowing "the dark side of earth" to blind him to "its other side, the theoretic bright one" (*MD* 528). Still worse was the indifference of a Stubb, who chose not to think, or a Flask, who lived his animal life incapable of thinking.

Agnostic spirituality descends from Ishmael's "Doubts of all things earthly, and intuitions of some things heavenly" (*MD* 374), but it casts spiritual life at a higher pitch. Unlike the agnosticism of scientific positivism (Huxley), of secular indifference (Stubb and Flask), and of jaunty, receptive intellectual play (Ishmael), it maintains the balanced suspension of belief and unbelief with a near-continuous intensity of engagement—what Tillich called the quality of "being unconditionally concerned."[45] "You cannot reach God," Tillich wrote, "by works of right thinking or by a sacrifice of the intellect or by a submission to strange authorities, such as the doctrines of the church and the Bible."[46] Neither, he adds, must godliness be attained through a victorious struggle with unbelief. It is enough, for the religious life, to bear oneself with "unconditional seriousness" in "the status of *doubt,*" which Tillich equates with living "in the status of truth," a distinctively modern form of the Protestant "justification through faith."[47]

The achievement of Rolfe is not simply to strike a mean between earnestness and geniality. His life is an effort such as Tillich describes (but without the title "Christian") to preserve an agnosticism that burns with the will to know while resisting temptations to closure that would slight the facts of suffering and evil (liberal meliorism), demean human nature (scientific materialism), or abridge intellectual sovereignty (Roman orthodoxy). Rolfe's trial is to endure the pressures of such a life alone, without a framework of doctrine and value to uphold him and confirm his sense of worth and without the sympathy of a sustaining community. His situation is that of the Indian Rama, whose fate Melville describes shortly after Rolfe's entry into the poem "A god he was, but knew it not; / Hence vainly puzzled at the wrong / Misplacing him in human lot" (C 1, 32: 2–4). All of Melville's tragic heroes (Babbalanja /Taji, Ahab, Pierre) are misplaced gods of one sort or another, exiled royalties stripped of their divine inheritance and left to roam as outcasts through an alien world. Rolfe shares this Wandering Jew's fate but is distinguished from the others in making no fuss about it and seeming oblivious to what Ahab calls his "royal rights" (MD 507). Like Rama, Rolfe is "a fugitive without redress / [who] never the Holy Spirit grieved, / Nor the divine in him bereaved, / Though what that was he might not guess" (C 1, 32: 8–11). Where Ahab and Pierre had gloried in a consciousness of grandeur, Rolfe is distinguished by a thorough unconsciousness of godlike merit, which it falls upon the narrator to commend. His godlikeness is not dependent on his finding, worshipping, or worshipfully defying a transcendent God; it resides in the elevation of the human personality that comes from living searchingly without illusion under the extraordinary demands of the agnostic life, not least of them the proscription that keeps the agnostic from ever suspecting his doubt is deifying.

Clarel's destiny, if he can rise to it, is to mature into Rolfe. He would not do so willingly. Rolfe unsettles him with his probing and his candor, yet Clarel instinctively realizes "this pressure . . . need be endured: / Weakness to strength must get inured" (C 2, 21: 127–28). As the poem unfolds, Clarel is drawn closer toward Rolfe, but it is Ruth's death more than any decision of his own that leaves Clarel alone amid the crowd of sufferers on the Via Crucis—"Cross-bearers all," Melville writes of them, yet different from Clarel, who "now, at close of rarer quest, / Finds so much more the heavier tree" (C 4, 34: 43, 47–48), the tree of consciousness. In terms of resolving the crisis with which it opened, the poem has gone virtually nowhere. Clarel's predicament has only deepened as he has grown more aware, yet depth and awareness are themselves indices of value in Melville's world. Clarel still "does not know"—about God, Christ, immortality, himself. Whether his unknowing will develop from youthful bewilderment into the religious areligion of Rolfe is left unhinted, and with it the future of his entire spiritual generation, which may or not consent to face the perplexities of being modern.

Ripened Pain

In 1884, eight years after he published *Clarel*, Melville joined the All Souls Unitarian Church not far from his home in New York City. Hershel Parker passes lightly over the event, suggesting that Melville may have been "mellowing toward youths of genteel capacity" like the church's new Clarel-like minister, Theodore Chickering Williams, or that perhaps he was trying to accommodate Lizzie in the wake of her brother Lemuel's recent death.[48] "The year 1884 was the worst for the [Melville] family since 1872," Parker observes.[49] The chief disaster was the death of Melville's younger brother Tom, which "meant the end of the Melvilles as a clan."[50] The church may have offered Melville promise of a substitute family; beyond that, it is hard to gauge what his act of membership meant. Heterogeneous as a sect, Unitarians differed among themselves even within particular congregations. As the Walter D. Kring, a former minister and historian of All Souls, points out, the covenant that members accepted "was not a creed," and "each individual member had the responsibility to make up his mind as to what he himself believed." In joining the church, Melville "simply agreed to search for the truth and to adopt whatever he believed to be the truth for his own use."[51] The search might even include the findings of the German Higher Criticism, whose acceptance in America "was greatest among Unitarians."[52] It is not known what part Melville took in the church, how often he attended it, or how he construed its basic principles.

In the absence of primary materials other than asides in letters and cryptic reading marginalia, *Clarel* is the chief evidence for the older Melville's religion, with the poem's epilogue perhaps the closest thing to his religious "testament." The epilogue begins with a doubly conditional question: "If Luther's day expands to Darwin's year, / Shall that exclude the hope—foreclose the fear?" (*C* 4, 35: 1–2). The first condition is historical: will scientific materialism establish itself through the indefinite future? The second is religious: if materialism does prevail, will it put an end to thoughts of God and immortality? Both questions are unanswerable. The measure of spirituality is thus thrown back upon temporal life to the nature of individual behavior during this long limbo: "The running battle of the star and the clod / Shall run forever—if there be no God" (*C* 4, 35: 16–17). The "star" is heavenly aspiration (or simply human idealism generally), the "clod" earthly gratification. The peculiar twist Melville gives the lines is to make the star independent of God's existence. The star is not God or belief in God; it is the ennobling quality within the human that seeks God against the downward pull of the clay and that will continue to do so, from its own tropism toward spiritual light, as long as God remains unrevealed. The "strife and old debate" between "ape and angel" (*C* 4, 35: 12) has been redefined in psychospiritual terms alone, without reference to a problematic Transcendent. To be "spiritual" is not to worship God; it is to live and think and feel as if on the stretch, not *at* but just *beyond* the height of the human.

Earlier in part 4 Melville foreshadowed this idea when he had Clarel respond to one of Ungar's polemics on human wickedness:

> If man in truth be what you say,
> And such the prospects for the clay,
> And outlook for the future—cease!
> What's left us but the senses' sway?
> Sinner, sin out life's petty lease:
> We are not worth the saving. Nay,
> For me, if thou speak true—but ah,
> Yet, yet there gleams one beckoning star—
> So near the horizon, judge I right
> That 'tis of heaven?
>
> (*C* 4, 22: 61–69)

For Clarel, a religion founded on human depravity and requiring that sinners "*be born anew*" (*C* 4, 22: 41) is as demoralizing as atheistic materialism. If human beings are not in their own nature "worth the saving," then it matters little to Clarel that God and Christ have the condescending power to save them. Clarel wants to believe (in Unitarian fashion) that life is steadfastly moral and that human beings define themselves as better or worse by their freely chosen commitments and behaviors. The star is his marker for such spiritual navigation, but located "so near the horizon," just above the boundary of the terrestrial world, the star is of uncertain origin; it may descend from heaven as a guide to mortals or it may rise from earth (like ideas of heaven itself?) as an expression of human idealism and aspiration. "An act of faith," Tillich said, "is an act of a finite being who is grasped by and turned toward the infinite."[53] Melville would have agreed, adding, that the site of the "infinite" is finally undeterminable; it may be outside the self, intuited by spirit, or inside the self, known chiefly through an exalted and exalting self-approbation at certain motions of one's being. The spiritual agnostic is one who swears by the star—the infinite—without knowing its metaphysical status and who lives with no more than a shadowy hope that his renunciation of "the senses' sway" will be vindicated in another world. The essential question for the agnostic is not whether man will be saved but, as Clarel says, whether he is worth the saving.[54]

"Wherefore ripen us to pain?" (C 4, 35: 21) Melville asks in the epilogue. This is Job's question, transferred to the realm of thought. Living in the modern age, when "the light is greater, hence the shadow more" (C 4, 35: 19), means being ripened by consciousness "*to* pain." Does it also mean being ripened to a higher spiritual life *by* pain? Surveying nineteenth-century British accounts of religious crisis, Frank M. Turner notes that

> doubters and unbelievers repeatedly presented their new lives pursued without the solace and support of their original faith as more difficult, rigorous, and in a sense less worldly than their earlier lives as conforming Christians. They had left the way of easy faith for a more arduous path. They had passed from a nominal religious life to a real one. In the process they had moved from an intellectually and morally inadequate position to one that accorded with the real, fundamental truth of morality, history, and nature.[55]

Against the contemporary vogue of "muscular Christianity," Turner's apostates posed their own muscular non-Christianity. The key word is "arduous," which suggests the rigors of a spiritual life that begins, not ends, with deconversion. The agnostic is as strenuously embattled a pilgrim as Bunyan's Christian, beset by the temptations of a materialist Vanity Fair and subject not to one but to multiple, recurrent Sloughs of Despond. The difference is that the agnostic has no guidebook to direct him, no wise counselors along the way, and no assurance of a Celestial City at the end of his journey, which, like the Wandering Jew's, has no end. Though hopeful of immortality, the agnostic must stake his life on the infinite within the finite and justify himself by a fidelity to impulses he intuitively grasps as "spiritual," whether or not God exists. He must ask, with Clarel, "how live / At all, if once a fugitive / From thy own nobler part, though pain / Be portion inwrought with the grain?" (C 4, 28: 81–84).

Clarel's enthusiasm for spiritual heroism is intermittent, but the poem's is not. The heroes of *Moby-Dick* and *Pierre* were heaven-stormers who sought their apotheosis through filial rebellion against the divine. The triumph of *Clarel* is to assert man's godlikeness in the absence or abeyance of the divine, and to do so with a quiet, unassuming dignity at once humble and regally proud, and manifest above all in the voice of the narrator. "Quiet" should not be taken to imply peaceful or settled, much less resigned. It means only that Melville's turbulence of spirit has been directed inward and, while still undammed, has been contained within levees and made to run straighter, deeper, and in courses that no longer threaten to inundate the landscape, save in overflow channels like "Mortmain" and "Ungar." Melville needs such figures, for he has not entirely overcome the bitterness of spiritual exile and literary neglect. The thrust of *Clarel*, however, is not to purge anger and frustration but to control them while shaping a spiritual life within the indeterminacy (agnosis) that Melville now accepts as the ineluctable condition of the modern intellectual. ·

10

Alms for Oblivion

Achilles: What, are my deeds forgot?

Ulysses: Time hath, my lord, a wallet at his back,

Wherein he puts alms for oblivion,

A great-siz'd monster of ingratitudes,

Those scraps of good deeds past, which are devour'd

As fast as they are made, forgot as soon

As done. Perseverance, dear my lord,

Keeps honor bright . . . .

    —Shakespeare, *Troilus and Cressida* (3, 3, 144–51)

It is possession of a great heart or a great head, and not

the mere fame of it, which is worth having and conducive

to happiness. Not fame, but that which deserves to be

famous, is what a man should hold in esteem.

    —Schopenhauer, *The Wisdom of Life*

The Gray Election

Shortly after Melville retired from the New York Custom House on December 31, 1885, his wife Lizzie wrote of a "great deal [of] unfinished work at his desk which will give him occupation."[1] A legacy from Lizzie's brother Lemuel Shaw had eased the family situation and placed Melville in the happy predicament he later allegorized in the poem "The Rose Farmer":

whether to cultivate the rose (experience) for its yield of evanescent pleasure or laboriously to distill and crystallize its attar in a timeless but solitary art. Although "The Rose Farmer" ends inconclusively, a cozy epicureanism was at most a wishful fantasy for Melville, who had outlived his generational male relatives, nearly all of his friends, and his times, but not his longstanding obsessions, metaphysics and the taunting dream of reputation. At home, while generally calmer than before, Melville was still prey to "moods and occasional uncertain tempers,"[2] surfacings of an emotional disquiet that hinted, as always with him, of an intellectual, spiritual, and vocational disquiet. Toward the outward world he adopted the stance of a recluse, less from misanthropy than from a silent, self-protective pride. In the nearly ten years since *Clarel* his life had been collapsing inward toward a center of private musing, which in his physically and emotionally weakened state he nurtured carefully against inordinate hopes and the chance of real or imagined slights. Invited to join the Authors Club, a group of New York literati, in 1882, Melville accepted, then withdrew his acceptance on the ground that "he had become too much of a hermit" and that "his nerves could not stand large gatherings."[3] In most things having to do with society, he preferred not to. "A few friends felt at liberty to visit him," wrote young Arthur Stedman, one of the privileged, but "he himself sought no one."[4]

Consonant with Melville's guarded life was "his marked unwillingness to speak of himself, his adventures or his writings in conversation," even to sympathetic listeners like Stedman,[5] as if his active life and literary career belonged to a buried past more wisely left undisturbed. "To forget is the great secret of strong and creative lives,—to forget utterly"[6]—a remark from Balzac he scored in or after August 1885. If Melville didn't forget, he at least simulated forgetfulness, down to telling a visitor that "he didn't own a single copy" of his books,[7] though he managed to unearth a copy of *Clarel* for English admirer James Billson in 1885, "fearing," as he said, "that you will never get at it by yourself" (*Corr* 486). The homage of Billson, with whom he corresponded for more than four years, and of Englishmen W. Clark Russell and H. S. Salt, was gratifying to Melville both as private testimonial and as it gave promise of belated or posthumous recognition without entailing risks. Otherwise, he seemed to visitors "contented to be forgotten."[8] At some point in his later life he checked an observation from William Rounseville Alger's *The Solitudes of Nature and of Man*, "It is not aspiration but ambition, this is the mother of misery in man," adding in the margin "H. M."[9] The great struggle of his last years, aside from summoning the physical and psychological energies to write,[10] was to separate aspiration (thought and art as transfiguring spiritual activities) from ambition (desire for fame).

By now his relationship with Lizzie had settled into what passed at least for "the companionable ease of husband and wife who have grown old together."[11] Of their children, Malcolm was long dead but scarcely forgotten; Stanwix, a dropout who never found himself, would die of tuberculosis in San Francisco in 1886; Bessie was an invalid and spinster living at home; and Frances, with her lifelong resentment toward her father, was comfortably married to Henry B. Thomas. In August 1884 Lizzie bought Melville a copy of Anglican clergyman Samuel Reynolds Hole's *A Book about Roses* (1883), and the urban Melville became, if was he was not already, a rose gardener. Hole's book was just the sort of quirky sui generis Melville treasured, a witty, allusive, hyperbolically heroic and mock-heroic celebration of the rose permeated with a genial, uninsistent moral and religious symbolism. For Hole, the rose garden was an enclave of serenity created by art, labor, and love that went as far toward repairing the ravages of the Fall as sublunary efforts could. "The Rosarium," Hole wrote of the garden in a passage Melville marked, "must be both exposed and sheltered; a place of both sunshine and of shade. The center must be clear and open, around it the protecting screen. It must be a fold wherein the sun shines warmly on the sheep, and the wind is tempered to the shorn lamb; a haven in which the soft breeze flutters the sails, but over which the tempest roars, and against whose piers the billow hurls itself, in vain."[12]

Hole might as easily have been describing the terms of Melville's life, a convent-like retreat that was carefully protected against incursions from the disorderly world without. Hole quotes Sir William Temple on "'the sweetness and satisfaction'" of his garden, "'where, since my resolution taken of never entering again into any public employments, I have passed five years without ever going once to town, though I am almost in sight of it, and have a house there ready to receive me.'"[13] Melville didn't have a second house, but he did have an austere, monastic room facing "bleakly north" and filled (his granddaughter Eleanor Melville Metcalf recalled) with a "great mahogany desk," "four shelves of dull gilt and leather books," "strange plaster heads," and a "small black iron bed." Posted on a sidewall by his desk, "well out of sight" to all but himself, "was a printed slip of paper" with a line from Schiller "that read simply, 'Keep true to the dreams of thy youth.'"[14] Metcalf understands those dreams as expressing "the deepest needs of the whole man" and reflecting "a desire to nourish the roots of life," which she believes "were religious in nature" for Melville.[15]

The rose garden and the study: these were the symbolic loci of Melville's world after 1885 as he asked himself whether an elderly man "come unto [his] roses late" ("WW" 44) should harvest the rose for enjoyment or profit or press its petals into art. "I did not care what it was all about," Hemingway's Jake Barnes says in *The Sun Also Rises*: "All I wanted to know was how to live in it. Maybe if you found out how to live in it you learned from that what it was all about."[16] Hemingway's title and epigraph are from Ecclesiastes, one of Melville's two favorite books of the Bible (Job was the other), and they suggest a futility that Melville himself must have felt as he looked back upon his sixty-odd years, on America's more than a hundred, and on Christendom's nearly two thousand. Melville never ceased caring what life was about, but, despairing of an answer through intellect or faith, he increasingly came to feel that living "aright," as instinctively grasped by the spirit, was the closest one might come to finding its meaning. In the poem "The Garden of Metrodorus" from *Timoleon*, Melville looks upon his cultivated life from outside and wonders about the adequacy of its seclusion:

> The Athenians mark the moss-grown gate
> And hedge untrimmed that hides the haven green:
> And who keeps here this quiet state?
> And shares he sad or happy fate
> Where never foot-path to the gate is seen?
>
> Here none come forth, here none go in,
> Here silence strange, and dumb seclusion dwell:
> Content from loneness who may win?
> And is this stillness peace or sin
> Which noteless thus apart can keep its dell?
>
> (*Poems* 317)

Melville knew Metrodorus from (among other sources) Schopenhauer's work *The Wisdom of Life*, which he read in 1891 and which alludes to Metrodorus as a disciple of Epicurus who titled one of his chapters "*The Happiness we receive from ourselves is greater than that which we obtain from our surroundings.*"[17] Melville was familiar with Schopenhauer in a general way from the early 1870s through Alger's book *The Solitudes of Nature and of Man*, though he probably did not read him until the first months of 1891.[18] When he did, he found what amounted to an ideology of leisure that crystallized his own thoughts expressed in several of the poems in *Timoleon* and "Weeds and Wildings." On one side, Schopenhauer commended the life of withdrawal Melville had chosen for himself: "The wise man will, above all, strive after freedom from pain and annoyance, quiet and leisure, consequently a tranquil modest life, with as few encounters as may be"; if "he is a man of great intellect," he may even elect to live "in solitude," having had enough of "his so-called fellowmen" (Schopenhauer, *The Wisdom of Life* 23–24). On the other side, Schopenhauer's wise man had a deep obligation to himself: "Mere leisure, that is to say, intellect unoccupied in the service of the will, is not of itself sufficient; . . . for as Seneca says, *otium sine litteris mors et vivi hominis sepultura*—illiterate leisure is a form of death, a living tomb" (Schopenhauer, *The Wisdom of Life* 36).

Otium is the virtue associated with literary pastoral, a "state of content and mental self-sufficiency" that is removed from the world but predicated, unlike Schopenhauer's retirement, on "the rejection of the aspiring mind."[19] The attraction of Metrodorus's "haven green" is its quiescence, but does quiescence also involve an ignoble *ac*quiescence? Is the "stillness" of the garden a genuine "peace" or does its "loneness" breed *dis*content and its languor constitute a "sin"? The question Melville asks concerns the moral quality of seclusion. The critical word is "noteless": is a leisure *sine litteris* (literally, without letters) "a living tomb" because it is mute and lacks the vindicating expression of the aspiring mind? "A man wants to use his strength, to see, if he can, what effect it will produce," Schopenhauer wrote: "those are happiest of all who are conscious of the power to produce great works animated by some significant purpose" (Schopenhauer, *Counsels and Maxims* 704, 705). A life of retirement (the garden) was valuable for Schopenhauer to the extent that it reoriented the gardener from the outer to the inner life, from the sensuous world to the monastic room of intellectual and artistic creation.

Melville's own retirement was anything but illiterate. Aside from his wide reading (it requires dedication and a faith in longevity for a septuagenarian to purchase eight volumes of Schopenhauer),[20] Melville wrote or revised poems for three late collections—*John Marr and Other Sailors* (1888), *Timoleon, Etc* (1891), and "Weeds and Wildings Chiefly: With a Rose of Two" (posthumous, 1924)—and began and narratively completed *Billy Budd, Sailor* (posthumous, 1924). Dating individual poems is mostly conjectural. With "Weeds and Wildings" in mind, Newton Arvin wrote of "the unprotesting tranquillity that Melville achieved at the end of his life,"[21] but in fact many of the pastorals in "Weeds and Wildings" were contemporaneous with the nautical poems in *John Marr* and were intended for an inclusive volume provisionally titled *Meadows and Seas*.[22] The mood of "Weeds and Wildings" is a function of genre and occasion, as are the moods of different sections of the other volumes. Within our construction of the mind and sensibility of Old Man Melville, the chronology of poetic publication cannot be taken straightforwardly as a guide to Melville's inner development.[23] The constant through nearly all of this period—what Hershel Parker calls "the single obsessive labor of Melville's last lustrum"[24]—was Melville's engagement with *Billy Budd*, whose phases of composition were datably identified by Harrison Hayford and Merton M. Sealts, Jr. If there is a "story" to be told about late Melville, it is to be inferred from the unfolding of the *Billy Budd* manuscript within the context of the poems (revised, if not always initially drafted during this period), as both novella and poems arise from, extend, resolve, or fail to resolve standing concerns of Melville's forty-five-year career.

Lone Founts

Privately printed in an edition of twenty-five copies, *John Marr* sounds some of the notes that will dominate Melville's final period: solitude and alienation; a feeling of having outlived his time; a yearning for the color and heroism of wooden ship days; and a grim, unflinching acceptance of life's mischances as they occur against the backdrop of nature's blankness. In the title poem with its long prose headnote, Melville projected his isolation into the figure of an aging ex-sailor living miles inland and drawn in his loneliness to memories of his former shipmates. The thematic center of the poem is a contrast between two human communities fronting nature: "staid" landsmen toiling on the oceanic prairie, their social "unresponsiveness . . . of a piece with the apathy of Nature itself" (*Poems* 265), and sailors from a romanticized past "hoisting up the storm-sail cheerly / *Life is storm—let storm!*" (*Poems* 266). In its evocation of loss—John Marr's wife and child have died; "the void at heart abides" (*Poems* 263)—the headnote draws upon Melville's grief at the death of Malcolm (and perhaps, depending on when it was written, of Stanwix) and upon his sense of life dwindling down to a bare minimum and lived out among an unsympathetic people.

Like a solitary child who creates imaginary playmates, John Marr "in eve's decline" conjures up the "shadowy fellowship" of distant or departed shipmates (*Poems* 268). "Eve" is "evening," the time of day and the approaching time of life, but "eve" may also be woman. As the female became less important for John Marr—and for Melville: his mother and three of his four sisters were dead by 1888; his daughter Frances lived with her husband—recollections of the male became more important. The theme of lost camaraderie recurs in "Bridegroom Dick," the monologue of a retired man-of-war's man spoken to his elderly wife and celebrating honor and heroism in pre-ironclad days "ere the Old order foundered . . . and we learned strange ways" (*Poems* 274). The name "Bridegroom Dick" may be a deliberate phallic pun; if so, homoeroticism in the poem is subsumed by an encompassing homosociality centered on the bonding of valorous men amid nature's hardships and the terrors of war. The poem is an *ubi sunt* commemoration of a life that is more vital and passionate for its speaker than the domestic and waningly sexual life around him. It is hard to tell from Melville's language where the gallant ends and the phallic may begin: "Wife, where be these blades, I wonder, / Pennoned fine fellows, so strong, so gay?" (*Poems* 278). Against her husband's intensities of and for the past, the wife feels eclipsed, and Bridegroom Dick is quick to reassure her that "an old man's passion / Amounts to no more than this smoke I puff" and to ask for a sexually rekindling kiss "in the good old fashion; / A died-down candle will flicker in the snuff" (*Poems* 280).

The open emphasis of the sailor poems is on magnanimity and geniality, the latter defined in the prologue to "John Marr" as "the flower of life springing from some sense of joy in it, more or less" (*Poems* 264). As death shrank his circle of intimates in the late 1870s and 1880s —Evert Duyckinck died in 1878, Thomas Melville in 1884, brother-in-law John C. Hoadley (the most admiring of family members) in 1886—the geniality Melville once displayed in family gatherings or evenings of wine and talk with friends was projected outward onto a group of imaginary friends (the Burgundy Club sketches of the 1870s), then backward in *John Marr* upon an idealized past. The volume's touchstone for geniality is the eponymous hero of "Jack Roy," "captain o' *Splendid*'s maintop: / A belted sea-gentleman; a gallant, off-hand / Mercutio indifferent in life's gay command" (*Poems* 283). The poem is Melville's eulogy to Jack Chase, his messmate from the *United States* and the beau idéal of *White-Jacket* whom Melville would honor again in the dedication to *Billy Budd*. Though an Englishman, Chase became Melville's image for the noble democracy that America seemed increasingly unlikely to produce, least of all in Melville's late nineteenth century. The midcentury vision of a nation of Americans of Shakespearean magnitude now belonged as much to the bygone past as Shakespeare himself, or as Melville's dream of becoming a Shakespeare.

As with other democrats of the 1840s (Emerson, for one), Melville's disenchantment with popular democracy took the form of an idealization of the exceptional individual against both the liberal's faith in human capacity and the conservative's reliance on social control. In "Bridegroom Dick" nostalgia assumes a political dimension relevant to *Billy Budd* as Melville revisits the naval world of *White-Jacket* and transforms his midcentury indictment of war and authoritarianism into a tribute to past gallantry and a near-Carlylean eulogy of government-by-the-hero. The great man in the poem is the "Kentuckian colossal" Captain Turret, who, unlike Captain Vere, overrides a naval statute and pardons a manly offender slated for punishment. "Magnanimous, you think?" Bridegroom Dick asks his wife (*Poems* 278), who assents with a generous tear. As the actualities of war and class exploitation receded in Melville's memory, the libertarian protest in his work gave way to a meditative conservatism devoted to order yet distinct from class-based conservatism in its antagonism to class and from institutional conservatism in its skepticism toward most institutions. What mattered chiefly for late Melville was less the governing system (short of absolute tyranny: the Articles of War) than the large-mindedness of the governors and the natural dignity of the governed. Like geniality, magnanimity may belong to any age, but *John Marr* reserves both qualities for the thither side of the great watershed it imagines between a poetic age and a mechanical one.

In contrast to the nostalgia of the sailor poems, the dozen or so "Sea Pieces" that complete *John Marr* are unillusioned to the verge of desolateness. Two of the poems, "The Good Craft 'Snow-Bird'" and "To the Master of the 'Meteor,'" are hymns of triumph over the elements, but more typically the poems record shipwrecks and disasters, often amid the pride of life and usually accomplished through some hidden treachery of reef, iceberg, or oozy, weed-choked floating wreck. Even "To the Master of the 'Meteor,'" first drafted in December 1860 during Melville's voyage to San Francisco on his brother Tom's ship, is brought into line with the chastened spirit of the Sea Pieces through Melville's revisions; the waves over which the "Meteor" sweeps in "To Tom" become "monstrous" in the final version, while the setting of the poem is shifted from the conventional "torrid deep" to "Off the Cape of Storms." The laureates of this world are the window box of "The Aeolian Harp," shrieking its mad plaint for life's victims, and the conch of the closing poem, "Pebbles," whispering of an "implacable" universe with nothing "that gives back man's strain— / The hope of his heart, the dream in his brain" (*Poems* 299). Although "Pebbles" ends with an accommodation of sorts—"Healed of my hurt, I laud the inhuman Sea" (*Poems* 299)—its stoicism amounts to a virtual surrender to amoral power. Its sense of nature is not substantially different from that in "John Marr"—"*Life is storm—let storm!*" (*Poems* 266)—but it is an old man's vision now, tired, gray, and austere. Divided structurally between the sailor poems and the Sea Pieces, *John Marr* is also divided in spirit, consigning heroism to a romanticized past while fronting the present neither reconciled to the universe nor consoled by any human victory beyond that of muted endurance.

Less visibly unified than *John Marr* in subject and theme, *Timoleon* is a richer volume whose best poems are among the finest Melville wrote. *Timoleon* assumes the pitiless universe of *John Marr* (as *Billy Budd* will) and asks the moral question of how therefore to live. The volume is particularly concerned with the renunciations and rewards of truth's votaries—the female astronomer in "After the Pleasure Party"; the artists of "The Weaver," "In a Garret," and "Art"; the insomniac thinker of "The Bench of Boors"; and the light-seeker of "The Enthusiast"—as if Melville, surveying his long career, were trying to persuade himself he had not been a Fool of Truth. As in *John Marr*, the title poem governs the collection. Adapted from Plutarch's story of the Corinthian soldier and statesman (with hints from Balzac's novel *The Two Brothers*), "Timoleon" is a compendium of Melville themes and a loose allegory of his fortunes: a docile second son overshadowed by his active brother, the mother's "pride" and "pet" (*Poems* 306); the son with self-conscious heroism committing himself to transcendent virtue (Timoleon slaying his tyrant-brother Timophanes; Melville pursuing truth in his fiction regardless of sales or reputation); and the son, repudiated by his mother and estranged from a weak-hearted populace, exiling himself from the city and railing at the silent gods for their apparent abandonment of him:

> To you, Arch Principals, I rear
> My quarrel, for this quarrel is with gods . . . .
> O, tell at last,
> Are earnest natures staggering here
> But fatherless shadows from no substance cast?
> Yea, *are* ye, gods? . . .
> But deign, some little sign be given—
> Low thunder in you tranquil skies;
> Me reassure, nor let me be
> Like a lone dog that for a master cries.
>
> (*Poems* 309)

In plot and rhetoric, "Timoleon" recalls *Pierre,* when, having sacrificed wordly happiness for truth, Pierre finds himself despised by earth and heaven, mother and divine Father, alike. Yet where Pierre dies scorning society, the gods, and the noblest part of himself, "Timoleon" ends with a vision of triumph in which the hero is recalled from his retirement to save the state, then—"Absolved and more!" (*Poems* 309)—spurns fickle Corinth's praise and returns to voluntary exile. The question that frames "Timoleon" is whether glory, belatedly won, is the result of "high Providence, or Chance" (*Poems* 305), a question prominently on Melville's mind as he pondered his long neglect, too proud or vulnerable to respond to the overtures of the New York literati yet scarcely indifferent to fame. Two passages that Melville marked in Schopenhauer bear on his situation. The first likens the man of genius to "some noble prisoner of state, condemned to work in the galleys with common criminals" and preserving his integrity through isolation; the second observes that "whether authors ever live to see the dawn of their fame depends on the chance of circumstances; and the higher and more important their works are, the less likelihood there is of their doing so. . . . [T]he more a man belongs to posterity, in other words, to humanity in general, the more of an alien he is to his contemporaries."[25]

In "Timoleon," "high Providence, or Chance" may signify time correcting life's inequities, as it does for Schopenhauer; yet imaged as an absent or withholding Father, "Providence" may also be a voice from without or within justifying the self-doubting hero for his sacrifices to truth. Beyond his desire for moral vindication and worldly repute, Timoleon is another of Melville's exiled royalties driven by a hunger for divine recognition. His most agonized suspicion is that humanity, after all, is made predominantly of clay and *for* clay, a thought that similarly torments Melville's astronomer awakened to her demanding sexuality in "After the Pleasure Party" and haunts his thought-burdened speaker in "The Bench of Boors." Nearly forty years after *Pierre* and fifteen after *Clarel*, Melville is still fighting "the running battle of the star and clod" (*C* 4, 35: 16); if anything, the battle has become more contested now that retirement and flagging energies have combined to make "illiterate leisure" a powerful temptation.

Setting aside its travel poems, whose initial drafts may date back as far as the late 1850s, *Timoleon* in large part is Melville's meditation on the value of spiritual struggle in the absence of any approbating voice. Its prime motif is solitude. Of the sequence of thirteen poems beginning with "The Garden of Metrodorus," seven include variations of the word "lone," and most of the rest involve triumphs of thought or art achieved in isolation and set against the sluggishness, materialism, or downright falsity of the world. The arrangement of the poems underscores the thematic contrast. "Lamia's Song," a siren-like appeal to sensualism—"Descend, descend! / Pleasant the downward way— / From your lonely Alp / With the wintry scalp / To our myrtles in valleys of May" (*Poems* 319)—is positioned between two counterpoems, "The Weaver" and "In a Garret," that exalt the ascetic rigors of art. Similarly, "The Bench of Boors" with its image of Teniers's drowsy, beer-soaked peasants, is flanked on one side by "The Enthusiast" ("Though light forsake thee, never fall / From fealty to light" [*Poems* 321]) and on the other by "Lone Founts":

> Though fast youth's glorious fable flies,
> View not the world with worldling's eyes;
> Nor turn with weather of the time.
> Foreclose the coming of surprise:
> Stand where posterity shall stand;
> Stand where the ancients stood before,
> And, dipping in lone founts thy hand,
> Drink of the never-varying lore:
> Wise once, and wise hence evermore.
> *(Poems* 320)

The lines might almost stand as an epigraph to this period. Through the notion of "lone founts"—living in solitude for timeless thought or art—Melville seems to be trying to shape an identic touchstone to help him come to terms with age, loneliness, and obscurity, and to persuade himself of the transcendent, if not the transcendental, value of his life. "Youth's glorious fable" is long behind him, but against the downward pull of time and the allure of quiescent leisure (*otium*) he seems to have been struggling to live by the motto from Schiller pasted on his wall: "Keep true to the dreams of thy youth."

The Rose and the Cross

In a poem from "Weeds and Wildings" titled "The New Rosicrucians" Melville imagines a latter-day order of philosophers whose talismanic symbol is the rose-vine wound about the Cross:

> To us, disciples of the Order,
> Whose rose-vine twines the Cross,
> Who have drained the rose's chalice
> Never heeding gain or loss;
> For all the preacher's din
> There is no mortal sin—
> —No, none to us but Malice!
>
> Exempt from that, in blest recline
> We let life's billows toss;
> If sorrows come, anew we twine
> The Rose-vine round the Cross.
>   ("WW" 38)

The question Melville's poem raises is one he must have been asking himself after 1885—whether a life of pleasure and ease can be wed to a life of spirituality. "Ascetics roses twine?" (*C* 1, 30: 2) *Clarel* asks. In *Clarel* they do not; the rose and the cross are opposing symbols identified, respectively, with worldly pleasure and unworldly striving. Derwent is rosy, the Lesbian merchant "light and rosy" (*C* 3, 26: 71), and the young Cypriote the poem's chief celebrant of the rose. The cross is associated with religionists like Salvaterra and the Syrian monk but also with unaffiliated seekers like Ungar, Celio, Mortmain, Rolfe, and Clarel; its distinguishing mark is earnestness of mind and temper.

"The New Rosicrucians" is one of eleven rose poems in "Weeds and Wildings" culminating in "The Rose Farmer." By the later 1880s Melville had cause to modify his association of the rose with shallow hedonism. Aside from being a rose gardener himself and delighting in Samuel Hole's practico-spiritual treatise on roses, Melville had read Edward Fitzgerald's *Rubáiyát of Omar Khayyám* in three editions, including an illustrated one by artist Elihu Vedder that rearranged Fitzgerald's stanzas (themselves a free adaptation of the original) and constituted virtually a new work of art. Through the *Rubáiyát* Melville came into contact with the "strong Epicurean revival voiced in the writings of Swinburne, Pater, Wilde, and the aesthetes,"[26] a movement that spoke to his own considerable interest in the visual arts and that raised sensualism into a serious philosophy of life. In Pater's *The Renaissance* (1873) (which Melville seems not to have read), aesthetic hedonism is made to derive from a naturalistic vitalism with affinities to a major strain in Melville's thought. "Not the fruit of experience, but experience itself, is the end" of life, Pater wrote:

> A counted number of pulses only is given to us of a variegated, dramatic life. How may we see in them all that is to be seen in them by the finest senses? How shall we pass most swiftly from point to point, and be present always at the focus where the greatest number of vital forces unite in their purest energy? To burn always with this hard, gem-like flame, to maintain this ecstasy, is success in life.[27]

In the rose poems of "Weeds and Wildings," "experience itself" is the rose, the spiritual "fruit of experience" the attar. In contrast to the lean, ascetic Parsee who "scimiters the living rose" to "get a mummified quintessence," the Persian whom Melville's narrator consults in "The Rose Farmer," though on one side a seller of roses and lover of gold, on another side is a Pateresque epicurean who believes that the bloom of the moment is everything: "'Quick, too, the redolence [of the rose] it stales. / And yet you have the brief delight, / And yet the next morn's bud avails; / and so on in sequence'" ("WW" 47). The Persian goes further and celebrates the earthly rose as heavenly, or preferable to the heavenly: "This evanescence is the charm! / And most it wins the spirits that be / Celestial, Sir. It comes to me / It was this fleeting charm in show / That lured the sons of God below, / Tired out with perpetuity" ("WW" 47).

The relationship between sense and spirit, temporality and perpetuity, is what the rose poems set themselves to explore. One form of perpetuity is the Christian afterlife. In "The Vial of Attar" a bereaved lover tries to console himself with the thought of the beloved's deathless spiritual essence (the attar) but comes to feel this a joyless compensation: "There is nothing like the bloom; / And the attar poignant reminds me / Of the bloom that's pass'd away" ("WW" 39).[28] In "The Rose Window" formulaic piety is again juxtaposed to the vividness of sense experience, whether beheld in reality or in a dream. The poem's speaker falls asleep in church during a sermon on the Resurrection and dreams of "an angel with a Rose" shedding red light on "the shrouds and mort-cloths" of the dead ("WW" 40). Has the speaker bypassed formal religion and arrived via dream vision at faith in eternal life? Is it eternal life that the dream even implies or does the angel simply peer at the dead, who like Emily Dickinson's "meek members of the Resurrection" lie "Safe in their Alabaster Chambers" awaiting a rebirth that may never come?[29] All that is certain is the pageant of color that greets the speaker as he awakens: dust motes transfigured by the light streaming through "the great Rose-Window high"—in Pater's words, "a group of impressions . . . in the mind of the observer . . . [,] unstable, flickering, inconsistent, which burn and are extinguished with our consciousness of them."[30] For John Bryant, the poem illustrates "the power of faith, beauty, art, and the rose to transfigure matter into spirit."[31] "Faith" and "art" are quite different things, however, as are the truth-claims they make about visible and invisible reality. The glories of sense experience as filtered through the art of the rose window are palpably real for the speaker; the promise of immortality is dim and conjectural. "Which is best?" Emily Dickinson asked in one of her many variations on this theme: "Heaven —/ Or only heaven to come / With that old codicil of doubt?" (Dickinson #1012). In the rose poems touching on this world and the next, the rose and the attar, Melville seems to feels as Dickinson does:

> I cannot help esteem
> The "Bird within the Hand"
> Superior to the one
> The "Bush" may yield me
> Or may not
> Too late to choose again.
>   (Dickinson #1012)[32]

As if in answer to a question like Dickinson's, Melville's next poem, "Rosary Beads," begins by locating heaven in a succession of intense perceptual moments:

> Adore the Roses; nor delay
> Until the rose-fane fall,
> Or ever their censers cease to sway;
> "To-day!" the rose-priests call.
>   ("WW" 40)

More than any other poem in "Weeds and Wildings," "Rosary Beads" borrows the idiom of religion to deck the secular hedonism of "that sublime old infidel" (*Corr* 497) Omar Khayyám. "After vainly endeavoring to unshackle his steps from destiny, and to catch some authentic glimpses of TO-MORROW," translator Fitzgerald wrote in a preface Melville marked, Omar Khayyám "fell back upon TO-DAY (which has outlasted so many to-morrows) as the only ground he had got to stand upon, however momentarily slipping from under his feet."[33] For the Sufi poets of Omar's time, "the traditional Persian imagery of wine, roses, and love became a code of mystical symbols" in which intoxication and the "contemplation of beauty" were seen as pathways to the divine.[34] Sense perception, gauzily idealized, was thus made a bridge between the natural and the supernatural by those disenchanted with orthodox theology or determined simply to have both worlds at once. "Omar," Fitzgerald wrote, "was too honest of heart as well as of head" for such "cloudy symbolism."[35] So was Melville, who reverses the Sufi process of poetic sublimation as he understood it from his reading. In the second stanza of "Rosary Beads" the language of Christian miracle (transubstantiation) is applied to the metamorphosis of sense experience into a continuing secular miracle of Paterian intensity: "But live up to the Rose's light, / Thy meat shall turn to roses red, / Thy bread to roses white" ("WW" 41). In these lines Melville comes as close as he will to an aesthete's religion of evanescent materialism. But the poem continues, ominously :

> Grain by grain the Desert drifts
> Against the Garden-Land;
> Hedge well thy Roses, heed the stealth
> Of ever-creeping Sand.
>
> ("WW" 41)

As in the *Rubáiyát*, time and encroaching death give an autumnal urgency, if not a wintry blight, to the pursuit of pleasure. "Rosary Beads" is Melville's staged version of the dialogue between a joyous naturalism and a horror at oblivion that marks the *Rubáiyát* and that Sufism (a form of Islamic "New Rosicrucianism") sought to resolve. During the revel at Mar Saba in *Clarel*, Derwent entertains the company by reciting a ditty about the Sufi poet Hafiz or a namesake meant to evoke the poet:

> "To Hafiz in grape-arbor comes
> Didymus, with book he thumbs:
> My lord Hafiz, priest of bowers—
> Flowers in such a world of ours?
> Who is the god of all these flowers?—
> "Signior Didymus, who knows?
> None the less I take repose—
> Believe, and worship here with wine
> In vaulted chapel of the vine
> Before the altar of the rose.
>
> (*C* 3, 13: 71–80)

Like Melville's New Rosicrucians, living "in blest recline," Derwent's Hafiz (like Derwent himself) takes "repose," waiving the strenuousness, pain, and consciousness of sin and evil that belonged to the religious life as Melville conceived it. For a believer of Hafiz's kind, temporal pleasure glides unproblematically into eternal pleasure, as if religion, as John Updike said, were something that "put[s] us at ease in this world" by "enabl[ing] us to ignore nothingness and get on with the jobs of life," chiefly work and sensuous enjoyment.[36] Ignoring nothingness is what a Melvillean hero can never do. Soon after Derwent's song Vine recites another, which he ascribes to an artist in Florence:

> "What is beauty? 'tis a dream
> Dispensing still with gladness;
> The dolphin haunteth not the shoal,
> And deeps there be in sadness.
> "The rose-leaves, see, disbanded be—
> Blowing, about me blowing;
> But on the death-bed on the rose
> My amaranths are growing."
>   (*C* 3, 14: 31–38)

As in *Pierre*, the amaranth in Vine's lyric is a symbol for aspiration toward God and immortality. Like a Sufi, the Florentine artist would make the ephemeral rose both the ground of pleasure in the temporal world and, in its passing, the compost nourishing eternal life. "*His amaranths*," Vine remarks scornfully: "a fond conceit, / Yes, last illusion of retreat!" (*C* 3, 14: 39). By "last illusion" Vine seems to mean the devolution of waning religion into a soft quasi-religion of aestheticism, a line of descent T. S. Eliot would trace in his essay "Arnold and Pater." More honest, Vine implies, to stand with Omar and take a rose as a rose than, like the Florentine artist or the Sufis, to make it a ladder to heaven.

Sufism or its equivalent—the rose as a vehicle for transcendence—continues to occupy Melville in "The Devotion of the Flowers to Their Lady," the climactic poem in the section "As they Fell," whose title suggests both the falling of rose petals into the stream of time (illustrated in Vedder's *Rubáiyát*) and the biblical or Romantic Fall. "The Devotion" is indeed about the Fall—the feeling of "banishment" from Eden and the "secret desire / For the garden of God" even amid the pleasure garden of the world ("WW" 42). The poem recalls Hole's remark in *A Book about Roses*, "What is our love of flowers, our calm happiness in our gardens, but a dim recollection of our first home in Paradise, and a yearning for the Land of promise!"[37] As a rose gardener-clergyman, Hole likes to imagine horticulture as a living lesson in "the truths of Revelation, the histories and prophecies of the Older Testament, [and] the miracles and parables of the New," but ultimately he must concede, as the speaker of "The Devotion" does, that "our gardens do not satisfy, are not meant to satisfy, our heart's desire."[38] As Melville's troubadour-turned-monk complains, "exile is exile though spiced be the sod."

William B. Dillingham sees late Melville as a New Rosicrucian who managed "to harmonize an ancient pagan emblem, the rose, with the

Christian symbol of the cross."[39] I doubt this strongly, with respect to both the rose poems themselves, which explore the possibility of harmony but fail to achieve it, and to the tenor of Melville's private life, the pleasures of which—his rose garden, his art collection, his reading and writing—were largely isolated and isolating. The picture of Melville and Lizzie enjoying a Darby-and-Joan old age is based chiefly on Melville's dedication of "Weeds and Wildings" "To Winnefred" (Lizzie). The prose of the dedication, however, is so arch and circumlocutious that it serves to mask rather than reveal Melville's deepest feelings; in its cloying pastoralism, reminiscent of the opening paragraphs of *Pierre*, the dedication even suggests an irony bordering on aggression. Against the "wild amaranths in a pasture"—"emblems of immortality"—Lizzie is associated with the humble red clover "sweet in the mouth of that brindled heifer whose breath [she] so loved to inhale" ("WW" 5). John Bryant praises Lizzie during these years as "patien[t] beyond any deep understanding of [Melville's] art and anxiety."[40] This may have been precisely the problem. Patience without intelligent sympathy is liable to breed "otium," an enervating content, which, by a slight shift of consonant and perspective, can shade into "odium" (hatred), the Latin root (according to Reinhard Kuhn) for the word "ennui."[41] From the Middle Ages onward, Kuhn observes, ennui "on the one hand . . . designated something, often of a petty nature, that proved vexatious and irritating" and "on the other hand" signified "a profound sorrow" or "deep spiritual distress."[42] Ennui in both these senses may have been the effect of the kindly-intentioned Lizzie on the irritable Melville, as her small domestic ineptitudes and incomprehensions aggravated his feeling of mental isolation. Neither side was wholly at fault; it was the logic of their interaction, smoothed by the years into (mostly) anaesthetized habit yet providing few positive satisfactions of the kind that Melville valued most.

Whether as a refined aestheticism or a common domestic happiness, the rose of temporal experience was not by itself an adequate dwelling place for late Melville, nor did it point upward from sense to spirit as it did for the Sufis or the New Rosicrucians. The attar of an afterlife was uncertain, but there was another kind of attar available through the austere distillations of art. "Essential oils—are wrung—," Emily Dickinson wrote of poetry: "The Attar from the Rose / Be not expressed by Suns—alone— / It is the gift of Screws—" (#675). Melville's own metaphor for creation in the poem "Art" is "wrestl[ing] with the angel," a fit image for the taxing struggle apparent even in the manuscript revisions of this brief poem.[43] As he departs from the "prosperous Persian," the speaker of "The Rose Farmer" reflects on a life that seems "rewarded / By sapient prudence not amiss, / Nor transcendental essence hoarded / In hope of quintessential bliss: / No, never with paintaking throes / Essays to crystallize the rose" ("WW" 45). "Sapient prudence" is a Plinlimmonesque virtue, not a Melvillean one; "painstaking throes" are what the poems in *Timoleon* celebrate. Through irony and multiple negatives Melville subtly damns the Persian his speaker appears to praise, yet what can he mean by "quintessential bliss"? In Dickinson's poem the vindication of art is its triumph over time:

> The General Rose—decay—
> But this —in Lady's Drawer
> Make Summer—When the Lady lie
> In Ceaseless Rosemary—
> (Dickinson #675)

The "General Rose" is the bloom of temporal experience; "this — in Lady's Drawer" is the poetry Dickinson kept in her bedroom, where it was discovered after her death by her sister, Lavinia. "Make Summer" for whom—and how? Not for the poet herself, later, when she lies in "Ceaseless Rosemary," with no implication that she is conscious or has earned immortality through her art. And not for a readership, since the poems are hidden away, as, in effect, were Melville's, privately printed and distributed in editions of twenty-five copies. "Summer" must lie in the value of the artifact itself, appreciated or not, and in how its wrought form testifies to what must have been a transfiguring struggle with the "angel." Art is "immortal" not merely because it endures, but because it calls forth, objectifies, and memorializes that part of human personality that used to be called the "spirit." In Woolf's *To the Lighthouse* Lily Briscoe knows that her painting will lie rolled up in an attic somewhere, yet the book ends in triumph: "I have had my vision."[44] *Have* had: as soon as it is completed, the work of art, along with the process that produced it, enters the stream of time. The artist must create another work and recreate herself or himself again.

Writing came hard for late Melville—it was an art of screws—and because of this it served him as a "cross." I do not mean that Melville arrived at an aesthete's religion of art or, as Dillingham claims, that "at times, [his] treatment of artistic inspiration so resembles a description of religious experience that the two are virtually indistinguishable."[45] What linked religion and art for Melville was their shared quality of pressing human faculties to their limit rather than acceding to the clay. Spiritual life was a process of working continuously to raise oneself above oneself. It is pleasant to imagine Old Man Melville redeemed from the struggles of his life by Christian faith, marital happiness, or the New Rosicrucians' "blest recline," but struggle (the "cross") was not something Melville wanted to be redeemed from; it was what redeemed. Religion for the late Melville was not belief; it was not even Tillich's holy doubt; it was the self-transfiguration that came from living in relation to the *next* thing, just beyond one's proven powers.

Telling the Sacrament

Billy Budd, Sailor is Melville's consummate work of screws. Begun modestly in or around 1886 with the poem "Billy in the Darbies," a sailor monologue akin to "Tom Deadlight" in *John Marr*, *Billy Budd* evolved through three phases that included "nine major stages of inscription with their substages,"[46] and was chronologically complete and awaiting final revision when Melville died in September 1891. The original Billy was "an older man, condemned for fomenting mutiny and apparently guilty as charged" (Hayford/Sealts 2), but at some point during the writing, Billy's story outgrew the ballad form and began to lead Melville in unforeseen directions. By November 1888 he had transformed his poem into what he then considered a complete narrative of more than 150 manuscript leaves (well under half the final number) in which Billy, now an Adamic innocent, is sentenced to hang for striking and killing his false accuser, Master-at-arms John Claggart. The focus of this second-phase *Billy Budd* was the fate of good-natured innocence in the man-of-war world, a theme that Melville had broached in *Typee* but that he now explored in a theological context that became more pronounced as he retouched his portrait of Claggart. Questions of justice and political morality were peripheral at this stage of composition, and "so minor was the commander's part . . . that only a few leaves stood between the killing of Claggart and the beginning of the ballad" (Hayford /Sealts 2). The lines of Melville's action were thus firmly in place before he returned to *Billy Budd* during the last three years of his life to develop the characterization of Captain Vere and to add the chapters between Claggart's death and Billy's that have longed claimed the bulk of critical attention. Melville was still refining the language and emphasis of his book when he died, leaving behind a narratively complete but not fully revised manuscript dotted with inconsistencies and in such disarray that an authoritative text of *Billy Budd* would not appear until the Hayford-Sealts edition of 1962.

    Billy Budd is an indeterminate text not only because it is unfinished but because the direction of Melville's late pencil revisions seem deliberately to have made it so, chiefly by undercutting what had formerly been the narrative's considered endorsement of Captain Vere.[47] The ambiguities introduced or underscored by these last changes has fueled what might in any case have been a tendency of readers to divide themselves over Vere's behavior according to their own moral, political, philosophical, or religious commitments. Evidence from the text can be marshaled to support a range of attitudes toward Vere and to unequivocally validate or refute very few of them. More than virtually any other text, *Billy Budd* is a doubloon reflecting back to the seer his or her own constitutive mind-set and inviting what John Wenke called "arguments that are in themselves political allegories in the form of literary criticism."[48]

There will never be a consensus about *Billy Budd*. That said, I would like to ask, first, what it meant for an elderly author in failing health to spend more than five years writing and rewriting a book he may never have intended for popular circulation and, second, whether the general thrust of Melville's alterations within each major phase can be taken to suggest anything about his intellectual and spiritual development during these years, which were also the years of his newly written or redrafted late poems. *Billy Budd* engaged Melville as it did because its fable resonated outwardly in ever widening circles of reference and inwardly in increasingly subtle complications of motive and judgment. Years earlier Melville had spoken of unfolding within himself virtually at three-week intervals (*Corr* 193). An old man has a slower metabolism, but as he worked on *Billy Budd* Melville must have felt himself developing in ways that he had not in close to a decade. "Whilst we converse with what is above us"—not the transcendent, but the next circle of our being—"we do not grow old, but grow young,"[49] Emerson remarked. Writing *Billy Budd*, demanding as the effort must have been, Melville grew young. So he may have meant to imply about writing generally when he prefaced "Weeds and Wildings" with an epigraph adapted from Hawthorne's *The Dolliver Romance*: "Youth is the proper, permanent, and genuine condition of man" ("WW" 1).

In its opening eulogy of the "'Handsome Sailor'" who flourished in "the less prosaic time" before steamships (*BB* 43), *Billy Budd* recalls the sailor poems in *John Marr*. What had been nostalgia in the verse, however, is immediately raised to the level of myth as the prelapsarian Billy is impressed from the *Rights-of-Man* and introduced to "the ampler and more knowing world of a great warship" (*BB* 50), Melville's symbol as in *White-Jacket* for the civilized world itself. By nature admirable, Billy is morally, intellectually, and spiritually undeveloped, an "upright barbarian" like Adam before the Fall (*BB* 52) but also, less honorifically, like a child, a baby (*BB* 4), and "a dog of St. Bernard's breed" (*BB* 52). Like the Typees, Billy belongs to the pre-cognitive, pre-societal world of pastoral, and, as happens in pastoral "from Aristotle to Milton," Hallett Smith remarks, "there is always some stern voice which announces, 'I will not praise a cloistered virtue.'"[50] In *Billy Budd* the stern voice is Claggart's with its "disdain of innocence—to be nothing more than innocent!" (*BB* 86)—but it is also the narrator's, which echoes Milton's *Areopagitica* in describing Billy as "much of a child-man" whose "utter innocence," like the child's, "is but its blank ignorance" (*BB* 86).

Melville's first intention in opposing Claggart to Billy was probably to illustrate the perils of simplicity in the devious world of a warship; this is how the Dansker views the situation, with his "grim internal merriment" (*BB* 70) and premonitions of disaster. As Melville reworked his manuscript, however, Claggart's motiveless spite became "'a mystery of iniquity'" that savored of "Holy Writ" (*BB* 76), and the story developed from an exemplary fable into a shipboard reenactment of the Fall. Melville's literary paradigm at this stage of composition was *Paradise Lost*, and hints of Milton's Satan resound in the expanded portrait of Claggart. Yet lacking the climactic execution scene that some readers take as Melville's Christian acceptance, the 1888 *Billy Budd* seems rather an anti–*Paradise Lost* designed to impugn the ways of God. The early narrative concluded with the garbled report of events from "News From the Mediterranean," upon which the narrator moralized: "Here ends a story not unwarranted by what sometimes happens in this [one undeciphered word] world of ours—Innocence and infamy, spiritual depravity and fair repute."[51] "Sometimes happens" implies a periodic divine negligence of the sort Ishmael called "an interregnum in Providence" (*MD* 320). God is thus arraigned on two counts: for his aboriginal responsibility for humanity's temptation and fall—Claggart acts out his part "like the scorpion for which the Creator alone is responsible" (*BB* 78)—and for his historical *ir*responsibility ever since. Also arraigned are those official versions of events (naval chronicles, Christian apologetics) that play havoc with the truth in order to demonstrate that all goes well. An "inside narrative," in this context, would be one that told the essential truth and, incidentally, adjusted the wrongs of worldly reputation.

That Melville should chafe against the problem of evil is hardly surprising; he had been doing so since *Mardi*. The curious thing is that after *Clarel*'s symposium on belief and skepticism he should press his language and symbols so far in the direction of Christian allegory. Perhaps the stark injustice of Billy's story reawakened a primal rage at the order of things, or perhaps a nostalgia for simplicity comparable to the historical nostalgia of *John Marr* drew him toward the totalizing explanation of theological myth. In any case, the impulse passed. Melville never erased the narrative's early anti-Christian allegory, but he did outgrow it as his quarrel with God expended itself in the telling and his interest passed to other matters. Two magazine articles on the *Somers* incident of 1842, the first appearing in the spring of 1888 as Melville worked on *John Marr*, may have kindled his memories of his cousin Guert Gansevoort, a first lieutenant on the *Somers* when an acting midshipman and two sailors were hanged for conspiracy,[52] and prompted Melville to brood on questions of justice and political authority. Whatever the reason, Melville returned to the manuscript he had once thought complete and addressed the thinly drawn figure of Vere, interpolating the character sketch of chapters 6 and 7 and carrying the action forward beyond Claggart's death without substantially recasting what he had written. Claggart with his unearthly violet eyes and Billy with his welkin-blue had been less—or more—than fully human characters, but with Claggart's death the Fall and its attendant issues become a given and the story descends to the historical world of gray-eyed Vere in which moral and political questions must be resolved in postlapsarian terms against "the monotonous blank of the twilight sea" (*BB* 109).

It was the tragedy of governance that absorbed Melville now—a subject he had touched upon with King Media in *Mardi* and Benito Cereno but never deeply explored—and that drew him outward beyond his metaphysical frustrations, first toward the political world, then toward the psyche, with an insight and breadth of comprehension unapproached in the late poetry. In part 4 of *Clarel* Melville had expressed the negatives of his social thought through the ex-Confederate officer Ungar, a part-Indian who rails at injustice with the bitterness of the dispossessed but also a lapsed-Catholic reactionary who berates radicals and meliorists for their neglect of original sin. *Billy Budd* preserves the terms, if not the full severity, of Ungar's neither/nor in its critical portrayal of French Jacobinism and British repression, but it focuses on the empowered ruler who must act. The long trial scene in chapter 21 is a masterpiece of ambiguity, with one class of readers taking Vere as an anguished but duty-bound representative of the political state and another seeing him as a myopic conservative whose narrow application of a wartime code tyrannical in itself is a double indictment of a martial society that sacrifices justice to order and dehumanizes even its most conscientious men.

That both these readings are not only supported but demanded by the text reflects the profound doubleness of Melville's social vision, for which terms like "radical" and "conservative" seem parochial and inept. Convinced of the need for "forms, measured forms" (*BB* 128), Melville knew that any particular set of forms were likely to be deeply flawed, sometimes tragically so. He also knew that forms had to be administered by human beings enmeshed in events and compromised by their tendencies, limitations, passions, and individual and group interests. In *Billy Budd* Melville presents a circumstanced case with more perspectives on it and attitudes toward it than certainty-seeking human consciousness can comfortably bear, and he challenges his readers to rise to it as a representation of experience "uncompromisingly told" (*BB* 128). As Melville revised *Billy Budd*, especially toward the last, he took pains, as John Wenke observed, to "thwart the determinate readings so characteristic of *Billy Budd* criticism,"[53] as if certainty in politics, no less than in religion, involved a leap of faith taken against the "ragged edges" of truth (*BB* 128). In practical politics, decisions had to be made and the leap taken, but for the political philosopher irony and ambiguity were the conditions of intellectual honesty. Melville is a political agnostic in *Billy Budd*—he "doesn't know" with finality—not because he is indifferent but because he sees too much.

Manuscript evidence suggests that Melville composed a substantial portion of the trial and execution scenes before he added the character analysis of chapters 6 and 7 that established Vere as a Burkean conservative of a peculiarly inward and idiosyncratic sort—bookish, prone to dreamy gazing "at the blank sea" (*BB* 61), and with "'a queer streak of the pedantic'" (*BB* 63). Melville's political themes were in place, that is to say, before he began exploring the roots of judgment in Vere's individual cast of mind and temper. Chapters 6 and 7 do not discredit Vere's arguments in the trial scene, but they do contextualize them as the views of a particular man in a particular historical situation rather than as universal and authorially sanctioned truths. If the composition of the trial scene turned *Billy Budd* from theological allegory to political debate, Melville's additions concerning Vere had the effect of redirecting the story once again, this time toward psychology, or political philosophy as refracted through psychology. Hershel Parker argues that Melville's late pencil revision of the surgeon's role—specifically, his insertion of the surgeon's view that Vere may be "unhinged" (*BB* 102) and that Billy's case should be referred to the admiral—contradicts Melville's earlier presentation of Vere and makes "the story . . . extremely difficult if not impossible to interpret as a whole."[54] This is true, but the process of qualifying Vere began almost as soon as Melville conceived him as a distinct personality.[55] Politics required political actors, and once the actors became more than mouthpieces for opinions, they assumed a dramatic interest that increasingly absorbed Melville in its own right.

Pertinent to this late emphasis on character is the history of Melville's digression on Lord Nelson (presently chapter 4), written in 1888 in the nostalgic spirit of "Bridegroom Dick" and under the direct influence of the British naval histories Melville had begun to consult and of Southey's *Life of Nelson*. In revising his manuscript later that year, Melville deleted the chapter, possibly because he found it inconsistent with the theological turn his story had taken. At the last, however, he decided to reinsert the leaves, apparently just preceding the newly written chapters on Vere and with additional comments disparaging "personal prudence" and glorifying Nelson's heroic death.[56] The significance of the change is underscored by the fact that "shortly after revising the Nelson chapter," Melville reworked the crucial scene between Vere and the surgeon.[57] What had originated as an exercise in Romantic escapism became, in its new context, an implied comment on a man "who whatever his sterling qualities was without any brilliant ones" (*BB* 61). Against Nelson—not a captain "to terrorize a crew into base subjection, but to win them" to allegiance "by force of his mere presence and heroic personality" (*BB* 59)—the legalistic Vere emerges as a type of the earnest but rigid humanity that makes us agents of avoidable suffering. Politically, the contrast between Nelson and Vere reaches beyond the specifics of Billy's case to illustrate the late Melville's "contention that man, at any level below that of the hero, is the victim of his own ambiguities and inconsistencies, and of history."[58] Psychologically, together with the surgeon's questions about Vere's sanity, it directs us further to the peculiarities of Vere's nature that may have operated within the framework of law and usage to necessitate Billy's death. Vere is not a villain; he is a virtuous but flawed human being acting under the press of circumstances and compounding society's institutional failures by private limitations of his own. His tragic deficiency is a want of that special quality evident in Nelson, which, in the absence of definite religious or political belief, Melville had come to value above all others: moral imagination as it makes for magnanimity.

After an initial movement upward from exemplary fable to theological myth, *Billy Budd* during its long gestation, traveled increasingly downward toward the particularized world of human action. Robert C. Ryan notes an analogous movement with the late poem "Rip Van Winkle's Lilac," from "Weeds and Wildings": beginning "with a skeleton narrative," Melville "progressively dramatize[d] its abstractly-drawn contrasts, adding human motivation and justification to previously shadowy characters" and working "to disengage himself from a total commitment" to a single point of view.[59] Novelists often speak of their characters escaping the roles assigned them and leading their creators into unmapped territories. The shift in Melville's earlier writings had typically come from another source—what Warner Berthoff called "that rush of interior development that served him for education"[60]—but in *Billy Budd* Melville seems genuinely to be responding to the latent possibilities of his story and, at the end, to the forward pull of Vere and Billy themselves. The defining changes in *Billy Budd* seem to have come upon Melville epiphanically, as new frames of understanding suggested themselves and returned him to a narrative that he must, on some level, have heartily wished to be done with. Yet within each phase he worked with the concentration of a miniaturist, altering words or phrases to achieve a maximum of precision on one side and a maximum of resonance on the other.

Billy's trial concluded, the focus of the narrative shifts again as issues of political justice and morality give way to the purely human circumstance of two men meeting the inevitable with generosity and strength. The Vere who had argued for coolness in the trial scene is "melt[ed] back into what remains primeval in our formalized humanity" (*BB* 115) and softened by the weight of a judgment made conscientiously and with full awareness of tragic sacrifice, disastrously wrong as it may be. Billy's role—to feel Vere's pain more than his own—is greater still, but his growth is made visible only at the last when, "spiritualized now through late experiences so poignantly profound" (*BB* 123), he becomes, not a symbol of Christ, but an example of humanity's Christlike capacity for transfiguration through suffering. Billy's "fortunate fall," reminiscent of Donatello's in *The Marble Faun* but without sin, is a justification neither of God's ways nor of the ways of state. Billy's triumph is personal and has reference to private moral and spiritual life alone. It is achieved, moreover, despite, or perhaps because of, the fact that Billy remains a "barbarian" (*BB* 120) to the end, unresponsive to the chaplain's gospel of "salvation and a Saviour" (*BB* 121) even as his final words—"God bless Captain Vere!" (*BB* 123)—amount to the "chronometrical return of good for evil" (*P* 215) that Melville considered the distinguishing moral feature of Christianity. Billy is Christ only to the extent that, as a man, he enacts an *imitatio Christi*.

In the execution scene Melville comes closest to dramatizing the relocation of the spiritual within the natural toward which he had been tending in and after *Clarel*. As Billy swings lifeless from the yardarm, the "soft glory" that "chanced" to illuminate "the vapory fleece hanging low in the east" (*BB* 124) seems a version of the divine signet craved by Timoleon and Pierre, but its promise is indistinct, like the hints of divinity in *Clarel*, and we are immediately recalled to the unsanctified world of a "great ship ponderously cannoned" (*BB* 124), which is the only world we indisputably know. Melville is not affirming a transcendent realm, nor is he denying it; the text is ambiguous. Waiving the matter of positive belief, Melville invokes the nimbus of Christianity to leave the possibility open but also, and chiefly, to canonize human beings trapped by circumstances and swayed by the imperatives of their nature yet capable at the last, like Nelson, of extraordinary gestures of heroism.

Like Shakespeare's late romances, as Northrop Frye described them, *Billy Budd* encloses tragedy within a movement "from a lower world of confusion to an upper world of order" and suggests the "transformation from one kind of life to another"; it "outrag[es] reality and at the same time introduc[es] us to a world of childlike innocence which has always made more sense than reality."[61] In Melville, this upper world belongs to the exceptional individual, whose transfiguration neither regenerates the social world nor is properly understood by it. It is fitting that *Billy Budd* should end with the garbled news report Melville retained from an earlier draft and with the crewmen fashioning a cult of Billy-as-Christ from an example of being it is theirs to imitate. Such will always be the world's misjudgments, Melville implies, whether of persons like Billy or, perhaps, of persons like himself. It hardly matters, so long as the individuals themselves feel their worth and so long as someone is present to record and ratify it in "an inside narrative."

Recording greatness—"telling the sacrament" (*BB* 115)—is the rationale for the closeted interview between Billy and Vere, so at odds with the emotional reserve of the rest of the text. As Vere communicates the sentence to Billy and is frank about his role in effecting it, his cross—"the agony of the strong" (*BB* 115)—is to bear the weight of a decision he knows is tragically unjust. Billy's cross is more demanding still: to perceive and honor the pain of his captain, which intellectually he cannot begin to fathom. Readers appalled at Vere's judgment and behavior have shrunk from the chapter's "quasi-liturgical language"—a "particularly offensive kind of moral casuistry,"[62] Laurie Robertson-Lorant called it—and posited a narrator distinct from Melville himself. This can neither be proved nor disproved, unreliable narrators residing often in the eye or heart of the beholder. One can, however, note the particular care Melville gave the chapter in revising it, along with the direction of his revisions. The Billy who in an early draft might only "have *discerned* the brave opinion of him" implied by Vere's frankness is elevated in a late pencil revision to one who "might have *appreciated*" it, or taken its symbolic measure. On his side, Vere "the *monkish* devotee of military duty" becomes, more temperately, "the *austere* devotee of duty," who "may in the end have caught Billy to his *heart*" rather than, as originally, "to his *arms*."[63] In contrast to the general movement of the revisions toward greater ambiguity, qualification, and authorial distance, Melville's changes in chapter 22 work to solemnify the scene so as virtually to preclude irony, however much surrounding events may anger or pain readers.

Hershel Parker claims that Vere's embrace of Billy, if it did occur, "had no overt consequences."[64] This depends on how one judges "overt." The interview scene culminating in the embrace is high among the "late experiences so poignantly profound" that "spiritualized" Billy (*BB* 123) and enabled him not merely to forgive but to bless the man about to execute him. Psychologically, the scene is indispensable. What is gratuitous is the manner in which it is told, which reverses the thrust of the late writing toward greater dramatization and involves the narrator in what Parker calls "a speculation so bold and so personal as to be all but indistinguishable from fantasy."[65] Though its subject is Vere and Billy, the language of the chapter, fraught with hypotheticals and reticences, continually recalls us to its origin in the mind and sensibility of the narrator. Eloquent in its reserve, the scene hints at depths that cannot be shared even with the reader, though they are evidently plumbed by the narrator and communicated with a reverence that reflects back upon himself as much as it ennobles his characters:

> But there is no telling the sacrament, seldom if in any case revealed to the gadding world, wherever under circumstances at all akin to those here attempted to be set forth two of Nature's nobler order embrace. There is privacy at the time, inviolable to the survivor; and holy oblivion, the sequel to each diviner magnanimity, covers all at last. (*BB* 115)

"Fantasy" the scene assuredly is, but fantasy is what we make ourselves known by as we shape an idealized self and memorialize it in our self-epitaphs as alms against "holy oblivion." To write sublimely of sublime behavior is, in some sense, to come to inhabit Byron's "life we imagine."[66] Reading Mme. de Staël's *Germany* in the 1860s, Melville boxed and checked her remark "Poetic genius is an internal disposition, of the same nature with that which renders us capable of a generous sacrifice."[67] Exalted writing is like heroic action; it testifies to largeness of being. *Billy Budd* extends this thought to the literary text and the creation of the text. The writer resembles the magnanimous hero through the act of conceiving the hero and struggling by means of an "art of Screws" to objectify that conception in a monument of language. Toward the end of the Nelson chapter, Melville develops this analogy himself when, defending the "priestly motive" that led Nelson at Trafalgar "to dress his person in the jewelled vouchers of his own shining deeds," he likens the decked out magnificence of the naval hero to the eloquence of the high mimetic writer:

> if thus to have adorned himself for the altar and the sacrifice were indeed vainglory, then affectation and fustian is each more heroic line in the great epics and dramas, since in such lines the poet but embodies in verse those exaltations of sentiment that a nature like Nelson, the opportunity being given, vitalizes into acts. (*BB* 58)

Nelson is not a Christian hero for Melville; his sign is not the cross but the "star" inserted in his ship's quarter-deck on the spot where he fell (*BB* 57). The star is the endpoint for what *Billy Budd* presents as the metamorphosis of the natural self (the rose) by means of aspiration or suffering (the cross) into the spiritual self (the star)—the "spiritual" understood as a quality of inner being within temporal life, beyond which everything is obscure. In this respect, Nelson's ship, the *Victory,* is aptly named. Heroism's "jest is the littleness of common life,"[68] Emerson remarked. Nelson's conduct at Trafalgar is a victory over that "littleness" and a reproach to the "martial utilitarians" who value "personal prudence" over "excessive love of glory, impassioning . . . the honest sense of duty" (*BB* 57, 58). Even "'Starry Vere'" (*BB* 61), whose "honest sense of duty" is his and Billy's undoing, is distinguished from his peers by the earnest, ruminative cast of mind that enables him to appreciate Billy and anguish over his role in condemning him. In "the running battle of the star and clod" (*C* 4, 35: 16) that Melville saw as the permanent condition of agnostic life, Vere, too, by virtue of his moral seriousness, belongs to "great Nature's nobler order" (*BB* 115) regardless of whether his behavior is right or wrong.

From *Clarel* onward, Melville increasingly came to believe that human beings defined themselves as star or clod by how they chose to live. Melville's own choice was to labor for most of six years on a story that refused imaginative closure. Years earlier he had Pierre acknowledge "the universal lurking insincerity of even the greatest and purest written thoughts. Like knavish cards, the leaves of all great books were covertly packed" (*P* 339). The expansions and revisions of *Billy Budd* down to the late pencil

stage were Melville's effort to *un*pack the fictive deck by tasking himself to
understand and express the meaning of his fable as it beckoned him on to
ever greater complication. If Melville had been content with craftsmanship
alone, he might have sent *Billy Budd* into the world in 1888 or mid-1891. It
was because there was more to discover and know, or *not*-know, that Melville
kept returning to his book, even as he saw that returning might keep him
from completing it at all. Forty-odd years earlier he had told Evert Duyckinck, "But live & push—tho' we put one leg forward ten miles—its no reason the other must lag behind—no, *that* must again distance the other—&
so on till we get the cramp and die" (*Corr* 128). At the age of seventy-two,
Melville was still pushing.

On August 4, 1891, or soon after, Melville wrote the flower-strewn dedication of "Weeds and Wildings" "To Winnefred." Eight weeks later he
was dead. The obituary in the *New-York Press* called him "once one of the
most popular writers in the United States," adding, "Probably, if the truth
were known, even his own generation has long thought him dead, so quiet
have been the later years of his life."[69] Had Melville been able to choose his
own obituary, it would have been consonant with his late conception of his
life to select the paraphrase from the *Aeneid* written and sent to him by his
brother-in-law John C. Hoadley in 1877, probably with *Clarel* in mind:

> Drawing the shaft
> Until its feathers touch his swelling breast,
> Its barb his out-stretched hand, he aims
> Full at the veiléd stars. Shrill twangs the string,
> The singing arrow flies, a gleam of light
> Athwart the blue, like a resurgent star
> Restored to heaven where the Mantuan bard
> Hath bid it shine for aye. The highest aim
> Hath won the highest prize.
> Aim high and do your best:
> Them though the mark be hid, the generous deed
> Shall ever shine,—itself the noblest prize.
> (*Corr* 717–18)

NOTES

Notes to Preface

1. Charles Olson to Merton M. Sealts, Jr., in "1952: Olson and the *New Republic*," in Sealts, *Pursuing Melville: 1940–1980* (Madison: University of Wisconsin Press, 1982), 119.

2. John Bryant, "From the Masthead," *Leviathan* 6 (March 2004): 2.

3. Bryant, "From the Masthead," 2.

4. Thomas Carlyle, "Jean Paul Friedrich Richter," in *Critical and Miscellaneous Essays, in Five Volumes* (London: Chapman and Hall, 1899), 2: 100–101.

5. Wayne C. Booth, *Critical Understanding: The Powers and Limits of Pluralism* (Chicago: University of Chicago Press), 270.

6. Warner Berthoff, *The Example of Melville* (Princeton: Princeton University Press, 1962), 47.

7. E. L. Grant Watson, "Melville's *Pierre*," in *Critical Essays on Herman Melville's "Pierre; or, The Ambiguities"* (Boston: G. K. Hall, 1983), 183.

8. Robert Milder, "Melville's 'Intentions' in *Pierre*," *Studies in the Novel* 6 (1974): 186–99.

9. George Gordon, Lord Byron, "Childe Harold's Pilgrmage," in *Lord Byron: The Major Works*, ed. Jerome J. McGann (Oxford: Oxford University Press, 1986), III, 697.

10. Lawrence Buell, "Melville and the Question of American Decolonization," *American Literature* 64 (1992): 217.

Notes to Chapter 1

1. Mary McCarthy, *Memories of a Catholic Girlhood* (New York: Harcourt Brace Jovanovich, 1957), 16–17.

2. Allan Melvill to Peter Gansevoort, quoted in Hershel Parker, *Herman Melville: A Biography*, vol. 1, *1819–1851* (Baltimore: John Hopkins University Press, 1996), 35.

3. Like everyone who writes on Melvile in the Pacific, I owe a great debt to Charles R. Anderson's *Melville in the South Seas* (New York: Columbia University Press, 1939). Valuable, too, has been T. Walter Herbert, Jr.'s *Marquesan*

Encounters: Melville and the Meaning of Civilization (Cambridge, Mass.: Harvard University Press, 1980).

4. Nathaniel Hawthorne, review of *Typee*, *Salem Advertiser*, quoted in Jay Leyda, *The Melville Log*, 2 vols. (New York: Harcourt Brace, 1951), 1:207. References to the *Log* are hereafter cited in the text.

5. Harrison Hayford, Hershel Parker, and G. Thomas Tanselle, Historical Note to *Typee: A Peep at Polynesian Life*, ed. Hayford, Parker, and Tanselle, vol. 1 of *The Writings of Herman Melville*, (Evanston, Ill., and Chicago: Northwestern University Press and The Newberry Library, 1968), 291. Hereafter cited in the notes as the Northwestern-Newberry edition.

6. John Bryant, introduction to *Typee* (New York: Penguin, 1996), xxii.

7. Bryant, introduction to *Typee*, xxiii.

8. Newton Arvin, *Herman Melville: A Biography* (New York: William Sloane, 1950), 57. Hereafter cited in the text.

9. I use the anthropological spelling "Tapivai" and "Taipi" for the actual place and people, considered independently of Melville, and "Typee" for Melville's personal experience and literary rendering of them.

10. Raymond Williams, *Marxism and Literature* (Oxford: Oxford University Press, 1977), 13–14. See also Herbert, *Marquesan Encounters*, 5.

11. William Ellis, *Polynesian Researches*, 4 vols. (London: Fisher, Son, and Jackson, 1831), 2:405. Hereafter cited in the text.

12. See Charles Wilkes, *Narrative of the United States Exploring Expedition, . . . 1838–1842*, 5 vols. (Philadelphia: Lea and Blanchard, 1845), 2:15; and Otto von Kotzebue, *A New Voyage Round the World . . .* , 2 vols. (London: Henry Colburn and Richard Bentley, 1830), 1:170.

13. Anonymous review of *Typee*, *Douglas Jerrold's Shilling Magazine* (April 1846), reprinted in *Critical Essays on Herman Melville's "Typee,"* ed. Milton R. Stern (Boston: G. K. Hall, 1982), 37.

14. Sigmund Freud, *Civilization and Its Discontents*, trans. James Strachey (New York: Norton, 1962), 33. Hereafter cited in the text as *CD*.

15. Clifford Geertz, *The Interpretation of Cultures* (New York: Basic Books, 1973), 346.

16. Anderson, *Melville in the South Seas*, 132.

17. John Sullivan Dwight, review of *Typee*, *Harbinger*, April 4, 1846, reprinted in Stern, *Critical Essays*, 25.

18. Dwight, review of *Typee*, 26.

19. William Heath, "Melville and Marquesan Eroticism," *Massachusetts Review* 29 (1988): 53.

20. David Porter, *Journal of a Cruise Made to the Pacific Ocean in the Frigate Essex . . .* , 2nd ed., 2 vols. (1822; reprint, Upper Saddle River, N.J.: Gregg Press, 1970), 2:59. Hereafter cited in the text.

21. Quoted in Herbert, *Marquesan Encounters*, 131.

22. Herbert Marcuse, *Eros and Civilization* (Boston: Beacon Press, 1955), 83. Hereafter cited in the text as Marcuse.

23. The chief exception to this monogamy was the custom, uncited by Melville, of extending sexual privileges (in the case of both husband and wife) to certain in-laws. See Anderson, *Melville in the South Seas*, 143; and Heath, "Melville and Marquesan Eroticism," 50–51.

24. See Rolfe's remark in *Clarel*, "'Tahiti should have been the place / For Christ in advent'" (*C* 4, 18: 43–44).

25. Caleb Crain, "Lovers of Human Flesh: Homosexuality and Cannibalism in Melville's Novels," *American Literature* 43 (March 1994): 32.

26. Herbert, *Marquesan Encounters*, 131.

27. Michel Foucault, *The History of Sexuality*, vol. 1, *An Introduction*, trans. Robert Hurley (New York: Random House, 1980), 69.

28. What Ellis apparently has in mind are verses 26 and 27: "26 . . . for even their women did change the natural use into that which is against nature: 27 And likewise also the men, leaving the natural use of the woman, burned in lust one toward another; men with men working that which is unseemly."

29. Herbert, *Marquesan Encounters*, 132.

30. Herbert, *Marquesan Encounters*, 129.

31. William Charvat, "Melville and the Common Reader," in *The Profession of Authorship in America: The Papers of William Charvat*, ed. Matthew J. Bruccoli (Columbus: Ohio State University Press, 1968), 265.

32. Horace Greeley, "Up the Lakes," in *New-York Weekly Tribune*, June 8, 1847, quoted in Leyda, *Log*, 1:248.

33. Nathaniel Hawthorne, *The Blithedale Romance*, in *"The Blithedale Romance" and "Fanshawe,"* vol. 3 of *The Centenary Edition of The Works of Nathaniel Hawthorne*, ed. William Charvat (Columbus: Ohio State University Press, 1964), 17.

34. Hawthorne, *Blithedale Romance*, 17.

35. Foucault, *History of Sexuality*, 1:57.

36. D. H. Lawrence, *Studies in Classic American Literature* (1923; reprint, New York: Viking Press, 1964), 137.

37. Walt Whitman, "Whitman to Emerson, 1856," in *Leaves of Grass*, ed. Sculley Bradley and Harold W. Blodgett (New York: Norton, 1973), 739.

38. Anderson, *Melville in the South Seas*, 241, 240.

39. Kotzebue, *New Voyage Round the World*, 1:167–69.

40. Ralph Waldo Emerson, "The Young American," in *Nature, Addresses, Lectures*, ed. Robert E. Spiller and Alfred R. Ferguson, vol. 1 of *The Collected Works of Ralph Waldo Emerson* (Cambridge, Mass: Harvard University Press, 1979), 231.

41. Emerson, "Emancipation in the British West Indies," *Complete Works of Ralph Waldo Emerson*, ed. Edward Waldo Emerson (Boston: Houghton Mifflin, 1903-4), 11:143.

42. On the difficulties and limits of reform, see *Redburn: His First Voyage*, ed. Harrison Hayford, Hershel Parker, and G. Thomas Tanselle, vol. 4 of the Northwestern-Newberry edition (1969), 139–40, 292–93.

43. Emerson, "Man the Reformer," in *Nature, Addresses, Lectures*, 148, 159.

44. C. Vann Woodward, *The Burden of Southern History*, rev. ed. (Baton Rouge: Louisiana State University Press, 1968), 28.

Notes to Chapter 2

1. Henry James, "The Figure in the Carpet," in *The Novels and Tales of Henry James* (New York: Scribner's, 1909), 15:241.

2. James, preface to *Novels and Tales*, 15:xvi.

3. See R. S. Crane, "Toward a More Adequate Criticism of Poetic Structure," in *The Languages of Criticism and the Structure of Poetry* (Toronto: University of Toronto Press, 1953), 140–94.

4. E. D. Hirsch, *Validity in Interpretation* (New Haven: Yale University Press, 1967), 223.

5. Albert Camus, "Herman Melville," in *Lyrical and Critical Essays*, trans. Philip Thody (London: Hamish Hamilton, 1967), 206.

6. Newton Arvin, *Herman Melville: A Biography* (New York: William Sloane, 1950), 79.

7. Northrop Frye, *A Study of English Romanticism* (New York: Random House, 1968), 17.

8. Friedrich von Schiller, "Naïve and Sentimental Poetry," in *"Naïve and Sentimental Poetry" and "On The Sublime,"* trans. Julius A. Elias (New York: Ungar, 1966), 103. Hereafter cited in the text as Schiller.

9. M. H. Abrams notes that "no thinker was of greater consequence than Friedrich Schiller in giving a distinctive Romantic formulation to the diagnosis of the modern malaise, to the assumptions about human good and ill which controlled this diagnosis, and to the overall view of the history and destiny of mankind of which the diagnosis was an integral part." Abrams, *Natural Supernaturalism* (New York: Norton, 1971), 199. Hereafter cited in the text as Abrams.

10. In exalting the moderns above the ancients, A. W. Schlegel went so far as to discount the works of Greek philosophy and poetry as "occasional exception[s]" to the rule. Although Schlegel felt that the Greeks had "accomplished all that the finite nature of man is capable of," he could not "concede any higher character to their civilisation than that of a refined and ennobled sensuality." "Lecture 1: Ancient and Modern Art and Poetry," in *Lectures on Dramatic Art and Literature*, trans. John Black (London: Bohn, 1846), 24.

11. Morse Peckham, "Hawthorne and Melville as European Authors," in *Melville and Hawthorne in the Berkshires*, ed. Howard P. Vincent (Kent, Ohio: Kent State University Press, 1968), 50.

12. Richard H. Brodhead, *"Mardi*: Creating the Creative," in *New Perspectives on Melville*, ed. Faith Pullin (Kent, Ohio: Kent State University Press, 1978), 48.

13. F. O. Matthiessen, *American Renaissance* (New York: Oxford University Press, 1941), 377.

14. Kerry McSweeney and Peter Sabor, introduction to *Sartor Resartus* by Thomas Carlyle, ed. McSweeney and Tabor (New York: Oxford University Press, 1987), vii.

15. For a chronology of *Mardi*'s composition, see Merrell R. Davis, *Melville's "Mardi": A Chartless Voyage* (New Haven: Yale University Press, 1952); and Elizabeth S. Foster, Historical Note to *Mardi; and a Voyage Thither*, ed. Harrison Hayford, Hershel Parker, and G. Thomas Tanselle, vol. 3 of the Northwestern-Newberry edition (1970), 657–64.

16. Ronald Mason, *The Spirit Above the Dust* (London: John Lehmann, 1951), 42.

17. Jerome C. McGann, *Fiery Dust* (Chicago: University of Chicago Press, 1968), 35.

18. See Brodhead, "Creating the Creative," 34.

19. See Foster, Historical Note to *Mardi*, 661; and Merton M. Sealts. Jr., *Melville's Reading*, rev. and enl. ed. (Columbia: University Of South Carolina Press), 102, 103.

20. Lilian R. Furst, *The Contours of European Romanticism* (Lincoln: University of Nebraska Press, 1979), 3.

21. Sigmund Freud, *Civilization and Its Discontents*, trans. James Strachey (New York: Norton, 1962), 15, 12.

22. Martin Bickman, *The Unsounded Centre: Jungian Studies in American Romanticism* (Chapel Hill: University of North Carolina Press, 1980), 39.

23. Shirley M. Dettlaff, "'Counter Natures in Mankind': Hebraism and Hellenism in *Clarel*," in *Melville's Evermoving Dawn*, ed. John Bryant and Robert Milder (Kent, Ohio: Kent State University Press, 1997), 195.

24. Foster, historical note to *Mardi*, 661.

25. George Ripley, review of *Mardi, New York Tribune*, May 10, 1849, reprinted in *The Recognition of Herman Melville*, ed. Hershel Parker (Ann Arbor: University of Michigan Press 1967), 16. As Harrison Hayford comments, "Melville's contemporary reviewers right away recognized his German streak. They recognized it, named it, and deplored its presence in *Mardi, Moby-Dick*, and *Pierre*." "Melville's German Streak," in *A Conversation in the Life of Leland R. Phelps: America and Germany: Literature, Art, and Music*, ed. Frank L. Borchardt and Marion C. Salinger (Durham, N.C.: Duke University Center for International Studies, 1987), 5.

26. Friedrich Schlegel, *Lyceum* aphorism 26, in *"Dialogue on Poetry" and Literary Aphorisms*, trans. Ernst Behler and Roman Struc (University Park: Pennsylvania State University Press, 1968), 123.

27. Friedrich Schlegel, *Athenaeum* aphorism 116, in *"Dialogue on Poetry" and Literary Aphorisms*, 140. Though Schlegel is referring to the role of Romantic poetry, he understands "poetry" in a transgeneric sense that includes the novel (*Roman*).

28. Friedrich Schlegel, "Letter about the Novel," in *"Dialogue on Poetry"* *and Literary Aphorisms*, 103.

29. See Paul de Man's discussion of symbolism and allegory in "The Rhetoric of Temporality," in *Blindness and Insight: Essays in the Rhetoric of Contemporary Criticism*, 2nd ed. (Minneapolis: University of Minnesota Press, 1983), 187–228.

30. Tilottama Rajan, *Dark Interpreter* (Ithaca: Cornell University Press, 1980), 21.

31. Robin Gilmour, *The Victorian Period: The Intellectual and Cultural Context of English Literature 1830–1890* (London: Longman, 1993), 86.

32. Matthew Arnold, "Memorial Verses," in *The Works of Matthew Arnold*, vol. 1 (London: Macmillan, 1903), ll. 44, 43. All references to Arnold's poetry will be to vols. 1 and 2 of this edition and will be cited in the text.

33. Elizabeth S. Foster, "Melville and Geology," *American Literature* 17 (1945): 50.

34. Matthiessen, *American Renaissance*, 122, 123.

35. This is the significance of the well-chosen adverb in Warner Berthoff's observation that Melville was "*manfully* absorbed, at the moment of writing his books, in the activity and astonishing development of his own mind." More than anything else, "manhood" for Melville signified an uncompromising determination to know and express the truth. Berthoff, *The Example of Melville* (Princeton: Princeton University Press, 1962), 8; my emphasis.

36. Elizabeth S. Foster observes that "although his knowledge of geology was spotty and amounted by no means to mastery in any area, nevertheless, early in his career Melville had studied, with enough care and interest to reproduce at least a part of the data with extraordinary accuracy, precisely those discoveries of the new science which were proving most dangerous to religious faith in the nineteenth century: the vast antiquity of our planet; the gradual changes of the earth through the operation of natural causes; the rise and extinction of species in era after era; the appearance, in succeeding ages, of related forms and increasingly higher forms, which tended to discredit doctrines of special creation; and perhaps the theory that species were not fixed but were developed from common antecedent types." "Melville and Geology," 65.

37. Alfred Lord Tennyson, "In Memoriam," in *The Complete Poetical Works of Tennyson*, ed. W. J. Rolfe (Cambridge, Mass.: Houghton Mifflin, 1898), stanza 50, ll. 13–16.

38. Leslie A. Marchand, *Byron's Poetry: A Critical Introduction* (Boston: Houghton Mifflin, 1965), 38.

39. George Gordon, Lord Byron, "Manfred," in *Lord Byron: The Major Works*, ed. Jerome J. McGann (Oxford: Oxford University Press, 1986), I, 1: 10–12. All references to Byron's poems are to this edition and will be cited in the text.

40. Henry A. Murray, Introduction to *Pierre* (New York: Hendricks House, 1962), xli. 41. Thomas Carlyle, *Sartor Resartus* (Berkeley: University of California Press, 2000), 119. Hereafter cited in the text as *Sartor*.

42. G. B. Tennyson, *Sartor Called Resartus* (Princeton: Princeton University Press, 1965), 3.

43. Tennyson notes that "Byron alone of the Romantics won Carlyle's quali-fied approval, but he felt that Byron never passed beyond the *Sturm und Drang* stage" (*Sartor Called Resartus*, 92 n. 35). More of Byron remained in Carlyle than Carlyle cared to admit.

44. Melville would mark this stanza with a double vertical line in his 1867 edition of Arnold, long after he had dramatized the idea in Ahab. See See Walter E. Bezanson, "Melville's Reading of Arnold's Poetry," *PMLA* 69 (1954): 381.

45. Arnold, "Author's Preface, 1853," in *The Poems of Matthew Arnold, 1840–1867* (London: Oxford University Press, 1913), 2–3.

46. See William Braswell, *Melville's Religious Thought* (Durham, N.C.: Duke University Press, 1943), 33.

47. De Man, "Rhetoric of Temporality," 215–16. See Melville's later com-ment in "Hawthorne in His Mosses" about "Lear the frantic King tear[ing] off the mask, and speak[ing] the sane madness of vital truth" (*PT* 244).

48. A. W. Schlegel, *Lectures on Dramatic Art and Literature*, 25.

49. A. W. Schlegel, *Lectures on Dramatic Art and Literature*, 24.

50. A. W. Schlegel, *Lectures on Dramatic Art and Literature*, 26.

51. Arvin, *Herman Melville*, 56–57.

52. Peckham, "Toward a Theory of Romanticism," in *Romanticism: Points of View*, ed. Robert F. Gleckner and Gerald E. Enscoe (Englewood Cliffs, N. J.: Prentice-Hall, 1962), 220.

53. I am speaking here of the attraction of Melville's dark, brooding char-acters, which is one of several forms homoeroticism takes in Melville's writings. The appeal of Marnoo in *Typee*, Harry Bolton and Carlo in *Redburn*, and the Lyonese Jew is *Clarel* is more aesthetic and physical. A good part of the confu-sion surrounding the question of Melville and same-sex attraction comes from a tendency to treat it as a single phenomenon with a single source; it is not.

54. Merlin Bowen, *The Long Encounter* (Chicago: University of Chicago Press, 1960), 209.

55. Lionel Trilling, "Hawthorne in Our Time," in *Beyond Culture* (New York: Viking Press, 1968), 200, 201.

56. Friedrich Schlegel, *Lyceum* fragment #37, quoted in Anne K. Mellor, *English Romantic Irony* (Cambridge, Mass.: Harvard University Press, 1980), 10.

Notes to Chapter 3

1. Walt Whitman, Preface 1855, in *Leaves of Grass*, ed. Sculley Bradley and Harold C. Blodgett (New York: Norton, 1973), 711. Hereafter cited in the text.

2. Whitman, "A Backward Glance O'er Travel'd Roads," in Bradley and Blodgett, *Leaves of Grass*, 568. Hereafter cited in the text.

3. "Introduction," *United States Magazine and Democratic Review* 1 (October 1837): 11.

4. Ralph Waldo Emerson, "Tragedy," in *The Early Lectures of Ralph Waldo Emerson*, 3 vols., ed. Stephen E. Whicher (Cambridge, Mass.: Harvard University Press, 1964), 2:110. As Lawrence W. Levine notes, "Shakespeare was taught in ineteenth-century schools and colleges as declamation or rhetoric, not as literature," while American stage presentations tended to favor a "vigorous, tempestuous, emotional style" rather than a reflective psychological one. Levine, *Highbrow/Lowbrow: The Emergence of Cultural Hierarchy in America* (Cambridge, Mass.: Harvard University Press, 1988), 37, 38.

5. At two points in his career, Melville was impelled by a belief that American writers might exercise a formative influence upon their culture. The first time was in 1850–51, when he was buoyed by the possibilities announced in "Hawthorne and His Mosses"; the second time was immediately after the Civil War, as he worked on *Battle-Pieces*. In both cases, Melville's optimism did not survive the reception of his book.

6. Walt Whitman, quoted in Richard M. Bucke, *Notes and Fragments Left by Walt Whitman* (London, Ontario: Talbot, 1899), 57.

7. Whitman, "One's-Self I Sing," in Bradley and Blodgett, *Leaves of Grass*, l. 2. All references to Whitman's poems hereafter are to this edition and are cited in the text. Larzer Ziff begins *Literary Democracy* by remarking that for the writers he will discuss, "America meant more than a new setting for time-honored forms; it meant a new way of perceiving reality." *Literary Democracy* (New York: Viking, 1981), xi.

8. *Aristotle's "Poetics,"* trans. S. H. Butcher (New York: Hill and Wang, 1961), 82.

9. Northrop Frye, *Anatomy of Criticism* (Princeton: Princeton University Press, 1957), 33.

10. Alexis de Tocqueville, *Democracy in America*, 2 vols., trans. Henry Reeve as revised by Francis Bowen, ed. Phillips Bradley (New York: Knopf, 1945), 1:3.

11. Tocqueville, *Democracy in America*, 2:77; see 2:78–81.

12. F. O. Matthiessen, *American Renaissance* (New York: Oxford University Press, 1941), 445. Hereafter cited in the text as Matthiessen.

13. Richard B. Sewall, "The Vision of Tragedy," in *Tragedy: Vision and Form*, 2nd ed., ed. Robert W. Corrigan (New York: Harper and Row, 1981), 49.

14. "Afford but the single nucleus of a system of administration of justice between man and man," the *Democratic Review* sermonized, "and, under the sure operation of [the voluntary] principle, the floating atoms will distribute and combine themselves, as we see in the beautiful process of crystallization, into a far more perfect and harmonious result than if government, with its 'fostering hand,' undertake to disturb, under the plea of directing, the process. The natural laws which will establish themselves and find their own level are the best laws." "Introduction," *United States Magazine and Democratic Review*, 7.

15. Emerson, "Tragedy," 110.

16. Lionel Trilling, "Reality in America," in *The Liberal Imagination* (London: Mercury, 1961), 9.

17. Julian Markels, *Melville and the Politics of Identity* (Urbana: University of Illinois Press, 1993), 56.

18. Melville's list of writers appears in the manuscript of "Hawthorne and His Mosses" but was omitted from the text in *The Literary World*, almost surely from editorial caution. The Northwestern-Newberry edition of Melville's prose restores the list (vol. 9, p. 247). In "Melville and Emerson's Rainbow," the most careful study of Melville's relationship to Emerson, Merton M. Sealts, Jr., concluded that "by August of 1850 [Melville] had indeed been reading Emerson, though probably not *Nature*." In *Pursuing Melville: 1940–1980* (Madison: University of Wisconsin Press, 1982), 266.

19. Emerson, "Literary Ethics," in *Nature, Addresses, Lectures*, ed. Robert E. Spiller and Alfred R. Ferguson, vol. 1 of *The Collected Works of Ralph Waldo Emerson* (Cambridge, Mass.: Harvard University Press, 1979), 105-6.

20. Emerson, "Nature," in *Nature, Addresses, Lectures*, 7.

21. Emerson, "Literary Ethics," 110.

22. Henry David Thoreau, *Walden*, ed. J. Lyndon Shanley (Princeton: Princeton University Press, 1971), 4.

23. Cornelius Mathews, "Nationality in Literature," *United States Magazine and Democratic Review* 20 (March 1847): 267.

24. Emerson, "Nature," 43.

25. Emerson, "The Poet," in *Essays, Second Series*, ed. Alfred R. Ferguson and Jean Ferguson Carr, vol. 3 of *The Collected Works of Ralph Waldo Emerson* (Cambridge, Mass.: Harvard University Press, 1983), 11.

26. W. Walker Cowen, "Melville's Marginalia" (Ph.D. diss., Harvard University, 1965), 5:5.

27. Albert Camus, *The Myth of Sisyphus*, trans. Justin O'Brien (New York: Random House, 1959), 21.

28. Camus, *Myth of Sisyphus*, 11.

29. Nina Baym, "Melville's Quarrel with Fiction," *PMLA* 94 (1979): 914.

30. See Frye, "Myth, Fiction, Displacement," in *Fables of Identity* (New York: Harcourt Brace, 1963), 21–38.

31. Thomas Carlyle, *On Heroes, Hero-Worship, and the Heroic in History*, ed. Michael K. Goldberg (Berkeley: University of California Press, 1993), 43. Hereafter cited in the text as *HHW*. Melville borrowed this volume of Carlyle, along with *Sartor Resartus*, from Evert Duyckinck in June or July (?) 1850. See Merton M. Sealts, Jr., *Melville's Reading*, rev. and enl. ed. (Columbia: University of South Carolina Press, 1988), nos. 122, 123.

32. Leon Howard, *Herman Melville: A Biography* (Berkeley: University of California Press, 1951), 169.

33. William James, *The Varieties of Religious Experience* (New York: New American Library, 1958), 162–63.

34. Howard P. Vincent, *The Trying-out of "Moby-Dick"* (Carbondale: Southern Illinois University Press, 1949), 37.

35. Evert A. Duyckinck, "Nathaniel Hawthorne," *United States Magazine and Democratic Review* 16 (April 1845): 378.

36. Duyckinck, "Nathaniel Hawthorne," 378.

37. Duyckinck, "Nathaniel Hawthorne," 384.

38. Duyckinck, "Nathaniel Hawthorne," 381.

39. Levine, *Highbrow/Lowbrow*, 4; see 41–42. Hereafter cited in the text.

40. Henry Norman Hudson, *Lectures on Shakespeare*, 2nd ed., 2 vols. (New York: Baker and Scribner, 1848), 2:278. Hereafter cited in the text.

41. John Stafford, "Henry Norman Hudson and the Whig Use of Shakespeare," *PMLA*, 66 (1951): 649–50.

42. Whitman, "An English and an American Poet," in *Walt Whitman: A Critical Anthology*, ed. Francis Murphy (Hammondsworth, England: Penguin, 1969), 38.

43. Hudson, "Whipple's Essays and Reviews," *American Whig Review* 9 (February 1849): 152.

44. Charles W. Webber, "Hawthorne," *American Whig Review* 9 (September 1846): 308. Hawthorne has frequently seemed a sympathetic writer for conservatives both within and without academia. This was especially true before the mid-1960s revolution in Hawthorne criticism initiated by Frederick Crews in *The Sins of the Fathers* and by the politically inspired criticism of the late 1960s and afterward. Among the earlier conservative readings of Hawthorne are Arlin Turner, "Hawthorne and Reform," *New England Quarterly* 15 (1942): 700–714; Russell Kirk, "The Moral Conservatism of Hawthorne," *Contemporary Review* 181 (December 1952): 361–66; and Darrel Abel, "Hawthorne's Skepticism About Social Reform," *University of Kansas City Review* 9 (1953): 181–93. Quentin Anderson, reacting partly to domestic disturbances during the Vietnam era, opposed Hawthorne to the Emersonian tradition of egoism in *The Imperial Self* (New York: Knopf, 1971), 59–87.

45. Webber, "Hawthorne," 308.

46. See Emerson, "The Conservative," in *Nature, Addresses, Lectures*, 196.

47. Hudson, "Whipple's Essays and Reviews," 151.

48. "Introduction," *United States Magazine and Democratic Review*, 11.

48. Emerson, "Conservative," 185–65.

50. See Charles H. Shattuck, *Shakespeare on the American Stage* (Washington, D.C.: Folger Shakespeare Library, 1976), 82–85; Richard Moody, *The Astor Place Riot* (Bloomington: Indiana University Press, 1958); and Dennis Berthold, "Class Acts: The Astor Place Riots and Melville's 'The Two Temples,'" *American Literature* 71 (1999): 429–61. All hereafter cited in the text.

51. Lawrence Buell, "Melville and the Question of American Decolonialization," *American Literature* 64 (1992): 217.

52. "Municipal Government," *United States Magazine and Democratic Review* 25 (June 1849): 485, 487.

53. Larry J. Reynolds, "Anti-Democratic Emphasis in *White-Jacket*," *American Literature* 48 (1976): 17.

54. Sealts, "Melville and Emerson's Rainbow," 258.

55. Emerson, "Natural Aristocracy," quoted in Sealts, "Melville and Emerson's Rainbow," 259.

56. Rush Welter, *The Mind of America 1820–1860* (New York: Columbia University Press, 1975), 83.

57. George Bancroft, "The Office of the People in Art, Government and Religion," reprinted in Joseph Blau, *Social Theories of Jacksonian Democracy* (Indianapolis: Bobbs-Merrill, 1954), 265–66. Tocqueville phrased this phenomenon rather differently: "The moral authority of the majority is partly based upon the notion that there is more intelligence and wisdom in a number of men than in a single individual. . . . The theory of equality is this applied to the intellects of men." *Democracy in America*, 1:265.

58. Daniel Aaron, *Men Of Good Hope* (1951; reprint, New York: Oxford University Press, 1969), 8.

59. Emerson, *Representative Men*, ed. Wallace E. Williams and Douglas Emory Wilson, vol. 4 of *The Collected Works of Ralph Waldo Emerson* (Cambridge, Mass.: Harvard University Press, 1987), 5.

60. Stanley Geist, *Herman Melville: The Tragic Vision and the Heroic Ideal* (1939; reprint, New York: Octagon Books, 1966), 63.

61. Geist, *Herman Melville*, 23.

62. A. C. Bradley, *Shakespearean Tragedy* (1904; reprint, Cleveland: Meridian, 1955), 228.

63. Emerson, *Representative Men*, 125.

64. Emerson, Divinity School Address, in *Nature, Addresses, Lectures*, 89.

65. Tocqueville, *Democracy in America*, 1:273.

66. Paul Lauter, "Melville Climbs the Canon," *American Literature* 66 (March 1994): 2.

67. William Charvat, "Melville and the Common Reader," in *The Profession of Authorship in America: The Papers of William Charvat*, ed. Matthew J. Bruccoli (Columbus: Ohio State University Press, 1968), 271.

68. Whitman, "Democratic Vistas," in *Leaves and Grass and Selected Prose*, ed. John Kouwenhoven (New York: Modern Library, 1950), 489.

69. Here I am following Benjamin T. Spencer's useful distinction in *The Quest for Nationality* (Syracuse: Syracuse University Press, 1957), 117.

70. Spencer, *Quest for Nationality*, 118.

71. Spencer, *Quest for Nationality*, 118

72. Emerson, "Literary Ethics," 113.

73. Leo Strauss, *Persecution and the Art of Writing* (New York: Free Press, 1952), 26.

74. "Behind [Hawthorne's] moralism, and often directly contradicting it," Crews wrote, lies a sure insight into everything that is terrible, uncontrollable,

and therefore *demoralizing* in human nature." *The Sins of the Fathers* (New York: Oxford University Press, 1966), 8.

75. Strauss, *Persecution and the Art of Writing*, 36.

76. Strauss, *Persecution and the Art of Writing*, 36.

77. Jay Leyda, *The Melville Log*, 2 vols. (New York: Harcourt Brace, 1951), 1:363–64.

78. See, for example, Sophia Hawthorne's description of Melville. Leyda, *Log*, 1:393–94.

79. Charles Fenno Hoffman, review of *Twice-Told Tales*, *American Monthly Magazine* (1838), reprinted in *Hawthorne: The Critical Heritage*, ed. J. Donald Crowley (New York: Barnes and Noble, 1970), 61.

Notes to Chapter 4

1. Walter E. Bezanson, "*Moby-Dick*: Work of Art" (1953), reprinted in *Moby-Dick*, ed. Hershel Parker and Harrison Hayford (New York: Norton, 2002), 644.

2. Robert Zoellner, *The Salt-Sea Mastodon* (Berkeley: University of California Press, 1973), xi.

3. Zoellner, *Salt-Sea Mastodon*, xi.

4. Harrison Hayford, "'Loomings': Yarns and Figures in the Fabric" (1975), reprinted in Parker and Hayford, *Moby-Dick*, 657.

5. Bezanson, "*Moby-Dick*: Work of Art," 657.

6. The first serious treatise on the novel, David Masson's *British Novelists and Their Styles*, would not be published until 1859.

7. Northrop Frye, *Anatomy of Criticism* (Princeton: Princeton University Press, 1957), 313.

8. Charles Olson, *Call Me Ishmael* (San Francisco: City Lights Books, 1947), 69.

9. R. S. Crane, *The Languages of Criticism and the Structure of Poetry* (Toronto: University of Toronto Press, 1953), 166. My working principle in thinking about the structure of *Moby-Dick* owes much to Crane's ideas of literary form and inductive literary method. "The problem, in any given poem," Crane wrote, "is what actually was, for its poet, the primary intuition of form which enabled him to synthesize his materials into an ordered whole . . . ; and this means that the first principle of our analysis must be an induction of which the only warrant is the evidence of the poem itself." (*The Languages of Criticism and the Structure of Poetry*, 146). I would alter Crane's "actually" to "hypothetically": critical "induction" is not even an imperfect science; it is an imperfect art, and its findings are always subject to debate.

10. R.W.B. Lewis, *The American Adam: Innocence, Tragedy, and Tradition in the Nineteenth Century* (Chicago: University of Chicago Press, 1955), 146.

11. See Allen Tate, "Tension in Poetry," in *The Man of Letters in the Modern World* (Cleveland: Meridian, 1955), 64–77.

12. Murray Krieger, *The Tragic Vision* (Chicago: University of Chicago Press, 1960), 255.

13. John Bryant, "*Moby-Dick* as Revolution," in *The Cambridge Companion to Herman Melville*, ed. Robert S. Levine (Cambridge: Cambridge University Press, 1998), 71.

14. Walt Whitman, "A Backward Glance O'er Travel'd Roads," in *Leaves of Grass*, ed. Sculley Bradley and Harold W. Blodgett (New York: Norton, 1973), 571. All references hereafter to Whitman's prose and poetry, unless otherwise noted, are to this edition.

15. Quoted in Richard M. Bucke, *Notes and Fragments Left by Walt Whitman* (London, Ontario: 1899), 57.

16. Northrop Frye, *The Return of Eden* (Toronto: University of Toronto Press, 1965), 5.

17. Olson, *Call Me Ishmael*, 102.

18. See Zoellner, *Salt-Sea Mastodon*, 53–71.

19. Walter J. Ong, *Interfaces of the Word* (Ithaca: Cornell University Press, 1977), 60–1.

20. Lawrence Buell, *Literary Transcendentalism* (Ithaca: Cornell University Press, 1973), 306.

21. See Buell, "Observer-Hero Narratives," *Texas Studies in Language and Literature* 21 (1979): 93–11; and Walter L. Reed, *Meditations on the Hero* (New Haven: Yale University Press, 1974).

22. Luther S. Mansfield and Howard P. Vincent, Explanatory Notes to *Moby-Dick*, ed. Mansfield and Vincent (New York: Hendricks House, 1952), 638. I gratefully acknowledge my debt to Mansfield and Vincent's exceptionally valuable work of scholarship and provocative interpretation.

23. *New Oxford Annotated Bible, Revised Standard Edition* (New York: Oxford University Press, 1973), 653.

24. Frye, *Anatomy of Criticism*, 189–90.

25. Frye, *Anatomy of Criticism*, 189.

26. Henry A. Murray, "Definitions of Myth," in *The Making of Myth*, ed. Richard M. Ohmann (New York: Putnam, 1962), 8, 16.

27. Richard H. Brodhead, *Hawthorne, Melville, and the Novel* (Chicago: University of Chicago Press, 1976), 139.

28. Warner Berthoff, *The Example of Melville* (Princeton: Princeton University Press, 1962), 45.

29. See I. A. Richards, *Practical Criticism* (1929; reprint, New York: Harcourt Brace, 1963), 255–74.

30. Murray, "Definitions of Myth," 25.

31. Murray, "Definitions of Myth," 25.

32. Kenneth Burke, *The Philosophy of Literary Form*, rev. ed. (New York: Random House, 1957), 40.

33. Simon O. Lesser, *Fiction and the Unconscious* (Boston: Beacon Press, 1957), 249. Hereafter cited in the text.

34. Norman N. Holland offers a parallel account of identification in *The Dynamics of Literary Response* (New York: Norton, 1975), 274–80.

35. T. Walter Herbert, Jr., presents *Moby-Dick* as Melville's effort to "dismantle" the Calvinist "scheme of theological ideas that was taken as an accurate description of ultimate reality in his time." *Calvinism and Moby-Dick* (New Brunswick, N.J.: Rutgers University Press, 1977), 5. I would see Melville's impulse extending beyond Calvinism to the hegemonic mindset of Christianity at large.

36. Joseph Campbell, "Transformations of the Hero," in Ohmann, *Making of Myth*, 122.

37. Thomas Carlyle, *On Heroes, Hero-Worship, and the Heroic in History*, ed. Michael K. Goldberg (Berkeley: University of California Press, 1993), 34–35.

38. Larzer Ziff, *Literary Democracy* (New York: Viking, 1981), 278.

39. Merton M. Sealts, Jr., "Melville and the Platonic Tradition," in *Pursuing Melville: 1940–1980* (Madison: University of Wisconsin Press, 1982), 301–3.

40. Albert Camus, *The Myth of Sisyphus and Other Essays*, trans. Justin O'Brien (New York: Random House, 1959), 37.

41. See Warwick Wadlington, "Ishmael's Godly Gamesomeness: Selftaste and Rhetoric in *Moby-Dick*," *ELH* 39 (1972): 309–31.

42. See Warner Berthoff's fine discussion of Stubb in *Example of Melville*, 105–8.

43. Camus, *Myth of Sisyphus*, 10.

44. Robert Alter, *Rogue's Progress* (Cambridge, Mass.: Harvard University Press, 1965) 10.

45. Ralph Waldo Emerson, "Nature," in *Nature, Addresses, Lectures*, ed. Robert E. Spiller and Alfred R. Ferguson, vol. 1 of *The Collected Works of Ralph Waldo Emerson*, (Cambridge, Mass.: Harvard University Press, 1979), 7.

46. As Nina Baym points out, "the anatomizing of the whale is conducted in the work's present time; it is presented as Ishmael's reflections as he is now, in the process of working on his book, and not as he was many years before on the *Pequod*." "Melville's Quarrel with Fiction," *PMLA* 94 (1979): 917.

47. Berthoff, *Example of Melville*, 121; John Keats, letter to George and Thomas Keats, December 21, 1817, in *Criticism: The Major Texts*, ed. Walter Jackson Bate (New York: Harcourt Brace, 1852), 349.

48. The title of John Bryant's chapter on Melville, "Ishmael: Sounding the Repose of If," suggests a kindred reading. In *Melville and Repose* (New York: Oxford University Press, 1993), 186–206.

49. *The Complete Poems of Emily Dickinson*, ed. Thomas H. Johnson (Boston: Little, Brown, 1960), #657, #1095.

50. Sigmund Freud, *Civilization and Its Discontents*, trans. James Strachey (1929; reprint, New York: Norton, 1962), 11–12.

51. Samuel Johnson, "Preface of Shakespeare," in *Works* (New York: George Dearborn, 1832), 2:473.

52. Camus, *Myth of Sisyphus*, 74.

53. Wadlington, "Ishmael's Godly Gamesomeness," 311.

54. Anne K. Mellor, *English Romantic Irony* (Cambridge, Mass.: Harvard University Press 1980), 4. Hereafter cited in the text. Mellor doesn't write about Melville, but I gratefully acknowledge her work and that of Ernst Behler and G. R. Thompson in helping me think about Ishmael. See Behler, "The Theory of Irony in German Romanticsm," in *Romantic Irony*, ed. Frederick Garber (Budapest: Akadémiai Kiadó, 1988), 43–81; and Thompson, "Romantic Arabesque, Contemporary Theory, and Postmodernism: The Example of Poe's *Narrative*," *ESQ* 35 (1989): 163-271. Herafter cited in the text.

55. See Behler, "Theory of Irony," 61; Thompson, "Romantic Arabesque," 217.

56. See Mellor, *English Romantic Irony*, 5; Paul de Man, "The Rhetoric of Temporality," in *Blindness and Insight*, 2nd rev. ed., (Minneapolis: University of Minnesota Press 1983), 187-228; and Thompson, "Romantic Arabesque," 187.

57. See de Man, "Rhetoric of Temporality," 215-16.

58. "We [Melville and Adler] talked metaphysics continually, & Hegel, Schlegel, Kant & c were discussed under the influence of the whiskey" (*J* 8). By "Schlegel" it is unclear whether Melville means Friedrich or his brother, August Wilhelm, whom he would also read. The index to the Northwestern-Newberry edition of the *Journals* has Melville referring to Friedrich Schlegel.

59. Friedrich Schlegel, "Dialogue on Poetry," in *"Dialogue on Poetry" and Literary Aphorisms*, trans. Ernst Behler and Roman Struc (University Park: Pennsylvania State University Press, 1968), 53.

60. As Tocqueville observed in 1840, "To evade the bondage of system and habit, of family maxims, class opinions, and, in some degree, of national prejudices; to accept tradition only as a means of information, and existing facts only as a lesson to be used in doing otherwise and doing better; to seek the reason of things for oneself, and in oneself alone; . . . and to strike through the form to the substance—such are the principal characteristics of what I shall call the philosophical method of the Americans." *Democracy in America*, 2 vols., trans. Henry Reeve as revised by Francis Bowen (New York: Random House, 1945), 2:3.

61. Arthur O. Lovejoy, "Schiller and the Genesis of German Romanticism," in *Essays in the History of Ideas* (1948; reprint, New York: Putnam's, 1960), 224.

62. Friedrich Schlegel, *Lyceum* aphorism 26, in *"Dialogue on Poetry" and Literary Aphorisms*, 123.

63. Friedrich Schlegel, *Athenaeum* aphorism 116, in *"Dialogue on Poetry" and Literary Aphorisms*, 140. See Northrop Frye's view of the epic mentioned earlier, *Return of Eden*, 5.

64. Schlegel, *Athenaeum* aphorism 116.

65. Schlegel, *Athenaeum* aphorism 116.

66. Friedrich Schlegel, "Dialogue on Poetry," 103.

67. Emerson, "Self-Reliance," in *Essays: First Series*, ed. Joseph Slater, Alfred R. Ferguson, and Jean Ferguson Carr, vol. 2 of *The Collected Works of Ralph Waldo Emerson* (Cambridge, Mass.: Harvard University Press, 1979), 45;

and Michel Foucault, "What Is an Author?" in *Language, Counter-Memory, Practice*, trans. Donald F. Bouchard and Sherry Simon (Ithaca: Cornell University Press, 1977), 131.

68. Friedrich Schlegel, *Athenaeum* aphorism 262, in *"Dialogue on Poetry" and Literary Aphorisms*, 146.

68. Emerson, "The American Scholar," in *Nature, Addresses, Lectures*, 65.

70. Whitman, Preface 1855, in *Leaves of Grass*, 731.

71. Evert A. Duyckinck, unsigned review of *Moby-Dick*, *Literary World*, November 22, 1851, reprinted in *Melville: The Critical Heritage*, ed. Watson G. Branch (London: Routledge and Kegan Paul, 1974), 267.

72. William Charvat, "Melville and the Common Reader," in *The Profession of Authorship in America: The Papers of William Charvat*, ed. Matthew J. Bruccoli (Columbus: Ohio State University Press, 1968), 268.

Notes to Chapter 5

1. Thomas Carlyle, *Sartor Resartus*, ed. Mark Engel and Rodger L. Tarr (Berkeley: University of California Press, 2000), 191. Hereafter cited in the text.

2. *Langenscheidt's New College Merriam-Webster English Dictionary* (New York: Langenscheidt, 1998), 99.

3. F. O. Matthiessen, *American Renaissance* (New York: Oxford University Press, 1941), 430. Philip Young quotes Matthiessen's words in his discussion of "The Candles," but he doesn't apply them to Melville. See *The Private Melville* (University Park: Pennsylvania State University Press, 1993), 129.

4. J. Hillis Miller, *The Disappearance of God: Five 19th-Century Writers* (New York: Schocken, 1965), 13, 14.

5. T. E. Hulme, *Speculations* (1924: reprint, New York: Harcourt, Brace), 118.

6. George Gordon, Lord Byron, "Manfred," in *Lord Byron: The Major Works*, ed. Jerome McGann (Oxford: Oxford University Press, 2000), I, 2: 39–45. All references to Byron's poems are to this edition and hereafter are cited in the text.

7. Leslie A. Marchand, *Byron's Poetry: A Critical Introduction* (Boston: Houghton Mifflin, 1965), 75.

8. Young, *The Private Melville*, 140. See Edwin Haviland Miller, *Melville* (New York: Braziller, 1975), 53–72.

9. Percy Bysshe Shelley, "Queen Mab," in *Shelley: Poetical Works*, ed. Thomas Hutchinson (Oxford: Oxford University Press, 1943), VII, 254, 259–61; See Luther S. Mansfield and Howard P. Vincent, Explanatory Notes to *Moby-Dick*, ed. Mansfield and Vincent (New York: Hendricks House, 1952), 671.

10. John Bryant, *Melville and Repose* (New York: Oxford Unversity Press, 1993), 206.

11. Paul Brodtkorb, Jr., *Ishmael's White World: A Phenomenological Reading of "Moby-Dick"* (New Haven: Yale University Press, 1965), 102.

12. Brodtkorb, *Ishmael's White World*, 112.

13. Charles Olson, *Call Me Ishmael* (San Francisco: City Light Books, 1947), 85.

14. Bryant, *Melville and Repose*, 207.

15. Olson, *Call Me Ishmael*, 52.

16. "Melville's Notes (1849–1851) in a Shakespeare Volume," in *Moby-Dick; or, The Whale*, ed. Harrison Hayford, Hershel Parker, and G. Thomas Tanselle, vol. 6 of the Northwestern-Newberry edition (1988), 970.

17. Geoffrey Sanborn, "The Name of the Devil: Melville's Other 'Extracts' for *Moby-Dick*," *Nineteenth-Century Literature* 47 (1992): 217, 220. Hereafter cited in the text.

18. See "Melville's Notes (1849–1851) in a Shakespeare Volume," 959, 969.

19. See Mansfield and Vincent, explanatory notes, 649.

20. See Mansfield and Vincent, explanatory notes, 649, 678–79; and Robert Milder, "*Nemo Contra Deum . . .* : Melville and Goethe's 'Demonic,'" in *Ruined Eden of the Present*, ed. G. R. Thompson and Virgil K. Lokke (West Lafayette, Ind.: Purdue University Press, 1981), 220–24 especially.

21. See Charles C. Walcutt, "The Fire Symbolism in *Moby-Dick*," *MLN* 59 (1944): 304–10.

22. William James, *The Varieties of Religious Experience* (New York: New American Library, 1958), 259.

23. Robin Gilmour, *The Victorian Period: The Intellectual and Cultural Context of English Literature 1830–1890* (London: Longman, 1993), 87.

24. William Ellery Channing, "Unitarian Christianity," in *Works* (Boston: American Unitarian Association, 1879), 376. See T. Walter Herbert, Jr., *"Moby-Dick" and Calvinism: A World Dismantled* (New Brunswick, N.J.: Rutgers University Press, 1977), 147.

25. Channing, "Unitarian Christianity," 377.

26. W. H. Auden, *The Enchafèd Flood* (1950; reprint, New York: Random House, 1967), 94, 95. As Paul Brodtkorb, Jr., said of Ahab's defiance, "everything depends upon whether one is willing to grant Ahab's assumptions, or their emotional bases. *Are* the gods as Ahab describes them . . . ? Are human ethics irrelevant to a divine ethic, which supersedes them, and which fallen man can no longer even begin to comprehend? Or, to put the case negatively, do the gods even take notice of man. *Are* there any gods?" *Ishmael's White World*, 72.

27. Henry Nash Smith, *Democracy and the Novel* (New York: Oxford University Press, 1968), 36.

28. Smith, *Democracy and the Novel*, 36.

29. See Thomas Vargish, "Gnostic Mythos in *Moby-Dick*," *PMLA* 81 (1966): 272; and Merton M. Sealts, Jr., *Melville's Reading*, rev. and enl. ed. (Columbia: University of South Carolina Press, 1988), 52.

30. Andrews Norton, *The Evidences of the Genuineness of the Gospels*, 3 vols., 2nd ed. (Cambridge, Mass.: George Nichols, 1848), 2:57.

31. James Hastings, *Encyclopaedia of Religion and Ethics* (New York: Scribner's, 1912) 6:236.

32. Norton, quoted in Vargish, "Gnostic Mythos in *Moby-Dick*," 275.

33. Hastings, *Encyclopaedia of Religion and Ethics*, 6:237.

34. Norton, *Evidences of the Genuineness of the Gospels*, 2:223.

35. *The Dictionary Historical and Critical of Mr. Peter Bayle*, 2nd ed. (London: Printed for J. J. and P. Knapton et al., 1738), 2:250.

36. Willam Blake's final painting in *Jerusalem* is a visual analogue to Melville's subject in "The Candles." As Phyllis Chesler characterized the painting, it is a "homosexually erotic" depiction of "the unmet yearnings of mortal sons for immortal and omnipotent father-gods, perhaps because their earthly fathers have failed them so, or because their earthly leaders have failed them so." *About Men* (New York: Simon and Schuster, 1978), 22.

37. Northrop Frye, *Anatomy of Criticism* (Princeton: Princeton University Press, 1957), 208, 207.

37. Matthiessen, *American Renaissance*, 456; Frye, *Anatomy of Criticism*, 212.

38. Frye, *Anatomy of Criticism*, 207, 210.

39. Robin Grey, "Melville's Quarrel with Milton: An Introduction," *Leviathan* 4 (2002): 5.

40. Melville's markings in *Paradise Lost*, in "Melville's Milton: A Transcription of Melville's Marginalia in His Copy of *The Poetical Works of John Milton*," ed. Robin Grey and Douglas Robillard, in consultation with Hershel Parker, *Leviathan* 4 (2002): 160.

41. Of the six phases of tragedy that Northrop Frye identifies—the first three ascending from romance, the last three descending toward irony—mutilation is characteristic only of the fifth and sixth. Frye describes *Oedipus Tyrannus*, for example, as "moving into the sixth phase of tragedy, a world of shock and horror in which the central images are images of *sparagmos*, that is, cannibalism, mutilation, and torture." *Anatomy of Criticism*, 222.

42. Karl Jaspers, "Basic Characteristics of the Tragic," in *Tragedy: Vision and Form*, 2nd ed., ed. Robert W. Corrigan (New York: Harper and Row, 1981), 65.

43. As Henry A. Murray remarked of the letter: "The implication is clear: all interpretations which fail to show that *Moby-Dick* is, in some sense, wicked have missed the author's avowed intention." "'In Nomine Diaboli,'" in *Melville: A Collection of Critical Essays*, ed. Richard Chase (Englewood Cliffs, N.J.: Prentice-Hall, 1962), 66. Unlike Murray, I don't believe Melville set out with the "intention" of writing "a wicked book" or deliberately changed his intention in order to do so. Ahab took possession of him, perhaps against his ruling "intention," because the hunt spoke so intimately to his own impulses and emotions. It may only have been in retrospect, when he descended from the exhilaration of writing the book, that Melville realized how far he had thrown himself into Ahab.

44. Sigmund Freud, "On Creative Writers and Daydreaming," in *The Freud Reader*, ed. Peter Gay (New York: Norton, 1989), 439.

45. Thomas Moore, *Letters and Journals of Lord Byron, with Notices of His Life* (London: John Murray, 1830), 1:186. Hereafter cited in the text.

46. Guinn Batten, *The Orphaned Imagination: Melancholy and Commodity Culture in English Romanticism* (Durham: Duke University Press, 1998), 26.

47. Batten, *Orphaned Imagination*, 27.

48. Murray, Introduction to *Pierre; or, The Ambiguities* (New York: Hendricks House, 1949), xl.

49. Murray, Introduction to *Pierre*, xli, lxxxvi; for Byron's influence on the young Melville, see also William H. Gilman, *Melville's Early Life and "Redburn"* (New York: New York University Press, 1951), 118, 119.

50. Anne Ridler, Introduction to *Poems and Some Letters of James Thomson* (Carbondale: Southern Illinois University Press, 1963), ix.

51. Thomas Carlyle, *On Heroes, Hero-Worship, and the Heroic in History*, ed. Michael K. Goldberg, Joel J. Brattin, and Mark Engel (Berkeley: University of California Press, 1993), 67–68.

52. T. S. Eliot, "Tradition and the Individual Talent," in *The Sacred Wood* (1920; reprint, London: Methuen, 1960), 55.

53. The "primogenitures of the gods" passage is one instance of this literary "self-satisfaction." This quality makes itself felt in other writers and works as well—in the last paragraph of Joyce's "The Dead," for example, or in virtuoso passages in Faulkner, Woolf, and James, among others, in which the prose seems almost to be admiring itself.

54. Carlyle, *On Heroes, Hero-Worship, and the Heroic in History*, 61.

55. In Jay Leyda, *The Melville Log*, 2 vols. (New York: Harcourt Brace, 1951), 1:369.

Notes to Chapter 6

1. Merton M. Sealts, Jr., calls the words "an unmistakable allusion" to Plato. "Melville and the Platonic Tradition," in *Pursuing Melville: 1940–1980* (Madison: University of Wisconsin Press, 1982), 299.

2. Edwin Haviland Miller, *Melville* (New York: Braziller, 1975), 36.

3. Ralph Waldo Emeron, "Friendship," in *Essays: First Series*, ed. Joseph Slater, Alfred R. Ferguson, and Jean Ferguson Carr, vol. 2 of *The Collected Works of Ralph Waldo Emerson* (Cambridge, Mass.: Harvard University Press, 1979), 113.

4. Emerson to Caroline Sturgis, quoted in Harmon Smith, *My Friend, My Friend* (Amherst: University of Massachusetts Press, 1999), 49; Emerson, "Friendship," 114.

5. Eve Kosofsky Sedgwick, *Epistemology of the Closet* (Berkeley: University of California Press, 1990), 44.

6. Carroll Smith-Rosenberg, *Disorderly Conduct* (New York: Oxford University Press, 1985), 58–59. Smith-Rosenberg argues that "rather than seeing a gulf between the normal and the abnormal, we [should] view sexual and emotional impulses as part of a continuum or spectrum of affect gradations strongly affected by cultural norms and arrangements," which in the centurynineteenth century "permit[ted] a great deal of freedom in moving across this spectrum" (*Disorderly Conduct*, 75–76). See also Sedgwick, *Between Men* (New York: Columbia University Press, 1985), 1–2.

7. David M. Halperin, *One Hundred Years of Homosexuality* (New York: Routledge, 1990), 28–29.

8. Virginia Woolf, "A Sketch of the Past," in *Moments of Being*, ed. Jeanne Schulkind (New York: Harcourt Brace, 1985), 108.

9. *The Diary of Virginia Woolf.* vol. 3, *1925–1930*, ed. Anne Olivier Bell (New York: Harcourt Brace, 1980), 51.

10. Robert K. Martin, "Knights-Errant and Gothic Seducers: The Representation of Male Friendship in Mid-Nineteenth-Century America," in *Hidden from History*, ed. Martin L. Duberman, Martha Vicinus, and George Chauncey, Jr. (New York: New American Library, 1989), 180.

11. Martin, "Knights-Errant," 182; Martin, *Hero, Captain, and Stranger: Male Friendship, Social Critique,and Literary Form in the Sea Novels of Herman Melville* (Chapel Hill: University of North Carolina Press, 1986), 14.

12. I emphasize "characteristic" along with overt because I do not think that participating in widespread shipboard sexual practices (if so he did) would be sufficient to categorize Melville as "homosexual" in a continuing identic sense of the term. Martin seems to agree: men in confined all-male institutions like prisons "remain heterosexual or homosexual, according to their principal sexual orientation, regardless of the sexual activity they may engage in while in a homosocial environment" (*Hero, Captain, and Stranger*, 13). As to the larger point, I think Martin obfuscates things when he chooses to apply "homosexual" to "feelings" that refer "to desires and not practices" (*Hero, Captain, and Stranger*, 13). The virtue of "homoerotic" is that it covers cases like this without discounting strong same-sex feelings but also without appropriating those who have them to the very different class of practicing homosexuals. Given the current status of the term, the claim that Melville was "homosexual" is not justified by anything that scholarship has been able to discover about him.

13. In *Hero, Captain, and Stranger*, Martin emphasizes that his "approach is in no way biographical and that what Melville actually 'did' is of absolutely no literary significance." (*Hero, Captain, and Stranger*, 14.)

14. Mellow, *Nathaniel Hawthorne in His Times* (Boston: Houghton Mifflin, 1980), 312.

15. Elizabeth Hardwick notes, apropos of *Redburn*, that "the readers of his own time, the publishers and booksellers do not seem to have paused before the enthusiastic and relishing adjectives surrounding male beauty." "Melville in Love," *New York Review of Books*, June 15, 2000, 18.

16. John Bryant, Introduction to *Typee: A Peep at Polynesian Life* (New York: Penguin, 1996), xx.

17. Lewis Mumford, *Herman Melville* (New York: Literary Guild, 1929), 201. Hershel Parker refers to Melville's "inexperience with intellectual women." *Herman Melville: A Biography*, vol. 2, *1815–1891* (Baltimore: Johns Hopkins University Press, 2002), 2.

18. Melville in W. Walker Cowen, *Melville's Marginalia* (New York: Garland, 1989), 650.

19. Melville in Cowen, *Melville's Marginalia*, 650.

20. Margaret Fuller, quoted in *Memoirs of Margaret Fuller Ossoli*, 2 vols., ed. R. W. Emerson, W. H. Channing, and J. F. Clarke (Boston: Roberts, 1874), 1:247.

21. I am not suggesting that Hawthorne was a substitute for Zenobia or, as Robert K. Martin and Leland S. Person believed me to imply in an earlier version of this chapter, that men with an interest in other men "simply have not met the right woman." My point is that Melville responded most deeply to a mixture of beauty, fearless intelligence, and noble grief, and that given what women were trained and allowed to be in his nineteenth-century New York/New England middle-class culture, he was not likely to meet such a woman there. Melville might well have been drawn to *both* Hawthorne and Zenobia. As it happened, he never met a Zenobia; he did meet Hawthorne. Robert K. Martin and Leland S. Person, "Missing Letters: Hawthorne, Melville, and Scholarly Desire," *ESQ* 46 (2000): 115.

22. Mellow, *Nathaniel Hawthorne in His Times*, 344.

23. Sealts, *Pursuing Melville*, 319.

24. Plato, *Symposium*, trans. Benjamin Jowett (Indianapolis: Bobbs-Merrill, 1956), 27; hereafter cited in the text. See Sealts, "Melville and the Platonic Tradition," in *Pursuing Melville*, 320.

25. *Langenscheidt New College Merriam-Webster English Dictionary* (New York: Langenscheidt, 1998), 892. My emphasis.

26. Margaret Fuller to Samuel Gray Ward, in *The Woman and the Myth: Margaret Fuller's Life and Writings*, ed. Bell Gale Chevigny (Old Westbury, N.Y.: Feminist Press, 1976), 112–13.

27. Sigmund Freud, *Beyond the Pleasure Principle*, trans. James Strachey (New York: Norton, 1961), 52.

28. Jonathan Lear, *Open Minded* (Cambridge, Mass.: Harvard University Press, 1998), 152.

29. Even "Hawthorne and His Mosses" is driven heavily by Melville's exhilaration about his own personality and prospective career, as he comes to envision them while meditating on his outward subject.

30. Miller, *Melville*, 250. Robert K. Martin went so far as to characterize "recent biographical criticism of Melville, notably the biography by Edwin Haviland Miller, [as] so offensive as to make almost anyone doubt the method." *Hero, Captain, and Stranger*, 14.

31. Nathaniel Hawthorne, *The English Notebooks 1856–1860*, ed. Thomas Woodson and Bill Ellis, vol. 22 of *The Centenary Edition of the Works of Nathaniel Hawthorne* (Columbus: Ohio State University Press, 1997), 162.

32. See Richard P. Stebbins, "Berkshire Quartet: Hawthornes and Tappans at Tanglewood, 1850–51," *Nathaniel Hawthorne Review*, 25 (1999): 1–20.

33. Walter E. Bezanson, Historical and Critical Note to *Clarel: A Poem and Pilgrimage in the Holy Land*, ed. Harrison Hayford, Alma A. MacDougall, Hershel Parker, and G. Thomas Tanselle, vol. 12 of the Northwestern-Newberry edition (1991), 596, 597.

34. In his introduction to the Hendricks House edition of *Clarel*, reprinted as the Historical and Critical Note to the Northwestern-Newberry edition, Bezanson argued persuasively that "Monody" was Melville's "tribute" to Hawthorne (Bezanson, Historical and Critical Note to *Clarel*, 602). Surveying the evidence in a tough-minded, if sometimes literalistic, fashion, Harrison Hayford took a more skeptical attitude in his pamphlet "Melville's 'Monody': Really for Hawthorne?" (Evanston, Ill.: Northwestern University Press, 1990), reprinted in abridged form in the Northwestern-Newberry edition of *Clarel* as "Melville's 'Monody': For Hawthorne?" 883–93. For a discussion of Hayford's reasoning, see Robert Milder, "Editing Melville's Afterlife," *Text* 9 (1997): 400–403.

35. Newton Arvin, *Herman Melville* (New York: Sloane, 1950), 206.

36. Melville, quoted in Jay Leyda, *The Melville Log*, 2 vols. (New York: Harcourt Brace,1951), 1:416.

37. William H. Gilman, *Melville's Early Life and "Redburn"* (New York: New York University Press, 1951), 60. Paul McCarthy similarly feels that "the loss of his father left Herman with a sense of rejection and loneliness he would never get over." *The Twisted Mind* (Iowa City: University of Iowa Press, 1990), 7. For Neal L. Tolchin, the failure of the Melvill(e) family and the culture at large to provide adequate outlets for grief left Melville with a "lifelong inability to finish mourning for his father." *Mourning, Gender, and Creativity in the Art of Herman Melville* (New Haven: Yale University Press, 1988), xii. Melville alludes to Burton's *Anatomy* in the opening sentence of his 1839 "Fragments from a Writing Desk" (*PT* 191).

38. "Mourning and Melancholia," in *Complete Psychological Works of Sigmund Freud*, vol. 14, trans. James Strachey (London: Hogarth Press), 246. Hereafter cited in the text as *MM*.

39. William Styron, *Darkness Visible* (New York: Random House, 1992), 56.

40. John Bowlby, *Attachment and Loss*, vol. 3, *Loss: Sadness and Depression* (New York: Basic Books, 1980), 217. Hereafter cited in the text as Bowlby.

41. Allan Melvill, quoted in Eleanor Melville Metcalf, *Herman Melville: Cycle and Epicycle* (Cambridge, Mass.: Harvard University Press, 1953), 8–9. See Hershel Parker, *Herman Melville: A Biography*, vol. 1, *1819–1851* (Baltimore: Johns Hopkins University Press, 1996) 34–39.

42. Allan Melvill, quoted in Metcalf, *Herman Melville*, 9.

43. Heinz Kohut, *The Analysis of the Self* (New York: International Universities Press, 1971), 25. Hereafter cited in the text as Kohut. Joseph Adamson has applied Kohut's theories to Melville in *Melville, Shame, and the Evil Eye* (Albany: State University of New York Press, 1997).

44. Parker, *Herman Melville*, 1:1.

45. Metcalf, *Herman Melville*, 135, 133.

46. Brian Higgins and Hershel Parker, Introduction to *Critical Essays on Herman Melville's "Pierre; or, The Ambiguities"* (Boston: G. K. Hall, 1983), 2.

47. Kay Redfield Jamison, *Touched with Fire: Manic-Depressive Illness and the Artistic Temperament* (New York: Free Press, 1993), 19. Newton Arvin also suggested Melville's disturbed mood when he wrote of "something . . . wrong psychologically with the distance between Melville and his material" (*Herman Melville*, 226–27), an opinion shared by several of *Pierre*'s contemporary reviewers who sensed that the literary problems of the book stemmed somehow from the psychological problems of its author. The "pervading" spirit of *Pierre* was "intolerably unhealthy," the critic for *Graham's* magazine reported (reprinted in Higgins and Parker, *Critical Essays*, 55), or as the *New York Day Book* extravagantly put it, in block letters: "HERMAN MELVILLE CRAZY" (reprinted in Higgins and Parker, *Critical Essays*, 55).

48. See Amy Puett Emmers, "Melville's Closet Skeleton: A New Letter About the Illegitimacy Incident in *Pierre*," *Studies in the American Renaissance* 1 (1977), 339–43; and Henry A. Murray, Harvey Myerson, and Eugene Taylor, "Allan Melvill's By-Blow," *Melville Society Extracts* 61 (1985): 1–6. Hershel Parker concludes that "there is, as of now, no way of knowing" whether Allan Melvill had an illegitimate daughter or, if so, who the daughter might have been (*Herman Melville*, 1:65).

49. Brian Higgins and Hershel Parker, "Reading *Pierre*," in *A Companion to Melville Studies*, ed. John Bryant (Westport, Conn.: Greenwood, 1986), 223.

50. F. O. Matthiessen, *American Renaissance* (New York: Oxford University Press, 1941), 471.

51. Matthiessen, *American Renaissance*, 480.

52. Arvin, *Herman Melville*, 224.

53. John Seelye, "'Ungraspable Phantom': Reflections on Hawthorne in *Pierre* and *The Confidence-Man*," *Studies in the Novel* 1 (1969): 438.

54. James Creech, *Closet Writing/Gay Reading* (Chicago: University of Chicago Press, 1993), 118, 119, 118. Hereafter cited in the text.

55. Phyllis Chesler, *About Men* (New York: Simon and Schuster: 1978), 22. See also Gene Patterson-Blake, "On Herman Melville," in *American Novelists Revisited: Essays in Feminist Criticism*, ed. Fritz Fleischmann (Boston: G. K. Hall, 1982), 107–42. I would like to thank both Chesler and Patterson-Black for helping me think about this elusive subject.

56. Janet Duckham revises the established views of Maria Melvill(e) as either a monstrous parent (as early biographers Raymond Weaver and Lewis Mumford saw her) or a nurturing Dutch-American matriarch (as for William H. Gil-

man and Alice Kenney). Working with family letters and carefully sifting the evidence, Duckham shows that Maria's attentiveness to and empathy with her second son were seriously compromised by her regular pregnancies and recoveries, her extended absences to visit her family, her illnesses, her fretfulness (which preceded Allan's financial difficulties), and her periods of depression. However affectionately she may have regarded Herman, she was simply not there for him, physically and/or emotionally, during a good part of his childhood. Duckam, "Melville and the M(Other): Object-Relations Theory and Melville's Metaphysical Quest" (Ph.D. diss., Washington University, 2001).

57. Matthiessen, *American Renaissance*, 468.

58. Arvin, *Herman Melville*, 202, 219.

59. Milton R. Stern, *The Fine Hammered Steel of Hernan Melville* (Urbana: University of Illinois Press, 1957), 16.

60. Henry A. Murray, Introduction to *Pierre* (New York: Hendricks House, 1949), lxxxiii.

61. Murray, Introduction to *Pierre*, lii, xliv.

62. Murray, Introduction *Pierre*, lii.

63. Murray, Introduction *Pierre*, xli.

64. Parker, *Herman Melville*, 1:795.

65. *The Journals and Miscellaneous Notebooks of Ralph Waldo Emerson*, 16 vols., ed. William H. Gilman, Ralph Orth (Cambridge, Mass.: Harvard University Press, 1960–82), 1:52–53.

66. Seelye,"'Ungraspable Phantom,'" 438.

67. Arvin, *Herman Melville*, 233.

68. Cornelius Mathews, in Leyda, *Log*, 1:323.

69. Parker, *Herman Melville*, 1:793.

70. Arvin, *Herman Melville*, 203.

71. To a degree, Melville's feeling was replicated in Hawthorne, but with greater ambivalence and native reserve. Hawthorne would not have been unreceptive to Melville's enthusiasm. The idyll of his first years of domesticity at the Old Manse had faded with the responsibilities of fatherhood, and by 1851–52, as Thomas Mitchell argues, he may well have been suffering "middle-aged discontent with his life and his work." *Hawthorne's Fuller Mystery* (Amherst: University of Massachusetts Press, 1998), 175. Hawthorne had reviewed *Typee* in 1846 with a paterfamilias's wistfulness at the life of adventure, geographical and erotic. Telling stories in his parlor, Melville was a surrogate self for Hawthorne and also, as Chillingworth the freethinker was for Dimmedale, a breath of intellectual fresh air to a mind that characteristically shrank before the metaphysically subversive.

72. Emerson, "Spiritual Laws," in *Essays: First Series*, 80; John Milton, *Paradise Lost*, in *John Milton: Complete Poems and Major Prose*, ed. Merritt Y. Hughes (New York: Odyssey Press, 1957), I, 351–52.

73. Matthiessen, *American Renaissance*, 480.

74. On November 3, Melville received an invitation to a farewell party to be given for the Hawthornes (Parker, *Herman Melville*, 1:876); it is unlikely that the invitation was the first Melville heard of Hawthorne's plans.

75. Bowlby, *Attachment and Loss*, 3:236.

76. Styron, *Darkness Visible*, 73.

77. Kohut, *The Restoration of the Self* (New York: International Universities Press, 1977), 4–5.

78. Warner Berthoff, *The Example of Melville* (Princeton: Princeton University Press, 1962), 57.

79. Julian Hawthorne, in Leyda, *Log*, 2:783.

80. Bezanson, Historical and Critical Note to *Clarel*, 596.

81. In adapting 2 Samuel 1:26 ("passing the love of *women*"), Melville makes females an entire gender ("woman") rather than a group of individuals, and he appends the adjective "fond": foolishly tender; weakly indulgent; doting.

82. Miller, *Melville*, 331.

83. Linda Dowling, *Hellenism and Homosexuality in Victorian Oxford* (Ithaca: Cornell University Press, 1994), 115.

84. Dowling, *Hellenism and Homosexuality*, 128.

85. Dowling, *Hellenism and Homosexuality*, 129.

86. Hawthorne, *English Notebooks*, 162.

87. Martin, *Hero, Captain, and Stranger*, 99–100.

88. Martin, *Hero, Captain, and Stranger*, 100.

89. See Martin and Person, "Missing Letters," 99–122.

Notes to Chapter 7

1. John Updike, *The Afterlife and Other Stories* (New York: Knopf, 1994).

2. Nathaniel Hawthorne, *The English Notebooks 1856–1860*, ed. Thomas Woodson and Bill Ellis, vol. 22 of *The Centenary Edition of the Works of Nathaniel Hawthorne* (Columbus: Ohio State University Press, 1997), 170.

3. Hawthorne, *English Notebooks*, 169–70.

4. Hawthorne, *English Notebooks*, 170.

5. Merton M. Sealts, Jr., *Melville as Lecturer* (Cambridge, Mass.: Harvard University Press, 1957), 111.

6. Dorothee Metlitsky Finkelstein, *Melville's Orienda* (New Haven: Yale University Press, 1961), 3.

7. William H. Shurr, *The Mystery of Iniquity* (Lexington: University Press of Kentucky, 1972), 168.

8. Ralph Waldo Emerson in *Emerson in His Journals*, ed. Joel Porte (Cambridge, Mass.: Harvard University Press, 1982), 119.

9. Howard C. Horsford with Lynn Horth, Historical Note to *Journals*, ed. Harrison Hayford, Hershel Parker, and G. Thomas Tanselle, vol. 15 of the Northwestern-Newberry edition (1989), 182.

10. Twenty years later, Mark Twain wrote of Constantinople in a similar vein: "Every where was dirt, and dust, and dinginess, and gloom; every where were signs of a hoary antiquity, but with nothing touching or beautiful about it." *The Innocents Abroad* (New York: Library of America, 1984), 287.

11. See Angela Miller, "Thomas Cole and Jacksonian America: *The Course of Empire* as Political Allegory,"in *Prospects*, vol. 14 (New York: Cambridge University Press, 1989), 65–66.

12. Barbara Novak, *American Painting of the Nineteenth Century*, 2nd ed. (New York: Harper and Row, 1979), 68.

13. Miller, "Thomas Cole and Jacksonian America," 77.

14. Herman Melville, "Naples in the Time of Bomba," in *"At the Hostelry" and "Naples in the Time of Bomba,"* ed. Gordon Poole (Naples: Istituto Universitario Orientale, 1989), ll. 150, 153–56.

15. Basem L. Ra'ad, "Melville's Art: Overtures from the Journal of 1856–57," in *Savage Eye*, ed. Christopher Sten (Kent, Ohio: Kent State University Press, 1991), 209.

16. John W. Davis, *The Landscape of Belief* (Princeton: Princeton University Press, 1996), 3. See also Hilton Obenzinger, *American Palestine: Melville, Twain, and the Holy Land Mania* (Princeton: Princeton University Press, 1999).

17. William Bradford, quoted in Jesper Rosenmeier, "'With Mine Owne Eyes': William Bradford's *Of Plymouth Plantation*," in *The American Puritan Imagination*, ed. Sacvan Bercovitch (Cambridge: Cambridge University Press, 1974), 77.

18. Twain, *Innocents Abroad*, 486.

19. Franklin Walker, *Irreverent Pilgrims* (Seattle: University of Washington Press, 1974), 28.

20. J. Ross Browne, *Yusef* (New York: Harpers, 1855), 360.

21. Twain, *Innocents Abroad*, 486.

22. Charles Dudley Warner, *In the Levant* (Boston: Houghton Mifflin, 1876), 221.

23. Hawthorne, *English Notebooks*, 163,

24. Newton Arvin, *Herman Melville* (New York: William Sloane, 1950), 253, 254.

25. See, for example, Martin Bernal's argument in *Black Athena: The Afro-Asiatic Roots of Classical Civilization*. vol. 1, *The Fabrication of Ancient Greece 1785–1985* (New Brunswick, N.J.: Rutgers University Press, 1987).

26. George William Curtis, *Nile Notes of a Howadji* (New York: Harpers, 1852), 64. Hereafter cited in the text.

27. See Shirley M. Dettlaff, "'Counter-Natures in Mankind': Hebraism and Hellenism in *Clarel*," in *Melville's Evermoving Dawn: Centennial Essays*, ed. John Bryant and Robert Milder (Kent, Ohio: Kent State University Press, 1998), 192–221.

28. Quoted in Eleanor Melville Metcalf, *Herman Melville: Cycle and Epicycle* (Cambridge, Mass.: Harvard University Press, 1953), 165.

29. Merton M. Sealts, Jr., Historical Note to *The Piazza Tales and Other Prose Pieces, 1839–1860,* ed. Harrison Hayford, Hershel Parker, and G. Thomas Tanselle, vol. 9 of the Northwestern-Newberry edition (1987), 517.

30. Nathaniel Hawthorne, *French and Italian Notebooks,* ed. Thomas Woodson, vol. 14 of *The Centenary Edition of the Works of Nathaniel Hawthorne* (Columbus: Ohio State University Press, 1980) 125, 298.

31. Shirley M. Dettlaff, "Ionian Form and Esau's Waste: Melville's View of Art in *Clarel,*" *American Literature* 54 (1982): 214.

32. Matthew Arnold, "Stanzas from the Grande Chartreuse," in *The Works of Matthew Arnold,* 15 vols. (London: Macmillan, 1903), I, ll. 85–86.

33. Merton M. Sealts, Jr., "Melville as Lecturer," in *Pursuing Melville: 1940–1980* (Madison: University of Wisconsin Press, 1982), 64.

34. Sealts, "Melville as Lecturer," 65.

35. Anonymous review, Cleveland *Daily Herald,* quoted in Jay Leyda, *The Melville Log* (New York: Harcourt Brace, 1951), 589.

36. Quoted in Leyda, *Log,* 2:591.

37. Quoted in Leyda, *Log,* 2:605.

38. Schiller, quoted in Dettlaff, "Ionian Form and Esau's Waste," 226.

39. Hawthorne, *French and Italian Notebooks,* 138.

40. Hawthorne, *English Notebooks,* 163.

Notes to Chapter 8

1. Henry James, *Hawthorne* (1879; reprint, Ithaca: Cornell University Press, 1956), 112. George M. Fredrickson also cites James at the beginning of *The Inner Civil War: Northern Intellectuals and the Crisis of the Union* (New York: Harper and Row, 1965), 1. Hereafter Fredrickson is cited in the text.

2. James, *Hawthorne,* 112.

3. James, *Hawthorne,* 112. Sacvan Bercovitch remarks that even those writers critical of American life were captive to "the symbol of America," which "compelled them to speak their defiance as keepers of the [national] dream." *The American Jeremiad* (Madison: University of Wisconsin Press, 1978), 180.

4. James, *Hawthorne,* 114.

5. There are no extratextual statements (letters, journal entries) testifying to Melville's "intentions" in *Battle-Pieces*; his intention is inferable from the broad outlines of the text itself. As Kenneth Burke remarked, "there is no need to 'supply' motives" to a literary text. . . . The motivation out of which [an author] writes is synonymous with the structural way in which he puts events and values together when he writes; and however consciously he may go about such work, there is a kind of generalization about these interrelations that he could not have been conscious of, since the generalization could be made by the kind of inspection that is possible only *after the completion* of the work." *The Philosophy of Literary Form,* rev. ed. (New York: Random House, 1957), 18.

6. Peter J. Rabinowitz, "Assertion and Assumption: Fictional Patterns and the External World," *PMLA* 96 (1981): 410.

7. See Stanton Garner, *The Civil War World of Herman Melville* (Lawrence: University Press of Kansas, 1993), 298.

8. William H. Shurr also discusses the metaphysical implications of the lines in *The Mystery of Iniquity: Melville as Poet, 1857–1891* (Lexington: University Press of Kentucky, 1972), 26.

9. Daniel Aaron, *The Unwritten War: American Writers and the Civil War* (New York: Knopf, 1973), 343.

10. Quoted in Fredrickson, *Inner Civil War*, 60.

11. Rush Welter, *The Mind of America, 1820–1860* (New York: Columbia University Press, 1975), 22.

12. Fredrickson, *Inner Civil War*, 48.

13. Quoted in Fredrickson, *Inner Civil War*, 80.

14. Michael Paul Rogin, *Subversive Genealogy: The Politics and Art of Herman Melville* (New York: Knopf, 1983), 267.

15. Shurr, "Melville's Poetry: The Late Agenda," in *A Companion to Melville Studies*, ed. John Bryant (Westport, Conn.: Greenwood Press, 1986), 355–56.

16. See Richard Harter Fogle, "Melville and the Civil War," *Tulane Studies in English* 9 (1959), 71.

17. Fogle, "Melville and the Civil War," 75.

18. Garner discusses the career of Bartlett in various sections of *Civil War World of Herman Melville*.

19. *Paradise Lost* IV, 393–94. See Hennig Cohen, note to *The Battle-Pieces of Herman Melville*, ed. Cohen (New York: Thomas Yoseloff, 1963), 260.

20. Garner, *Civil War World of Herman Melville*, 386.

21. The pattern of "'The Apparition'"—first, an idyllic optimism, figured as a sleep; second, a catastrophe that serves as a revelation of nature's terror; and third, a meditation of the folly of innocence and the necessity of tragic awareness—replicates the movement of Wordsworth's "Elegiac Stanzas," which, like "'The Coming Storm,'" was suggested by a painting of nature in a storm.

22. Aaron, *Unwritten War*, xiii–xiv.

23. See Bercovitch, *American Jeremiad*, chap. 1.

24. *Uncle Tom's Cabin* is a Northern Jeremiad warning against the catastrophe of the war; Faulkner's *Go Down, Moses* is a Southern Jeremiad reflecting back upon the sins that caused it and that have been perpetuated in other forms through the book's present.

25. C. Vann Woodward, "The Irony of Southern History," in *The Burden of Southern History*, rev. ed. (Baton Rouge: Louisiana State University Press, 1968), 134–35. Woodward's essay was originally published in 1953.

26. Cohen, note to *Battle-Pieces of Herman Melville*, 293.

27. I write this on November 7, 2004.

28. Garner, *Civil War World of Herman Melville*, 424; Henry Adams, *The Education of Henry Adams* (1919; reprint, Boston: Houghton Mifflin, 1961), 266.

29. See Walter D. Kring and Jonathan S. Carey, "Two Discoveries Concerning Herman Melville," *Proceedings of the Massachusetts Historical Society* 87 (1975): 137–41. The Kring/Carey article is reprinted, along with an introduction by Kring and commentaries by eleven Melvilleans, in *The Endless, Winding Way in Melville: New Charts by Kring and Carey*, ed. Donald Yannella and Hershel Parker (Glassboro, N.J.: Melville Society, 1976). Hereafter cited in the text as *EWW*.

30. Elizabeth Renker, "Herman Melville, Wife-Beating, and the Written Page," *American Literature* 66 (1994): 126, 143 n. 12; Edwin Haviland Miller, *Herman Melville* (New York: Braziller, 1975), 321; Eleanor Melville Metcalf, *Herman Melville: Cycle and Epicycle* (Cambridge, Mass: Harvard University Press, 1953), 215.

31. Quoted in Jay Leyda, *The Melville Log*, 2 vols. (New York: Harcourt, Brace, 1951), 2:605.

32. Miller 321. Laurie Robertson-Lorant, *Melville: A Biography* (New York: Clarkson Potter, 1996), 509; Garner, *Civil War World of Herman Melville*, 41. Contra Miller's notion of alcoholic "orgies" (Miller, *Herman Melville*, 321), Melville celebrates drinking as festive and, at its best, conducive to philosophical talk. The closest extended example of an alcoholic "orgy" in Melville is the revel at Mar Saba in Part 3 of *Clarel*, which Melville presents as coarsely sensuous but innocent.

33. Virginia Woolf, "A Sketch of the Past," in *Moments of Being*, ed. Jeanne Schulkind (New York: Harcourt, Brace, 1976), 145.

34. Parker, *Herman Melville: A Biography*, vol. 2, *1851–1891* (Baltimore: Johns Hopkins University Press, 2002), 631.

35. Garner, *Civil War World of Herman Melville*, 41.

36. Maria Morewood, quoted by her daughter Margaret, in Metcalf, *Herman Melville*, 259.

37. Metcalf, *Herman Melville*, 55.

38. Parker, *Herman Melville*, 2:795. Parker goes harshly on Lizzie—rather a surprise, after his fanciful account earlier in the biography of Melville falling madly in love with her—but even biographer Laurie Robertson-Lorant, who is generally sympathetic to Lizzie, calls her "an average woman of her time." *Melville*, 528.

39. Parker argues strongly for the want of support as a contributing factor to Melville's behavior toward Lizzie: "In all the intervening years until 1867, Lizzie still wholly lacked the capacity for making a personal judgment that her husband was a great writer; and if she retained much lingering faith in his greatness, . . . she lacked the strength to interpose her opinion against the well-educated authorities in the Boston newspapers. . . . It is hopeless to try to separate whatever Melville did to Lizzie to make her feel ill treated from everything she and the other Shaws read about him in the papers and magazines." *Herman Melville*, 2:633–34.

40. On this same subject, Robertson-Lorant speculates that Melville might "have unconsciously resented her passivity at times, as a woman's goodness

often makes a man feel all the more guilty for his abusive behavior. Lizzie's docility may even have sparked some of her husband's outbursts and reinforced unhealthy repressions that adversely affected their four children." *Melville*, 509.

41. I am citing Elizabeth Renker's quotation from Forrest G. Robinson's 1992 biography of Murray, which excerpts words from Murray's manuscript. "Herman Melville, Wife-Beating, and the Written Page,"128.

42. Samuel Shaw to Henry Whitney Bellows, in Kring and Carey, "Two Discoveries Concerning Herman Melville," 139.

43. Kay Redfield Jamison, *Touched with Fire: Manic-Depressive Illness and the Artistic Temperament* (New York: Free Press, 1993), 217.

44. Parker, *Herman Melville*, 2:635.

45. Cited in Leyda, *Log*, 2:686.

46. Cited in Leyda, *Log*, 2:686.

47. Parker, *Herman Melville*, 2:641.

48. Robertson-Lorant, *Melville*, 509, 511–12.

49. Robertson-Lorant, *Melville*, 517.

50. I owe this suggestion to John Bryant.

Notes to Chapter 9

1. Stan Goldman discusses Melville's technique of "delayed identification" in his thoughtful book *Melville's Protest Theism: The Hidden and Silent God in "Clarel"* (DeKalb: Northern Illinois University Press, 1993), 110.

2. William Rounseville Alger, *The Solitudes of Nature and of Man* (Boston: Roberts, 1867), 308.

3. Alger, *Solitudes of Nature and of Man*, 307.

4. Paul Tillich, *The Protestant Era*, trans. James Luther Adams (Chicago: University of Chicago Press, 1948), xiv.

5. Thomas Henry Huxley, "Agnosticism," in *Collected Essays* (1897; reprint, New York: Greenwood, 1968), 5:246.

6. Tillich, *The Dynamics of Faith* (New York: Harper & Row, 1957), 1.

7. Newton Arvin, *Herman Melville* (New York: William Sloane, 1950), 273.

8. Walter E. Bezanson, Historical and Critical Note to *Clarel: A Poem and Pilgrimage in the Holy Land*, ed. Harrison Hayford, Alma A. MacDougall, Hershel Parker, and G. Thomas Tanselle, vol. 12 of the Northwestern-Newberry edition (1991), 587. Hereafter cited in the text as Bezanson.

9. Matthew Arnold, "Stanzas from the Grande Chartreuse," in *The Works of Matthew Arnold*, 15 vols. (London: Macmillan 1903), vol. 1, ll. 205-8. Unless otherwise noted, all references to Arnold's poems will be to this volume of the 1903 *Works*.

10. Bezanson, "Melville and Arnold's Poetry," *PMLA* 69 (1954): 390.

11. "The Second Coming," in *The Collected Poems of W. B. Yeats*, 2nd ed. (London: Macmillan, 1950), l. 22.

12. *The Complete Poems of Emily Dickinson*, ed. Thomas H. Johnson (Boston: Little, Brown, 1960), #1551, ll. 6–9. All references to Dickinson's poems will be to this edition and are cited hereafter in the text.

13. "Melville's Milton: A Transcription of Melville's Marginalia in His Copy of *The Poetical Works of John Milton*," ed. Robin Grey and Douglas Robillard in consultation with Hershel Parker, *Leviathan* 4 (2002): 152.

14. Niccolò Tommaseo, quoted in Tim Parks, "In Love with Leopardi," *New York Review of Books*, March 23, 2000: 39.

15. Bernard Rosenthal, "Herman Melville's Wandering Jews," in *Puritan Influences in American Literature*, ed. Emory Elliott (Urbana: University of Illinois Press, 1970), 171.

16. Quoted in Eleanor Melville Metcalf, *Herman Melville: Cycle and Epicycle* (Cambridge, Mass.: Harvard University Press, 1953), 232, 237.

17. Hershel Parker, *Herman Melville: A Biography*, vol. 2, *1851–1891* (Baltimore: Johns Hopkins University Press, 2002), 757, 767.

18. See Robert Milder, "In Behalf of 'Dearth,'" *Leviathan* 1 (1999): 63–69.

19. Nathaniel Hawthorne, *The English Notebooks 1856–1860*, ed. Thomas Woodson and Bill Ellis, vol. 22 of *The Centenary Edition of The Works of Nathaniel Hawthorne*, ed. William Charvat (Columbus: Ohio State University Press, 1997), 163.

20. Parker incisively remarks that "compulsive moralizing [of Vine's sort] can be a means of shielding oneself from the ambiguities inherent in any complex ethical situation. . . . [Vine] never concerns himself with right or wrong, never weighs the conflicting ethics of a problematical situation any more than he grapples with an aesthetic problem." *Herman Melville*, 2:698.

21. In 1884, Melville told Julian Hawthorne "that he was convinced that there was some secret in my father's life which had never been revealed, and which accounted for the gloomy passages in his books." Julian Hawthorne, *Hawthorne and His Circle* (New York: Harper, 1903), 33.

22. Hawthorne, *The American Notebooks*, ed. Claude M. Simpson and Bill Ellis, vol. 8 of *The Centenary Edition of the Works of Nathaniel Hawthorne*, 429.

23. Cited in Jay Leyda, *The Melville Log*, 2 vols. (New York: Harcourt, Brace, 1951), 2:674.

24. Hawthorne, *American Notebooks*, 429.

25. I don't agree with Parker that Melville "shows Vine changing, for the worse, reflecting [his own] altering comprehension of Hawthorne" as he wrote; the recoil at Vine's whimsical mockery is present virtually from the start (see *C* 1, 30: 107–16). *Herman Melville*, 2:780.

26. Parker, *Herman Melville*, 2:486–87.

27. See Shirley M. Dettlaff, "'Counter Natures in Mankind': Hebraism and Hellenism in *Clarel*," in *Melville's Evermoving Dawn*, ed. John Bryant and Robert Milder (Kent, Ohio: Kent State University Press, 1997), 192–221.

28. Matthew Arnold, *Culture and Anarchy* (Cambridge: Cambridge University Press, 1963) 133. Although Melville did not purchase a copy of *Culture and*

Anarchy until 1883, Arnold, as Dettlaff notes, "used the dichotomy [Hebraism and Hellenism] but not the terms in *Essays in Criticism*," which Melville read at the time of *Clarel*. Dettlaff, "Counter Natures in Mankind," 197.

29. Madame the Baroness De Staël-Holstein, *Germany*, 2 vols. (Boston: Houghton, Osgood, 1879), 1:199.

30. A. W. Schlegel, *Lectures on Dramatic Art and Literature*, trans. John Black (London: Bohn, 1824), 24. See slso Dettlaff, "Counter Natures in Mankind," 194.

31. Hawthorne, "The Maypole of Merry-Mount," in *Twice-Told Tales*, vol. 9 of *Centenary Edition of the Works of Nathaniel Hawthorne*, 59.

32. George Herbert, "The Pulley," in *The Poems of George Herbert* (London: Oxford University Press, 1961), l. 17.

33. Arvin, *Herman Melville*, 276.

34. Bezanson, "Melville and Arnold's Poetry," 376.

35. Arnold, preface to *Literature and Dogma*, in *Works*, 7:xi, xiii.

36. Leon Gottfried, *Matthew Arnold and the Romantics* (London: Routledge and Kegan Paul, 1963), 212.

37. Lawrence Buell, "Melville the Poet," in *The Cambridge Companion to Herman Melville*, ed. Robert S. Levine (Cambridge: Cambridge University Press, 1998), 144.

38. As Stan Goldman rightly observes, "the real basis for theism in *Clarel* is human need." *Melville's Protest Theism*, 131.

39. Sigmund Freud, *The Future of an Illusion*, trans. W. D. Robson-Scott, revised and edited by James Strachey (Garden City, N.Y.: Doubleday, 1964), 48.

40. Freud, *Future of an Illusion*, 47–48.

41. Hawthorne, *English Notebooks*, 163.

42. William James, "The Will to Believe," in *The Will to Believe and Other Essays in Popular Philosophy*, ed. Frederick H. Burkhardt, Fredson Bowers, and Ignas K. Skrupskelis (Cambridge, Mass.: Harvard University Press, 1979), 20, 30.

43. Freud, *Future of an Illusion*, 51.

44. James, *Pragmatism*, ed. Frederick H. Burkhardt, Fredson Bowers, and Ignas K. Skrupskelis (Cambridge. Mass.: Harvard University Press, 1975), 101.

45. Tillich, *Protestant Era*, xv.

46. Tillich, *Protestant Era*, 65.

47. Tillich, *Protestant Era*, xv.

48. Parker, *Herman Melville* 2:863.

49. Parker, *Herman Melville*, 2:857.

50. Parker, *Herman Melville*, 2:860.

51. Walter Donald Kring, *Herman Melville's Religious Journey* (Raleigh, N.C.: Pentland Press, 1997), 130.

52. Mark Heidman, "The Markings in Melville's Bibles," in *Studies in the American Renaissance*, ed. Joel Myerson (Charlottesville: University Press of Virginia, 1990), 347.

53. Tillich, *Dynamics of Faith*, 16.

54. In Shirley Dettlaff's words, "about the only way of determining whether man is 'ape or angel,' star or clod, is the purely subjective evidence of man's yearning for the infinite." "Counter Natures in Mankind," 218.

55. Frank M. Turner, *Contesting Cultural Authority* (Cambridge: Cambridge University Press, 1993), 80–81.

Notes to Chapter 10

1. Elizabeth Melville to Catherine Lansing, quoted in Jay Leyda, *The Melville Log*, 2 vols. (New York: Harcourt Brace, 1951), 2:796.

2. Frances Cuthbert and Thomas Osborne, "Herman Melville Through a Child's Eyes," in Merton M. Sealts, Jr., *The Early Lives of Melville* (Madison: University of Wisconsin Press, 1974), 180.

3. Charles De Kay, quoted in Leyda, *Log*, 2:781.

4. Arthur Stedman, "Herman Melville," in Sealts, *Early Lives of Melville*, 152.

5. Stedman, "Marquesan Melville," in Sealts, *Early Lives of Melville*, 106.

6. Cited in Leyda, *Log*, 2:791.

7. O. G. Hilliard, quoted in Leyda, *Log*, 2:787. Hilliard's obituary letter to the *New York Times* (October 6, 1891) is mistitled "The Late Henry Melville," an irony Melville would ruefully have appreciated.

8. O. G. Hilliard, quoted in Leyda, *Log*, 2:787.

9. Wilson Walker Cowen, *Melville's Marginalia* (New York: Garland, 1987), 4.

10. As William B. Dillingham observes, "old age was a crisis of tremendous proportions in his emotional life, a crisis brought on by a distressing drop in energy, a diminishment of interest, a leveling of emotions, a loss of enthusiasm, a disrelish of others' company, [and] a dislike of noise and busy activities." *Melville and His Circle: The Last Years* (Athens: University of Georgia Press, 1996), 87. Hereafter cited in the text as Dillingham.

11. William H. Shurr, "Melville's Poems," in *A Companion to Melville Studies*, ed. John Bryant (Westport, Conn.: Greenwood Press, 1986), 365.

12. Samuel Reynolds Hole, *A Book About Roses* (New York: William S. Gottsberger, 1883), 56.

13. Sir William Temple, quoted in Hole, *Book About Roses*, 177.

14. Eleanor Melville Metcalf, *Herman Melville: Cycle and Epicycle* (Cambridge, Mass.: Harvard University Press, 1953), 283, 284.

15. Metcalf, *Herman Melville*, 2:284.

16. Ernest Hemingway, *The Sun Also Rises* (New York: Scribners, 1957), 152.

17. Arthur Schopenhauer, "The Wisdom of Life," in *The Pessimist's Handbook: A Collection of Popular Essays by Arthur Schopenhauer*, trans. T. Bailey Saunders, ed. Hazel E. Barnes (Lincoln: University of Nebraska Press, 1964), 4. All references to Schopenhauer will be to this edition, which also includes *Coun-*

sels and Maxims. Melville acquired both *The Wisdom of Life* and *Counsels and Maxims* in the Saunders translation in February 1891.

18. See Dillingham, *Melville and His Circle,* 48–49.

19. Hallett Smith, *Elizabethan Poetry* (Cambridge, Mass.: Harvard University Press, 1966), 10.

20. See Merton M. Sealts, Jr., *Melville's Reading,* rev. and enl. ed. (Columbia: University of South Carolina Press, 1988), nos. 443–48.

21. Newton Arvin, *Herman Melville* (New York: William Sloane, 1950), 280.

22. See Robert C. Ryan, introduction to "'Weeds and Wildings Chiefly: With a Rose or Two,' by Herman Melville: Reading Text and Genetic Text, Edited from the Manuscripts, with Introduction" (Ph. D. diss., Northwestern University, 1967), vii. The text of "Weeds and Wildings" is problematic. Howard P. Vincent included the collection, with errors and arguable editorial judgments, in his edition, *Collected Poems of Herman Melville* (Chicago: Packard, 1947), but until the appearance of the Northwestern-Newberry edition of the unpublished manuscripts, the most reliable text (cited here in all references) is Ryan's 1967 reading text.

23. Hershel Parker notes that Melville seems to have "pushed one project forward, then another." *Herman Melville: A Biography,* vol. 2, *1851–1891* (Baltimore: Johns Hopkins University Press, 2002), 880. In discussing the poetry, I follow chronology chiefly as a matter of convenience in addressing aspects of Melville during this period.

24. Parker, *Reading "Billy Budd"* (Evanston, Ill.: Northwestern University Press, 1990), 32.

25. Cited in Leyda, *Log,* 2:832–33.

26. Walter E. Houghton and G. Robert Stange, introduction to Edward Fitzgerald, *Victorian Poetry and Poetics* (Boston: Houghton Mifflin: 1959), 328.

27. Walter Pater, *The Renaissance,* in *Walter Pater: Three Major Texts,* ed. William E. Buckler (New York: New York University Press, 1986), 219.

28. See John Bryant's discussion of the poem in "Melville's Rose Poems: As They Fell," *Arizona Quarterly* 53 (1997): 70–72.

29. *The Complete Poems of Emily Dickinson,* ed. Thomas H. Johnson (Boston: Little, Brown 1969), #216. Hereafter cited in the text by poem number.

30. Pater, *Renaissance,* 218.

31. Bryant, "Melville's Rose Poems," 67.

32. The theme of Dickinson's poem is echoed in several of the quartrains in Fitzgerald's *Rubáiyát,* among them quatrain 13: "Some for the Glories of This World; and some / Sigh for the Prophet's Paradise to come; / Ah, take the Cash, and let the promise go, / Nor heed the music of a distant drum." *The Rubáiyát of Omar Khayyám (First and Second Eds.) and Six Plays of Calderon,* trans. Edward Fitzgerald (London: J. M. Dent, 1928), 2nd ed., quatrain 13.

33. Fitzgerald, "Omar Khayyám: The Astronomer-Poet of Persia," in *Rubáiyát of Omar Khayyám,* 9.

34. Dorothee Metlitsky Finkelstein, *Melville's Orienda* (New Haven: Yale University Press, 1961), 104, 241.

35. Fitzgerald, "Omar Khayyám," 7.

36. John Updike, *Self-Consciousness* (New York: Fawcett, 1989), 245, 240.

37. Hole, *Book About Roses*, 105.

38. Hole, *Book About Roses*, 104, 106.

39. Dillingham, *Melville and His Circle*, 145.

40. Bryant, "Melville's Rose Poems," 50. Eleanor Melville Metcalf believes that Melville's "challenging" of Lizzie "must have ceased during the last eight or ten years of his life" as he "grew calmer and quieter," but she ascribes this development either to Melville's "lack of energy" (her mother Frances's view) or to his relief from the burden of the Custom House. She does not suggest that Melville's underlying feelings toward Lizzie changed. Metcalf, *Herman Melville*, 259.

41. Reinhard Kuhn, *The Demon at Noontide* (Princeton: Princeton University Press, 1976), 5.

42. Kuhn, *Demon at Noontide*, 5, 6.

43. See Robert C. Ryan, "Melville Revises 'Art,'" in *Melville's Evermoving Dawn: Centennial Essays*, ed. John Bryant and Robert Milder (Kent, Ohio: Kent State University Press, 1997), 307-20.

44. Virginia Woolf, *To the Lighthouse* (1927; reprint, New York: Harcourt, Brace, 1981), 209.

45. Dillingham, *Melville and His Circle*, 91.

46. See Harrison Hayford and Merton M. Sealts, Jr., Editor's Introduction to *Billy Budd, Sailor (an Inside Narrative)* (Chicago: University of Chicago Press, 1962), 239. For a compositional history, see Hayford and Sealts, 1-12. References to Hayford and Sealts's introduction and notes and commentary are hereafter cited in the text as Hayford/Sealts.

47. See Hershel Parker, *Reading "Billy Budd"* (Evanston, Ill.: Northwestern University Press, 1990), 174.

48. John Wenke, "Melville's Indirection: *Billy Budd*, the Genetic Text, and 'The Deadly Space Between,'" in *New Essays on "Billy Budd,"* ed. Donald Yanella (Cambridge: Cambridge University Press, 2002), 116.

49. Ralph Waldo Emerson, "Circles," in *Essays, First Series*, ed. Joseph Slater, Alfred R. Ferguson, and Jean Ferguson Carr, vol. 2 of *The Collected Works of Ralph Waldo Emerson* (Cambridge, Mass.: Harvard University Press, 1979), 189.

50. Smith, *Elizabethan Poetry*, 57.

51. Manuscript quoted in Hayford and Sealts, Editor's Introduction to *Billy Budd, Sailor*, 8.

52. The articles on the *Somers* incident, which Melville may or may not have read, are Lieutenant H. D. Smith, "The Mutiny of the *Somers*," *American Magazine* 8 (June 1888): 109-14; and Gail Hamilton, "The Murder of Philip Spen-

cer," *Cosmopolitan* 7 (June, July, August 1889): 134–40, 248–55, 345–54. Guert Gansevoort, a compelling, star-crossed figure within family legend, is recalled twice in "Bridegroom Dick," the second time as Tom Tight, "no fine fellow finer," a "lieutenant in the brig-o'-war famed / Where an officer was hung for an arch-mutineer" (*Poems* 274, 275).

53. Wenke, "Melville's Indirection," 117.

54. Parker, *Reading "Billy Budd,"* 174.

55. See Hayford and Sealts, genetic text of *Billy Budd, Sailor (An Inside Narrative)* (Chicago: University of Chicago Press, 1962), 309.

56. Hayford and Sealts, genetic text of *Billy Budd, Sailor*, 306–7.

57. Hayford and Sealts, "Table and Discussion of Foliation," in *Billy Budd, Sailor (an Inside Narrative)* (Chicago: University of Chicago Press, 1962), 246.

58. Ralph W. Willett, "Nelson and Vere: Hero and Victim in *Billy Budd, Sailor, PMLA* 82 (1967): 373.

59. Ryan, introduction to "Weeds and Wildings," xi.

60. Warner Berthoff, *The Example of Melville* (Princeton: Princeton University Press, 1962), 15.

61. Northrop Frye, *Anatomy of Criticism* (Princeton: Princeton University Press, 1957), 184.

62. Laurie Robertson-Lorant, *Melville: A Biography* (New York: Clarkson Potter, 1996), 591–92.

63. Hayford and Sealts, genetic text of *Billy Budd, Sailor*, 440; my emphasis; *Billy Budd*, 115.

64. Parker, *Reading "Billy Budd,"* 145.

65. Parker, *Reading "Billy Budd,"* 145.

66. See George Gordon, Lord Byron, "Childe Harold's Pilgrimage," in *Lord Byron: The Major Works*, ed. Jerome McGann (Oxford: Oxford University Press, 2000), III, 46–49.

67. Cowen, *Melville's Marginalia*, 632.

68. Emerson, "Heroism," in *Essays, First Series*, 149.

69. Leyda, *Log*, 2:836.

INDEX

3 5282 00619 1194